Karl Mar[...]
of a Germ[...]
to Christia[...]
and Berlin [...]
Hegel's dia[...] [...] he later reacted
against idealist philosophy and began
to develop his theory of historical
materialism. He related the state of
society to its economic foundations
and means of production, and
recommended armed revolution on the
part of the proletariat. In Paris in 1844
Marx met Frederick Engels, with whom
he formed a life-long partnership.
Together they prepared the *Manifesto
of the Communist Party* (1848) as a
statement of the Communist League's
policy. In 1848 Marx returned to
Germany and took an active part in
the unsuccessful democratic revolution.
The following year he arrived in
England as a refugee and lived in
London until his death in 1883. Helped
financially by Engels, Marx and his
family nevertheless lived in great
poverty. After years of research (mostly
carried out at the British Museum), he
published in 1867 the first volume of
his great work, *Capital*. From 1864
to 1872 Marx played a leading role
in the International Working Men's
Association, and his last years saw the
development of the first mass workers'
parties founded on avowedly Marxist
principles. Besides the two posthumous
volumes of *Capital* compiled by Engels,
Karl Marx's other writings included
*The German Ideology, The Poverty of
Philosophy, A Contribution to the Critique
of Political Economy*, and *Theories of
Surplus Value*.

KARL MARX

The Revolutions of 1848

Political Writings   Volume 1

Edited and Introduced
by David Fernbach

Penguin Books
in association with New Left Review

Penguin Books Ltd, Harmondsworth,
Middlesex, England
Penguin Books Inc., 7110 Ambassador Road,
Baltimore, Maryland 21207, U.S.A.
Penguin Books Australia Ltd, Ringwood,
Victoria, Australia

New Left Review, 7 Carlisle Street, London W1V 5RG

Made and printed in Great Britain by
Hazell Watson & Viney Ltd, Aylesbury, Bucks
Set in Monotype Times

Contents

References to Marx and Engels's works in the most frequently quoted editions have been abbreviated as follows:

MEW 1–39   *Marx-Engels-Werke*, Dietz Verlag, Berlin, 1956–64.

MESW   Marx and Engels, *Selected Works* [one-volume edition], Lawrence & Wishart, 1968.

MESC   Marx and Engels, *Selected Correspondence*, Lawrence & Wishart, 1965.

AOB   Marx and Engels, *Articles on Britian*, Progress Publishers, Moscow, 1971.

MEOI   Marx and Engels, *On Ireland*, Lawrence & Wishart, 1971.

IWMA I–V   International Working Men's Association, *Documents of the First International*, Lawrence & Wishart, 1964–6.

Introduction

From Philosophy to Politics

Karl Marx was born in Trier, in the Prussian Rhineland, on 5 May 1818. His parents were of Jewish origin, but were baptized into the Prussian state church while Marx was still a small child. The ideology of the French Enlightenment had won a strong base in the Rhineland, which had been annexed to France from 1798 to 1815, and from his father and schoolteachers Marx acquired a liberal and humanist education.

The Germany in which Marx grew up was still a backward country by comparison with its western neighbours. It was overwhelmingly agricultural; urban production was still dominated by the guild system, and modern industry was making its first inroads only in the northern Rhineland. The German cities had grown little, if at all, since the sixteenth century, and the total urban population of Germany was only half as much again as the population of Paris. This economic backwardness was reflected in German political structures. Germany had not experienced any form of bourgeois revolution, and was still divided between thirty-nine states, mainly absolutist, in a confederation underwritten by the Holy Alliance of Prussia, Austria and Russia.

However backward, German history was not static. The French Revolution had inspired a strong democratic sentiment among the artisans and intelligentsia in the German cities. This had not been entirely eradicated by the experience of Napoleonic domination, and was still available to inspire a popular revolution. The 'War of Liberation' of 1813, although fought under Prussian leadership, aroused enthusiasm for German unification, which merged with the democratic current and led to the formation of secret societies known as the Burschenschaften (students' associations). Although confined to the universities, their demonstrations, particularly at the Wartburg festival of 1817, provided a focus for the national-democratic movement. In 1819 the repressive measures of the Karlsbad decrees, dictated by the Holy Alliance, were introduced to suppress this movement, which flared up again after the French July revolution of 1830 and received a new dose of repression.

Industrial development, both in textiles and heavy industry, got seriously under way in the 1830s, and took advantage from the first of the technological advances made in England over the past sixty years. Railway building followed rapidly in the 1840s. The North German Zollverein (customs union) had been set up under Prussian auspices in 1834 to pre-empt bourgeois demands for national unification, but as capitalist development advanced, liberal pressure for a constitution built up in Prussia, particularly in the Rhineland, intensifying after the accession of Frederick William IV in 1840. The German population increased by 50 per cent between 1816 and 1846, despite a steady emigration to America, and this aggravated the pressure on the land, particularly in the eastern provinces of Prussia. The indebtedness of the peasantry in south and west Germany also intensified. In the 1840s an agrarian and trade depression began to cause rural and urban unrest. Economic, political and ideological factors were thus being formed, which would fuse in the revolutionary conjuncture of 1848.

A paradoxical effect of German backwardness marked intellectual life, one sphere in which Germany was unquestionably advanced. From the time of the French Revolution onwards German philosophy underwent a peculiar 'overdevelopment', producing the powerful idealist systems of Kant, Fichte, Schelling and Hegel. In the context of their national historical backwardness, German intellectuals were forced, as Marx put it, to 'think what others had done',[1] and this forced abstraction of their thought made the German philosophy of this period unequalled in the scope of its syntheses, culminating in Hegel's systematic integration of the natural sciences, logic and social theory.

In 1836 Marx began his university career at Bonn, but transferred the next year to Berlin. He had originally intended to read law, but his theoretical inclination soon drew him towards philosophy. In 1831 Hegel had died in office as Professor of Philosophy at Berlin, but by the middle of the decade his legacy

1. Karl Marx, 'Contribution to the Critique of Hegel's Philosophy of Right: Introduction', in *Early Writings*, Allen Lane/Penguin Books, in preparation.

was already in dispute, as the 'Left' or Young Hegelians fired their first shot at orthodoxy with the publication of David Strauss's *Life of Jesus*.[2]

In the peculiar German circumstances of economic and political backwardness coupled with theoretical overdevelopment, the Hegelian philosophy, with its ambiguous political implications and internal tension between system and method, was for the next decade to provide a terrain for political battles that could not yet be fought out in the arena of open class struggle.

The 'Right', i.e. orthodox Hegelians, fought for conservatism by defending Hegel's *system*, which under the dictum that 'the real is the rational' provided a legitimation for everything that existed, in particular the Christian religion and the Prussian monarchy. The 'Left' Hegelians used Hegel's dialectical *method* to criticize existing institutions as non-rational and therefore 'non-real', i.e. having outlived their historical moment and due to be changed. They thus refought, though in more sophisticated terms, the battles against religion and absolutism that the French Enlightenment had fought in the previous century. Rather than deny the truth of religion on its own ground, the Young Hegelians sought to explain religious dogma in terms of a different level of reality, which in the first instance was that of ethics. In 1841 Ludwig Feuerbach achieved what appeared to the Young Hegelians as a decisive 'abolition' of religion with his book *The Essence of Christianity*,[3] in which he transformed Hegel's idealism into a radical humanism by substituting for the abstract subject of Hegel's *Philosophy of Mind* the human species, and explaining religion as man's alienation of his own powers or essence and his subsequent domination by his own creations. In Prussia and the other absolutist states of Germany, religion was the natural starting point of rationalist criticism, as the state and the traditional social order still founded their legitimacy on a religious basis. Marx himself eagerly plunged into religious criticism, and his doctoral thesis, completed in 1841, was conceived as an anti-religious work.[4]

Marx approached politics under the aegis of his Young Hegelian colleague Bruno Bauer, who made the transition from reli-

2. English translation by Marian Evans (George Eliot), London, 1854.
3. English translation by George Eliot, London, 1853.
4. 'On the Difference between the Democritian and Epicurian Philosophies of Nature', *MEW Ergänzungsband* [Supplementary Volume] I.

gious to explicitly political criticism with his book *The Christian State*. In the summer of 1841 Marx joined Bauer in Bonn and worked with him for a while on an abortive plan for a journal, hoping also to obtain a place beside Bauer at the university. A few months later, however, Bauer's subversive activities led to his dismissal from Bonn, an event which simultaneously ditched Marx's own hopes of an academic career.

Marx's first political article was published in February 1842 in the Young Hegelian journal *Anekdota*. Commenting on the Prussian censorship, Marx exposed the inherent contradictions of the censorship system, and argued a liberal and rationalist defence of a free press and public opinion.[5]

During the course of 1842 Marx became increasingly involved with the recently founded *Rheinische Zeitung* (*Rhenish Gazette*), and was eventually appointed its editor. The *Rheinische Zeitung*, published in Cologne, represented a short-lived alliance between the Young Hegelian philosophers, already verging on radicalism, and the liberal Rhineland bourgeoisie who were restless with the failure of the new king to grant the long promised constitution. In the *Rheinische Zeitung* Marx dealt with current political questions within the limits of the liberal opposition, for he still believed possible and necessary the 'thankless and painful task of conquering political liberty step by step'.[6] It was while working on the *Rheinische Zeitung* that Marx first came into contact with French socialist and communist ideas, which became current in Germany in 1842 with the propaganda of Moses Hess[7] and the publication of Lorenz von Stein's book *The Socialism and Communism of Contemporary France*. But Marx's attitude to French communism was still extremely cautious. When Hess came under attack for articles he had written in the *Rheinische Zeitung*, Marx wrote editorially, 'The *Rheinische Zeitung* . . . cannot even concede *theoretical reality* to communistic ideas in their present form, and can even less wish to consider possible their practical realization.' However he conceded that 'writings such as those by Leroux,

5. 'Comments on the Latest Prussian Censorship Instruction', in L. D. Easton and K. H. Guddat, *Writings of the Young Marx on Philosophy and Society*, Doubleday, New York, 1967.

6. Marx to Oppenheim, 25 August 1842; *MEW* 27, p. 410.

7. Moses Hess was at this time predominantly influenced by Fourier, the French utopian socialist, and was soon to be a founder of German 'true socialism'. He was later a member of the Communist League, although he never accepted Marx and Engels's scientific communism.

Considérant, and above all Proudhon's penetrating work, can be criticized only after long and deep study'.[8]

It was more immediately important for Marx's development that as editor of the *Rheinische Zeitung* he was confronted practically with the 'social question'. Previously Marx had been concerned exclusively with religion and politics, in which fields he had been able to ascribe conflicts between men, in the idealist fashion, simply to the truth or falsity of their ideas. Now Marx came up against conflicts of material interest for the first time, in connection with the Rhineland Diet's[9] legislative encroachment on common timber rights, and the destitution of the Moselle grape growers caused by the Zollverein. Marx criticized the Rhineland Diet for its class-biased legislation, but still believed that political reason could resolve such conflicts, the conditions for this being a free press and public debate.[10] As Marx later acknowledged, however, it was the problems presented by these issues that first led him away from the mainstream of Young Hegelian philosophical criticism and towards the theory of historical materialism.[11]

*

The suppression of the *Rheinische Zeitung* in March 1843 marked the end of the hope that Prussia could progress through constitutional monarchy to democratic freedom. The Young Hegelians now branched in different directions. Some, like Bruno and Edgar Bauer, and Max Stirner, went on to develop increasingly radical theoretical positions, but kept safely away from all practical activity; others, particularly Arnold Ruge,[12] Moses Hess, Karl Marx and Frederick Engels, began to seek the means of

8. Easton and Guddat, op. cit., pp. 134–5. Pierre Leroux was a Saint-Simonian, and Victor Considérant a Fourierist. On Saint-Simon, Fourier and Proudhon see below, pp. 22–3.

9. The Rhineland, as one of the eight provinces of the Prussian monarchy, had its own parliament. These Diets were, however, dominated by the aristocracy, and had no more than advisory powers.

10. See 'The Defence of the Moselle Correspondent: Economic Distress and Freedom of the Press', abridged in Easton and Guddat, op. cit.; German original in *MEW* 1.

11. See Marx's brief and only account of his intellectual development in the 'Preface to *A Contribution to the Critique of Political Economy*', *MESW*, pp. 181–5.

12. Arnold Ruge, however, did not go with Marx as far as communism. In 1848 he sat with the Radical-Democratic party in the Frankfurt Assembly and later became a National Liberal.

turning the 'arm of criticism' into the 'criticism of arms'.[13] To that end Ruge and Marx left Germany in October 1843 for Paris, where Hess was already living, and where they planned to produce a journal, the *Deutsche-Französische Jahrbücher* (*Franco-German Yearbooks*). The move to Paris was not only necessitated by the Prussian censorship. As the title of their journal implied, Marx and his colleagues hoped to combine their philosophic results with the achievements of French political theory, and thus to arrive at the guiding principles of the radical revolution that they now believed necessary in Germany.

During the course of 1843 Marx had become an ardent follower of Feuerbach, who had developed his full position in that year with the publication of his *Provisional Theses for the Reform of Philosophy*. Feuerbach had already taught that the religious account of God as subject and Man as predicate had only to be inverted in order to reveal the true relationship. In the *Provisional Theses* he claimed that this 'transformative method' was the means to criticize all speculative philosophy (such as German idealism), since this was nothing more than religion in a secular guise. Feuerbach's key critical concept was that of *Gattungswesen* or species-being, which he used to denote the sum of humanity's collective powers, and it is this that Marx sought to apply, first to the political state, then to the capitalist economy, in two major texts written in 1843 and 1844.

Marx wrote his *Critique of Hegel's Doctrine of the State* in the summer of 1843. He had just married Jenny von Westphalen, to whom he had been engaged for seven years, and was shortly to move with her to Paris. In this text Marx attacked Hegel's presentation of the relation between the state and civil society (i.e. economic life) as a typical case of speculative philosophy. For Hegel, civil society was the sphere of material needs, while the state was the higher sphere of reason in which conflicts of material interest were resolved. Marx based himself on Feuerbach's humanism to assert that civil society, not the state, was the sphere of man's real life as a 'species-being', and that the 'reason' that governed the state presented man's real relations in an inverted form. Far from the state bureaucracy rationally mediating conflicts of material interest, it weighed on man's real existence as an oppressive force.

13. 'Contribution to the Critique of Hegel's Philosophy of Right: Introduction' in *Early Writings*.

In this critique Marx already saw the resolution of the antagonism between state and civil society as requiring the dissolution of the former into the latter, a position he was later to integrate into his scientific communism. But at this stage in his development Marx had as yet only a vague conception of class antagonisms. He believed that universal suffrage would spell the dissolution of the oppressive state, and the liberation of man's species-life, and did not yet recognize the abolition of private property – i.e. communism – as the essential condition of this liberation.

However Feuerbach's doctrine of the species-being easily led in the direction of communism, and Marx was rapidly to take this further step. Marx's conversion to communism came soon after his move to Paris, where he studied at first hand the French socialist and communist tendencies, and engaged in discussion with the militants of the French workers' movement. In the class-conscious workers of Paris Marx found the solution to the problems he had analysed in the *Critique of Hegel's Doctrine of the State*, and his first mention of the proletariat is in the Introduction published in the *Deutsche-Französische Jahrbücher* to a projected edition of that manuscript. Here Marx argues that the only class that can make a radical revolution in Germany (i.e. one that would realize the goals of Feuerbach's humanist philosophy) is,

a class with *radical chains*, a class in civil society which is not a class of civil society, a class which has a universal character because its sufferings are universal, and which does not claim a *particular redress* because the wrong done to it is not a *particular wrong* but *wrong in general* . . . This dissolution of society, as a particular class, is the proletariat.

With his stay in Paris in 1843–4, Marx outgrew his early formation in German philosophy. He not only continued his study of French political theory, intending at one point to write a history of the French revolutionary Convention, but also, under the stimulus of his contacts with the proletarian movement, began to read the English economists who analysed the 'anatomy' of bourgeois society. Yet in the first text in which Marx dealt with the problems of economic theory and communism – the *Economic and Philosophical Manuscripts* of 1844 – he still attempted, for the first and last time, to integrate this new subject matter into the framework of Feuerbachian humanism.

In the 1844 Manuscripts Marx applied Feuerbach's critical method to political economy, criticizing the bourgeois economic system and its apologists for inverting the true relations of labour and capital. Instead of capital being the subject of the economic process and labour its predicate, in reality it is human labour, the natural activity of man's species-being that is estranged or alienated, and turned into the capital which oppresses the labourer. Communism is defined in these terms as the reappropriation of man's estranged productive powers, and thus as the form of society conforming to man's species-being.

These Manuscripts are often considered the sign of Marx's arrival at the basic themes of his mature theory. It is certainly true that the notion of capital as 'estranged labour' presages Marx's later analysis of surplus value, and that Marx for the first time here explicitly avows communism as the solution to social antagonisms. However the decisive break in Marx's theoretical development was still ahead. In the Manuscripts Marx did not take issue with the descriptive content of bourgeois economic theory, but criticized as inhuman the reality that it described, and the ideologists who accepted and justified this reality. In *Capital*, however, Marx no longer criticized capitalist society simply on the basis of external humanistic criteria, but criticized bourgeois economic theory for its inadequate scientific comprehension of the capitalist economy, and explained how the *reality* of the capitalist economy contains inherent contradictions that impel it into crisis. And although in 1844 Marx already accepted a communist solution to the antagonisms of capitalist society, he in fact criticized the communist tendencies of the day, represented by Blanqui and Cabet, on the grounds that their politics were based on the greed and envy that capitalism itself engendered, rather than transcending this 'selfish' motivation. Not long after, Marx was to accept that the 'selfish' class struggle was the motive force of history and would lead to communism, and criticize Cabet and Blanqui for quite different reasons.

The 1844 Manuscripts certainly foreshadow Marx's future concerns, and they undoubtedly contain important insights that Marx was to integrate into his theory of historical materialism. Yet rather than heralding the birth of the new theory, they represent in fact Marx's last staging-post within the realm of 'German ideology', as he was soon to call it, a desperate but untenable attempt to integrate the realities of political economy and communism into the philosophical humanism of Ludwig Feuerbach.

Historical Materialism and Scientific Communism

Before explaining the theoretical break that led Marx to elaborate the theory of historical materialism, it is necessary to introduce Frederick Engels, who, as Marx himself wrote, 'had by another road . . . arrived at the same result'.[14]

Engels was born in 1820 in Barmen, Westphalia, into a Calvinist mill-owning family. He did not undergo formal higher education, but made his mark as a literary figure while still extremely young with articles and pamphlets of religious criticism, often very satirical in character. From October 1841, shortly after Marx had left Berlin, Engels spent a year posted there on military service, and eagerly joined in the heady current of Young Hegelian philosophy. He became, like Marx, an ardent follower of Feuerbach. In November 1842 Engels travelled to England to work in Manchester for his family's cotton business, and there he came into first-hand contact with both working-class misery and the Chartist movement. In England Engels gathered material for his book on *The Condition of the Working Class in England in 1844*,[15] in which he presented, more clearly than Marx had yet done, the thesis that the movement of the industrial working class on the basis of its material conditions of life would be the agency of communist revolution. In September 1844 Engels travelled to Paris. He spent some weeks in discussion with Marx, and the two found themselves in close agreement on their basic theoretical positions. Their partnership continued unbroken from that time onwards.

Marx and Engels's first joint venture was a book entitled *The Holy Family*,[16] a polemical work directed against the verbally radical, but idealist and apolitical, Young Hegelians, Bruno and Edgar Bauer and Max Stirner. This is very much a transitional work between Marx's early writings and the theory of historical materialism, and bears the marks of being written for hasty publication. Soon after finishing *The Holy Family* Marx moved to Brussels, being expelled from Paris at the request of the Prussian government for his activities among the German exiles. In spring 1845 Engels visited Marx in Brussels, and the two began a period of intensive study, travelling to England together to do further

14. 'Preface to *A Contribution to the Critique of Political Economy*', *MESW*, p. 182.

15. English translation by Florence Kelley [1887], Allen & Unwin, 1968.

16. English translation by R. Dixon, Foreign Languages Publishing House, Moscow, 1956.

research on political economy. The fruits of their work were the two volumes of *The German Ideology*, written in 1845–6, but published posthumously only in 1932.[17]

The German Ideology represents Marx and Engels's arrival at the theory of historical materialism that was to govern all their future work. It must be stressed that the materialist conception of history did not emerge fully-fledged from the brains of its creators. In the two decades that lay between *The German Ideology* and *Capital*, Marx's general social theory was to be modified in certain important respects. In particular, *The German Ideology* is not free from a certain evolutionism, which presents the different modes of production which have characterized human history as a unilinear, if dialectical, series. Nevertheless, the basic framework of *The German Ideology*, for all its inadequacies, constitutes a radical rupture with Young Hegelian philosophy in general, and Feuerbachian humanism in particular. Whatever development the new theory was to undergo, its basis, like that of all new sciences, was laid in *The German Ideology* by an 'epistemological break'[18] that established an entirely new perspective for the understanding of history. *The German Ideology* is explicitly presented as a comprehensive critique of the same 'modern German philosophy'[19] which Marx and Engels had until recently accepted as their own theoretical framework. The fundamental theses of historical materialism are spelled out in the first chapter of the book, which is specifically devoted to the critique of Ludwig Feuerbach, the doyen of the Young Hegelians and Marx's own former mentor.

Marx opens *The German Ideology* by criticizing the Young Hegelian philosophers for seeking only to effect a change in consciousness, 'to interpret reality in another way'.[20] Young Hegelian philosophy, which started from the critique of religion, had criticized the dominant metaphysical, political, juridical and moral conceptions by exposing their religious basis, but it forgot that it was only counterposing its phrases to other phrases, and not combating the real existing world. In this respect the *Deutsche-*

17. English translation by C. Dutt, W. Lough and C. P. Magill, Lawrence & Wishart, 1965.

18. On this concept see Louis Althusser, *For Marx*, Allen Lane The Penguin Press, 1969, pp. 32–4.

19. The full subtitle of *The German Ideology* is *Critique of Modern German Philosophy According to Its Representatives Feuerbach, Bruno Bauer and Stirner, and of German Socialism According to Its Various Prophets*.

20. Lawrence & Wishart edition, 1965, p. 30.

Französische Jahrbücher had certainly been less guilty than the 'critical critics' Bruno and Edgar Bauer, whom Marx had recently attacked in *The Holy Family*. But Marx goes on to criticize Feuerbach's equation of communism with humanism, and thus by implication his own position in the *Economic and Philosophical Manuscripts*. 'Feuerbach's whole deduction ... goes only so far as to prove that men need and *have always needed* each other', whereas communist 'in the real world means the follower of a definite revolutionary party'.[21]

Marx founds this distinction between philosophical and 'real' communism on a general sketch of historical development that situates communism as a 'definite revolutionary party', not in the world of ideas but as a determined product of social conditions. From this schema the basic concepts of historical materialism emerge. Marx presents his interpretation of history as radically different from that of German philosophy in that it proceeds 'from earth to heaven' instead of vice versa. It is the way in which men produce their material means of subsistence, how they 'work under definite material limits, presuppositions and conditions independent of their will' that determines 'the production of ideas, of conceptions, of consciousness'. 'Morality, religion, metaphysics, all the rest of ideology ... thus no longer retain the semblance of independence. They have no history, no development; but men, developing their material production and their material intercourse, alter, along with their real existence, their thinking and the products of their thinking.'[22]

The dynamic of historical development is provided by the development of the productive forces, and the changes in property relations that this requires. With the statement that 'the various stages of development in the division of labour are just so many different forms of ownership',[23] Marx introduces the historical periodization that is so crucial to his theory, positing tribal property, ancient (i.e. Graeco-Roman) 'communal and state property' and feudal property as the three major pre-bourgeois forms. Since consciousness has no independent development, then 'if this theory, theology, philosophy, ethics, etc. comes into contradiction with the existing relations, this can only occur because existing social relations have come into contradiction with existing forces of production',[24] i.e. because the development of

21. ibid., p. 54.   22. ibid., pp. 37–8.
23. ibid., p. 32.   24. ibid., p. 43.

productive forces requires a new form of property that conflicts with that at present existing.

Each division of labour defines a number of social classes, which are mutually antagonistic from the time that private property first develops, involving as it does 'the *unequal* distribution, both quantitative and qualitative, of labour and its products'.[25] Ownership of property gives one class domination over others, and the political state becomes necessary in order to mediate the ensuing conflicts. 'All struggles within the state, the struggle between democracy, aristocracy and monarchy, the struggle for the franchise, etc., etc., are merely the illusory forms in which the real struggles of the different classes are fought out . . . Every class which is struggling for mastery . . . must first conquer for itself political power in order to represent its interest in turn as the general interest.'[26] The rule of the dominant class is always ideologically legitimated, since 'the class which has the means of material production at its disposal, has control at the same time over the means of mental production', and 'the ruling ideas are nothing more than the ideal expression of the dominant material relationships . . . the relationships which make one class the ruling one.'[27]

Within this interpretation of history Marx's conception of 'real' communism becomes intelligible. The ideas of communism are not the logical outcome of the history of philosophy, for philosophy has no independent history. Communist consciousness comes into being because the existing bourgeois relations of production can no longer contain the developing productive forces.

In the development of the productive forces there comes a stage when productive forces and means of intercourse are brought into being, which, under the existing relationships, only cause mischief, and are no longer productive but destructive forces (machinery and money); and connected with this a class is called forth, which has to bear all the burdens of society without enjoying its advantages, which, ousted from society, is forced into the most decided antagonism to all other classes; a class which forms the majority of all members of society, and from which emanates the consciousness of the necessity of a fundamental revolution.[28]

In short, it is the material premises for communism that generate the communist consciousness that leads to social transformation.

25. ibid., p. 44.   26. ibid., p. 45.   27. ibid., p. 60.   28. ibid., p. 85.

'Communism is not for us a *state of affairs* which is to be established, an *ideal* to which reality (will) have to adjust itself. We call communism the *real* movement which abolishes the present state of things.'[29]

With *The German Ideology* Marx decisively rejected the concepts of Feuerbachian humanism which assumed an ideal human nature to which social institutions should be remoulded, in favour of objective scientific investigation of the real world, combined with political practice to change it. Following the discovery of historical materialism, Engels later wrote,

Communism among the French and Germans, Chartism among the English, now no longer appeared as something accidental which could just as well not have occurred. These movements now presented themselves as a movement of the modern oppressed class, the proletariat, as the more or less developed forms of its historically necessary struggle against the ruling class, the bourgeoisie ... And communism now no longer meant the concoction, by means of the imagination, of an ideal society as perfect as possible, but insight into the nature, the conditions and the consequent general aims of the struggle waged by the proletariat.[30]

Although Marx and Engels now realized that it was the actual workers' movement that had led them to communism, the ideology of this movement, even when it called itself communist and envisaged the abolition of private property, betrayed a quite inadequate conception of the society in which it had arisen, and of the possibilities and means of social transformation. Moreover, England was still the only country where industrial capitalism was unquestionably the dominant form of material production, where agriculture already involved less than half of the labouring population, and where earlier forms of urban production such as handicrafts and manufacture had been almost entirely squeezed out by machine industry. In the 1830s there had developed in England the first historic movement of a mass character that was based on the industrial proletariat: Chartism. Recognizing this fact, Marx and Engels gave consistent support to the Chartists and were to work closely with the Chartist left wing led by Ernest Jones and Julian Harney.

(Ernest Jones, born into the minor aristocracy, became the most

29. ibid., p. 47.
30. 'On the History of the Communist League', *MESW*, p. 437.

consistent representative of the revolutionary wing of the Chartist movement, and the main surviving Chartist leader in the 1850s. For his part in the Chartist uprisings of 1848 he was imprisoned for two years in such conditions that two of his comrades imprisoned with him died of privation. Jones was the only British working-class leader in the nineteenth century who understood Marx's theory of scientific communism. Although in 1858, with the final collapse of Chartism, Jones broke with Marx and collaborated with the bourgeois radicals, Engels nevertheless wrote to Marx on Jones's death in 1869 that he was 'the only *educated* Englishman ... who was, at bottom, entirely on our side'.[31] George Julian Harney, although influenced by Marx and Engels, was more of a revolutionary romantic. From 1843 to 1850 he was *de facto* editor of the main Chartist newspaper, Feargus O'Connor's *Northern Star*. Later, in his own newspaper, the short-lived *Red Republican*, he published in November 1850 the first English translation of the Communist Manifesto. In 1851, however, Harney broke with Marx and allied himself with the Schapper-Willich faction (see below, pp. 58–9). The following year Harney's erratic and subjective politics led him to quarrel with Ernest Jones, and he soon after dropped out of the Chartist movement altogether.)

Chartism as such was by no means a communist or even a socialist movement, but was based simply on the programme of manhood suffrage. Communistic ideas, though not in the Marxist sense of the 'real movement', were represented in England by the followers of Robert Owen, who renounced the class struggle and hoped to lay the basis for their utopia by means of rational persuasion. When Engels arrived in England in October 1843, like Marx at the time a Feuerbachian humanist, his first political contacts were with the Owenists, and he frequently contributed to their paper the *New Moral World* for nearly two years before, in the light of the new theory, he switched his allegiance to the Chartist *Northern Star*.

In France, although capitalist development was considerably more backward than in England, political ideology was more sophisticated and complex, having developed in the hot-house of the revolution of 1789 and its aftermath. Modern socialism had first originated in France with the utopian writings of Henri de Saint-Simon and Charles Fourier, who envisaged the planned

31. *MEW* 32, p. 253.

direction of industrial technology in the general interest. However the utopian socialists did not demand the abolition of all private property, and did not see the industrial working class, still very undeveloped in early nineteenth-century France, as the agent of social transformation. By the 1840s the followers of Saint-Simon and Fourier only survived in the form of quasi-religious sects, but their writings continued to inspire all sorts of plans for solving the 'social question', i.e. the social upheaval caused by the beginnings of industrialization and the working-class unrest that accompanied it.

Among these socialist doctrines of the 1840s, two were not only particularly important in the history of socialist thought, but also won considerable support from the French workers. Louis Blanc pioneered modern 'democratic socialism' with his scheme for self-governing 'national workshops' set up by government action. Pierre-Joseph Proudhon, although he is sometimes classed rather as the founder of modern anarchism for his rejection of the state as an unnecessary evil, also had his socialist panacea. Proudhon counterposed the 'organization of credit' to Blanc's 'organization of labour', and held that exploitation would be abolished if associated groups of workers could produce and exchange on the basis of unlimited interest-free loans. Blanc believed that his workshops would eventually supersede the market economy, whereas Proudhon, in true petty-bourgeois spirit, equated the free market with freedom in general.[32]

The term 'communism' in the France of the 1840s denoted a very different phenomenon, an offshoot of the Jacobin tradition of the first French revolution. It was rather crude in its ideas, but – unlike the contemporary socialism – directly related to the struggles of the masses. This communism went back to Gracchus Babeuf's Conspiracy of Equals of 1795, which aimed to install, by means of a conspiratorial coup, a dictatorship of 'true republicans' that would expropriate the rich, allocate work according to each individual's capacity, and fix wages on the basis of strict equality. This egalitarian or 'crude' communism, as Marx

32. During Marx's stay in Paris he maintained fraternal relations with Proudhon and sought to influence him. In 1847, however, Marx's first published presentation of the theory of historical materialism took the form of a polemic against Proudhon, *The Poverty of Philosophy*. For a shorter critique of Proudhon, see Marx's letter to Schweitzer of 24 January 1865; *MESC*, pp. 151–8.

called it, originated before the great development of machine industry. It appealed to the Paris *sans-cullottes* – artisans, journeymen and unemployed – and potentially to the poor peasantry in the countryside. However Babeuf's Conspiracy, as related by his disciple Buonarotti,[33] provided the model for revolutionary organizations formed under the July monarchy of 1830–48, and by this time both the class character of their social base and the objective possibilities of social transformation were rapidly changing with the development of machine industry. The idea of a communism of production based on machine industry was now popularized in Étienne Cabet's utopian novel, *Voyage en Icarie*, published in 1839.

The outstanding figure of French communism in the period before 1848 was Auguste Blanqui, whose Société des Saisons organized the revolutionary wing of the French workers' movement, and carried out an attempt at insurrection in May 1839. Blanqui neither elaborated a utopia nor an economic doctrine. His economic writings are muddled, and he expressly censured Cabet and Proudhon for speculating on the details of the future social order. Blanqui believed it sufficient that the capitalist economy led to growing extremes of wealth and poverty, and must be replaced by some form of workers' cooperation, and went on to concentrate on the problem of overthrowing the state that he correctly saw as the organized power of the propertied classes. Following Babeuf and Buonarotti, Blanqui argued his communism from the principle of equality. He saw France as divided between a small minority of the 'rich', and '30 million proletarians' (i.e. including the peasantry and urban artisans as well as the industrial working class), and counted on overthrowing the state power by means of a coup carried out by a secret society. On all those points Marx was to take issue with Blanqui. Yet Blanquism was unique among pre-Marxist socialism and communism in being a revolutionary proletarian movement, and in June 1848 the first real challenge to bourgeois class rule was to take place under Blanquist inspiration. It was Blanqui who coined the phrase 'dictatorship of the proletariat', and although Marx was to transform the concept of the proletariat, and to reject Blanqui's conspiratorial tactics, he retained Blanqui's stress on the violent overthrow of the bourgeois state as the precondition for communism.

33. Philippe Buonarotti, *History of Babeuf's Conspiracy of Equals*, London, 1836.

We can now situate the basic principles of Marx's scientific communism in relation to the socialist and communist doctrines of the 1840s. Marx insisted against the great utopians, Saint-Simon, Fourier and Owen, that the common goal of a rational reorganization of production could not be achieved simply by appeal to reason, and, against the reformist schemes of Proudhon and Louis Blanc, that the working class could only be liberated by revolutionary political action to expropriate private property. Communism could only come about as a result of the antagonisms of capitalist society, by the victory of the working class over the bourgeoisie in class struggle. Yet while agreeing with Blanqui that the present ruling class had to be defeated politically, Marx rejected Blanqui's conception of the proletariat, i.e. the dispossessed social base of the revolution, as including all the labouring classes. For Marx, the new society was only possible on the basis of modern industry, and it was only the industrial working class, who did not own their means of production, that could be relied on to overthrow the capitalist order. But the obverse of Marx's restriction of the social base of the revolution was his extension of its political agency. Communist society could not be brought about, as Blanqui would have it, by a conspiratorial coup and the dictatorship of a political elite ruling on the proletariat's behalf, but only by the political organization of the industrial working class itself. Here Marx took his model from the English Chartists, the first mass organization of the modern working class. This political subject, the organized proletariat, was to expropriate the means of production, and to exercise collective control over the productive process. With the abolition of antagonistic classes, political power would give way, as Saint-Simon had envisaged, to the mere administration of production.

The Communist League

At the beginning of 1846, having elaborated the basic principles of scientific communism, Marx and Engels moved to engage themselves practically in the proletarian movement. Yet the country to which they primarily directed their attention was not advanced England, but backward Germany. To some extent this choice was dictated to them. They already possessed a certain following among the German intelligentsia, while their capacity to intervene in English or French politics was severely limited. But besides this,

Marx and Engels felt as Germans a special responsibility to their native land that they were to retain throughout their decades of exile, and in the late 1840s German absolutism was moving conspicuously and rapidly towards crisis. In the forthcoming German revolution, which Marx and Engels expected to overthrow the old regimes and transform German society along bourgeois lines, they saw a necessary step towards the final, communist revolution.

Germany in the 1840s still showed little sign of organized activity on the part of the industrial working class. Despite the economic development of the 1830s and 1840s, the proletariat, in the Marxist sense, was still a small minority of the population, concentrated particularly in the cotton mills of the northern Rhineland. The Silesian weavers' revolt of 1844 was not a movement of the modern proletariat, but one of traditional artisans starved out of production by the competition of machine industry. Among German skilled workers, however, there was already a significant political ferment, which, if it found little expression in Germany itself, where police conditions made this almost impossible, blossomed in the great centres of German emigration: Paris, Brussels, London, Geneva and New York. (In Paris alone, there were by 1843 some 85,000 emigrant German workers.)

The main organization of the German workers' movement of this time, which was also, in the circumstances of the emigration, 'the *first international workers' movement* of all time',[34] was the League of the Just. This secret society, formed by German émigrés in Paris in 1836, had been closely connected with Blanqui's Société des Saisons, and had suffered together with it in the defeated insurrection of 1839. In the 1840s, although the nominal centre of the League was still Paris, its real centre of gravity moved with the League's leading members to London, where the German Workers Educational Association was founded in 1840 as a public front for the League's activities.[35] In London in the 1840s the League of the Just learned from the English Chartists the possibilities of mass working-class organization consequent on the development of modern industry. Though the League kept the

34. Engels, 'On the History of the Communist League', *MESW*, p. 431.
35. The German Workers Educational Association, with its meeting hall in Great Windmill Street, Soho, served as the London centre of the German workers' movement for many years. It survived the dissolution of the Communist League in 1852, and was later associated with the German Social-Democratic Party, until in 1918 it was dissolved by the British government.

structure of a conspiratorial organization, it began to distance itself from the tactics of Blanquism, and sought alternative means to bring about its communist goal.

It was evidently towards the League of the Just that Marx and Engels had to orient themselves. Engels had already been in contact with the League circle in London, and both he and Marx respected the League for its militancy and recognized its importance as a workers' organization. At this time, however, the League was under the influence of the utopian communist Wilhelm Weitling,[36] and Marx and Engels were unwilling to join forces with it until it understood and accepted their scientific communism. They therefore decided, as an intermediate step, to set up a Communist Correspondence Committee based in Brussels, where Marx was still living, to conduct propaganda among the ranks of the German communists, and to win them over to their own theoretical position. The Communist Correspondence Committee was little more than a small group of Marx's personal followers, but it held meetings and exchanged letters with working-class militants in England, France and Germany, and in particular with the sections of the League of the Just, which it gradually succeeded in influencing. On 23 October 1846, for example, Engels could write to the Committee from Paris, that, after several weeks of discussion he had won the majority of the League circle to accept that, as communists, they pursued the interests of the proletariat in opposition to the bourgeoisie, aiming at the abolition of private property by means of a 'democratic revolution by force'.[37]

Early in 1847 the League had come close enough to Marx and Engels's theoretical position for them to be able to determine its future organization and tactics. In June 1847 a congress was held in London, attended by Engels and Wilhelm Wolff[38] on behalf of the Communist Correspondence Committee, which transformed the League of the Just into the Communist League, reorganized its structure on democratic lines (though the League necessarily

36. Wilhelm Weitling was the first working-class publicist of communism in Germany. His *Guarantees of Harmony and Freedom* was inspired primarily by Fourier, and Marx had praised it highly in his Paris period.

37. *MESC*, p. 32.

38. Wilhelm Wolff, a journalist, remained a close comrade of Marx and Engels throughout the revolutionary period of 1848 and in exile in England. In 1867 Marx dedicated to Wolff the first volume of *Capital*, describing him as an 'intrepid, faithful, noble protagonist of the proletariat'.

remained secret), and laid down, as the first article of its new rules, 'The aim of the League is the overthrow of the bourgeoisie, the rule of the proletariat, the abolition of the old, bourgeois society based on class antagonisms and the foundation of a new society without classes and without private property.'[39] After the June Congress, Marx and his followers set up a public German Workers Association in Brussels on the lines of the League's successful front organization in London, through which to influence the emigrant German workers. In November 1847 Marx and Engels travelled to London to attend the second congress of the Communist League, held secretly in the Great Windmill Street premises over a ten day period. This congress discussed at length the principles of scientific communism presented by Marx and Engels, and at the end of the congress the two were mandated to draft a statement of principles for the League. Marx sent the *Manifesto of the Communist Party* to London at the end of January 1848, and it was published there in German just before revolution broke out in Paris on 21 February.[40]

The Communist Manifesto is justly Marx's most famous political text, for it formulates in polemical form his general conception of the proletarian revolution, as it follows from the materialist concept of history. In the Manifesto Marx did not merely set out to demonstrate the thesis that opens its first section, 'The history of all hitherto existing societies is the history of class struggles.'[41] Commenting on the Manifesto some four years later, Marx insisted,

No credit is due to me for discovering the existence of classes in modern society or the struggle between them. Long before me bourgeois historians had described the historical development of this class struggle and bourgeois economists the economic anatomy of the classes. What I did that was new was to prove: 1) that the *existence of classes* is only bound up with *particular historical phases in the development of production*, 2) that the class struggle necessarily leads to the *dictatorship of the proletariat*, 3) that this dictatorship itself only constitutes the transition to the *abolition of all classes* and to a *classless society*.[42]

39. Quoted by Engels, 'On the History of the Communist League', *MESW*, p. 440.

40. The Manifesto originally appeared without the names of its authors, and its title does not refer to the secret Communist League (Bund der Kommunisten). 'Party' (*Partei*) has here a meaning more like the modern 'movement'; it was a very loose word in mid nineteenth century usage, both German and English.

41. See below, p. 67.

42. Marx to Weydemeyer, 5 March 1852; *MESC*, p. 69.

Marx's concern in the first section of the Manifesto is to explain in what way capitalist relations of production have become fetters on the development of the productive forces, and why the class that is exploited by capital, the industrial proletariat, is both capable of overthrowing this mode of production and indeed compelled by its position to do so. By way of comparison, Marx opens the Manifesto by outlining the transition from feudalism to capitalism, portraying the bourgeoisie in heroic guise as the representative of the new forces of production and exchange (manufacture, international trade) whose development was restricted by feudal social relations. To attain the free market it needed, the bourgeoisie had to overthrow the feudal organization of agriculture and industry, and the political superstructures built upon this, and it 'has at last, since the establishment of modern industry and of the world market, conquered for itself, in the modern representative state, exclusive political sway'.[43]

Just as the manufacturing system could not be contained within the feudal guilds, so bourgeois society is increasingly unable to control the means of production it has itself created, as evidenced by the periodic commercial and industrial crises caused by overproduction – 'an epidemic that, in all earlier epochs, would have seemed an absurdity'.[44] In the Manifesto Marx is content merely to indicate overproduction crises as the sign of the 'revolt of modern productive forces against modern conditions of production', and his theoretical explanation of this phenomenon and its implications was to wait until *Capital*. What must be stressed here, however, is the distinction that Marx makes between the constantly developing productive forces that are fettered by capitalist property relations, and which Marx describes as 'weapons' that are 'turned against the bourgeoisie itself', and 'the men who are to wield these weapons – the proletarians'.[45] The industrial working class is the *political agency* that will overthrow existing social relations, but it can only do so because the development of the productive forces places this task on the historical agenda.

Marx proceeds to analyse the process by which the proletariat is organized into a class and onto the political arena by the very conditions of its social existence. What spurs its development from sporadic and inchoate rebellion, originally against the instruments of labour rather than the capitalists (e.g. Luddism), to sustained mass organization, is the development of machine

43. See below, p. 69.   44. See below, p. 73.   45. ibid.

industry itself, which concentrates the workers together in great masses. In these conditions, *combinations* of workers, originally formed to bargain with the individual capitalist over wages, inevitably expand and develop, and in modern conditions the workers achieve a national union more quickly than did the burghers of the Middle Ages. As the union of the workers expands to include their whole class, their struggle becomes *ipso facto* a political one. Meanwhile, the development of capitalism causes intermediate classes that remain over from pre-capitalist modes of production (petty bourgeois, peasants, artisans, etc.) to disappear into the proletariat. Class antagonisms are thus simplified into the single antagonism between bourgeois and proletarians, and 'the proletarian movement is the self-conscious, independent movement of the immense majority, in the interests of the immense majority'. 'What the bourgeoisie, therefore, produces, above all, are its own grave-diggers. Its fall and the victory of the proletariat are equally inevitable.'[46]

In the second section of the Manifesto, Marx summarizes the goal of the proletarian revolution 'in the single sentence: Abolition of private property,' specifying, 'Modern bourgeois private property is the final and most complete expression of the system of producing and appropriating products that is based on class antagonisms, on the exploitation of the many by the few.' Since capital is already a 'social power', in the sense that 'only by the united action of all members of society, can it be set in motion',[47] and the vast majority of the population – i.e. the proletariat – is already devoid of private property, all that is necessary for the realization of a non-antagonistic, classless mode of production is to convert capital into common property, the property of society as a whole. And the agent of this transformation can only be the proletariat that is forming itself 'into a class, and consequently into a political party'[48] in the course of its struggle against its immediate exploiters. This is the point at which the distinctively Marxist synthesis of the social and the political revolution is made, and Marx goes on to specify that 'the proletariat will use its political supremacy to wrest, by degrees, all capital from the bourgeoisie, to centralize all instruments of production in the hands of the state, i.e. of the proletariat organized as the ruling class.'[49]

But the class struggle of the proletariat is itself only a necessary

46. See below, pp. 78–9.   47. See below, pp. 80–81.
48. See below, p. 76.   49. See below, p. 86.

transitional stage towards the achieved communist society. Since 'political power . . . is merely the organized power of one class for oppressing another', then when the proletariat

sweeps away by force the old conditions of production, it will, along with these conditions, have swept away the conditions for the existence of class antagonisms and of classes generally, and will thereby have abolished its own supremacy as a class . . . In place of the old bourgeois society, with its classes and class antagonisms, we shall have an association, in which the free development of each is the condition for the free development of all.[50]

In the third section of the Manifesto, Marx undertakes a fairly detailed critique of the various types and sub-types of contemporary socialist and communist literature. This polemic is directed against the whole welter of doctrines of social reform that flourished under the name of socialism and even communism in the 1840s, when the social conflicts generated by capitalist industrialization became an increasingly urgent problem for all classes in England, France and Germany. Although the particular doctrines and panaceas that Marx attacks here were specific to this period, Marx's critique still provides a paradigm of ideological analysis informed by the theory of historical materialism. The last sub-section 'Critical-Utopian Socialism and Communism' is particularly important as it presents an explanation of the development of socialist ideology from utopia to science, and introduces the concept of sectarianism which Marx saw as the main obstacle in the way of the development of a revolutionary workers' movement.

As mentioned above, the basic economic theory of communism, i.e. a rationally planned and collectively controlled mode of production based on modern industry, was first formulated by Saint-Simon in opposition to the anarchic character of capitalist production and the extremes of wealth and poverty it produced, although Saint-Simon and the other utopians were elitist and anti-democratic, and saw no connection between their own ideas and the workers' movement. Marx attributed this original distance between the critique of capitalism and the actual working-class movement to the still undeveloped stage of industrial capitalism, and consequently of the proletariat, in the early nineteenth century. Since the founders of the utopian systems saw the proletariat as 'a class without any historical initiative or any indepen-

50. See below, p. 87.

dent political movement',[51] they sought to realize their plans for social reconstruction by an appeal to society at large, especially to the educated and ruling classes. Although their writings 'attack[ed] every principle of existing society' and were therefore 'full of the most valuable materials for the enlightenment of the working class',[52] their ideas of the future society and the means to achieve it were inevitably characterized by all sorts of idiosyncracies. But as the struggle of the proletariat against the bourgeoisie developed, it became possible for the first time to conceive of communism as being brought about not by the reconciliation of class antagonisms from outside, but by the victory of the proletariat over the bourgeoisie in class struggle. The subjective and arbitrary schemes of the utopians now acquired a reactionary significance, since they still endeavoured 'to deaden the class struggle and to reconcile the class antagonisms'.[53]

It is against this characterization of the utopian socialism and communism which attempted to foist its subjective plans on the real proletarian movement, that Marx defines the tasks of the Communists in the second section of the Manifesto. As opposed to the utopians, 'the theoretical conclusions of the Communists ... merely express, in general terms, actual relations springing from an existing class struggle, from an historical movement going on under our very eyes'. The Communists therefore 'do not form a separate party opposed to other working-class parties'[54], and 'do not set up any sectarian principles of their own, by which to shape and mould the proletarian movement'.[55] The particular task of the Communists, distinguished only by their theoretical insight into the historical process, is to struggle for the proletariat to recognize the revolutionary role that it is compelled to play by the objective dynamic of bourgeois society, to 'point out' to the proletariat as a whole its own international and long-term interests.

The Manifesto should not be regarded as the *summa* of Marx's political thought. It is certainly the most general formulation of the principles of scientific communism, and Marx himself was to

51. See below, p. 95. In the first section of his 'Socialism: Utopian and Scientific', Engels expands on this analysis of the utopian socialists; see *MESW*, pp. 394–405.

52. See below, p. 96.   53. ibid.

54. See above, p. 28, n. 40. The Communist League, if not a separate *party* in the contemporary sense of this term, was certainly separate from other working-class *organizations*, and indeed frequently opposed to them.

55. See below, pp. 79–80.

refer to it as a touchstone throughout his life. However the Manifesto leaves many problems unresolved and gives untenable solutions to others. The paramount problem is of course whether the 'historical movement going on under our very eyes' leads as straightforwardly to communism as Marx in 1848 believed, and we shall return to this in the Introduction to *The First International and After* (Political Writings, Volume 3). Other problems include those of how the working class organizes politically for the seizure of power, and how it confronts the state apparatus, as well as the problems of national antagonisms and intermediate classes, and these will be discussed as they arise in the context of Marx's political practice. The greatness of the Manifesto is that it lays down the most general implications of the theory of historical materialism for the proletarian class struggle in a form that is fundamentally as valid today as when it was first written: the fetters that capitalist relations of production impose on the productive forces render inevitable the replacement of capitalism by communism; capitalist relations can only be abolished by the class struggles that they themselves engender; the proletariat can only transform capitalist into communist society by organizing itself as the ruling class and using its state power to expropriate the owners of capital; and the abolition of classes consequent on the instauration of communism will lead to the withering away of the state itself.

The Problem of Tactics

In the Communist League Marx and Engels developed a working-class cadre that accepted their theory of scientific communism. For this embryonic workers' party, as for every German opposition party at the time, a formulation of ultimate aims was not sufficient. It had been apparent since the beginning of the decade that the Prussian absolutist regime was moving into crisis. When in 1846 the liberal bourgeois opposition demanded the promulgation of a constitution before they would vote further taxation, the Communists, in common with all democrats,[56] began to expect the outbreak of revolution in the near future. The approach of revolu-

56. In this period, when the proletarian movement was only just beginning to distinguish itself from the movement of the petty bourgeoisie, the term 'democrat' was generally used in the wide sense to denote all who stood for rule by the people, hence including the Communists.

tion required the Communist League to define its tactical goals, which, given the infancy of German industrial capitalism, could not simply coincide with the strategic goal of the seizure of power by the working class.

The situation that the Communist League faced in the approaching German revolution seems at first sight inexplicable in terms of the historical schema presented in the Manifesto. The Manifesto was principally oriented to the problems of the proletarian movement in the most advanced capitalist countries, which had long since experienced their bourgeois revolutions (e.g. England in the seventeenth and France in the eighteenth century), and where Marx expected the contradiction between the proletariat and the bourgeoisie to rapidly intensify and lead to communist revolution. But in Germany, which was so far behind the western countries in its economic and social development that the bourgeoisie had not yet taken power, how could there already be a proletarian movement directed against the bourgeoisie, and what should the German Communists do in such a situation?

The root cause of Germany's idiosyncratic political course is explained in Marxist theory by the concept of uneven development, which, though it forms the object of many of Marx's analyses, only later received its name from the Russian Marxist George Plekhanov. In the historical process, societies originally separate from one another, which have developed at different rates, enter into relation with each other exhibiting different modes of production, and mutually affect each other's historical course by means of trade, war, the spread of technology, etc. It is this process of interaction that gives history its intricate complexity. And although Marx believed that capitalism was tending to level out national differences, it has itself generated new forms of uneven development (see the Introduction to *Surveys from Exile*, Political Writings, Volume 2). Only with world communism can we expect, at last, a single human history.

The survey of capitalist development that Marx presented in *The German Ideology* and the *Manifesto of the Communist Party* is a theoretical schema, not an empirical description. Marx was quite well aware that real history is more complicated, and he never expected every country to follow an identical historical path. In the final section of the Manifesto Marx himself alluded to the effects of uneven development with respect to Germany, although he did not explain its particular causes. With historical hindsight, these appear to be essentially of the following kind. Germany's previous history had left the country considerably behind its western neighbours in the transition from feudalism to capitalism (largely as a result of the Peasant War in the Reformation period and the Thirty Years War in the seventeenth century, which blocked the formation of a unified nation state). Germany had not developed a strong commercial and financial bourgeoisie based on international trade, such as had overthrown the old regimes in England and France, but this did not prevent the rise of an industrial capitalist class in the nineteenth century, based on the new technology of machine industry, which had gradually been developed in the most advanced countries. Because of this, the German bourgeoisie did not confront 'its' revolution until it had already produced its *alter ego*, the industrial proletariat[56a]. In the Manifesto, however, although Marx asserted that German history would take a different course from the 'classic' scenario of the English and French bourgeois revolutions, he presented this merely in terms of a condensed time-scale: the bourgeois revolution in Germany, 'to be carried out under more advanced conditions of European civilization, and with a much more developed proletariat, than that of England was in the seventeenth, and of France in the eighteenth century', would be 'the prelude to an immediately following proletarian revolution'.[57]

From early in 1846, when Marx and Engels began their systematic propaganda for scientific communism, they also put forward a specific tactic for the working class in the German revolution. Given that the coming revolution would bring the bourgeoisie to power in Germany, the proletariat should actively support the bourgeoisie in its struggle against absolutism, and refrain from pursuing its own struggle against the bourgeoisie until the old regime had been decisively defeated. The first public statement of this position was in an article by Engels on 'The State of Germany', published in the Chartist *Northern Star* (4 April 1846), where he wrote that the German workers' movement would subordinate itself to the bourgeoisie until the day that the bourgeoisie held full power, but that from that very day its struggle against the bourgeoisie would begin. A similar formulation is reproduced in Section IV of the Manifesto, with the proviso that the Communists 'never cease, for a single instant, to instil into the working class the clearest possible recognition of the hostile antagonism

56a. See below, p. 123.   57. See below, p. 98.

between bourgeoisie and proletariat',[58] so as to prepare the workers for the future battle against their present ally.

It is interesting to compare this new tactical position with that expressed by Marx before he developed his materialist conception of history. When Marx first committed himself to the proletariat, in 1844, it was as the class with 'radical chains', the agent of a revolution that had to 'surmount', in *'salta mortale'* (a mortal leap), both Germany's 'limitations' and those of the modern nations, because 'the development of the social conditions, and the progress of political theory, show that [the middle class's] point of view is already antiquated or at least disputable'.[59] By 1846, however, Marx's theory of historical materialism had led him to the conclusion that the German proletariat could not simply ignore the 'disputable' position of the bourgeoisie, and that, in the revolution now approaching, the working class must at first throw in its lot with its own immediate exploiter until feudalism and absolutism had been defeated. As we shall see, Marx was to insist on the need for this alliance with the bourgeoisie even at the expense of losing allies in the German working-class movement.[60]

In line with this tactic, Marx and Engels concentrated on attacking utopian ideas that held that communism was already possible in Germany, and in particular the ideas of 'true socialism' which dominated German socialist ideology at this time,[61] and which used a critique of capitalism drawn from the French utopians to deflect the workers from participating in the growing democratic movement. At a discussion between the Communist Correspondence Committee and Weitling when the latter visited Brussels in March 1846, Marx denounced the 'fantastic hopes' of the utopians and argued his characteristic position that communism could not be achieved in Germany without the bourgeoisie first coming to power. On the basis of this position Marx and Engels could also work within the ranks of the general democratic exile of petty bourgeois and intellectuals, attempting to weld a solid alliance of Communists and democrats on a com-

58. See below, p. 98.

59. 'Contribution to the Critique of Hegel's Philosophy of Right: Introduction', in *Early Writings*.

60. Though rejected by Marx in 1846, the theory of the 'mortal leap' presaged the tactic of 'permanent revolution' which Marx developed in 1850, this time within the framework of scientific communism. See below, pp. 54–6.

61. See Section III 1.c. of the Communist Manifesto, below, pp. 90–93.

mon programme of the overthrow of feudalism and absolutism, and the unification of Germany as a democratic republic. Marx therefore collaborated, from its foundation in the spring of 1847, with the *Deutsche-Brüsseler-Zeitung* (*Brussels German Gazette*), a German paper published in Brussels which was quite influential in the immediate pre-revolutionary period, and which towards the end of the year became the virtual organ of Marx and his followers. Marx represented German democracy in the Democratic Association for the Unification of All Countries, set up in November 1847, a Belgian organization in correspondence with the English Fraternal Democrats, which united workers and petty-bourgeois democrats and campaigned in solidarity with the nations and peoples of Europe oppressed by absolutism. (See p. 99, n. 1.)

Despite Marx's undoubtedly correct insistence on the primacy of the struggle against absolutism, his position on the relationship of the proletariat to the bourgeoisie in the bourgeois revolution was still rather ambivalent. According to the Manifesto, the communists were to 'instil into the working class the clearest possible recognition of the hostile antagonism between bourgeoisie and proletariat', while simultaneously mobilizing the proletariat to 'fight with the bourgeoisie whenever it acts in a revolutionary way'.[62] These two aims would seem in practice very difficult to reconcile, particularly as the German workers' movement was still at a very embryonic and spontaneous stage, and could not yet act as a disciplined unity. It is therefore not surprising that *The Demands of the Communist Party in Germany* which Marx and Engels drew up after the March revolutions in Germany as their basic programmatic document, and which summarizes in seventeen points the prerequisites of the radical-democratic overthrow of feudalism and absolutism, mentions not a word of the 'hostile antagonism between bourgeoisie and proletariat' that the Manifesto had promised to stress. Forced to choose between present and future needs, Marx now decided to sacrifice for the time being the anti-capitalist education of the proletariat to the immediate struggle against the old regime.

As we shall see, Marx's tactic of a short-term alliance with the bourgeoisie proved untenable. In the context of Germany's uneven development, the very existence of a proletarian movement threatening it from behind seriously checked the revolutionary ardour of the bourgeoisie – a fact that Marx should perhaps have

62. See below, p. 97.

foreseen when he wrote that the German bourgeois revolution was 'the prelude to an immediately following proletarian revolution'. When the 1848 revolution broke out, however, Marx was still counting on the German bourgeoisie to take the initiative in the first stage of the revolution, as the French bourgeoisie had done in 1789. His policy was to spur on the bourgeoisie from an independent base on the left, organizing the plebeian classes separately from the bourgeoisie in order to strike together at the old regime, and to prepare this democratic bloc of proletariat, petty bourgeoisie and peasantry to step temporarily into the vanguard should the bourgeoisie show signs of cold feet, by analogy with the Jacobin government in France of 1793–4. (*The Demands of the Communist Party in Germany* were explicitly presented as representing the common interest of these three classes.) However, events were soon to show that the proletariat could not allay the fears it roused in the bourgeoisie merely by supporting it in the struggle against the old regime. Even if its political representatives refrained from mentioning the hostile antagonism between it and the bourgeoisie, the real existence of this threat could not be covered up, and the development of the revolution was to force Marx to abandon any hope that the bourgeoisie would move decisively against the old order.

The German Revolution

The February revolution in Paris, which overthrew the constitutional monarchy of Louis Philippe, rapidly detonated a revolutionary movement in Germany. On 13 March a popular uprising in Vienna crippled the Habsburg monarchy, and on 18 March the revolution spread to Berlin. Frederick William IV of Prussia was forced to allow free political activity, and to promise not to stand in the way of democratic national unification.

Following the February revolution, Marx immediately left Brussels for Paris, where, by way of compensation for his expulsion three years earlier, the Provisional Government granted him honorary French citizenship. Marx had been authorized by the Communist League to set up a new Central Committee in Paris, which he formed out of his closest followers: Engels, Wilhelm Wolff from Brussels, and Bauer, Moll and Schapper from London.[63] The largest group of German exiles in Paris formed a

63. Joseph Moll, a watchmaker, and Karl Schapper, a compositor, were both leading members of the League of the Just before its transformation into

legion which optimistically aimed at spreading revolution to Germany by force of arms, but Marx and his friends spent their energies on sending several hundred Communist League members and supporters back clandestinely, until the March days in Berlin made open return possible. It was during their stay in Paris that Marx and Engels drew up *The Demands of the Communist Party in Germany*, which were distributed on a wide scale in Germany over the next few months.

Marx and Engels returned to Germany in April and decided to settle in Cologne. This choice was motivated by several considerations. Cologne was a Prussian city, from where they could confront one of the two German great powers. It was in the Rhineland province, economically the most advanced part of Germany, and which also retained the more liberal press laws of the Code Napoléon as a legacy from its French occupation. Cologne had been a centre of opposition activity throughout the 1840s, and already possessed an active Communist League organization. Finally, Marx himself was remembered in Cologne from the days of the *Rheinische Zeitung* of 1842–3. This was particularly important given Marx's tactic of a bloc of all democratic forces, and on their return to Cologne Marx and Engels set out to obtain sufficient political and financial support from the Rhineland democrats to launch a daily paper. The *Neue Rheinische Zeitung* (*New Rhenish Gazette*) duly appeared on 1 June, subtitled *Organ der Demokratie* (*Organ of Democracy*).

The twelve months that he spent in Germany in 1848–9 provide an unparalleled occasion to see Marx as a revolutionary militant, and we shall therefore examine his political practice in some detail. Throughout this period, Marx's base of operations was not the Communist League but the *Neue Rheinische Zeitung*, a fact that requires some explanation. Engels was certainly justified in attributing this move to the fact that 'the League proved to be much too weak a lever as against the popular mass movement that had now broken out'.[64] But there was more to it than that.

---

the Communist League. Both worked with Marx in Cologne during the 1848 revolution, and Moll was killed in 1849 during the Reich Constitution Campaign (see p. 48). Schapper broke with Marx when the Communist League split in September 1850 (see below, pp. 57–9), though their differences were later reconciled. Heinrich Bauer, a shoemaker, also a leading member of the League of the Just, was not related to the Young Hegelian brothers Edgar and Bruno Bauer.

64. 'On the History of the Communist League', *MESW*, p. 442.

Although Engels avoids mentioning it, there is every indication that Marx himself deliberately sabotaged the League, following the dispute that developed between him and Gottschalk.[65]

Andreas Gottschalk was the dominant figure in the Cologne district of the League, and had used his position as a physician to build up a following among the workers and unemployed. After the March days he established an openly functioning Workers Society, which Marx and Engels made contact with when they returned to Cologne. Similar societies had been formed in many German towns, though not always with Communists in a leading position, and in Berlin the League member Stefan Born was attempting to unite these into a national association. Initially the Communist League hoped to control the open workers' societies through its secret 'communes', but by the end of April this hope had to be abandoned as illusory. The League was too thin on the ground numerically, its communications were poor, and – most crucially – the workers' societies were too strongly permeated by the old guild spirit and organized themselves along craft lines, reflecting their domination by artisans, and not workers in modern industry.

In the Cologne Workers Society, which rapidly acquired 5,000 members, Gottschalk pandered to the artisanal consciousness of the membership in a way that Marx considered intolerable. Not only did Gottschalk sanction the division of the society on craft lines; he supported its concentration on the particular problems of unemployment, etc. faced by the workers, and compromised with politically backward elements on the crucial question of the republic, sticking at the demand for a federal constitutional monarchy. In April Gottschalk won the Workers Society, against Marx's counsel, for a boycott of the elections to the German National Assembly at Frankfurt, which were admittedly indirect and inegalitarian, and in May, more seriously, he actually opposed a demonstration against the return of the ultra-reactionary Prince William, who had fled to England at the outbreak of revolution. Gottschalk's supporters formed a majority of the Communist League's Cologne district, although Marx controlled the Central Committee by virtue of the powers conferred on him from London. When Gottschalk refused League discipline, Marx appears to

65. This assertion is still contentious, but in my view amply demonstrated by B. Nicolaevsky in an article, 'On the History of the Communist League', *International Review of Social History*, vol. I, no. 2, Amsterdam, 1956.

have decided that the League was, for the time being, more trouble than it was worth. He dissolved the Central Committee, thus leaving the League headless in the flux of the revolution, and worked from his base in the *Neue Rheinische Zeitung* with the handful of his closest supporters. Joseph Moll was sent to work in the Workers Society, where he conducted an educational campaign, dividing the meetings into small groups to discuss the League's Demands. But Marx's supporters were far from controlling the Workers Society, and when the *Neue Rheinische Zeitung* showed that its main concerns were removed from the immediate economic problems of the working class, the Workers Society weekly paper began to attack the *Organ of Democracy* for a 'callous' and 'exploitative' attitude towards the workers.[66]

By the time the *Neue Rheinische Zeitung* commenced publication, the revolutionary movement of March had forced democratic concessions in Prussia, Austria and the smaller German states; the all-German National Assembly had started its deliberations in Frankfurt, while a Prussian Assembly was sitting in Berlin. But in Germany, as in Europe as a whole, the first wave of the revolutionary movement, which had won extensive if fragile victories, had already spent its main force. In Italy, revolutionary Milan and Venice were on the defensive against the Austrian troops. In France the elections held in April with universal male suffrage had resulted in the defeat of the Provisional Government of 'red republicans' and socialists by an immense reactionary majority elected by the countryside. In Britain the 'monster' Chartist demonstration of 10 April had ended in a demobilizing shambles, and in Belgium the bourgeoisie had successfully contained the workers' movement by conceding reforms. In Germany itself, the Prussian and Austrian monarchies, though they had made concessions to the popular movement, were still secure in command of their armies and bureaucracies, and behind them loomed the power of tsarist Russia, their partner in the counter-revolutionary Holy Alliance.

In this political setting Marx was more than ever determined to concentrate single-mindedly on the struggle against the absolutist regimes. Not only did the *Neue Rheinische Zeitung* avoid all talk of communism, but Marx was quite unmoved by the Workers Society's complaints that his paper ignored the workers' economic

66. Oscar J. Hammen, *The Red '48ers*, Charles Scribner's Sons, New York, 1969, p. 224.

R. – 3

interests. As Engels later wrote, 'The political programme of the *Neue Rheinische Zeitung* consisted of two main points: a single, indivisible, democratic German republic, and war with Russia, which included the restoration of Poland.'[67] On the home front, Marx and Engels bent all their efforts to preparing and organizing the democratic forces for a decisive insurrection. And the importance that they attributed to offensive war against Russia was not only to pre-empt the threat of intervention and to restore Poland as a bastion of '20 million heroes' between Russia and the West.[68] War against Russia would also have demanded the marshalling of Germany's economic and military resources in an unprecedented manner, and thus more than anything else have required the centralization of power in a single national state and favoured the most decisive of the revolutionary parties in its bid for power. In this scenario as in so much else in the 1848 revolution, Marx had in mind the model of the first French revolution, in this case the stimulus that foreign war had on its radicalization.

During the first weeks of the *Neue Rheinische Zeitung*'s existence, its chief concern was with the Frankfurt and Berlin Assemblies, belabouring them mercilessly for their 'parliamentary cretinism', i.e. their failure to recognize the crucial question of power.[69] In the columns of his paper Marx attempted to drive home to the Frankfurt Assembly the folly of its concern with constitution-making when it had no executive arm of its own and did not even sit in a city with a 'strong revolutionary movement' to defend it.[70] The *Neue Rheinische Zeitung* nicknamed the Berlin Assembly the '*Vereinbarungsversammlung*' ('assembly of agreement'), for its passive acceptance of its royal mandate to draw up a constitution for Prussia 'by agreement with the Crown'. Despite the fact that the Berlin Assembly, unlike the Frankfurt, did have a 'strong revolutionary movement' behind it, it shared the illusion that history is made by parliamentary debate and not by the class struggle, whereas both assemblies owed their very existence to the barricade fighting of the March days. When the liberal Camphausen ministry in Prussia promised the abolition of feudal obliga-

67. 'Karl Marx and the *Neue Rheinische Zeitung*', *MESW* [two-volume edition], Lawrence & Wishart, 1950, vol. II, p. 300.
68. See Engels, 'Speech on Poland' below, pp. 105–8.
69. See 'Camphausen's Declaration in the Sitting of 30 May', and 'The 15 June Sitting of the "*Vereinbarungsversammlung*"', below.
70. 'The Programmes of the Radical-Democratic Party and the Left in the Frankfurt Assembly', below, p. 121.

tions, Marx wrote in heavy type beneath his report, 'But the Bastille has still not been stormed.'[71]

For the first three months of the German revolution, it appeared that the liberal bourgeoisie, though irresolute, might well be pushed by circumstances into decisive action, leading the plebeian classes in an offensive against the remaining institutions of the old regime. The *Neue Rheinische Zeitung* therefore sought to spur this class into action by appeal to its own interests. However it soon became clear that this tactic was unviable. After the June insurrection in Paris, the showdown between the Constituent Assembly and the socialist workers who had made the February revolution, the Communists and the more consistent of their democratic allies could no longer hope to unite with the liberal bourgeoisie in a common front against the old regime. As Marx later wrote in *The Class Struggles in France*, the June days were 'the first great battle ... between the two great classes which divide modern society. It was a fight for the preservation or destruction of the bourgeois order.'[72] The significance of the June days was immediately apparent throughout Europe, and the spectre of proletarian revolution which, for the first time in history, had shown itself a practical possibility, consolidated all the exploiting classes in Germany on the side of reaction. Needless to say, the *Neue Rheinische Zeitung* came out unflinchingly on the side of the vanquished insurgents, exposing the brutal solidarity against the working class under the slogan of 'Order' that ran right through from the monarchists to the 'red republicans'.[73] But the timorous German bourgeoisie did not need Marx to spell out the lessons of the June days.

During the summer, and with the increasing stagnation of the Berlin and Frankfurt Assemblies, Marx and his comrades in Cologne concentrated their efforts on extending their organizational base, so as to be prepared for any future contingencies. The arrest of Gottschalk, after the Workers Society held rallies in support of the Paris insurgents, provided a fortuitous occasion for Marx to augment his influence over the society. In July Moll and Schapper were elected as its president and vice-president, and the society was reorganized with a smaller, directly elected executive committee to replace the old one elected on a guild basis, and with

71. 'The 15 June Sitting of the "*Vereinbarungsversammlung*",' below, p. 125.
72. In *Surveys from Exile*, pp. 58–9.
73. See 'The June Revolution', below.

fixed dues. The June days had caused severe tensions in the ranks of the democrats, but in the increasing climate of repression Marx, who was himself accused under the press laws, consolidated his support in the Cologne Democratic Society, where he now argued openly in favour of a revolutionary government brought about by new popular insurrection, which would represent all the 'heterogeneous elements' that made the revolution, i.e. not merely the bourgeoisie.[74] During the summer Marx and Engels pressed the Workers Society into starting agitation amongst the peasantry, and by September substantial Peasant Unions had been started up and down the Rhineland, as well as a peasant newspaper.

September 1848 saw a crisis in Prussia after the fiasco of the war against Denmark over the disputed territories of Schleswig-Hol-stein. The war had become a symbol of the movement for national unity, and even an occasion for German chauvinism, and the Frankfurt Assembly, having no armed forces of its own, had had to ask the Prussian monarchy to fight on behalf of the German nation. The Malmö armistice of 26 August, which Prussia accept-ed in deference to England and Russia, sparked off a wave of anger against the Prussian regime, leading to clashes between soldiers and citizens in Berlin, Cologne and other cities.[75]

On 16 September the crisis intensified, as the Frankfurt Assem-bly finally ratified the Malmö armistice. A popular insurrection broke out in Frankfurt, in which the peasantry played a major role, and the Frankfurt 'Reich ministry' called in Prussian, Austrian and Hessian troops to restore order. In Cologne, the Democratic and Workers Societies called a mass meeting to denounce the Frankfurt Assembly, and by 25 September, when a Rhineland Democratic Congress was scheduled to meet in Cologne, that city was also on the verge of insurrection. Marx, who had kept a low profile during the previous three weeks' agita-tion, and preferred where possible to work behind the scenes, realized that if the Democratic Congress met, a suicidal insurrec-tion confined to Cologne was inevitable. While attempts by the police to arrest the most active leaders were delayed by popular action, Marx succeeded in getting the Congress cancelled, and persuading the Workers and Democratic Societies not to be provoked into insurrection. Barricades were erected in Cologne in the evening, but the defenders quickly dispersed as the army

74. Hammen, *The Red '48ers*, p. 266.
75. See 'The Crisis and the Counter-Revolution', below.

advanced. Martial law was proclaimed, with the support of the constitutionalist city council, the civic guard was disbanded, and the *Neue Rheinische Zeitung* and three other papers banned. Engels, expecting imminent arrest for his role on the Committee of Public Safety formed to prepare for insurrection, fled to France, where he remained until the new year, and most of Marx's other chief supporters also either fled or were imprisoned.[76]

The *Neue Rheinische Zeitung* was allowed to reappear on 12 October, but took time to regain its former strength. On 17 October, in the absence of Moll and Schapper, Marx was himself elected president of the Workers Society, and a few weeks later delivered there his lectures on *Wage Labour and Capital*.[77]

Meanwhile, the German revolution came to its decisive stage. The high point of the revolution had been reached with the October events in Vienna, when the imminent departure of Habsburg troops against Hungary provoked a successful insurrection, and the city was liberated for three weeks. After heavy siege, the Vienna insurrection succumbed on 1 November, and the Prussian monarchy now also felt strong enough to move to the counter-offensive.[78] The king appointed an explicitly counter-revolutionary ministry under Count Brandenburg, and, when the Prussian Assembly passed a vote of no confidence, signed, on 9 November, a decree dissolving the Assembly, moved 10,000 troops into Berlin and declared martial law. The Assembly attempted to carry on its sessions, but reacted only passively to increasing harrassment. Rather than take the opportunity to organize armed resistance, its members dispersed across the country to organize a campaign of tax refusal.[79]

At first the *Neue Rheinische Zeitung* participated in this campaign, as Marx hoped that the liberal bourgeoisie might once again rally to the side of the revolution. But when it became apparent that the bourgeois opposition would not go beyond peaceful protest, Marx made an attempt to turn passive into active resistance, and the *Neue Rheinische Zeitung* and the Workers Society called for the forcible deposition of government officials, the

76. See 'The "Cologne Revolution"', below.
77. *MESW*, pp. 71–93.
78. See 'Revolution in Vienna', and 'The Victory of the Counter-Revolution in Vienna', below.
79. See 'The Counter-Revolution in Berlin' and 'No More Taxes!!!', below.

establishment of committees of public safety, and the formation of democratic troops of the military reserve into a people's militia. By 21 November the Cologne revolutionaries had their own armed forces, but two days later these collapsed without a struggle against the overwhelming force of the Prussian garrison. The Cologne city council refused to halt tax collection, and the Frankfurt Reich ministry declared a National Assembly motion to this end null and void. In December Frederick William, having used the red scare to entice the bourgeoisie back into the monarchist fold, consolidated his new reactionary bloc by granting a superficially liberal constitution, and waited for the occasion when the forces of revolution could be decisively routed.

In December 1848, in the series of articles 'The Bourgeoisie and the Counter-Revolution', Marx analysed the Prussian bourgeoisie's backsliding into the camp of reaction. Whereas in the Manifesto Marx had predicted, from the fact that Germany was entering her bourgeois revolution with a more developed proletariat than had England and France at the corresponding stage of their development, that the German proletariat would seize power hard on the heels of the bourgeoisie, he was now forced to the realization that the effect of this uneven development was that the German bourgeoisie would not seize power at all.

The German bourgeoisie had developed so sluggishly, so pusillanimously and so slowly, that it saw itself threateningly confronted by the proletariat, and all those sections of the urban population related to the proletariat in interests and ideas, at the very moment of its own threatening confrontation with feudalism and absolutism ... The Prussian bourgeoisie was not, like the French bourgeoisie of 1789, the class which represented the *whole* of modern society in face of the representatives of the old society, the monarchy and the nobility. It had sunk to the level of a type of *estate* ... inclined from the outset to treachery against the people ... because it itself already belonged to the old society.[80]

The bourgeois revolution in Germany could thus expect no help from the bourgeoisie itself – this was the paradoxical yet vitally important conclusion that Marx formulated for the first time in December 1848.

How then could the bourgeois revolution succeed, and what tactic should the proletariat follow? Marx had as yet no definite plan for this new contingency, and was only to formulate one after

80. Below, pp. 193–4.

the defeats of 1849. But if the bourgeoisie had decisively gone over to the counter-revolution, then there was no need for the proletariat to play down its antagonism to the bourgeoisie, and it was free to concentrate on building up its own independent organization, the better to prepare for the next round of the revolution. In the early part of 1849 Marx gradually moved to separate himself from the democrats and press for the construction of the independent workers' party which he had earlier blocked by dissolving the League's Central Committee. In the February elections under the new Prussian constitution, undemocratic as they were, Marx had still insisted on the Cologne Workers Society backing the democratic candidates, thereby incurring the vehement opposition of Gottschalk's faction, who charged Marx with 'asking the workers to endure the rule of capital'.[81] But on 18 February a new note crept into the columns of the *Neue Rheinische Zeitung*, when Marx referred to the paper as representing, not the democratic party, but 'the party of the people, which until now has existed only in elementary form'.[82] The *Neue Rheinische Zeitung* now turned decisively towards the working class, publishing Wilhelm Wolff's articles on the fraudulent 'emancipation' of the Silesian peasantry, and Marx's lectures *Wage Labour and Capital*. On 14 April Marx and his group formally severed their ties with the democrats, and declared that they would work instead 'for a closer union of workers' societies'.[83] Two days later the Cologne Workers Society called a regional congress of all workers' societies of Rhineland and Westphalia for 6 May, and sent out reprints of *Wage Labour and Capital*, its own statutes and other documents by way of preparation.

In spring 1849 Marx and Engels counted on support from without as the only salvation of the German revolution. The Hungarian national army was successfully fending off Austrian invasion, and was expected at one point to march on Vienna. In France the Constituent Assembly dissolved itself, and it looked as if a further advance of the revolution was possible there. Meanwhile, however, the ground was being prepared for the final battle of the German revolution in a way that Marx and Engels did not anticipate. On 4 March the Austrian government declared the Habsburg empire an indivisible monarchy, effacing for the first time all economic

81. In *Freiheit, Arbeit*, the paper of the Workers Society, quoted in Hammen, *The Red '48ers*, p. 372.

82. 'Stein', *MEW* 6, p. 298.   83. 'Declaration', ibid., p. 426.

and military distinctions between the German and non-German provinces, and thus pre-empting the Frankfurt Assembly's claims for German unity. The Frankfurt Assembly had now completed its constitution-making, and, abdicating its claims over German Austria, offered the crown of a 'little Germany' to Frederick William of Prussia, which on 12 April he refused. The previously impotent Assembly now acquired a last spurt of energy, and the Left found itself for the first time in the majority. The petty bourgeoisie, who had clung to the illusion of peaceful development until the last possible moment, decided, faced with the prospect of a return to unmediated absolutism, to engage in struggle behind the Frankfurt constitution, and began an agitation that rapidly led to insurrection in Dresden, in the Prussian Rhineland and in Baden.

Marx and Engels were slow to respond to this Reich Constitution Campaign, since it did not aim at a unified democratic republic but only a constitutional monarchist federation. However, when the movement developed into insurrection, Marx and his followers placed their full weight behind it. In the Rhineland, the rising was rapidly defeated. The petty bourgeoisie, after taking the initiative in launching armed struggle, began to compromise once insurrection had broken out, and in Elberfeld, for instance, where Engels went to give military advice, the revolution was even disowned by its erstwhile leaders. On 16 May Marx was served with an expulsion order, and the final issue of the *Neue Rheinische Zeitung* appeared on the 19th, printed in red, with the leading article 'To the Workers of Cologne'[84] advising against premature and isolated insurrection. Simultaneously, however, the *Neue Rheinische Zeitung* optimistically predicted that 'in a few weeks, even days, the revolutionary armies of France, Poland, Hungary and Germany will be in Berlin.'[85]

Marx and Engels left Cologne for Frankfurt, where they vainly attempted to rouse the collapsing Assembly to give a decisive political leadership to the revolutionary forces. However, only in Baden and the Palatinate, where the entire state fell into the hands of the insurrection, did military operations last for more than a week. Engels joined the Baden army which resisted the Prussians until July, while Marx left for Paris, and, soon expelled by the Cavaignac government, for London.

84. Below, p. 264.
85. '"To My People"', *MEW* 6, p. 515.

The National Question

The first of *The Demands of the Communist Party in Germany* was 'The whole of Germany shall be declared a single and indivisible republic.'[86] In central and eastern Europe, dominated by the trans-national empires of Austria and Russia, nationalism and democracy inevitably went hand in hand. The bourgeois revolution could only triumph if it broke up the Habsburg empire, fused together the petty German princedoms, and established a barrier against Russian intervention.

Marx and Engels inherited from their bourgeois-democratic forebears the view of Russia as a barbarous Asiatic presence outside the pale of European civilization. In their later years they overcame this Europocentrism, but they were at least justified at this time in their indiscriminate antipathy to all things Russian. In the 1848 period there was no possibility of support for the revolutionary movement from any class of Russian society, and since 1815 the tsarist regime had never hesitated, as the strongest partner in the Holy Alliance, to use its influence in Europe as the ultimate bulwark of reaction. It was generally believed that Russian military intervention against the French revolution of 1830 had only been prevented by the insurrection in Poland, and the tsar was to send Russian troops to put down the Hungarian revolution in 1849.

Poland had been completely partitioned between Prussia, Austria and Russia since 1795, and support for Polish independence was naturally common ground for all democrats. Next to German unification itself, Polish independence was the foundation stone on which Marx and Engels built up their position on the national questions of central and eastern Europe. In their speeches of 29 November 1847, a few weeks before the outbreak of the 1848 revolutions, Marx and Engels first began to integrate a national policy into their communist programme, a policy in which the restoration of Poland had a crucial place. Marx's own speech still betrays the rather idealistic euphoria that often characterized the early formulations of scientific communism from 1846 to the crucible of the 1848 revolution, in so far as Marx tended to reduce the struggle for Polish independence to an epiphenomenon of the universal proletarian revolution he believed impending. 'The victory of the proletariat over the

86. Below, p. 109.

bourgeoisie also signifies the emancipation of all downtrodden nations', and as 'of all countries it is England where the opposition between the proletariat and the bourgeoisie is most highly developed', 'Poland, therefore, must be freed, not in Poland, but in England'.[87] Engels, however, was already at this stage concerned with the tactical significance of the Polish movement to the German revolution. German democracy and Polish liberation were allied because 'the first condition for the freeing of both Germany and Poland is the overthrow of the present political regime in Germany . . ., and the withdrawal of Russia to the Dniester and the Dvina'.[88]

During the 1848 revolution, as editors of the *Neue Rheinische Zeitung*, Marx and Engels had to develop their national policy at a more specific and detailed level. Given that the overthrow of absolutism required the establishment of strong national states, Engels, who generally acted as the pair's spokesman on national questions, put forward the theory of the 'great historic nations', Germany, Poland, Hungary and Italy, as the four peoples that could successfully create viable nation states in central and eastern Europe.

The reason why Engels was led to discriminate in this way between 'great historic nations' and lesser nationalities doomed to subordination was that the trans-national empires contained an intricate patchwork of overlapping populations, at different stages of social development. Although the Communist Manifesto had asserted that 'national differences, and antagonisms between peoples, are daily more and more vanishing',[89] consequent on capitalist development, these antagonisms were at this very time bursting forth into open conflict in the eastern part of Europe, and were as significant a factor in the revolutions of 1848 as were antagonisms of class. Given the overlap of national groups, these antagonisms could never be solved according to principles of abstract justice, and Marx and Engels in any case rejected as idealist the so-called 'principle of nationalities', by which each national group was considered entitled to self-determination as an absolute right. The Germans, Poles, Hungarians and Italians had long proved their viability in struggling for unity and independence, and Marx and Engels decided to hitch the proletarian wagon to these national stars. In the process, the claims of the smaller and

87. Below, p. 100.   88. 'Speech of 22 February 1848', below, p. 108.
89. See below, p. 85.

less vocal nationalities – Czechs, Slovaks, Croats, Serbs, etc. – went by the board.

Marx and Engels had never been guilty of crude German chauvinism, as Engels could himself demonstrate by reference to their pre-1848 writings.[90] During the 1848 revolution itself, they struggled against the chauvinist degeneration of German nationalism when the Frankfurt National Assembly claimed for Germany a share of the Prussian and former Polish province of Posen [Poznań] which included a majority of Poles. Their error in 1848 was rather a general great-nation chauvinism, based on the major miscalculation that the smaller peoples of Europe were doomed by the logic of history, and had irrevocably lost their autonomy.

The national policy of the *Neue Rheinische Zeitung* was premised on the assumption that the economic and cultural differences between the 'great historic nations' and the other nationalities was substantial enough to allow the former to divide up the map between them. But the gap between these two groups was simply not great enough to make this possible. The case of the Czechs is the most outstanding example of this error. The predominantly Czech provinces of Bohemia and Moravia had formed part of the old Holy Roman Empire, and it was on the grounds of this historic attachment to Germany, not simply because of their substantial German minorities, that the Frankfurt Assembly claimed them from Austria in the name of a united Germany. It was undoubtedly true that the Slavic nationalities were on the whole less advanced than the Germans, and that the cultural and economic development of the central and southern Slavs had owed a lot to their German neighbours. Yet it showed a substantial gap in Engels's historical knowledge, to say the least, to assert that the Czechs had 'never had a history'.[91] And, arguing against Bakunin's[92] programme of 'democratic pan-Slavism', Engels went so

90. See 'Democratic Pan-Slavism', below, p. 237. 91. ibid., p. 232.

92. Michael Bakunin is chiefly remembered as the founder of revolutionary anarchism as a tendency in the working-class movement. For his disputes with Marx in this regard see the Introduction to *The First International and After*. In the mid 1840s Bakunin had been a member of the Young Hegelian circle in Germany, and was close to Marx at the inception of the *Deutsche-Französische Jahrbücher*. Still a revolutionary democrat, Bakunin took an active part in the 1848 revolution. In May 1849 during the Reich Constitution Campaign he played a leading role in the Dresden insurrection, was captured and handed over to the Russian government, and subsequently spent twelve years in prison before escaping.

far as to claim that 'apart from the Poles, the Russians, and at most the Slavs of Turkey, no Slav people has a future, for the simple reason that all the other Slavs lack the primary historical, geographical, political and industrial conditions for a viable independence.'[93] However, far from accepting their permanent incorporation into Germany, the Czechs were already in the sway of a great cultural renaissance that blossomed in 1848 into a political movement for national independence. Slovaks, Croats, Serbs and others were later to follow in their wake.

The four 'great historic nations' were thus an insufficient base for Marx and Engels's national policy, and this untenable tactic itself contributed to the failure of the 1848 revolution. The opposition of all classes in Germany to Czech independence, which the *Neue Rheinische Zeitung* shared, helped to drive Czech nationalism onto a pro-Russian path, while the Magyar suppression of Croat nationalism, which the *Neue Rheinische Zeitung* actively encouraged, enabled the Habsburg monarchy to use the Croatian army against revolutionary Vienna. Bakunin's 1848 programme of a democratic pan-Slavist movement was certainly utopian, given the great diversity of conditions in the Slavic lands. And the 'principle of nationalities' which Bakunin accepted was both idealist and impossible to put into practice, as Engels argued. But Bakunin at least recognized the strength of the Slavic nationalisms and attempted to exploit their anti-tsarist potential. The Habsburg monarchy survived the 1848 revolution precisely because of its skill in playing off its subject nations against one another. Marx and Engels, however, completely failed to formulate a policy designed to counter this.

The Split in the Communist League

For the first year of his exile in England, Marx believed that the defeats of 1849 had been a temporary setback. He therefore applied his main energies to rebuilding the Communist League. Towards this end, he also worked in the German Workers Educational Association and the Social-Democratic Refugee Committee and organized the publication, in Hamburg, of the monthly *Neue Rheinische Zeitung Revue*. The Central Committee of the League had been reconstituted in London in autumn 1848, by the first of the new exiles who left Germany after the September crisis, though

93. ibid., p. 231.

its links with Germany had so far remained fragile. Although Marx had himself dissolved the former Central Committee in May 1848, he recognized that a secret organization was again necessary, now that open political activity was once more impossible, and was unanimously voted onto the new Central Committee as soon as he arrived in London. Engels, who had taken refuge in Switzerland after the defeat of the Baden insurrection, joined Marx in London in October.

During this period Marx and Engels wrote two circular letters on behalf of the Central Committee, the *Addresses of the Central Committee to the Communist League of March and June 1850*. The March Address is the more important of these, and draws theoretical and tactical conclusions from the experience of 1848, to be applied in the next round of the German revolution which was expected shortly. Although written by Marx and Engels, it opens with a criticism of unnamed persons who are really none other than themselves. If 'a large number of members who were directly involved in the movement thought that the time for secret societies was over and that public action alone was sufficient', then the leaders of this tendency had unmistakably been Marx and Engels, and their allies on the *Neue Rheinische Zeitung*. And if 'the individual districts and communes allowed their connections with the Central Committee to weaken and gradually become dormant', the responsibility for this fell directly on Marx, who, entrusted with full executive power, had unilaterally dissolved the Central Committee and thus effectively prevented the League from functioning during the critical period of the revolution. As for the charge that, with the disorganization of the League, the workers' party had 'come under the complete domination and leadership of the petty-bourgeois democrats', again it was Marx and Engels who had deliberately blocked the Cologne Workers Society from putting up independent workers' candidates in the elections, and had worked to subordinate the workers' movement to the broad democratic front right up to February 1849.[94]

The unexpected blow that had vitiated Marx's previous tactical position and led to this implicit self-criticism was the passage of the Prussian liberal bourgeoisie to the reactionary camp, analysed by Marx in 'The Bourgeoisie and the Counter-Revolution'. Marx had held in the Communist Manifesto that the proletarian revolu-

94. See below, pp. 319–20.

tion in Germany would follow hard on the heels of the bourgeois revolution. Now that the bourgeois revolution had been deserted by its natural leader, the bourgeoisie, and the task of destroying feudalism and absolutism therefore fell to the plebeian classes alone, it seemed that the bourgeois revolution would directly merge into the first stages of the proletarian revolution. With this perspective, Marx developed in the March Address the tactic of 'permanent revolution'. Although the petty-bourgeois democrats are expected to take the initiative in the next revolutionary outbreak (carrying on the struggle they began with the Reich Constitution Campaign), Marx sets the German working class the task of inserting into the anti-feudal struggle its own leadership, and carrying the revolution forward from the overthrow of absolutism to the overthrow of capital itself.

Marx stresses, therefore, that the workers, after they fought with the petty bourgeoisie against the existing governments, must not lay down their arms with the advent of the new regime, even if they themselves could not yet take and hold power. The workers must remain armed and organized so that, even if the petty-bourgeois democrats would seize power in the first instance, they could 'make it as difficult as possible for the petty bourgeoisie to use its power against the armed proletariat, and ... dictate such conditions to them that the rule of the bourgeois democrats, from the very first, will carry within it the seeds of its own destruction, and its subsequent displacement by the proletariat will be made considerably easier'.[95]

Although 'the German workers cannot come to power and achieve the realization of their class interests without passing through a protracted revolutionary development',[96] it is the exercise of their own independent political power that the workers must now be concerned with.

In this context, Marx develops two important points of revolutionary theory. Firstly, the state apparatus is not a mere machine that passes from the control of one class to another, and the working class must prepare for taking power by building up its own state apparatus alongside and in opposition to that of the propertied classes. The workers will need their own armed and representative counter-state organizations, which Marx refers to as 'revolutionary local councils' or 'revolutionary workers' governments'. These were later to take on a concrete historical

95. Below, p. 325.   96. See below, p. 330.

existence in the form of the Paris Commune of 1871, and the Russian Soviets of 1905 and 1917. Secondly, the need for these counter-state organizations presented a new task for the Communists. Whereas in the Manifesto Marx had confined the Communists' specific task to propaganda work within the proletarian party, he now made it clear that it was the task, not just of the workers' party, but particularly of the organized Communists as its most advanced section, to ensure that this counter-state power was in fact set up.

The March Address marks a significant theoretical advance for the politics of scientific communism, but in practice, the tactic of permanent revolution was quite inapplicable in the circumstances of Germany in 1850. Marx and Engels had entered the revolutionary period of 1848 with a basically false assumption, that the impending revolutionary storm marked the beginning of the end for the bourgeois order. With the advantage of hindsight, it is clear that industrial capitalism was still in its early stages even in England, while on the Continent the new mode of production was only in its infancy. Throughout the 1848 period, Marx and Engels tended to read into the present what was still a long way in the future, an error of judgement which can be attributed to the novelty of the ideas of scientific communism and their birth so far ahead of their time.[97] We have already seen how, in the revolution of 1848–9, the spectre of proletarian revolution led the German bourgeoisie to compromise its own goals and thus vitiated Marx and Engels's original tactic of alliance with the bourgeoisie in the bourgeois revolution. Once the bourgeoisie had passed over to the side of reaction, the assumption that socialism was on the historical agenda in Germany, and that only the class-conscious organization of the proletariat was necessary to overthrow capitalism, led Marx and Engels to a new tactical error. The tactic of permanent revolution could not have worked, as the weakness of the German working class at the time was due not simply to its political and ideological immaturity, but to the economic immaturity of German capitalism. There was not the slightest

97. See Engels's 1895 Introduction to *The Class Struggles in France, MESW*, p. 647: 'History has proved us, and all who thought like us, wrong. It has made clear that the state of economic development on the Continent at that time was not, by a long way, ripe for the elimination of capitalist production; it has proved this by the economic revolution which, since 1848, has seized the whole of the Continent . . .'

chance of the German proletariat, whatever the political circumstances, overthrowing capitalism and setting up a socialist economy.

In the event, the revolutionary movement of 1848 had already been decisively defeated. Capitalism was to triumph in Germany without the revolutionary overthrow of the old regime, which would instead undertake its own 'modernization', and Germany was to be unified from above by Prussian arms. In the absence of a revolutionary situation, the tactics of the March Address were not put to the test, and the problem of the position of the proletariat in the bourgeois revolution disappeared from Marxist theory for half a century. Only in 1905 was Marxism finally to deal with the situation produced by the abdication of the bourgeoisie in the face of 'its own' revolution, when Lenin developed for the Russian revolution of that year a tactic that fully matched up to the torsions of this form of uneven development, that of the 'revolutionary-democratic dictatorship of the proletariat and the peasantry'. According to Lenin, the proletariat in this situation should struggle for leadership of the bourgeois revolution, even going so far as to temporarily seize state power with a provisional revolutionary government. The proletariat could thereby ensure what the petty bourgeoisie would not, the decisive defeat of all feudal and absolutist vestiges, and therefore the most favourable conditions for pursuing its own ultimate goals. It could do this without any illusions of the possibility of passing directly to socialism, and indeed it had to forgo the attempt to advance towards socialism at this stage, as it still needed the support of the peasantry as a whole (and not just the rural proletariat) in order to decisively defeat the old regime.[98]

The tactic of permanent revolution, although inapplicable in the Germany of 1850, remained as a valuable political legacy for the workers' movement. It was proposed by Trotsky for Russia in 1905, though Lenin still considered it premature to attempt to convert the bourgeois–democratic revolution into a proletarian one. In 1917, however, in the context of the all-European crisis brought about by the World War, Lenin and the Bolshevik party were able to apply successfully the tactic of permanent revolution, leading the Russian revolution of that year forward from the overthrow of tsarism to the overthrow of capital itself.

98. See 'Two Tactics of Social-Democracy in the Democratic Revolution', in Volume 1 of Lenin's *Selected Works*, Moscow, 1970.

The June Address witnesses to the revival of the Communist League's organization in Germany, despite the difficult conditions created by the repression. It is noteworthy for its insistence on the organizational unity of the Communists as the precondition for tactical action, and for the importance it attaches to the international alliances that the League had built with the left wing of the English Chartists, and with the exiled French Blanquists and Hungarian revolutionaries. In April 1850 the Central Committee of the League had founded, together with the Blanquists and left Chartists, a secret international organization confined to leading cadres, the 'World Society of Revolutionary Communists', based on the expectation of a new revolutionary outbreak and pledging mutual support. The first two articles of its constitution, signed by Adam and J. Vidil (Blanquists), G. Julian Harney (Chartist), and Marx, Engels and August Willich (Communist League), specified:

1. The aim of the association is the overthrow of all privileged classes and their subjugation to the dictatorship of the proletariat, which will carry through the permanent revolution until the realization of communism, the ultimate form of organization of the human family.
2. Towards the realization of this goal the association will form a bond of solidarity between all tendencies of the revolutionary communist party, while, in accordance with the principle of republican brotherhood, it dispenses with all national restrictions.[99]

Soon after writing the June Address, however, Marx underwent a substantial change of perspective, perhaps the most important during his entire political work as a Communist. In the summer of 1850, he returned to the economic studies he had abandoned in 1848, and undertook a thorough analysis of the economic basis of the political upheavals of the past few years. The conclusion he came to was that the 1848 revolutions had been provoked by the trade crisis of the previous year, and that, with the economic recovery that was now in progress, 'There can be no question of a real revolution. Such a revolution is only possible at a time when two factors come into conflict: the *modern productive forces* and the *bourgeois forms of production* . . . A new revolution is only possible as a result of a new crisis; but it will come, just as surely as the crisis itself.'[1]

99. *MEW* 7, pp. 553–4.
1. Review: 'May–October 1850', below, p. 303 n. 47.

This analysis had substantial implications for Communist political practice, and a dispute arose between Marx's group and the 'Willich-Schapper faction'.[2] In the private context of this dispute, Marx went further than in his review, and admitted that a successful proletarian revolution, in Germany at least, depended not simply on the next periodic trade crisis, but also on a considerable further development of the productive forces.

On 15 September 1850 the Central Committee of the League concluded its debate on 'the position of the German proletariat in the coming revolution'.[3] Schapper had argued to the Central Committee that the activities of the Communists only had meaning if the proletariat could come to power immediately with the next round of the revolution. Otherwise, they might as well give up political activity altogether. Arguing against Schapper, Marx subtly but decisively jettisoned the tactic of permanent revolution put forward in the March Address. While the Address had spoken of the working class having to undergo a 'protracted revolutionary development' before it could achieve its goal, Marx now mentioned 'fifteen, twenty or fifty years' of class struggle as the time-scale involved, ascribing this to the immaturity of economic conditions. Even if the workers' party did come to power now, it could only carry out petty-bourgeois measures (i.e. it could not socialize production, which was still predominantly small-scale).[4] Both sides agreed that this difference in perspective was too great to enable them to continue working together, and the League split in two.

Despite Willich and Schapper's fine revolutionary spirit, they had, as Marx claimed, renounced the scientific communism of the

2. August Willich, a former Prussian officer, joined with Karl Schapper in leading this 'left' opposition to Marx; in 1853 he emigrated to the U.S.A. and later fought for the North in the Civil War, like many other German communist émigrés.

3. See the 'Minutes of the Central Committee Meeting of 15 September 1850', below, p. 341.

4. It might nevertheless be very important for the proletariat to come to power and carry out petty-bourgeois measures, as Lenin was to hold. Although Marx never developed the tactic of the 'revolutionary–democratic dictatorship', he had himself stressed in the March Address that the petty bourgeoisie would flinch from sufficiently radical measures to destroy all vestiges of feudalism, and this had already been shown in practice with the Reich Constitution Campaign. But in the light of Marx's thesis that 'there can be no question of a real revolution', the question had become, at least for the time being, an academic one.

Manifesto. Unable to refute Marx's economic arguments, they ignored them, and stressed 'the *will*, rather than the actual conditions . . . as the chief factor in the revolution'.[5] This was in fact the position of the Blanquists, who held as a principle that only the activity of the vanguard was ever necessary in order to reopen the revolutionary process. When Marx rejected the possibility of a new revolution in the near future, there was no longer any occasion for his alliance with the Blanquists. After the split in the League, Marx, Engels and Harney wrote to the Blanquist leaders that they had 'long considered the association as *de facto* dissolved' (i.e. the World Society of Revolutionary Communists), and requesting a meeting to burn the founding agreement.[6] Willich and Schapper, however, whose supporters formed the majority both in the Communist League's London district and in the German Workers Educational Association, slid from a tactical alliance with the Blanquists to a principled one. Rather than 'work for the creation of an independent organization of the workers' party, both secret and open, alongside the official democrats',[7] which the March Address had laid down as the task of the Communist League in the immediate, pre-revolutionary period, they turned to conspiratorial activity precisely in harness with the petty-bourgeois democrats, who from the safety of exile in London were hatching all sorts of schemes that came to nothing. Marx's group, on the other hand, moved their Central Committee to Cologne, where it continued for a while to conduct propaganda work. In spring 1851, however, both groups' German organizations were totally destroyed by the Prussian police, and after the conviction of the accused in the Cologne Communist Trial of October 1852, Marx had his League formally wound up.

The first major phase of Marx's political practice as a scientific communist comes to an end with the close of the revolutionary period of 1848, and with Marx's recognition of this fact. The communist revolution had proved to be a much longer and harder struggle than Marx had originally anticipated. Marx had in fact seen the revolution of 1848 as an ultimate and general crisis of capitalism, when this was, like all crises, specific and particular. As the revolutionary tide ebbed, he began to stand back and take the measure of the events of the past few years. During the 1850s Marx returned to the economic studies that were to result in *Capital*, and

5. 'Minutes . . .,' p. 341.   6. *MEW* 7, p. 415.
7. See below, p. 324.

sharpened his general theory of historical materialism, which was still very incomplete in the 1848 period. Politically, however, Marx was very isolated during the decade of reaction. After the Communist League was dissolved in 1852, he no longer belonged to any political organization, and he saw eye to eye with very few of his former comrades. Most of these had either followed Schapper and Willich, or abandoned political activity altogether. Between 1852 and 1864, Marx was to comment voluminously on political developments in Europe and overseas, but he had resigned himself temporarily to the role of a spectator.

When the European workers' movements recovered from the defeats of 1848, Marx's overall perspective had substantially broadened. His horizon, originally simply European, was increasingly becoming a world one. And while Marx by no means abandoned his thesis of the necessity of violent revolution, he was to lay more stress on the gradual building of a mass workers' party as a necessary prerequisite for this. This process was set under way with the foundation, in 1864, of the International Working Men's Association – the First International – in which Marx himself played a leading role.

*

Besides several texts that Marx and Engels co-authored, a few articles written by Engels alone have been included in this volume where these are necessary to the understanding of Marx's own politics. Although Engels's positions sometimes diverged slightly from Marx's, the two did operate a very close division of labour from 1846 through to Marx's death, in which Marx generally left to Engels the fields of international politics and military affairs. Not only did Marx and Engels invariably consult together before publishing any significant political statement, but Engels often wrote pieces at Marx's express request. Although Engels's individual work, these are nevertheless an essential dimension of Marx and Engels's joint political practice. In the Introduction and Notes to this volume 'Marx' is sometimes used for 'Marx and Engels' in this sense, and when Marx alone is involved and it is necessary to avoid ambiguity, this is made explicit.

All texts written by Marx and Engels in German and French have been newly translated for this volume, with the exception of the Communist Manifesto, for which we have used the authorized English translation by Samuel Moore, edited by Engels. The articles from the *Neue Rheinische Zeitung* and the Reviews from the *Neue Rheinische Zeitung Revue* were annotated by Ben Fowkes.

DAVID FERNBACH

The following books and articles are suggested for the further study of Marx's politics, with particular reference to the period covered in this volume.

G. Becker, *Karl Marx and Friedrich Engels in Köln*, Berlin, 1963.

W. Blumenberg, *Karl Marx*, New Left Books, 1972.

W. Blumenberg, 'Zur Geschichte des Bundes der Kommunisten', *International Review of Social History*, vol. IX, no. 1, Amsterdam, 1964.

E. H. Carr, *Karl Marx: A Study in Fanaticism*, J. M. Dent, 1934.

A. Cornu, *Karl Marx et Friedrich Engels: Leur Vie et leur Oeuvre* (three vols), Paris, 1955–62.

H. B. Davis, *Nationalism and Socialism*, Monthly Review Press, New York, 1967.

H. Förder, *Marx und Engels am Vorabend der Revolution*, Berlin, 1960.

F. Engels, 'On the History of the Communist League', *MESW*.

F. Engels, 'Karl Marx and the *Neue Rheinische Zeitung*', *MESW* [two-volume edition], Lawrence & Wishart, 1950.

O. Hammen, *The Red '48ers*, Charles Scribner's Sons, New York, 1969.

M. Johnstone, 'Marx and Engels and the Concept of the Party', in R. Miliband and J. Saville, eds., *The Socialist Register 1967*, Merlin Press, 1967.

F. Mehring, *Karl Marx: The Story of His Life*, Allen & Unwin, 1966.

B. Nicolaevsky, 'Towards a History of the "Communist League", 1847–1852', *International Review of Social History*, vol. I no. 2, Amsterdam, 1956.

B. Nicolaevsky and O. Mänchen-Helfen, *Karl Marx: Man and Fighter*, Methuen 1934; 2nd ed., Allen Lane, 1973.

D. Riazanov, *The Communist Manifesto of Marx and Engels*, Martin Lawrence, 1930.

D. Riazanov, *Karl Marx and Frederick Engels*, Martin Lawrence, 1927.

E. Rosdolsky, 'Friedrich Engels und das Problem der "geschichtslosen Völker"', *Archiv für Sozialgeschichte*, Bd.4, Bonn, 1964.

Manifesto of the Communist Party

PREFACE TO THE ENGLISH EDITION OF 1888[1]

The Manifesto was published as the platform of the Communist League, a working men's association, first exclusively German, later on international, and, under the political conditions of the Continent before 1848, unavoidably a secret society. At a congress of the League, held in London in November 1847, Marx and Engels were commissioned to prepare for publication a complete theoretical and practical party programme. Drawn up in German, in January 1848, the manuscript was sent to the printer in London a few weeks before the French revolution of 24 February. A French translation was brought out in Paris shortly before the insurrection of June 1848. The first English translation, by Miss Helen Macfarlane, appeared in George Julian Harney's *Red Republican*, London, 1850. A Danish and a Polish edition had also been published.

The defeat of the Parisian insurrection of June 1848 – the first great battle between proletariat and bourgeoisie – drove again into the background, for a time, the social and political aspirations of the European working class. Thenceforth, the struggle for supremacy was again, as it had been before the revolution of February, solely between different sections of the propertied class; the working class was reduced to a fight for political elbow-room, and to the position of extreme wing of the middle-class radicals. Wherever independent proletarian movements continued to show signs of life, they were ruthlessly hunted down. Thus the Prussian police hunted out the Central Board[2] of the Communist League, then

1. This translation of the Communist Manifesto was made by Samuel Moore in 1888, and edited by Engels. His notes are identified in this edition by [Engels]. Besides printer's errors, inconsistent and old-fashioned punctuation and orthography, a very few linguistic archaisms have also been amended.

2. i.e. the Central Committee, as it is referred to elsewhere in this edition.

located in Cologne. The members were arrested, and, after eighteen months' imprisonment, they were tried in October 1852. This celebrated 'Cologne Communist Trial' lasted from 4 October till 12 November; seven of the prisoners were sentenced to terms of imprisonment in a fortress, varying from three to six years. Immediately after the sentence, the League was formally dissolved by the remaining members. As to the Manifesto, it seemed thenceforth to be doomed to oblivion.

When the European working class had recovered sufficient strength for another attack on the ruling classes, the International Working Men's Association sprang up.[3] But this association, formed with the express aim of welding into one body the whole militant proletariat of Europe and America, could not at once proclaim the principles laid down in the Manifesto. The International was bound to have a programme broad enough to be acceptable to the English trade unions, to the followers of Proudhon in France, Belgium, Italy and Spain, and to the Lassalleans[4] in Germany. Marx, who drew up this programme to the satisfaction of all parties, entirely trusted to the intellectual development of the working class, which was sure to result from combined action and mutual discussion. The very events and vicissitudes of the struggle against capital, the defeats even more than the victories, could not help bringing home to men's minds the insufficiency of their various favourite nostrums, and preparing the way for a more complete insight into the true conditions of working-class emancipation. And Marx was right. The International, on its breaking up in 1874,[5] left the workers quite different men from what it had found them in 1864. Proudhonism in France, Lassalleanism in Germany were dying out, and even the conservative English trade unions, though most of them had long since severed their connection with the International, were gradually advancing towards that point at which, last year at Swansea, their President could say in their name, 'Continental socialism has lost its terrors

3. On the International, see the Introduction to *The First International and After*.

4. Lassalle personally, to us, always acknowledged himself to be a disciple of Marx, and, as such, stood on the ground of the Manifesto. But in his public agitation, 1862–4, he did not go beyond demanding cooperative workshops supported by state credit [Engels].

5. In fact the International was not officially wound up until 1876, although it effectively ceased to function when the General Council was transferred to New York in 1872.

for us.'[6] In fact: the principles of the Manifesto had made considerable headway among the working men of all countries.

The Manifesto itself thus came to the front again. The German text had been, since 1850, reprinted several times in Switzerland, England and America. In 1872, it was translated into English in New York, where the translation was published in *Woodhull and Claflin's Weekly*.[7] From this English version, a French one was made in *Le Socialiste* of New York. Since then at least two more English translations, more or less mutilated, have been brought out in America, and one of them has been reprinted in England. The first Russian translation, made by Bakunin, was published at Herzen's *Kolokol*[8] office in Geneva, about 1863; a second one, by the heroic Vera Zasulich,[9] also in Geneva, 1882. A new Danish edition is to be found in *Socialdemokratisk Bibliothek*, Copenhagen, 1885; a fresh French translation in *Le Socialiste*, Paris, 1885. From this latter a Spanish version was prepared and published in Madrid, 1886. The German reprints are not to be counted, there have been twelve altogether at the least. An Armenian translation, which was to be published in Constantinople some months ago, did not see the light, I am told, because the publisher was afraid of bringing out a book with the name of Marx on it, while the translator declined to call it his own production. Of further translations into other languages I have heard, but have not seen them. Thus the history of the Manifesto reflects, to a great extent, the history of the modern working-class movement; at present it is undoubtedly the most wide-spread, the most international production of all socialist literature, the common platform acknowledged by millions of working men from Siberia to California.

Yet, when it was written, we could not have called it a 'Socialist'

6. W. Bevan, in his address to the TUC Congress, reported in the *Commonweal*, 17 September 1887.

7. This paper was published by two American feminists, Victoria Woodhull and her sister Tennessee Claflin, whose campaign Marx considered 'middle-class humbug' and who were eventually expelled from the International. (See *IWMA* V, pp. 323–32). It carried an abridged translation of the Manifesto on 30 December 1871.

8. Alexander Herzen was a Russian philosopher and revolutionary democrat. His paper *Kolokol* (The Bell) was the leading organ of the Russian emigration in the 1860s. Bakunin's translation of the Manifesto was in fact published in 1869.

9. Engels celebrates Vera Zasulich for her attempted assassination of the governor of St Petersburg, General Trepov, in 1878. The translation was in fact by George Plekhanov, the founder of Russian Marxism.

manifesto. By 'socialists', in 1847, were understood, on the one hand, the adherents of the various utopian systems: Owenites in England, Fourierists in France, both of them already reduced to the position of mere sects, and gradually dying out; on the other hand, the most multifarious social quacks, who, by all manners of tinkering, professed to redress, without any danger to capital and profit, all sorts of social grievances; in both cases men outside the working-class movement, and looking rather to the 'educated' classes for support. Whatever portion of the working class had become convinced of the insufficiency of mere political revolutions, and had proclaimed the necessity of a total social change, that portion then called itself communist. It was a crude, rough-hewn, purely instinctive sort of communism; still, it touched the cardinal point and was powerful enough amongst the working class to produce the utopian communism, in France, of Cabet, and in Germany, of Weitling. Thus, socialism was, in 1847, a middle-class movement, communism a working-class movement. Socialism was, on the Continent at least, 'respectable'; communism was the very opposite. And as our notion, from the very beginning, was that 'the emancipation of the working class must be the act of the working class itself', there could be no doubt as to which of the two names we must take. Moreover, we have, ever since, been far from repudiating it.

The Manifesto being our joint production, I consider myself bound to state that the fundamental proposition, which forms its nucleus, belongs to Marx. That proposition is: that in every historical epoch, the prevailing mode of economic production and exchange, and the social organization necessarily following from it, form the basis upon which is built up, and from which alone can be explained, the political and intellectual history of that epoch; that consequently the whole history of mankind (since the dissolution of primitive tribal society, holding land in common ownership) has been a history of class struggles, contests between exploiting and exploited, ruling and oppressed classes; that the history of these class struggles forms a series of evolutions in which, nowadays, a stage has been reached where the exploited and oppressed class – the proletariat – cannot attain its emancipation from the sway of the exploiting and ruling class – the bourgeoisie – without, at the same time, and once and for all, emancipating society at large from all exploitation, oppression, class distinctions and class struggles.

This proposition which, in my opinion, is destined to do for history what Darwin's theory has done for biology, we, both of us, had been gradually approaching for some years before 1845. How far I had independently progressed towards it is best shown by my *Condition of the Working Class in England*. But when I again met Marx at Brussels, in spring 1845, he had it ready worked out, and put it before me, in terms almost as clear as those in which I have stated it here.

From our joint preface to the German edition of 1872, I quote the following:

However much the state of things may have altered during the last twenty-five years, the general principles laid down in this Manifesto are, on the whole, as correct today as ever. Here and there some detail might be improved. The practical application of the principles will depend, as the Manifesto itself states, everywhere and at all times, on the historical conditions for the time being existing, and, for that reason, no special stress is laid on the revolutionary measures proposed at the end of section II. That passage would, in many respects, be very differently worded today. In view of the gigantic strides of modern industry since 1848, and of the accompanying improved and extended organization of the working class; in view of the practical experience gained, first in the February revolution, and then, still more, in the Paris Commune, where the proletariat for the first time held political power for two whole months, this programme has in some details become antiquated. One thing especially was proved by the Commune, viz., that 'the working class cannot simply lay hold of the ready-made state machinery, and wield it for its own purposes'. (See 'The Civil War in France', section III, where this point is further developed.) Further, it is self-evident that the criticism of socialist literature is deficient in relation to the present time, because it comes down only to 1847; also, that the remarks on the relation of the Communists to the various opposition parties (section IV), although in principle still correct, yet in practice are antiquated, because the political situation has been entirely changed, and the progress of history has swept from off the earth the greater portion of the political parties there enumerated.

But then, the Manifesto has become a historical document which we have no longer any right to alter.

The present translation is by Mr Samuel Moore, the translator of the greater portion of Marx's *Capital*. We have revised it in common, and I have added a few notes explanatory of historical allusions.

London, 30 January 1888   FREDERICK ENGELS

MANIFESTO OF THE COMMUNIST PARTY

A spectre is haunting Europe – the spectre of Communism. All the powers of old Europe have entered into a holy alliance to exorcize this spectre: Pope and Tsar, Metternich[10] and Guizot,[11] French radicals and German police spies.

Where is the party in opposition that has not been decried as communistic by its opponents in power? Where the opposition that has not hurled back the branding reproach of Communism, against the more advanced opposition parties, as well as against its reactionary adversaries?

Two things result from this fact.

1. Communism is already acknowledged by all European powers to be itself a power.

2. It is high time that Communists should openly, in the face of the whole world, publish their views, their aims, their tendencies, and meet this nursery tale of the Spectre of Communism with a manifesto of the party itself.

To this end, Communists of various nationalities have assembled in London, and sketched the following manifesto, to be published in the English, French, German, Italian, Flemish and Danish languages.

1. Bourgeois and Proletarians[12]

The history of all hitherto existing society[13] is the history of class struggles.

10. Clemens Lothar, prince Metternich, was the leading Austrian statesman from 1809 to 1848 and the architect of the counter-revolutionary Holy Alliance.

11. François Guizot was a French historian and *de facto* Prime Minister from 1840 to 1848 under the Orleanist 'July' monarchy of Louis Philippe.

12. By bourgeoisie is meant the class of modern capitalists, owners of the means of social production and employers of wage labour. By proletariat, the class of modern wage labourers who, having no means of production of their own, are reduced to selling their labour power in order to live [Engels].

13. That is, all *written* history. In 1847, the pre-history of society, the social organization existing previous to recorded history, was all but unknown. Since then, Haxthausen discovered common ownership of land in Russia, Maurer proved it to be the social foundation from which all Teutonic races started in history, and by and by village communities were found to be, or to have been the primitive form of society everywhere from India to Ireland. The inner organization of this primitive communistic society was laid bare, in its typical form, by Morgan's crowning discovery of the true nature of the

Freeman and slave, patrician and plebeian, lord and serf, guild-master[14] and journeyman, in a word, oppressor and oppressed, stood in constant opposition to one another, carried on an uninterrupted, now hidden, now open fight, a fight that each time ended, either in a revolutionary reconstitution of society at large, or in the common ruin of the contending classes.

In the earlier epochs of history, we find almost everywhere a complicated arrangement of society into various orders, a manifold gradation of social rank. In ancient Rome we have patricians, knights, plebeians, slaves; in the Middle Ages, feudal lords, vassals, guild-masters, journeymen, apprentices, serfs; in almost all of these classes, again, subordinate gradations.

The modern bourgeois society that has sprouted from the ruins of feudal society has not done away with class antagonisms. It has but established new classes, new conditions of oppression, new forms of struggle in place of the old ones.

Our epoch, the epoch of the bourgeoisie, possesses, however, this distinctive feature: it has simplified the class antagonisms. Society as a whole is more and more splitting up into two great hostile camps, into two great classes directly facing each other: bourgeoisie and proletariat.

From the serfs of the Middle Ages sprang the chartered burghers of the earliest towns. From these burgesses the first elements of the bourgeoisie were developed.

The discovery of America, the rounding of the Cape, opened up fresh ground for the rising bourgeoisie. The East Indian and Chinese markets, the colonization of America, trade with the colonies, the increase in the means of exchange and in commodities generally, gave to commerce, to navigation, to industry, an impulse never before known, and thereby, to the revolutionary element in the tottering feudal society, a rapid development.

The feudal system of industry, under which industrial production was monopolized by closed guilds, now no longer sufficed for the growing wants of the new markets. The manufacturing

---

gens and its relation to the *tribe*. With the dissolution of these primeval communities society begins to be differentiated into separate and finally antagonistic classes. I have attempted to retrace this process of dissolution in: *Der Ursprung der Familie, des Privateigenthums und des Staats* (*The Origin of the Family, Private Property and the State*) [Engels].

14. Guild-master, that is, a full member of a guild, a master within, not a head of a guild [Engels].

system took its place. The guild-masters were pushed on one side by the manufacturing middle class; division of labour between the different corporate guilds vanished in the face of division of labour in each single workshop.

Meantime the markets kept ever growing, the demand ever rising. Even manufacture no longer sufficed. Thereupon, steam and machinery revolutionized industrial production. The place of manufacture was taken by the giant, modern industry, the place of the industrial middle class, by industrial millionaires, the leaders of whole industrial armies, the modern bourgeois.

Modern industry has established the world market, for which the discovery of America paved the way. This market has given an immense development to commerce, to navigation, to communication by land. This development has, in its turn, reacted on the extension of industry; and in proportion as industry, commerce, navigation, railways extended, in the same proportion the bourgeoisie developed, increased its capital, and pushed into the background every class handed down from the Middle Ages.

We see, therefore, how the modern bourgeoisie is itself the product of a long course of development, of a series of revolutions in the modes of production and of exchange.

Each step in the development of the bourgeoisie was accompanied by a corresponding political advance of that class. An oppressed class under the sway of the feudal nobility, an armed and self-governing association in the medieval commune;[15] here independent urban republic (as in Italy and Germany), there taxable 'third estate' of the monarchy (as in France), afterwards, in the period of manufacture proper, serving either the semi-feudal or the absolute monarchy as a counterpoise against the nobility, and, in fact, corner-stone of the great monarchies in general, the bourgeoisie has at last, since the establishment of modern industry and of the world market, conquered for itself, in the modern representative state, exclusive political sway. The executive of the modern state is but a committee for managing the common affairs of the whole bourgeoisie.

15. 'Commune' was the name taken, in France, by the nascent towns even before they had conquered, from their feudal lords and masters, local self-government and political rights as the 'third estate'. Generally speaking, for the economic development of the bourgeoisie, England is here taken as the typical country; for its political development, France [Engels].

The bourgeoisie, historically, has played a most revolutionary part.

The bourgeoisie, wherever it has got the upper hand, has put an end to all feudal, patriarchal, idyllic relations. It has pitilessly torn asunder the motley feudal ties that bound man to his 'natural superiors', and has left remaining no other nexus between man and man than naked self-interest, than callous 'cash payment'. It has drowned the most heavenly ecstasies of religious fervour, of chivalrous enthusiasm, of philistine sentimentalism, in the icy water of egotistical calculation. It has resolved personal worth into exchange value, and in place of the numberless indefeasible chartered freedoms, has set up that single, unconscionable freedom – free trade. In one word, for exploitation, veiled by religious and political illusions, it has substituted naked, shameless, direct, brutal exploitation.

The bourgeoisie has stripped of its halo every occupation hitherto honoured and looked up to with reverent awe. It has converted the physician, the lawyer, the priest, the poet, the man of science, into its paid wage labourers.

The bourgeoisie has torn away from the family its sentimental veil, and has reduced the family relation to a mere money relation.

The bourgeoisie has disclosed how it came to pass that the brutal display of vigour in the Middle Ages, which reactionists so much admire, found its fitting complement in the most slothful indolence. It has been the first to show what man's activity can bring about. It has accomplished wonders far surpassing Egyptian pyramids, Roman aqueducts, and Gothic cathedrals; it has conducted expeditions that put in the shade all former exoduses of nations and crusades.

The bourgeoisie cannot exist without constantly revolutionizing the instruments of production, and thereby the relations of production, and with them the whole relations of society. Conservation of the old modes of production in unaltered form, was, on the contrary, the first condition of existence for all earlier industrial classes. Constant revolutionizing of production, uninterrupted disturbance of all social conditions, everlasting uncertainty and agitation distinguish the bourgeois epoch from all earlier ones. All fixed, fast-frozen relations, with their train of ancient and venerable prejudices and opinions, are swept away, all new-formed ones become antiquated before they can ossify. All that is solid melts into air, all that is holy is profaned, and man is at last compelled to face with sober senses, his real conditions of life, and his relations with his kind.

The need of a constantly expanding market for its products chases the bourgeoisie over the whole surface of the globe. It must nestle everywhere, settle everywhere, establish connections everywhere.

The bourgeoisie has through its exploitation of the world market given a cosmopolitan character to production and consumption in every country. To the great chagrin of reactionists, it has drawn from under the feet of industry the national ground on which it stood. All old-established national industries have been destroyed or are daily being destroyed. They are dislodged by new industries, whose introduction becomes a life and death question for all civilized nations, by industries that no longer work up indigenous raw material, but raw material drawn from the remotest zones; industries whose products are consumed, not only at home, but in every quarter of the globe. In place of the old wants, satisfied by the productions of the country, we find new wants, requiring for their satisfaction the products of distant lands and climes. In place of the old local and national seclusion and self-sufficiency, we have intercourse in every direction, universal interdependence of nations. And as in material, so also in intellectual production. The intellectual creations of individual nations become common property. National one-sidedness and narrow-mindedness become more and more impossible, and from the numerous national and local literatures, there arises a world literature.

The bourgeoisie, by the rapid improvement of all instruments of production, by the immensely facilitated means of communication, draws all, even the most barbarian, nations into civilization. The cheap prices of its commodities are the heavy artillery with which it batters down all Chinese walls, with which it forces the barbarians' intensely obstinate hatred of foreigners to capitulate. It compels all nations, on pain of extinction, to adopt the bourgeois mode of production; it compels them to introduce what it calls civilization into their midst, i.e., to become bourgeois themselves. In one word, it creates a world after its own image.

The bourgeoisie has subjected the country to the rule of the towns. It has created enormous cities, has greatly increased the urban population as compared with the rural, and has thus rescued a considerable part of the population from the idiocy of rural life.

Just as it has made the country dependent on the towns, so it has made barbarian and semi-barbarian countries dependent on the civilized ones, nations of peasants on nations of bourgeois, the East on the West.

The bourgeoisie keeps more and more doing away with the scattered state of the population, of the means of production, and of property. It has agglomerated population, centralized means of production, and has concentrated property in a few hands. The necessary consequence of this was political centralization. Independent, or but loosely connected provinces, with separate interests, laws, governments and systems of taxation, became lumped together into one nation, with one government, one code of laws, one national class interest, one frontier and one customs tariff.

The bourgeoisie, during its rule of scarce one hundred years, has created more massive and more colossal productive forces than have all preceding generations together. Subjection of nature's forces to man, machinery, application of chemistry to industry and agriculture, steam navigation, railways, electric telegraphs, clearing of whole continents for cultivation, canalization of rivers, whole populations conjured out of the ground – what earlier century had even a presentiment that such productive forces slumbered in the lap of social labour?

We see then: the means of production and of exchange, on whose foundation the bourgeoisie built itself up, were generated in feudal society. At a certain stage in the development of these means of production and of exchange, the conditions under which feudal society produced and exchanged, the feudal organization of agriculture and manufacturing industry, in one word, the feudal relations of property became no longer compatible with the already developed productive forces; they became so many fetters. They had to be burst asunder; they were burst asunder.

Into their place stepped free competition, accompanied by a social and political constitution adapted to it, and by the economical and political sway of the bourgeois class.

A similar movement is going on before our own eyes. Modern bourgeois society with its relations of production, of exchange and of property, a society that has conjured up such gigantic means of production and of exchange, is like the sorcerer, who is no longer able to control the powers of the nether world whom he has called up by his spells. For many a decade past, the history of industry and commerce is but the history of the revolt of modern productive forces against modern conditions of production, against the property relations that are the conditions for the existence of the bourgeoisie and of its rule. It is enough to mention the commercial crises that by their periodical return put on trial, each time more threateningly, the existence of the entire bourgeois society. In these crises a great part not only of the existing products, but also of the previously created productive forces, are periodically destroyed. In these crises there breaks out an epidemic that, in all earlier epochs, would have seemed an absurdity – the epidemic of overproduction. Society suddenly finds itself put back into a state of momentary barbarism; it appears as if a famine, a universal war of devastation had cut off the supply of every means of subsistence; industry and commerce seem to be destroyed; and why? Because there is too much civilization, too much means of subsistence, too much industry, too much commerce. The productive forces at the disposal of society no longer tend to further the development of the conditions of bourgeois property; on the contrary, they have become too powerful for these conditions, by which they are fettered, and so soon as they overcome these fetters, they bring disorder into the whole of bourgeois society, endanger the existence of bourgeois property. The conditions of bourgeois society are too narrow to comprise the wealth created by them. And how does the bourgeoisie get over these crises? On the one hand by enforced destruction of a mass of productive forces; on the other, by the conquest of new markets, and by the more thorough exploitation of the old ones. That is to say, by paving the way for more extensive and more destructive crises, and by diminishing the means whereby crises are prevented.

The weapons with which the bourgeoisie felled feudalism to the ground are now turned against the bourgeoisie itself.

But not only has the bourgeoisie forged the weapons that bring death to itself; it has also called into existence the men who are to wield those weapons – the modern working class – the proletarians.

In proportion as the bourgeoisie, i.e., capital, is developed, in the same proportion is the proletariat, the modern working class, developed – a class of labourers, who live only so long as they find work, and who find work only so long as their labour increases capital. These labourers, who must sell themselves piecemeal, are a commodity, like every other article of commerce, and are consequently exposed to all the vicissitudes of competition, to all the fluctuations of the market.

Owing to the extensive use of machinery and to division of labour, the work of the proletarians has lost all individual character, and, consequently, all charm for the workman. He becomes an appendage of the machine, and it is only the most simple, most monotonous, and most easily acquired knack, that is required of him. Hence, the cost of production of a workman is restricted, almost entirely, to the means of subsistence that he requires for his maintenance, and for the propagation of his race. But the price of a commodity, and therefore also of labour,[16] is equal to its cost of production. In proportion, therefore, as the repulsiveness of the work increases, the wage decreases. Nay more, in proportion as the use of machinery and division of labour increases, in the same proportion the burden of toil also increases, whether by prolongation of the working hours, by increase of the work exacted in a given time or by increased speed of the machinery, etc.

Modern industry has converted the little workshop of the patriarchal master into the great factory of the industrial capitalist. Masses of labourers, crowded into the factory, are organized like soldiers. As privates of the industrial army they are placed under the command of a perfect hierarchy of officers and sergeants. Not only are they slaves of the bourgeois class, and of the bourgeois state; they are daily and hourly enslaved by the machine, by the overseer, and, above all, by the individual bourgeois manufacturer himself. The more openly this despotism proclaims gain to be its end and aim, the more petty, the more hateful and the more embittering it is.

The less the skill and exertion of strength implied in manual labour, in other words, the more modern industry becomes developed, the more is the labour of men superseded by that of women. Differences of age and sex have no longer any distinctive social validity for the working class. All are instruments of labour, more or less expensive to use, according to their age and sex.

No sooner is the exploitation of the labourer by the manufacturer so far at an end that he receives his wages in cash, than he is set upon by the other portions of the bourgeoisie, the landlord, the shopkeeper, the pawnbroker, etc.

16. In Marx's later theory of surplus value, he concluded that it is the worker's *labour power*, not his labour, that is sold to the capitalist as a commodity. (See 'Wages, Prices and Profit', in *MESW*.)

The lower strata of the middle class – the small tradespeople, shopkeepers, and *rentiers*, the handicraftsmen and peasants – all these sink gradually into the proletariat, partly because their diminutive capital does not suffice for the scale on which modern industry is carried on, and is swamped in the competition with the large capitalists, partly because their specialized skill is rendered worthless by new methods of production. Thus the proletariat is recruited from all classes of the population.

The proletariat goes through various stages of development. With its birth begins its struggle with the bourgeoisie. At first the contest is carried on by individual labourers, then by the work-people of a factory, then by the operatives of one trade, in one locality, against the individual bourgeois who directly exploits them. They direct their attacks not against the bourgeois conditions of production, but against the instruments of production themselves; they destroy imported wares that compete with their labour, they smash to pieces machinery, they set factories ablaze, they seek to restore by force the vanished status of the workman of the Middle Ages.

At this stage the labourers still form an incoherent mass scattered over the whole country, and broken up by their mutual competition. If anywhere they unite to form more compact bodies, this is not yet the consequence of their own active union, but of the union of the bourgeoisie, which class, in order to attain its own political ends, is compelled to set the whole proletariat in motion, and is moreover yet, for a time, able to do so. At this stage, therefore, the proletarians do not fight their enemies, but the enemies of their enemies, the remnants of absolute monarchy, the landowners, the non-industrial bourgeois, the petty bourgeoisie. Thus the whole historical movement is concentrated in the hands of the bourgeoisie; every victory so obtained is a victory for the bourgeoisie.

But with the development of industry the proletariat not only increases in number; it becomes concentrated in greater masses, its strength grows, and it feels that strength more. The various interests and conditions of life within the ranks of the proletariat are more and more equalized, in proportion as machinery obliterates all distinctions of labour, and nearly everywhere reduces wages to the same low level. The growing competition among the bourgeois, and the resulting commercial crises, make the wages of the workers ever more fluctuating. The unceasing improvement of machinery, ever more rapidly developing, makes their livelihood more and more precarious; the collisions between individual workmen and individual bourgeois take more and more the character of collisions between two classes. Thereupon the workers begin to form combinations (trade unions) against the bourgeois; they club together in order to keep up the rate of wages; they found permanent associations in order to make provision beforehand for these occasional revolts. Here and there the contest breaks out into riots.

Now and then the workers are victorious, but only for a time. The real fruit of their battles lies, not in the immediate result, but in the ever expanding union of the workers. This union is helped on by the improved means of communication that are created by modern industry, and that place the workers of different localities in contact with one another. It was just this contact that was needed to centralize the numerous local struggles, all of the same character, into one national struggle between classes. But every class struggle is a political struggle. And that union, to attain which the burghers of the Middle Ages, with their miserable highways, required centuries, the modern proletarians, thanks to railways, achieve in a few years.

This organization of the proletarians into a class, and consequently into a political party, is continually being upset again by the competition between the workers themselves. But it ever rises up again, stronger, firmer, mightier. It compels legislative recognition of particular interests of the workers, by taking advantage of the divisions among the bourgeoisie itself. Thus the Ten Hours Bill in England was carried.[17]

Altogether, collisions between the classes of the old society further, in many ways, the course of development of the proletariat. The bourgeoisie finds itself involved in a constant battle: at first with the aristocracy; later on, with those portions of the bourgeoisie itself, whose interests have become antagonistic to the progress of industry; at all times, with the bourgeoisie of foreign countries. In all these battles it sees itself compelled to appeal to the proletariat, to ask for its help, and thus to drag it into the political arena. The bourgeoisie itself, therefore, supplies the proletariat with its own elements of political and general education, in other words, it furnishes the proletariat with weapons for fighting the bourgeoisie.

17. In 1846. See Engels's article 'The English Ten Hours Bill', *A O B*, pp. 96–108.

Further, as we have already seen, entire sections of the ruling classes are, by the advance of industry, precipitated into the proletariat, or are at least threatened in their conditions of existence. These also supply the proletariat with fresh elements of enlightenment and progress.

Finally, in times when the class struggle nears the decisive hour, the process of dissolution going on within the ruling class, in fact within the whole range of old society, assumes such a violent, glaring character, that a small section of the ruling class cuts itself adrift, and joins the revolutionary class, the class that holds the future in its hands. Just as, therefore, at an earlier period, a section of the nobility went over to the bourgeoisie, so now a portion of the bourgeoisie goes over to the proletariat, and in particular, a portion of the bourgeois ideologists, who have raised themselves to the level of comprehending theoretically the historical movement as a whole.

Of all the classes that stand face to face with the bourgeoisie today, the proletariat alone is a really revolutionary class. The other classes decay and finally disappear in the face of modern industry; the proletariat is its special and essential product.

The lower middle class, the small manufacturer, the shopkeeper, the artisan, the peasant, all these fight against the bourgeoisie, to save from extinction their existence as fractions of the middle class. They are therefore not revolutionary, but conservative. Nay more, they are reactionary, for they try to roll back the wheel of history. If by chance they are revolutionary, they are so only in view of their impending transfer into the proletariat, they thus defend not their present, but their future interests, they desert their own standpoint to place themselves at that of the proletariat.

The 'dangerous class',[18] the social scum, that passively rotting mass thrown off by the lowest layers of old society, may, here and there, be swept into the movement by a proletarian revolution; its conditions of life, however, prepare it far more for the part of a bribed tool of reactionary intrigue.

In the conditions of the proletariat, those of old society at large are already virtually swamped. The proletarian is without property; his relation to his wife and children has no longer anything in common with the bourgeois family relations; modern industrial labour, modern subjection to capital, the same in England as in

18. i.e. the lumpenproletariat of casual labourers and unemployed, which was very extensive in the cities of nineteenth-century Europe.

France, in America as in Germany, has stripped him of every trace of national character. Law, morality, religion, are to him so many bourgeois prejudices, behind which lurk in ambush just as many bourgeois interests.

All the preceding classes that got the upper hand, sought to fortify their already acquired status by subjecting society at large to their conditions of appropriation. The proletarians cannot become masters of the productive forces of society, except by abolishing their own previous mode of appropriation, and thereby also every other previous mode of appropriation. They have nothing of their own to secure and to fortify; their mission is to destroy all previous securities for, and insurances of, individual property.

All previous historical movements were movements of minorities, or in the interest of minorities. The proletarian movement is the self-conscious, independent movement of the immense majority, in the interest of the immense majority. The proletariat, the lowest stratum of our present society, cannot stir, cannot raise itself up, without the whole superincumbent strata of official society being sprung into the air.

Though not in substance, yet in form, the struggle of the proletariat with the bourgeoisie is at first a national struggle. The proletariat of each country must, of course, first of all settle matters with its own bourgeoisie.

In depicting the most general phases of the development of the proletariat, we traced the more or less veiled civil war, raging within existing society, up to the point where that war breaks out into open revolution, and where the violent overthrow of the bourgeoisie lays the foundation for the sway of the proletariat.

Hitherto, every form of society has been based, as we have already seen, on the antagonism of oppressing and oppressed classes. But in order to oppress a class, certain conditions must be assured to it under which it can, at least, continue its slavish existence. The serf, in the period of serfdom, raised himself to membership in the commune, just as the petty bourgeois, under the yoke of feudal absolutism, managed to develop into a bourgeois. The modern labourer, on the contrary, instead of rising with the progress of industry, sinks deeper and deeper below the conditions of existence of his own class. He becomes a pauper, and pauperism develops more rapidly than population and wealth. And here it becomes evident that the bourgeoisie is unfit any longer to be the ruling class in society, and to impose its conditions of existence upon society as an overriding law. It is unfit to rule because it is incompetent to assure an existence to its slave within his slavery, because it cannot help letting him sink into such a state that it has to feed him, instead of being fed by him. Society can no longer live under this bourgeoisie, in other words, its existence is no longer compatible with society.

The essential condition for the existence, and for the sway of the bourgeois class, is the formation and augmentation of capital; the condition for capital is wage labour. Wage labour rests exclusively on competition between the labourers. The advance of industry, whose involuntary promoter is the bourgeoisie, replaces the isolation of the labourers, due to competition, by their revolutionary combination, due to association. The development of modern industry, therefore, cuts from under its feet the very foundation on which the bourgeoisie produces and appropriates products. What the bourgeoisie therefore produces, above all, are its own grave-diggers. Its fall and the victory of the proletariat are equally inevitable.

II. Proletarians and Communists

In what relation do the Communists stand to the proletarians as a whole?

The Communists do not form a separate party opposed to other working-class parties.

They have no interests separate and apart from those of the proletariat as a whole.

They do not set up any sectarian principles of their own, by which to shape and mould the proletarian movement.

The Communists are distinguished from the other working-class parties by this only:

1. In the national struggles of the proletarians of the different countries, they point out and bring to the front the common interests of the entire proletariat, independently of all nationality.

2. In the various stages of development which the struggle of the working class against the bourgeoisie has to pass through, they always and everywhere represent the interests of the movement as a whole.

The Communists, therefore, are on the one hand, practically, the most advanced and resolute section of the working-class parties of every country, that section which pushes forward all others; on the other hand, theoretically, they have over the great mass of the proletariat the advantage of clearly understanding the line of march, the conditions, and the ultimate general results of the proletarian movement.

The immediate aim of the Communists is the same as that of all the other proletarian parties: formation of the proletariat into a class, overthrow of the bourgeois supremacy, conquest of political power by the proletariat.

The theoretical conclusions of the Communists are in no way based on ideas or principles that have been invented, or discovered, by this or that would-be universal reformer.

They merely express, in general terms, actual relations springing from an existing class struggle, from a historical movement going on under our very eyes. The abolition of existing property relations is not at all a distinctive feature of communism.

All property relations in the past have continually been subject to historical change consequent upon the change in historical conditions.

The French Revolution, for example, abolished feudal property in favour of bourgeois property.

The distinguishing feature of communism is not the abolition of property generally, but the abolition of bourgeois property. But modern bourgeois private property is the final and most complete expression of the system of producing and appropriating products that is based on class antagonisms, on the exploitation of the many by the few.

In this sense, the theory of the Communists may be summed up in the single sentence: Abolition of private property.

We Communists have been reproached with the desire of abolishing the right of personally acquiring property as the fruit of a man's own labour, which property is alleged to be the ground work of all personal freedom, activity and independence.

Hard-won, self-acquired, self-earned property! Do you mean the property of the petty artisan and of the small peasant, a form of property that preceded the bourgeois form? There is no need to abolish that; the development of industry has to a great extent already destroyed it, and is still destroying it daily.

Or do you mean modern bourgeois private property?

But does wage labour create any property for the labourer? Not a bit. It creates capital, i.e., that kind of property which exploits wage labour, and which cannot increase except upon conditions of begetting a new supply of wage labour for fresh exploitation. Property, in its present form, is based on the antagonism of capital and wage labour. Let us examine both sides of this antagonism.

To be a capitalist, is to have not only a purely personal, but a social status in production. Capital is a collective product, and only by the united action of many members, nay, in the last resort, only by the united action of all members of society, can it be set in motion.

Capital is, therefore, not a personal, it is a social power.

When, therefore, capital is converted into common property, into the property of all members of society, personal property is not thereby transformed into social property. It is only the social character of the property that is changed. It loses its class character.

Let us now take wage labour.

The average price of wage labour is the minimum wage, i.e., that quantum of the means of subsistence which is absolutely requisite to keep the labourer in bare existence as a labourer. What, therefore, the wage labourer appropriates by means of his labour, merely suffices to prolong and reproduce a bare existence. We by no means intend to abolish this personal appropriation of the products of labour, an appropriation that is made for the maintenance and reproduction of human life, and that leaves no surplus wherewith to command the labour of others. All that we want to do away with, is the miserable character of this appropriation, under which the labourer lives merely to increase capital, and is allowed to live only in so far as the interest of the ruling class requires it.

In bourgeois society, living labour is but a means to increase accumulated labour. In communist society, accumulated labour is but a means to widen, to enrich, to promote the existence of the labourer.

In bourgeois society, therefore, the past dominates the present; in communist society, the present dominates the past. In bourgeois society capital is independent and has individuality, while the living person is dependent and has no individuality.

And the abolition of this state of things is called by the bourgeois, abolition of individuality and freedom! And rightly so. The abolition of bourgeois individuality, bourgeois independence, and bourgeois freedom is undoubtedly aimed at.

By freedom is meant, under the present bourgeois conditions of production, free trade, free selling and buying.

R.—5

But if selling and buying disappears, free selling and buying disappears also. This talk about free selling and buying, and all the other 'brave words' of our bourgeoisie about freedom in general, have a meaning, if any, only in contrast with restricted selling and buying, with the fettered traders of the Middle Ages, but have no meaning when opposed to the communistic abolition of buying and selling, of the bourgeois conditions of production, and the bourgeoisie itself.

You are horrified at our intending to do away with private property. But in your existing society, private property is already done away with for nine tenths of the population; its existence for the few is solely due to its non-existence in the hands of those nine tenths. You reproach us, therefore, with intending to do away with a form of property, the necessary condition for whose existence is the non-existence of any property for the immense majority of society.

In one word, you reproach us with intending to do away with your property. Precisely so; that is just what we intend.

From the moment when labour can no longer be converted into capital, money, or rent, into a social power capable of being monopolized, i.e., from the moment when individual property can no longer be transformed into bourgeois property, into capital, from that moment, you say, individuality vanishes.

You must, therefore, confess that by 'individual' you mean no other person than the bourgeois, than the middle-class owner of property. This person must, indeed, be swept out of the way, and made impossible.

Communism deprives no man of the power to appropriate the products of society; all that it does is to deprive him of the power to subjugate the labour of others by means of such appropriation.

It has been objected that upon the abolition of private property all work will cease, and universal laziness will overtake us.

According to this, bourgeois society ought long ago to have gone to the dogs through sheer idleness; for those of its members who work, acquire nothing, and those who acquire anything, do not work. The whole of this objection is but another expression of the tautology that there can no longer be any wage labour when there is no longer any capital.

All objections urged against the communistic mode of producing and appropriating material products have, in the same way, been urged against the communistic mode of producing and appropriating intellectual products. Just as, to the bourgeois, the disappearance of class property is the disappearance of production itself, so the disappearance of class culture is to him identical with the disappearance of all culture.

That culture, the loss of which he laments, is, for the enormous majority, a mere training to act as a machine.

But don't wrangle with us so long as you apply, to our intended abolition of bourgeois property, the standard of your bourgeois notions of freedom, culture, law, etc. Your very ideas are but the outgrowth of the conditions of your bourgeois production and bourgeois property, just as your jurisprudence is but the will of your class made into a law for all, a will whose essential character and direction are determined by the economical conditions of existence of your class.

The selfish misconception that induces you to transform into eternal laws of nature and of reason the social forms springing from your present mode of production and form of property – historical relations that rise and disappear in the progress of production – this misconception you share with every ruling class that has preceded you. What you see clearly in the case of ancient property, what you admit in the case of feudal property, you are of course forbidden to admit in the case of your own bourgeois form of property.

Abolition of the family! Even the most radical flare up at this infamous proposal of the Communists.

On what foundation is the present family, the bourgeois family, based? On capital, on private gain. In its completely developed form this family exists only among the bourgeoisie. But this state of things finds its complement in the practical absence of the family among the proletarians, and in public prostitution.

The bourgeois family will vanish as a matter of course when its complement vanishes, and both will vanish with the vanishing of capital.

Do you charge us with wanting to stop the exploitation of children by their parents? To this crime we plead guilty.

But, you will say, we destroy the most hallowed of relations, when we replace home education by social.

And your education! Is not that also social, and determined by the social conditions under which you educate, by the intervention direct or indirect, of society, by means of schools, etc.? The Communists have not invented the intervention of society in education;

they do but seek to alter the character of that intervention, and to rescue education from the influence of the ruling class.

The bourgeois claptrap about the family and education, about the hallowed co-relation of parent and child, becomes all the more disgusting, the more, by the action of modern industry, all family ties among the proletarians are torn asunder, and their children transformed into simple articles of commerce and instruments of labour.

But you Communists would introduce community of women, screams the whole bourgeoisie in chorus.

The bourgeois sees in his wife a mere instrument of production. He hears that the instruments of production are to be exploited in common, and, naturally, can come to no other conclusion than that the lot of being common to all will likewise fall to the women.

He has not even a suspicion that the real point aimed at is to do away with the status of women as mere instruments of production.

For the rest, nothing is more ridiculous than the virtuous indignation of our bourgeois at the community of women which, they pretend, is to be openly and officially established by the Communists. The Communists have no need to introduce community of women; it has existed almost from time immemorial.

Our bourgeois, not content with having the wives and daughters of their proletarians at their disposal, not to speak of common prostitutes, take the greatest pleasure in seducing each other's wives.

Bourgeois marriage is in reality a system of wives in common, and thus, at the most, what the Communists might possibly be reproached with, is that they desire to introduce, in substitution for a hypocritically concealed, an openly legalized community of women. For the rest, it is self-evident that the abolition of the present system of production must bring with it the abolition of the community of women springing from that system, i.e., of prostitution both public and private.

The Communists are further reproached with desiring to abolish countries and nationality.

The working men have no country. We cannot take from them what they have not got. Since the proletariat must first of all acquire political supremacy, must rise to be the leading class of the nation, must constitute itself as the nation, it is, so far, itself national, though not in the bourgeois sense of the word.

National differences, and antagonisms between peoples, are daily more and more vanishing, owing to the development of the bourgeoisie, to freedom of commerce, to the world market, to uniformity in the mode of production and in the conditions of life corresponding thereto.

The supremacy of the proletariat will cause them to vanish still faster. United action, of the leading civilized countries at least, is one of the first conditions for the emancipation of the proletariat.

In proportion as the exploitation of one individual by another is put an end to, the exploitation of one nation by another will also be put an end to. In proportion as the antagonism between classes within the nation vanishes, the hostility of one nation to another will come to an end.

The charges against communism made from a religious, a philosophical, and, generally, from an ideological standpoint, are not deserving of serious examination.

Does it require deep intuition to comprehend that man's ideas, views and conceptions, in one word, man's consciousness, changes with every change in the conditions of his material existence, in his social relations and in his social life?

What else does the history of ideas prove, than that intellectual production changes its character in proportion as material production is changed? The ruling ideas of each age have ever been the ideas of its ruling class.

When people speak of ideas that revolutionize society, they do but express the fact that within the old society, the elements of a new one have been created, and that the dissolution of the old ideas keeps even pace with the dissolution of the old conditions of existence.

When the ancient world was in its last throes, the ancient religions were overcome by Christianity. When Christian ideas succumbed in the eighteenth century to rationalist ideas, feudal society fought its death battle with the then revolutionary bourgeoisie. The ideas of religious liberty and freedom of conscience merely gave expression to the sway of free competition within the domain of knowledge.

'Undoubtedly,' it will be said, 'religious, moral, philosophical and juridical ideas have been modified in the course of historical development. But religion, morality, philosophy, political science and law constantly survived this change.'

'There are, besides, eternal truths, such as freedom, justice, etc., that are common to all states of society. But communism abolishes eternal truths, it abolishes all religion and all morality, instead of constituting them on a new basis; it therefore acts in contradiction to all past historical experience.'

What does this accusation reduce itself to? The history of all past society has consisted in the development of class antagonisms, antagonisms that assumed different forms at different epochs.

But whatever form they may have taken, one fact is common to all past ages, viz., the exploitation of one part of society by the other. No wonder, then, that the social consciousness of past ages, despite all the multiplicity and variety it displays, moves within certain common forms, or general ideas, which cannot completely vanish except with the total disappearance of class antagonisms.

The communist revolution is the most radical rupture with traditional property relations; no wonder that its development involves the most radical rupture with traditional ideas.

But let us have done with the bourgeois objections to communism.

We have seen above, that the first step in the revolution by the working class is to raise the proletariat to the position of ruling class, to win the battle of democracy.

The proletariat will use its political supremacy to wrest, by degrees, all capital from the bourgeoisie, to centralize all instruments of production in the hands of the state, i.e., of the proletariat organized as the ruling class, and to increase the total of productive forces as rapidly as possible.

Of course, in the beginning, this cannot be effected except by means of despotic inroads on the rights of property, and on the conditions of bourgeois production; by means of measures, therefore, which appear economically insufficient and untenable, but which, in the course of the movement, outstrip themselves, necessitate further inroads upon the old social order, and are unavoidable as a means of entirely revolutionizing the mode of production.

These measures will of course be different in different countries.

Nevertheless, in the most advanced countries, the following will be pretty generally applicable.

1. Abolition of property in land and application of all rents of land to public purposes.

2. A heavy progressive or graduated income tax.

3. Abolition of all right of inheritance.

4. Confiscation of the property of all emigrants and rebels.

5. Centralization of credit in the hands of the state, by means of a national bank with state capital and an exclusive monopoly.

6. Centralization of the means of communication and transport in the hands of the state.

7. Extension of factories and instruments of production owned by the state; the bringing into cultivation of waste lands, and the improvement of the soil generally in accordance with a common plan.

8. Equal liability of all to labour. Establishment of industrial armies, especially for agriculture.

9. Combination of agriculture with manufacturing industries; gradual abolition of the distinction between town and country, by a more equable distribution of the population over the country.

10. Free education for all children in public schools. Abolition of children's factory labour in its present form. Combination of education with industrial production, etc.

When, in the course of development, class distinctions have disappeared, and all production has been concentrated in the hands of a vast association of the whole nation, the public power will lose its political character. Political power, properly so called, is merely the organized power of one class for oppressing another. If the proletariat during its contest with the bourgeoisie is compelled, by the force of circumstances, to organize itself as a class; if, by means of a revolution, it makes itself the ruling class, and, as such, sweeps away by force the old conditions of production, then it will, along with these conditions, have swept away the conditions for the existence of class antagonisms and of classes generally, and will thereby have abolished its own supremacy as a class.

In place of the old bourgeois society, with its classes and class antagonisms, we shall have an association, in which the free development of each is the condition for the free development of all.

III. Socialist and Communist Literature

1. Reactionary Socialism

a. Feudal Socialism. Owing to their historical position, it became the vocation of the aristocracies of France and England to write pamphlets against modern bourgeois society. In the French revolution of July 1830, and in the English Reform agitation,[19] these aristocracies again succumbed to the hateful upstart. Thenceforth, a serious political contest was altogether out of question. A literary battle alone remained possible. But even in the domain of literature the old cries of the Restoration period[20] had become impossible.

In order to arouse sympathy, the aristocracy were obliged to lose sight, apparently, of their own interests, and to formulate their indictment against the bourgeoisie in the interest of the exploited working class alone. Thus the aristocracy took their revenge by singing lampoons on their new master, and whispering in his ears sinister prophecies of coming catastrophe.

In this way arose feudal socialism: half lamentation, half lampoon; half echo of the past, half menace of the future; at times, by its bitter, witty and incisive criticism, striking the bourgeoisie to the very heart's core; but always ludicrous in its effect, through total incapacity to comprehend the march of modern history.

The aristocracy, in order to rally the people to them, waved the proletarian alms-bag in front for a banner. But the people, so often as it joined them, saw on their hindquarters the old feudal coats of arms, and deserted with loud and irreverent laughter.

One section of the French Legitimists,[21] and 'Young England',[22] exhibited this spectacle.

In pointing out that their mode of exploitation was different to that of the bourgeoisie, the feudalists forget that they exploited under circumstances and conditions that were quite different, and that are now antiquated. In showing that, under their rule, the modern proletariat never existed, they forget that the modern bourgeoisie is the necessary offspring of their own form of society.

For the rest, so little do they conceal the reactionary character of their criticism that their chief accusation against the bourgeoisie amounts to this, that under the bourgeois regime a class is being developed, which is destined to cut up root and branch the old order of society.

19. Of 1830–32.
20. Not the English Restoration 1660 to 1689, but the French Restoration 1814 to 1830 [Engels].
21. The supporters of the restored Bourbon monarchy of 1814–30, representing the landed aristocracy.
22. A literary circle attached to the Tory party. Benjamin Disraeli's *Sybil: or Two Nations*, and Thomas Carlyle's pamphlets, were among its typical expressions.

What they upbraid the bourgeoisie with is not so much that it creates a proletariat, as that it creates a *revolutionary* proletariat.

In political practice, therefore, they join in all coercive measures against the working class; and in ordinary life, despite their high-falutin phrases, they stoop to pick up the golden apples dropped from the tree of industry, and to barter truth, love, and honour for traffic in wool, beetroot-sugar, and potato spirits.[23]

As the parson has ever gone hand in hand with the landlord, so has clerical socialism with feudal socialism.

Nothing is easier than to give Christian asceticism a socialist tinge. Has not Christianity declaimed against private property, against marriage, against the state? Has it not preached in the place of these, charity and poverty, celibacy and mortification of the flesh, monastic life and Mother Church? Christian socialism is but the holy water with which the priest consecrates the heart-burnings of the aristocrat.

b. Petty-Bourgeois Socialism. The feudal aristocracy was not the only class that was ruined by the bourgeoisie, not the only class whose conditions of existence pined and perished in the atmosphere of modern bourgeois society. The medieval burgesses and the small peasant proprietors were the precursors of the modern bourgeoisie. In those countries which are but little developed, industrially and commercially, these two classes still vegetate side by side with the rising bourgeoisie.

In countries where modern civilization has become fully developed, a new class of petty bourgeois has been formed, fluctuating between proletariat and bourgeoisie and ever renewing itself as a supplementary part of bourgeois society. The individual members of this class, however, are being constantly hurled down into the proletariat by the action of competition, and, as modern industry develops, they even see the moment approaching when they will completely disappear as an independent section of modern society, to be replaced, in manufacture, agriculture and commerce, by overseers, bailiffs, and shop assistants.

23. This applies chiefly to Germany where the landed aristocracy and squirearchy have large portions of their estates cultivated for their own account by stewards, and are, moreover, extensive beetroot-sugar manufacturers and distillers of potato spirits. The wealthier British aristocracy are, as yet, rather above that; but they, too, know how to make up for declining rents by lending their names to floaters of more or less shady joint-stock companies [Engels].

In countries like France, where the peasants constitute far more than half of the population, it was natural that writers who sided with the proletariat against the bourgeoisie should use, in their criticism of the bourgeois regime, the standard of the peasant and petty bourgeois, and from the standpoint of these intermediate classes should take up the cudgels for the working class. Thus arose petty-bourgeois socialism. Sismondi[24] was the head of this school, not only in France but also in England.

This school of socialism dissected with great acuteness the contradictions in the conditions of modern production. It laid bare the hypocritical apologies of economists. It proved, incontrovertibly, the disastrous effects of machinery and division of labour; the concentration of capital and land in a few hands; overproduction and crises; it pointed out the inevitable ruin of the petty bourgeois and peasant, the misery of the proletariat, the anarchy in production, the crying inequalities in the distribution of wealth, the industrial war of extermination between nations, the dissolution of old moral bonds, of the old family relations, of the old nationalities.

In its positive aims, however, this form of socialism aspires either to restoring the old means of production and of exchange, and with them the old property relations and the old society, or to cramping the modern means of production and of exchange within the framework of the old property relations that have been, and were bound to be, exploded by those means. In either case, it is both reactionary and utopian.

Its last words are: corporate guilds for manufacture; patriarchal relations in agriculture.

Ultimately, when stubborn historical facts had dispersed all intoxicating effects of self-deception, this form of socialism ended in a miserable fit of the blues.

c. German or 'True' Socialism.　The socialist and communist literature of France, a literature that originated under the pressure of a bourgeoisie in power, and that was the expression of the struggle against this power, was introduced into Germany at a time when the bourgeoisie, in that country, had just begun its contest with feudal absolutism.

German philosophers, would-be philosophers and *beaux esprits* eagerly seized on this literature, only forgetting that when these

24. Sismondi's *Principles of Political Economy* first appeared in 1803.

writings immigrated from France into Germany, French social conditions had not immigrated along with them. In contact with German social conditions, this French literature lost all its immediate practical significance, and assumed a purely literary aspect.[25] Thus, to the German philosophers of the eighteenth century, the demands of the first French revolution were nothing more than the demands of 'practical reason' in general, and the utterance of the will of the revolutionary French bourgeoisie signified in their eyes the laws of pure will, of will as it was bound to be, of true human will generally.

The work of the German *literati* consisted solely in bringing the new French ideas into harmony with their ancient philosophical conscience, or rather, in annexing the French ideas without deserting their own philosophic point of view.

This annexation took place in the same way in which a foreign language is appropriated, namely by translation.

It is well known how the monks wrote silly lives of Catholic saints *over* the manuscripts on which the classical works of ancient heathendom had been written. The German *literati* reversed this process with the profane French literature. They wrote their philosophical nonsense beneath the French original. For instance, beneath the French criticism of the economic functions of money, they wrote 'alienation of humanity', and beneath the French criticism of the bourgeois state they wrote, 'dethronement of the category of the general', and so forth.

The introduction of these philosophical phrases at the back of the French historical criticisms they dubbed 'philosophy of action', 'true socialism', 'German science of socialism', 'philosophical foundation of socialism', and so on.

The French socialist and communist literature was thus completely emasculated. And, since it ceased in the hands of the German to express the struggle of one class with the other, he felt conscious of having overcome 'French one-sidedness' and of representing, not true requirements, but the requirements of truth; not the interests of the proletariat, but the interests of human nature, of man in general, who belongs to no class, has no reality, who exists only in the misty realm of philosophical fantasy.

This German socialism, which took its schoolboy task so seri-

25. In the German editions of the Manifesto there is an additional sentence here which reads (1872): 'It was bound to appear as idle speculation about the realization of the essence of man.'

ously and solemnly, and extolled its poor stock-in-trade in such mountebank fashion, meanwhile gradually lost its pedantic innocence.

The fight of the German, and especially the Prussian bourgeoisie, against feudal aristocracy and absolute monarchy, in other words, the liberal movement, became more earnest.

By this, the long wished-for opportunity was offered to 'true' socialism of confronting the political movement with the socialist demands, of hurling the traditional anathemas against liberalism, against representative government, against bourgeois competition, bourgeois freedom of the press, bourgeois legislation, bourgeois liberty and equality, and of preaching to the masses that they had nothing to gain, and everything to lose, by this bourgeois movement. German socialism forgot, in the nick of time, that the French criticism, whose silly echo it was, presupposed the existence of modern bourgeois society, with its corresponding economic conditions of existence and the political constitution adapted thereto, the very things whose attainment was the object of the pending struggle in Germany.

To the absolute governments, with their following of parsons, professors, country squires and officials, it served as a welcome scarecrow against the threatening bourgeoisie.

It was a sweet finish after the bitter pills of floggings and bullets with which these same governments, just at that time, dosed the German working-class risings[26].

While this 'true' socialism thus served the governments as a weapon for fighting the German bourgeoisie, it, at the same time, directly represented a reactionary interest, the interest of the German philistines. In Germany the petty-bourgeois class, a relic of the sixteenth century, and since then constantly cropping up again under various forms, is the real social basis of the existing state of things.

To preserve this class is to preserve the existing state of things in Germany. The industrial and political supremacy of the bourgeoisie threatens it with certain destruction – on the one hand, from the concentration of capital; on the other, from the rise of a revolutionary proletariat. 'True' socialism appeared to kill these two birds with one stone. It spread like an epidemic.

The robe of speculative cobwebs, embroidered with flowers of rhetoric, steeped in the dew of sickly sentiment, this transcenden-

26. i.e. the Silesian weavers' revolt of 1844.

tal robe in which the German socialists wrapped their sorry 'eternal truths', all skin and bone, served to wonderfully increase the sale of their goods amongst such a public.

And on its part, German socialism recognized, more and more, its own calling as the bombastic representative of the petty-bourgeois philistine.

It proclaimed the German nation to be the model nation, and the German petty philistine to be the typical man. To every villainous meanness of this model man it gave a hidden, higher, socialistic interpretation, the exact contrary of its real character. It went to the extreme length of directly opposing the 'brutally destructive' tendency of communism, and of proclaiming its supreme and impartial contempt of all class struggles. With very few exceptions, all the so-called socialist and communist publications that now (1847) circulate in Germany belong to the domain of this foul and enervating literature.

2. Conservative or Bourgeois Socialism

A part of the bourgeoisie is desirous of redressing social grievances, in order to secure the continued existence of bourgeois society.

To this section belong economists, philanthropists, humanitarians, improvers of the condition of the working class, organizers of charity, members of societies for the prevention of cruelty to animals, temperance fanatics, hole-and-corner reformers of every imaginable kind. This form of socialism has, moreover, been worked out into complete systems.

We may cite Proudhon's *Philosophie de la Misère*[27] as an example of this form.

The socialistic bourgeois want all the advantages of modern social conditions without the struggles and dangers necessarily resulting therefrom. They desire the existing state of society minus its revolutionary and disintegrating elements. They wish for a bourgeoisie without a proletariat. The bourgeoisie naturally conceives the world in which it is supreme to be the best; and bourgeois socialism develops this comfortable conception into various more or less complete systems. In requiring the proletariat to carry out such a system, and thereby to march straightway into

27. It was in reply to Proudhon's *Philosophy of Poverty* (1846) that Marx wrote his *Poverty of Philosophy* (1847).

the social New Jerusalem, it but requires in reality that the proletariat should remain within the bounds of existing society, but should cast away all its hateful ideas concerning the bourgeoisie.

A second and more practical, but less systematic, form of this socialism sought to depreciate every revolutionary movement in the eyes of the working class, by showing that no mere political reform, but only a change in the material conditions of existence, in economical relations, could be of any advantage to them. By changes in the material conditions of existence, this form of socialism, however, by no means understands abolition of the bourgeois relations of production, an abolition that can be effected only by a revolution, but administrative reforms, based on the continued existence of these relations; reforms, therefore, that in no respect affect the relations between capital and labour, but, at the best, lessen the cost, and simplify the administrative work, of bourgeois government.

Bourgeois socialism attains adequate expression when, and only when, it becomes a mere figure of speech.

Free trade: for the benefit of the working class. Protective duties: for the benefit of the working class. Prison reform: for the benefit of the working class. This is the last word and the only seriously meant word of bourgeois socialism.

It is summed up in the phrase: the bourgeois is a bourgeois – for the benefit of the working class.

3. Critical-Utopian Socialism and Communism

We do not here refer to that literature which, in every great modern revolution, has always given voice to the demands of the proletariat, such as the writings of Babeuf and others.

The first direct attempts of the proletariat to attain its own ends, made in times of universal excitement, when feudal society was being overthrown, these attempts necessarily failed, owing to the then undeveloped state of the proletariat, as well as to the absence of the economic conditions for its emancipation, conditions that had yet to be produced, and could be produced by the impending bourgeois epoch alone. The revolutionary literature that accompanied these first movements of the proletariat had necessarily a reactionary character. It inculcated universal asceticism and social levelling in its crudest form.

The socialist and communist systems properly so called, those of Saint-Simon, Fourier, Owen and others, spring into existence in the early undeveloped period, described above, of the struggle between proletariat and bourgeoisie (see section I, 'Bourgeoisie and Proletariat').

The founders of these systems see, indeed, the class antagonisms, as well as the action of the decomposing elements in the prevailing form of society. But the proletariat, as yet in its infancy, offers to them the spectacle of a class without any historical initiative or any independent political movement.

Since the development of class antagonism keeps even pace with the development of industry, the economic situation, as they find it, does not as yet offer to them the material conditions for the emancipation of the proletariat. They therefore search after a new social science,[28] after new social laws, that are to create these conditions.

Historical action is to yield to their personal inventive action, historically created conditions of emancipation to fantastic ones, and the gradual, spontaneous class organization of the proletariat to an organization of society specially contrived by these inventors. Future history resolves itself, in their eyes, into the propaganda and the practical carrying out of their social plans.

In the formation of their plans they are conscious of caring chiefly for the interests of the working class, as being the most suffering class. Only from the point of view of being the most suffering class does the proletariat exist for them.

The undeveloped state of the class struggle, as well as their own surroundings, cause socialists of this kind to consider themselves far superior to all class antagonisms. They want to improve the condition of every member of society, even that of the most favoured. Hence, they habitually appeal to society at large, without distinction of class; nay, by preference, to the ruling class. For how can people, when once they understand their system, fail to see in it the best possible plan of the best possible state of society?

Hence, they reject all political, and especially all revolutionary, action; they wish to attain their ends by peaceful means, and

28. Here, as in other writings of the 1840s, Marx and Engels still used 'science' in a now archaic sense of the term, roughly equivalent to the modern 'doctrine'. Although the substance of their argument remained the same, the change in usage led them later to refer to their own theory as 'scientific', in contrast to the utopianism of their predecessors. See, for example, Marx's Preface to the first German edition of *Capital*, and Engels's 'Socialism: Utopian and Scientific', both in *MESW*.

endeavour, by small experiments, necessarily doomed to failure, and by the force of example, to pave the way for the new social gospel.

Such fantastic pictures of future society, painted at a time when the proletariat is still in a very undeveloped state and has but a fantastic conception of its own position, correspond with the first instinctive yearnings of that class for a general reconstruction of society.

But these socialist and communist publications contain also a critical element. They attack every principle of existing society. Hence they are full of the most valuable materials for the enlightenment of the working class. The practical measures proposed in them – such as the abolition of the distinction between town and country, of the family, of the carrying on of industries for the account of private individuals, and of the wage system, the proclamation of social harmony, the conversion of the functions of the state into a mere superintendence of production – all these proposals point solely to the disappearance of class antagonisms which were, at the time, only just cropping up, and which, in these publications, are recognized under their earliest, indistinct and undefined forms only. These proposals, therefore, are of a purely utopian character.

The significance of critical-utopian socialism and communism bears an inverse relation to historical development. In proportion as the modern class struggle develops and takes definite shape, this fantastic standing apart from the contest, these fantastic attacks on it, lose all practical value and all theoretical justification. Therefore, although the originators of these systems were, in many respects, revolutionary, their disciples have, in every case, formed mere reactionary sects. They hold fast by the original views of their masters, in opposition to the progressive historical development of the proletariat. They therefore endeavour, and that consistently, to deaden the class struggle and to reconcile the class antagonisms. They still dream of experimental realization of their social utopias, of founding isolated '*phalanstères*', of establishing 'home colonies', of setting up a 'little Icaria'[29] – duodecimo editions of the New Jerusalem – and to realize all these castles in the air, they are compelled to appeal to the feelings and purses of the

29. *Phalanstères* were socialist colonies on the plan of Charles Fourier; Icaria was the name given by Cabet to his utopia and, later on, to his American communist colony [Engels].

bourgeois. By degrees they sink into the category of the reactionary conservative socialists depicted above, differing from these only by more systematic pedantry, and by their fanatical and superstitious belief in the miraculous effects of their social science.

They therefore violently oppose all political action on the part of the working class; such action, according to them, can only result from blind unbelief in the new gospel.

The Owenites in England, and the Fourierists in France, respectively oppose the Chartists and the Réformistes.

IV. Position of the Communists in Relation to the Various Existing Opposition Parties

Section II has made clear the relations of the Communists to the existing working-class parties, such as the Chartists in England and the agrarian reformers[30] in America.

The Communists fight for the attainment of the immediate aims, for the enforcement of the momentary interests of the working class; but in the movement of the present, they also represent and take care of the future of that movement. In France the Communists ally themselves with the Social-Democrats,[31] against the conservative and radical bourgeoisie, reserving, however, the right to take up a critical position in regard to phrases and illusions traditionally handed down from the great Revolution.

In Switzerland they support the Radicals, without losing sight of the fact that this party consists of antagonistic elements, partly of democratic socialists, in the French sense, partly of radical bourgeois.

In Poland they support the party that insists on an agrarian revolution as the prime condition for national emancipation, that party which fomented the insurrection of Cracow in 1846.[32]

In Germany they fight with the bourgeoisie whenever it acts in a revolutionary way, against the absolute monarchy, the feudal squirearchy, and the petty bourgeoisie.[33]

30. This seems to be a reference to the Free Soil movement, which demanded the free distribution of uncultivated land to small farmers.

31. The party then represented in parliament by Ledru-Rollin, in literature by Louis Blanc, in the daily press by *La Réforme*. The name 'Social-Democracy' signified, with these its inventors, a section of the democratic or republican party more or less tinged with socialism [Engels].

32. See below, p. 102 n. 1.

33. *Kleinbürgerei* in the original. 'Petty-bourgeois conditions' would be a more accurate translation.

But they never cease, for a single instant, to instil into the working class the clearest possible recognition of the hostile antagonism between bourgeoisie and proletariat, in order that the German workers may straightway use, as so many weapons against the bourgeoisie, the social and political conditions that the bourgeoisie must necessarily introduce along with its supremacy, and in order that, after the fall of the reactionary classes in Germany, the fight against the bourgeoisie itself may immediately begin.

The Communists turn their attention chiefly to Germany, because that country is on the eve of a bourgeois revolution that is bound to be carried out under more advanced conditions of European civilization, and with a much more developed proletariat, than that of England was in the seventeenth, and of France in the eighteenth century, and because the bourgeois revolution in Germany will be but the prelude to an immediately following proletarian revolution.

In short, the Communists everywhere support every revolutionary movement against the existing social and political order of things.

In all these movements they bring to the front, as the leading question in each, the property question, no matter what its degree of development at the time.

Finally, they labour everywhere for the union and agreement of the democratic parties of all countries.

The Communists disdain to conceal their views and aims. They openly declare that their ends can be attained only by the forcible overthrow of all existing conditions. Let the ruling classes tremble at a communistic revolution. The proletarians have nothing to lose but their chains. They have a world to win.

WORKING MEN OF ALL COUNTRIES, UNITE!

Speeches on Poland (29 November 1847)[1]

Deutsche-Brüsseler-Zeitung, 9 December 1847

SPEECH BY KARL MARX

The unification and brotherhood of nations is a phrase which is nowadays on the lips of all parties, particularly of the bourgeois free traders. A kind of brotherhood does indeed exist between the bourgeois classes of all nations. It is the brotherhood of the oppressors against the oppressed, of the exploiters against the exploited. Just as the bourgeois class of one country is united in brotherhood against the proletarians of that country, despite the competition and struggle of its members among themselves, so the bourgeoisie of all countries is united in brotherhood against the proletarians of all countries, despite their struggling and competing with each other on the world market. In order for peoples to become really united their interests must be common. For their interests to be common the existing property relations must be abolished, since the exploitation of one nation by another is caused by the existing property relations. And it is only in the interests of the working class to abolish the existing property relations; only

1. These speeches were delivered by Marx and Engels at a meeting in London commemorating the seventeenth anniversary of the Polish revolution of 1830. The meeting was organized by the Fraternal Democrats, an organization that served as the international department of the Chartists and campaigned in solidarity with the oppressed nations of Europe. Marx spoke as the representative of the Democratic Association in Brussels, of which he was in fact vice-president. The Democratic Association, like the Fraternal Democrats, included both petty-bourgeois democrats and Communists. The meeting coincided with the opening of the secret second congress of the Communist League, which was the real reason for Marx and Engels's journey to London. The speeches are translated here from the text of the *Deutsche-Brüsseler-Zeitung* (9 December 1847) a German democratic paper in Brussels in which Marx was editorially involved, as reproduced in *MEW* 4. The Polish uprising of November 1830 was led by the nobles and intellectuals of Russian Poland. A provisional government was set up in Warsaw, which attempted to bargain with the tsar for reforms. In February 1831 a Russian army invaded Poland, which took until the end of the year to restore 'order', and conducted vicious reprisals.

they have the means to achieve it. The victory of the proletariat over the bourgeoisie represents at the same time the victory over national and industrial conflicts, which at present create hostility between the different peoples. Therefore, the victory of the proletariat over the bourgeoisie also signifies the emancipation of all downtrodden nations.

The old Poland is certainly lost, and we should be the last to wish for its restoration. But not only is the old Poland lost. The old Germany, the old France, the old England, the old social order in general is lost. The loss of the old social order, however, is not a loss for those who have nothing to lose in the old society, and at the present time this is the case for the large majority of people in all countries. They have, in fact, everything to gain from the destruction of the old society, for it is a precondition for the formation of a new society no longer based on class antagonisms.

Of all countries it is England where the opposition between the proletariat and the bourgeoisie is most highly developed. Thus the victory of the English proletariat over the English bourgeoisie is of decisive importance for the victory of all oppressed peoples over their oppressors. Poland, therefore, must be freed, not in Poland, but in England. You Chartists should not express pious wishes for the liberation of nations. Defeat your own enemies at home and then you may be proudly conscious of having defeated the old social order in its entirety.

SPEECH BY FREDERICK ENGELS

My friends, allow me today to appear for once in my capacity as a German. For we Germans have a particular interest in the liberation of Poland. German princes have profited from the partition of Poland[2] and German soldiers are still exercising oppression in Galicia and Posen. It must be the concern of us Germans, above all, of us German democrats, to remove this stain from our nation. A nation cannot be free and at the same time continue to oppress other nations. Thus Germany cannot be liberated without the liberation of Poland from oppression by Germans. And for this reason Poland and Germany have a common interest, for

2. After the three partitions of Poland, in 1772, 1793 and 1795, the country was entirely divided between Austria, Prussia and Russia, with the nominally independent district of Cracow itself occupied by the three powers. Galicia was in Austrian hands, and Posen (now Poznań) in Prussian.

this reason Polish and German democrats can work together for the liberation of both nations.

I, too, am of the opinion that the first decisive blow from which the victory of democracy, the liberation of all European countries will ensue, will be delivered by the English Chartists; I have been in England for several years and during this time I have openly joined in the Chartist movement. The English Chartists will rise up first because it is precisely here that the struggle between bourgeoisie and proletariat is at its fiercest. And why is it at its fiercest? Because in England, as a result of modern industry and machines, all the oppressed classes have been thrown together into one huge class with common interests, the class of the proletariat; because, conversely, as a result of these developments all the oppressing classes have likewise been united into a single class, the bourgeoisie. Thus the struggle has been simplified; thus it will be resolved at one great decisive stroke. Is this not so? The aristocracy has no more power in England; the bourgeoisie alone rules and has taken the aristocracy in tow. The bourgeoisie, however, is faced by the great mass of the people, united in a terrible phalanx, whose victory over the ruling capitalists is drawing nearer and nearer. And this destruction of the divergent interests which earlier divided the different sections of the workers, this reduction of the lives of all workers to the same level you owe to machinery; without machinery there would be no Chartism, and even though your situation may be becoming worse at present as a result of machinery, it is, for this very reason, making our victory possible. But it has had this result not just in England but also in all other countries. In Belgium, in America, in France, in Germany it has reduced the conditions of all workers to the same level and it is making them increasingly similar day by day; in all these countries the workers have the same interest, that is, to overthrow the class which is oppressing them, the bourgeoisie. This levelling out of conditions, this international identity of interest of the workers' party is the result of machinery; machinery therefore, remains an enormous historical advance. What conclusions can be drawn from this? Because the position is the same for the workers of all countries, because their interests are the same and their enemies are the same, for this reason they must also fight together, they must oppose the brotherhood of the bourgeoisie of all nations with the brotherhood of the workers of all nations.

R. – 6

Speeches on Poland (22 February 1848)[1]

SPEECH BY KARL MARX

Gentlemen,

There are some striking analogies in history. The Jacobin of 1793 has become the communist of our own day. In 1793, when Russia, Austria and Prussia divided Poland, the three powers justified themselves by citing the constitution of 1791, which was condemned by general agreement on the grounds of its reputedly Jacobin principles.

And what had the Polish constitution of 1791 proclaimed? No more and no less than constitutional monarchy: legislation to be placed in the hands of the country's representatives, freedom of the press, freedom of conscience, judicial hearings to be made public, serfdom to be abolished, etc. And all this was at that time simply called Jacobinism! So, gentlemen, you see how history has progressed. The Jacobinism of that time has today become, in the form of liberalism, all that is most moderate.

The three powers have moved with the times. In 1846, when they took away the last vestiges of Polish nationality by incorporating Cracow into Austria, they referred to what they used to call Jacobinism as communism.

1. These speeches were delivered by Marx and Engels in Brussels at a meeting to commemorate the Cracow insurrection. They were published in the pamphlet *Célébration, à Bruxelles, du deuxième anniversaire de la Révolution Polonaise du 22 Février 1846*, Brussels, 1848, and are translated here from the texts reproduced by D. Ryazanov in *Archiv für die Geschichte des Sozialismus*, vol. VI, Leipzig, 1916.

The Polish uprising of 1846 was led by revolutionary democrats. It began on 22 February with an insurrection in the 'free state' of Cracow. The national government in Cracow proclaimed a radical programme that included the abolition of feudal dues, the redistribution of land, and 'social' workshops. However it failed, from insufficient organizational preparation, to ensure rapid enough support from the peasantry. Cracow was recaptured by the beginning of March, although sporadic resistance in the countryside continued for several weeks. In November 1846, Cracow was annexed to Austria.

But what was communist about the Cracow revolution? Was it communist to want to re-establish Polish nationality? One might equally say that the war of the European Coalition against Napoleon to save the various nationalities was a communist war, and that the Congress of Vienna was made up of communists with crowned heads. Or was the Cracow revolution communist for wanting to set up a democratic government? No one would accuse the millionaires of Berne or New York of communist tendencies.

Communism denies the need for classes to exist: it wants to get rid of all classes and all class distinctions. But the Cracow revolutionaries merely wanted to get rid of *political* distinctions between the classes; they wanted to give all classes equal rights.

Just what then was communist about that Cracow revolution?

Was it possibly that it was trying to break the chains of the feudal system, to liberate land subject to tribute and transform it into free, modern property?

If one were to say to French landowners: 'Do you realize what the Polish democrats want? They want to bring into their country the form of ownership already existing in your country'; then the French landowners would answer: 'They are doing the right thing'. But say, like M. Guizot, to the French landowners: 'The Poles want to get rid of landownership as established by you in the 1789 revolution, and as it still exists in your country.' 'Good God!' they would cry, 'then they are revolutionaries, communists! These evil men must be crushed.' The abolition of guild wardens and corporations, and the introduction of free competition, is now in Sweden called communism. The *Journal des Débats* goes further: abolishing the income which the two hundred thousand electors' right of corruption brings in – that means abolishing a source of revenue, destroying an existing property, communism.[2] Certainly the Cracow revolution also wanted to abolish a form of property. But what kind of property? A kind which can no more be destroyed anywhere else in Europe, than can the Sonderbund[3] in Switzerland, because it simply does not exist any more.

2. The *Journal des Débats* was the official newspaper of the July monarchy of 1830–48. Marx is alluding to the electoral corruption that the restricted franchise of this regime fostered.

3. The Swiss Sonderbund (separatist league) was formed by the reactionary Catholic 'founding cantons' in 1847, to resist the greater centralization that the federal government was mandated to carry out. The Sonderbund was defeated with a short military campaign in November 1847.

No one will deny that in Poland the political question is linked with a social question. The one is always inseparable from the other.

You can ask the reactionaries about that! Under the Restoration,[4] were they only struggling against political liberalism and its necessary corollary, Voltaireanism? One respected reactionary writer freely admitted that the highest metaphysic of a de Maistre and a de Bonald[5] came down ultimately to a question of money, and is not every question of money a social question? The men of the Restoration did not hide the fact that to return to sound politics, they had to bring back sound property, feudal property, moral property. Everyone knows that faithful royalism cannot manage without tithes and *corvée*.

Let us go back further: in 1789 the political question of human rights concealed the social question of free competition.

And what is happening in England? In all matters from the Reform Bill[6] to the repeal of the Corn Laws,[7] have the political parties fought for anything but changes of property, questions of property – social questions?

Here, in Belgium itself, is the battle between liberalism and Catholicism anything other than a battle between industrial capital and the large landowners?

And all the political questions that have been debated for the past seventeen years[8] – are they not all at bottom social questions?

So whatever point of view you may adopt, whether it be liberal, radical or even aristocratic, you can hardly still dare to blame the Cracow revolution for having attached a social question to a political one.

The men who led the revolutionary movement in Cracow were absolutely convinced that only a democratic Poland could be free, and that there could be no democratic Poland without the abolition of all feudal rights, and without an agrarian movement which would transform the peasants from landowners forced to pay tribute into free, modern landowners.

If the Russian autocrat were to be replaced by Polish aristo-

4. i.e. the restored Bourbon monarchy in France, 1814–30.
5. Joseph-Marie, comte de Maistre, and Louis-Gabriel-Ambroise, vicomte de Bonald, were both ideologists of the aristocratic and clerical reaction in the Restoration period.
6. 1832.
7. 1846.
8. i.e. since Belgium gained independence in 1831.

crats, then despotism would merely have taken out naturalization papers. Thus the Germans, in their battle against the foreigner, exchanged one Napoleon for thirty-six Metternichs.[9] Though the Polish lord would no longer have a Russian lord over him, the Polish peasant would still have a lord over him – only a lord who was free rather than one who was a slave. This particular political change involves no social change at all.

The Cracow revolution has given all of Europe a magnificent example by identifying the cause of nationhood with the cause of democracy and the liberation of the oppressed class.

Though that revolution has for the time been stifled by the bloodstained hands of paid assassins, it is rising again in glory and triumph in Switzerland and Italy.[10] It is finding its principles confirmed in Ireland, where the purely nationalist party has gone to the grave with O'Connell, and the new national party is above all reforming and democratic.[11]

It is still Poland that has taken the initiative – not the feudal Poland of the past, but democratic Poland – and from now on its liberation has become a point of honour for all the democrats in Europe.

SPEECH BY FREDERICK ENGELS

Gentlemen,

The rising whose anniversary we are celebrating today failed. After a few days of heroic resistance, Cracow was taken, and the bloody ghost of Poland, which had for a moment risen before the eyes of her assassins, returned to the tomb.

The Cracow revolution was a defeat, a most deplorable defeat. We must pay our last honours to the fallen heroes, lament their failure, and express our sympathies to the twenty million Poles whose chains have been drawn tighter by it.

9. Marx refers to the result of the 'War of Liberation' of 1813–14. See Introduction, p. 9.

10. The defeat of the Sonderbund in November 1847 was seen as a victory for the democratic revolution. Revolution broke out in Palermo on 12 January 1848.

11. The Irish Confederation was formed in June 1847 by radical democrats, mainly intellectuals from the Young Ireland group, who broke with the liberal bourgeois Repeal Association founded by Daniel O'Connell. In 1848 the left wing of the Irish Confederation attempted an insurrection on the basis of Thomas Meagher's Proclamation which linked national independence with democratic reforms. O'Connell died in 1847.

But, gentlemen, is that all we have to do? Is it enough to drop a tear on the tomb of an unhappy country, and swear implacable hatred towards its oppressors – implacable, but hitherto impotent?

No, gentlemen! The anniversary of Cracow is not only a day of mourning, but for us democrats it is also a day of rejoicing; for even in that defeat there is contained a victory, and the fruits of that victory are something that will live, whereas the results of the defeat will pass.

That victory is the victory of the young democratic Poland over the old aristocratic Poland.

Yes, Poland's last struggle against her foreign oppressors was preceded by a hidden, unseen but decisive struggle inside Poland herself; the struggle of the oppressed Poles against the oppressing Poles, of Polish democracy against Polish aristocracy.

Compare 1830 and 1846: compare Warsaw and Cracow. In 1830, the ruling class in Poland was as selfish, as limited, as cowardly in the legislature as it was dedicated, enthusiastic and brave on the battlefield. What did the Polish aristocracy want in 1830? To preserve its own entrenched rights as against the tsar. It restricted its rebellion to that little area which it pleased the Congress of Vienna to designate the Kingdom of Poland;[12] it restrained the fighting spirit of the other Polish provinces, and did nothing to mitigate the degrading slavery of the peasants or the iniquitous conditions of the Jews. Though, during the course of the rebellion, the aristocracy was forced to make concessions to the people, by the time they made them it was too late and the rebellion had already failed.

We may say categorically: the 1830 rebellion was neither a national revolution (it excluded three quarters of Poland), nor a social or political revolution; it did nothing to change the situation of the people inside the country; it was a conservative revolution.

But within that conservative revolution, actually within the national government, there was one man who forcefully attacked the narrow views of the ruling class. He proposed genuinely revolutionary measures which appalled the aristocrats in the Diet by their boldness. He wanted to make the national cause the cause of liberty, and to identify the interest of all peoples with that of the

12. The Grand Duchy of Warsaw created by Napoleon in 1807 as a satellite state was handed to Russia by the Congress of Vienna. Tsar Alexander I made this 'Congress Poland' into his 'Kingdom of Poland', granting it a minimal autonomy in the hope of staving off nationalist agitation.

Polish people, by calling all of what was formerly Poland to arms, and thus making the Polish war of independence a European war, by emancipating the Jews and the peasants, by giving the latter a share in land ownership, and by reconstructing Poland on a basis of democracy and equality. It seems hardly necessary to name the man whose genius conceived this plan at once so immense and so simple – it was Lelewel.[13]

In 1830, those proposals were repeatedly rejected, owing to the self-interested blindness of the majority of the aristocracy. But those principles, ripened and developed by the experience of fifteen years' slavery, are the principles we have since seen emblazoned on the flag of the Cracow revolution. In Cracow, as we saw, there was no one left with a lot to lose, there were no aristocrats, and every step that was taken bore the mark of that democratic, almost proletarian boldness which has nothing to lose but its poverty, and a country, indeed a whole world, to gain. There was no hanging back, no scruple, there: they attacked all three powers at once; they proclaimed freedom for the peasants, agrarian reform, emancipation of the Jews – and all this without a moment's anxiety as to whether it might go counter to this or that aristocratic interest.

The Cracow revolution sought neither to re-establish the Poland of the past, nor to preserve such of the old Polish institutions as the foreign governments had left in existence; it was not reactionary, nor was it conservative.

No, it was even more hostile to Poland herself than to her foreign oppressors; hostile to the Poland of the past, barbarous, feudal, aristocratic, founded on the slavery of the majority of the people. Far from re-establishing that old Poland, it sought to turn it entirely upside down, and to found upon what remained, with an entirely new class, with the majority of the people, a new, civilized, democratic, modern Poland, worthy of the nineteenth century, which would be a real advance post of civilization.

The difference between 1830 and 1846, the immense progress achieved inside even that unhappy, bleeding, shattered country; the Polish aristocracy completely separated from the people and thrown into the arms of their country's oppressors; the Polish

13. Joachim Lelewel was a Polish historian, who after the defeat of the 1830–31 revolution became the leader of the democratic wing of the Polish refugees. At this time he lived in Brussels and was an executive member of the Democratic Association.

people wholly won over to the cause of democracy; and finally the struggle of class against class, which is the prime mover of all social progress, established in Poland just as it is here – that is the victory of democracy achieved by the Cracow revolution, the result that will still bear fruit when the defeat of the rebels has long been avenged.

Yes, gentlemen, the Cracow rebellion has made the Polish cause, nationalist though it may be, the cause of all peoples; from being merely a matter for sympathy, it has become a matter of interest to all democrats. Until 1846 we had a crime to avenge; from now on, we have allies to support, and we shall support them.

It is especially our own Germany which can congratulate herself for that explosion of democratic feeling in Poland. We ourselves are on the point of having a democratic revolution; we shall have to fight the barbarian hordes of Austria and Russia. Before 1846, we had some hesitation as to which side Poland might support in a democratic revolution in Germany, but the Cracow revolution has resolved all our doubts. Henceforth the German and Polish peoples are forever allied. We have the same enemies, the same oppressors, for the Russian government weighs us down as heavily as the Poles. The first condition for the freeing of both Germany and Poland is the overthrow of the present political regime in Germany, the fall of Prussia and Austria, and the withdrawal of Russia to the Dniester and the Dvina.

Thus, the alliance of our two nations is far from being a beautiful dream, a delightful illusion; no, gentlemen, it is an inevitable necessity, given the common interests of the two countries, and it is the Cracow revolution that has made it a necessity. The German people who, up to now, have had little more than words to use on their own behalf, will have actions for their brothers in Poland. And just as we German democrats who are here today hold out our hand to the Polish democrats, so the entire German people will celebrate their alliance with the people of Poland on the battlefield on which we win our first victory together over our common oppressors.

The Demands of the Communist Party in Germany[1]

Karl Marx and Frederick Engels

Proletarians of all countries, unite!

1. The whole of Germany shall be declared a single and indivisible republic.

2. Every German over twenty-one years of age shall be able to vote and be elected, provided he has no criminal record.

3. Representatives of the people shall be paid, so that workers, too, will be able to sit in the parliament of the German people.

4. The whole population shall be armed. In future, the armed forces are to be forces of workers as well, so that the army will not merely be a consumer, as it was in the past, but will produce even more than the cost of its upkeep.

Furthermore, this will be a means of organizing labour.

5. The exercise of justice shall be free of charge.

6. All the feudal dues, tributes, duties, tithes, etc., which have oppressed the rural population until now, shall be abolished, with no compensation whatsoever.

7. The estates of princes and other feudal lords, and all mines and pits, etc., shall become state property. On these estates, large-scale agriculture is to be introduced for the benefit of all and using the most modern scientific aids.

8. Mortgages on peasant lands shall be declared state property. The peasants are to pay the interest on these mortgages to the state.

9. In those regions where there is a developed system of lease-holding, the ground rent or the 'lease shilling' shall be paid to the state as tax.

1. These Demands were drawn up by Marx and Engels on behalf of the Central Committee of the Communist League in Paris during the last week of March 1848. They were published there on 31 March as a leaflet, and at the beginning of April in various democratic German newspapers. In summer 1848 the Demands were reprinted in Cologne. They are translated here from the text of the Cologne leaflet, as printed in *MEW* 5.

All the measures listed in 6, 7, 8 and 9 are designed to reduce public and other burdens on peasants and small tenant farmers, without reducing the requisite means for paying the expenses of the state and without endangering production itself.

The real landowner, who is neither a peasant nor a tenant, has no part in production. His consumption is therefore nothing but misuse.

10. One state bank shall replace all the private banks, and its note issue shall be legal tender.

This measure will make it possible to regulate credit in the interests of the *whole* population and thus undermine the domination of the big money-men. The gradual replacement of gold and silver by paper money will reduce the cost of the indispensable instrument of bourgeois commerce, the universal means of exchange, and reserve gold and silver for effective use abroad. Finally, this measure is needed in order to bind the interests of the conservative bourgeois to the revolution.[2]

11. All means of transport: railways, canals, steamships, roads, stations, etc. shall be taken over by the state. They are to be transformed into state property and put at the free service of the needy.

12. All civil servants shall receive the same pay, without any distinction other than that those *with* a family, i.e. with more needs, will also receive a higher salary than the rest.

13. The complete separation of Church and State. Ministers of all confessions are to be paid only by their congregations.

14. Restriction of the right of inheritance.

15. The introduction of severely progressive taxation and the abolition of taxes on consumption.

16. The establishment of national workshops. The state is to guarantee all workers their existence and care for those unable to work.

17. Universal and free education for the people.

It is in the interests of the German proletariat, petty bourgeoisie and peasantry to work energetically for the implementation of the above measures. Through their realization alone can the millions

2. The original text of the tenth Demand, in place of '*an die Revolution zu knüpfen*' (to bind [the interests of the conservative bourgeois] to the revolution), read '*an die Regierungen zu fesseln*' (to chain [the interests of the conservative bourgeois] to the governments).

of German people, who have up till now been exploited by a small handful, and whom some will attempt to maintain in renewed oppression, get their rights, and the power that they are due as the producers of all wealth.

The Committee:

KARL MARX	F. ENGELS
KARL SCHAPPER	J. MOLL
H. BAUER	W. WOLFF

Articles from the *Neue Rheinische Zeitung*[1]

THE DEMOCRATIC PARTY[2]

N.Rh.Z., 2 June 1848

Cologne, 1 June

Any new organ of public opinion commonly has to fulfil certain requirements: enthusiastic support for the party whose principles it professes; unlimited confidence in its strength; constant readiness both to gloss over real weakness with the lustre of principle and to use real strength to make up for an absence of principle. However, we shall not comply with these demands. We shall not seek to gild the defeats that have been suffered with misleading illusions.

The democratic party has suffered defeats; the fundamental principles which it proclaimed at the moment of its triumph have been put in question, the terrain which it had actually won has been progressively converted back into debatable ground. It has already suffered heavy losses, and we shall soon have to ask what is still left to it.

What we are concerned about is that the democratic party should become aware of its situation. We may well be asked why we address ourselves to a party, why we do not instead simply keep in view the goal of democratic endeavour, the good of the people, the salvation of everyone without distinction.

This is our right and the normal practice of the struggle. The salvation of the new age can only grow from the *struggle* of parties, not from apparently clever compromises or a sham association of contradictory views, interests and aims.

1. These articles are selected from approximately two hundred and twenty that Marx and Engels wrote for the *Neue Rheinische Zeitung* between 1 June 1848 and 19 May 1849. They are translated here from the texts printed in *MEW* 5 and 6.

2. This article was based on a draft by Heinrich Bürgers, who was taken onto the editorial board of the *Neue Rheinische Zeitung* as a concession to the local Cologne Communists in return for their allowing Marx and Engels to determine the policy of the newspaper. Marx edited the article, making extensive alterations to one half of it, and striking out the other half.

The 'democratic party' of this article refers to the broad democratic movement, not to any particular organized group.

We demand that the democratic party become aware of its situation. This demand has arisen from the experiences of the last few months. The democratic party has abandoned itself far too much to the ecstatic celebration of its first victories. Drunk with joy at being permitted at last to declare its principles loudly and frankly, it imagined that it was only necessary to proclaim them to be certain of their immediate realization. After its first triumph and the concessions directly linked to this, the democratic party never did more than proclaim its principles. But while, in its generosity, it embraced as a brother anyone who did not venture immediately to contradict it, other people, who had either been left in power or just presented with it, were taking action. And the results of their activity are not to be despised. They kept their principles in the background, only allowing them to obtrude in so far as they were directed against the old situation overthrown by the revolution. Cautiously they restricted the movement, wherever the interest of the newly created legal framework or the establishment of external order could serve as an excuse. They made apparent concessions to the friends of the old order, to be the more certain of their support in carrying out their plans. Then they gradually introduced their own political system in its basic features, and finally succeeded in winning the middle ground between the democratic party and the absolutists. Looked at from one side they are moving forwards, from the other side they are pushing backwards. They are at once progressive – against absolutism, and reactionary – against democracy.

This is the party of the prudent, moderate bourgeoisie, by which the party of the people in its initial drunkenness allowed itself to be outsmarted, until finally its eyes were opened when it was contemptuously rejected, denounced as subversive, and had all possible reprehensible tendencies attributed to it. Then the democratic party realized that basically it had achieved no more than what the gentlemen of the bourgeoisie regarded as compatible with their own well-understood interests. Involved in self-contradiction by undemocratic electoral laws, and beaten in the elections, the democratic party now sees itself confronted with two representative bodies,[3] and the only disputable point about them is which one opposes the strongest resistance to its demands.

3. The two representative bodies were the German National Assembly, which met at Frankfurt on 18 May 1848, and the Prussian National Assembly, which met at Berlin on 22 May 1848.

With this, of course, its enthusiasm has cooled off, and given place to the sober recognition that a powerful reaction has attained power, and, peculiarly enough, before any action of a revolutionary kind has taken place.

Although all this is indubitable, it would be dangerous now if the democratic party allowed itself to be persuaded, by the bitterness of the first defeat, for which it is itself partly responsible, to return to that accursed idealism, unfortunately so dear to the German character, in virtue of which a principle which cannot immediately be put into practice is recommended for the remote future, but for the present left to the harmless elaborations of the 'thinkers'.

We must give a direct warning against those hypocritical friends who declare their agreement with the principle, but who are doubtful of its feasibility because the world is not yet ripe for it. They have no intention of bringing this ripeness about, but prefer rather to revert, in this depraved earthly existence, to man's general fate of depravity. If these are the crypto-republicans, so feared by Hofrat Gervinus,[4] we must agree with him wholeheartedly: such men are dangerous.

CAMPHAUSEN'S DECLARATION IN THE SITTING
OF 30 MAY 1848

N.Rh.Z., 3 June 1848

Cologne, 2 June

Post hoc et non propter hoc. Herr Camphausen[5] did not become Prime Minister *on account of* the March revolution but merely *after* the March revolution. On 30 May 1848 he revealed the subsequent character of his cabinet in a solemn, highly declamatory manner, with that so to speak serious corporeality which conceals the lack of a soul,[6] to the Berlin Assembly agreed on between the

4. Georg Gottfried Gervinus was a historian, court councillor (Hofrat), and member of the Frankfurt National Assembly. As a supporter of the constitutional monarchist Right Centre, Gervinus opposed the 'crypto-republicans' of the Left Centre, referred to here by Marx.

5. Ludolf Camphausen was a Cologne banker, one of the leading Rhineland liberals before 1848, and Prime Minister of Prussia from March to June 1848.

6. A quotation from Book I, chapter 11 of Lawrence Sterne's novel *Tristram Shandy*.

indirect electors[7] and himself. 'The ministry of state which was formed on 29 March', says the *thinking friend of history*,[8] 'met together shortly *after* an occurrence the significance of which it has not failed to appreciate and will not fail to appreciate.'

The evidence for Herr Camphausen's assertion that he did *not* form a cabinet *before* 29 March will be found in the last few months' issues of the *Preussische Staats-Zeitung*.[9] And we may reliably assume that the date which forms at least the chronological starting-point for Herr Camphausen's ascension into heaven possesses a great 'significance' for him. What reassurance for the dead of the barricades, that their cold corpses should figure as a signpost, a pointer towards the ministry of 29 March! What an honour!

To put it briefly: after the March revolution a Camphausen ministry was formed; that same Camphausen ministry recognizes the 'great significance' of the March revolution; at any rate it does not *fail to appreciate* it. The revolution itself is a mere bagatelle, but we are speaking of its *significance*. What it *signifies* is the Camphausen ministry, at any rate retrospectively. 'This occurrence' – the formation of the Camphausen ministry or the March revolution? – 'belongs among the most essential contributory causes of the reconstruction of our *internal* constitution.'

He apparently means that the March revolution was an 'essential contributory cause' of the formation of the ministry of 29 March, i.e. of Camphausen's ministry. Or is he merely saying: the Prussian March revolution has revolutionized Prussia? We might very well expect a solemn tautology of this nature from a 'thinking friend of history'. 'We stand at the entrance to the same' (namely the reconstruction of the internal relations of our state), 'and we have a long road ahead of us, as the government recognizes.'

In short, the Camphausen ministry recognizes that it still has a long road ahead of it, i.e. it expects to last a long time. Short is art, i.e., the revolution, and long is life, i.e. the subsequent ministry. What a superfluity of self-recognition! Or should Camphausen's words be interpreted in some other way? One would certainly not expect from the *thinking friend of history* the

7. The Prussian National Assembly was elected on a two-tier voting system which was intended to cancel out the effect of universal suffrage.

8. This is Marx's ironic description of Camphausen, and refers to the dedication of Karl von Rotteck's well-known *Allgemeine Geschichte* (Freiburg, 1834), which was compiled 'for thinking friends of history'.

9. The semi-official organ of the Prussian government from 1819 to April 1848.

trivial statement that peoples which stand on the threshold of a new historical epoch stand at its threshold, and that the road which every epoch has *ahead of it* is precisely as long as the *future*.

Thus far the *first* part of the laborious, serious, formal, upright and shrewd speech of Prime Minister Camphausen. It can be summed up in three phrases: *after* the March revolution the Camphausen ministry; great significance of the Camphausen ministry; long road *ahead* of the Camphausen ministry.

Now the *second* part. 'We have by no means', pontificates Herr Camphausen, .

conceived the situation to be that this occurrence [he means the March revolution] has brought about a complete upheaval, that the entire constitution of our state has been overthrown, that what we see before us has ceased to exist in law, and that all our institutions require a new legal foundation. On the contrary. Immediately they had met together, the ministers agreed to view it as a matter of the ministry's very existence that the United Diet[10] called at that time should actually meet, despite the petitions handed in against it. We agreed that the passage from the existing constitution to the new constitution should take place through the legal means provided by the former, and without cutting off the bond which links the old to the new. We strictly maintained this unquestionably correct course. The electoral law was presented to the United Diet and issued with its concurrence. Later on the attempt was made to empower the government to alter the law out of the plenitude of its own power, namely to change the indirect into the direct electoral system. The government did not give way to this. The government has not exercised a dictatorship; it has not been able to, nor has it *wanted* to. The electoral law has in fact been brought into operation in the form in which it exists legally. The electors, the deputies, have been elected on the basis of this electoral law. They are here on the basis of this electoral law with full powers to agree jointly with the Crown upon a constitution for the future which it is hoped will be a lasting constitution.

A kingdom for a doctrine! A doctrine for a kingdom! First comes the 'occurrence', shamefaced title of the *revolution*. Then along comes the doctrine and swindles the 'occurrence'.

10. The first United Diet (Vereinigte Landtag) sat in Berlin from April to June 1847. It consisted of representatives of the eight Provincial Diets of Prussia, assembled in two Curias, or chambers, one for the nobility and the other for the three mock-medieval estates of knights, towns and rural districts. A second United Diet was called on the same basis after the March revolution, but only for the purpose of passing the electoral law for the forthcoming National Assembly and granting the loan refused by the first United Diet. It was dissolved on 10 April 1848.

The unlawful 'occurrence' makes Herr Camphausen a *responsible* Prime Minister, makes him a being both out of place and meaningless in the old regime, under the existing constitution. With a breathtaking leap we brush aside the old order and are fortunate enough to find a responsible minister. But the responsible minister is still luckier: he finds a doctrine. The absolute monarchy expired, perished, at the first breath of the *responsible Prime Minister*. The late lamented 'United Diet', that repulsive mixture of Gothic fantasy and modern falsehood,[11] was the first victim of the responsible ministry. The 'United Diet' was the 'faithful follower', the 'little donkey' of the absolute monarchy. The German republic can only celebrate its triumphal entry over the dead body of Herr Venedey,[12] the responsible ministry only over the dead body of the 'faithful follower'. The responsible minister now seeks out the missing corpse, or conjures up the *ghost* of the faithful 'United', which does indeed appear but dangles unhappily in the air, cutting the most peculiar capers since it no longer finds any *ground* beneath its feet, the old *legal and moral foundation* having been swallowed up by the earthquake of the 'occurrence'. The magician informs the ghost that he has called it up in order to liquidate its remains and to be able to behave as its loyal heir. This polite mode of action is beyond all praise, he says, for in ordinary life the dead are not permitted to draw up their wills posthumously. The highly flattered ghost nods like an oriental figurine to all the magician's commands, makes his obeisance on the way out, and vanishes. The law of indirect election is his posthumous testament.

This is the doctrinal sleight-of-hand by which Herr Camphausen makes the transition 'from the existing constitution to the new constitution, through the legal means provided by the former'. An illegal occurrence makes Herr Camphausen an *illegal* person in the sense of the 'existing constitution' of the 'old order'. It makes him a responsible Prime Minister, a *constitutional minister*. The constitutional minister illegally makes the *anti-constitutional, pre-democratic*, faithful *United Diet* a *constituent* assembly. The faithful 'United' illegally establishes indirect suffrage. Indirect suffrage

11. Heinrich Heine, 'Germany: A Winter's Tale', English translation in F. Ewen (ed.), *The Poetry and Prose of Heinrich Heine*, Citadel, New York, 1948.

12. Jakob Venedey was a radical journalist, and sat in the Frankfurt National Assembly as a member of the Radical-Democratic party.

produces the Berlin Assembly, the Berlin Assembly produces the constitution, the constitution produces all subsequent assemblies and so on *ad infinitum*.

In this way the egg comes out of the goose, and the goose comes out of the egg. However the people soon realize, from the cackling that saved the Capitol, that someone has filched the golden eggs of Leda,[13] laid by the goose during the revolution. Even deputy Milde[14] does not seem to be the son of Leda, the ever-shining Castor.

THE CAMPHAUSEN MINISTRY

N.Rh.Z., 4 June 1848

Cologne, 3 June

It is well known that an Assembly of Notables preceded the French National Assembly of 1789, and that this assembly, like the Prussian United Diet, was composed of *estates*. In the decree in which minister Necker convoked the National Assembly, he referred to the wish the notables had expressed for the convocation of the Estates General. Necker therefore had a considerable advantage over Camphausen. He did not need to await the storming of the Bastille and the fall of the absolute monarchy in order to link the old and the new in doctrinaire fashion, so as to maintain with great effort the *appearance* that France had achieved its new Constituent Assembly by the lawful means provided by the old constitution. He had other advantages too. He was a minister of France and not of Alsace-Lorraine, whereas Herr Camphausen is not a minister of Germany but of Prussia. And with all these advantages, Necker did not succeed in making a quiet reform out of a revolutionary movement. The great sickness was not to be healed with attar of roses.[15] So much the less will Herr Camphausen change the character of the movement with an artificial theory which draws a straight line between his ministry and the previous situation in the Prussian monarchy. The March revolution, and the German revolutionary movement in general, will not

13. According to the Greek legend, the children of the Spartan queen Leda and the god Zeus came out of an egg.

14. Karl August Milde was a Silesian cotton manufacturer, a liberal monarchist, chairman of the Prussian National Assembly and Prussian Minister of Trade from June to September 1848.

15. Heine, 'Germany: A Winter's Tale.'

allow themselves to be transformed into *incidents* of greater or lesser importance by any kind of stratagem. Was Louis Philippe chosen king of the French *because* he was a Bourbon? Was he chosen *although* he was a Bourbon? Remember that this question divided the parties shortly after the July revolution. What did the question itself signify? That the revolution had been put in question, and that the interest of the revolution was not the interest of the class that had achieved mastery, nor of its political representatives.

This is also the meaning of Herr Camphausen's declaration that his ministry did not come into the world *on account of* the March revolution, but *after* it.

THE PROGRAMMES OF THE RADICAL-DEMOCRATIC PARTY AND THE LEFT IN THE FRANKFURT ASSEMBLY

N.Rh.Z., 7 June 1848

Cologne, 6 June

Yesterday we communicated to our readers the 'Reasoned Manifesto of the Radical-Democratic Party in the Constituent National Assembly at Frankfurt-am-Main'. Today, under the heading 'Frankfurt', you will find the manifesto of the Left.[16] The two manifestoes appear at first sight to be scarcely distinguishable except in form, in that the Radical-Democratic party's writer is clumsy while the Left's is skilful. On closer inspection, however, there stand out certain essential points of difference. The Radical manifesto demands a National Assembly 'on the basis of *direct elections* without property qualifications'. The Left's manifesto calls for 'free election by everyone'. *Free election by everyone* excludes the property qualifications but by no means excludes the *indirect* method. And what indeed is the reason for this indefinite, ambiguous expression?

We are once again confronted with the greater scope and the flexibility of the demands of the Left, as opposed to the demands of the Radical party. The Left calls for 'an executive central authority, elected *by* the National Assembly for a specified period,

16. The left wing of the Frankfurt National Assembly split into two parts in May 1848. The larger and more moderate group was the Left proper, led by Robert Blum; the smaller, more extreme group was the Radical-Democratic party.

and responsible to it'. It leaves undecided whether this central authority is to emerge *from the ranks of the National Assembly*, as expressly laid down by the Radical manifesto.

Finally, the manifesto of the Left demands that the fundamental rights of the German people be immediately determined, proclaimed, and protected against all possible attacks by the individual German governments. The Radical manifesto does not content itself with this, but declares: 'The Assembly already contains within itself the full powers of the whole state; it must *immediately* put into operation its various powers and the forms of political life it has been called to decide, and deal with the internal and external policy of the whole state'.

Both manifestoes agree that they want to leave the 'establishment of the German constitution to the National Assembly alone', excluding the participation of the governments. Both agree in leaving each individual state the choice of its constitution, whether it is to be a constitutional monarchy or a republic, 'without prejudice to the rights of the people, to be proclaimed by the National Assembly'. Finally, both agree that they want to transform Germany into a confederation or federal state.

At least the Radical manifesto expresses the *revolutionary* nature of the National Assembly. It enlists the aid of the revolutionary activities appropriate to it. The very existence of a *constituent* National Assembly shows, does it not, that a constitution no longer *exists*. But if a constitution no longer exists, a government no longer exists. If there is no longer a government, the National Assembly itself must govern. Its first sign of life ought to have been the six-word decree: 'The Federal Diet[17] is permanently abolished.'

A constituent National Assembly should above all be an *active* assembly, active in a revolutionary sense. The Assembly in Frankfurt performs parliamentary exercises and lets the governments act. Even assuming that this learned council succeeds in contriving the best agenda and the best constitution, what use is the best agenda and the best constitution when in the meantime the governments have placed bayonets on the agenda?

The German National Assembly, leaving aside the fact that its members were elected *indirectly*, suffers from a peculiarly Ger-

17. The Federal Diet (Bundestag) was the assembly of representatives of the thirty-nine German states in the German confederation (Deutscher Bund), formed in 1815 by the Congress of Vienna.

manic disease. Its seat is Frankfurt-am-Main, and Frankfurt is only an ideal centre, corresponding to the previously existing ideal, i.e. only imagined, unity of Germany. Moreover, Frankfurt-am-Main is not a big city with a strong revolutionary movement capable of standing behind the National Assembly, partly to protect it, partly to drive it forwards. For the first time in world history, the constituent assembly of a great nation has held its meetings in a small town. This was a result of Germany's previous development. Whereas the French and the English national assemblies stood on the volcanic soil of Paris and London, the German National Assembly was content to find a piece of *neutral* ground, where it could reflect on the best possible constitution and the best possible order of business without its peace of mind being disturbed. Despite this, the present situation in Germany offered the Assembly the opportunity of overcoming its unfortunate material position. It needed only to oppose the reactionary encroachments of the antiquated German governments in a dictatorial fashion, and it would have conquered a position in the public esteem impregnable to bayonets and rifle-butts. Instead, the Assembly knowingly left Mainz to the mercy of the soldiery, and delivered German-speaking foreigners to the chicaneries of the philistine citizens of Frankfurt. It bores the German people, instead of inspiring them or being itself inspired by them. It admits the existence of a *public*, which in the meantime still observes the comical antics of the resurrected spirit of the Holy Roman German Imperial Diet[18] with generous good humour, but not the existence of a *nation*, rediscovering its national life in and through the life of the Assembly. Far from being the central organ of the revolutionary movement, it has so far not even been its echo.

Even if the National Assembly should give birth to a central authority[19] we can expect little satisfaction from this provisional government, in view of the Assembly's present composition and its failure to grasp the most favourable moment for action. If no central authority is set up, however, the Assembly will have

18. Marx is alluding to the archaic nature of the German Federal Diet.

19. The question of a possible central authority (*Zentralgewalt*) occupied the centre of the discussions of the Frankfurt Assembly in June 1848, and was finally settled by the decision of 28 June 1848 to set up the Provisional Central Authority of Germany, consisting of a Reich regent (Reichsverweser) and a Reich ministry (Reichsministerium) appointed by him. Archduke John of Austria was chosen as the regent.

abdicated of its own accord, and will be scattered in all directions by the weakest puff of the revolutionary wind.

It is to the credit of both the Left and the Radical-Democrats that they have understood this necessity and included the central authority in their programmes. Both programmes also proclaim, with Heine:

> Considering how matters stand,
> We need no king at all.[20]

and the difficulty of deciding *who* shall be kaiser, as well as the fact that both the elective and the hereditary systems have good grounds in their favour, will also compel the conservative majority of the Assembly to cut the Gordian knot by choosing *no kaiser at all*.

What is incomprehensible is how the so-called Radical-Democratic party has been able to proclaim a *federation* of constitutional monarchies, principalities and mini-republics as the ultimate constitution for Germany. For the proposed central committee (an idea naturally accepted by the Left, but now also by the Radical party) is nothing more than a republican government at the head of a monarchical federation composed of the above heterogeneous elements.

There is no doubt about it. The German central government elected by the National Assembly must first emerge *alongside* the individual governments, which still exist *de facto*. But the struggle with the individual governments commences with its very existence, and in this struggle either the central government and with it the unity of Germany will go under, or the individual governments will, i.e. the constitutional princes and the obscure little republics.

We are not making here the utopian demand that a united, indivisible German republic be proclaimed here and now, but rather that the so-called Radical-Democratic party cease to confuse the starting-point of the struggle and the revolutionary movement with its final goal. German unity and a German constitution can only emerge as a result of a movement in which the internal conflicts as well as the war with the East[21] will reach their decision. The definitive constitution cannot be *decreed*; it coincides with the

20. *The Poetry and Prose of Heinrich Heine*, p. 215.
21. i.e. with Russia.

process we shall have to pass through. It is not a question of the realization of this or that opinion, of this or that political idea; it is a question of understanding the course of development. The task of the National Assembly is simply to take the immediately possible practical steps.

Despite his assertion that 'every man is happy to get rid of his confusions', there is nothing more confused than the idea put forward by the writer of the Radical-Democratic manifesto that the German constitution should take as its example the constitution of the *federal state in North America*!

The United States of America, apart from the fact that they all have similar constitutions, extend over an area as large as civilized Europe. An analogy could only be found in a *European* federation. And before Germany can federate with other countries it must itself first become a *single* country. In Germany, the struggle of centralization with federalism is the struggle between modern civilization and feudalism. Germany decayed into a bourgeoisified feudalism at the very moment when the great monarchies of western Europe were established, and it was excluded from the world market at the very moment when that market was opened to western Europe. Germany declined into poverty, whilst the others enriched themselves. Germany became ruralized, whilst the others became urbanized. Even if Russia were not at the gates, Germany's economic condition alone would compel the most rigid centralization. Even from a purely bourgeois standpoint, absolute unity is the first requirement for saving Germany from its previous misery and building up the national economy. Indeed, how could any modern social tasks be accomplished on the basis of a land divided into thirty-nine parts?

The writer of the Democratic programme did not in any case find it necessary to deal with the petty question of material economic relations. His justification remained at the level of the concept of federation. A *federation* is a *union of free and equal people. Therefore*, Germany must be a *federal state*. But couldn't the Germans also federate themselves into a *single* great state, without sinning against the concept of a union of free and equal people?

THE 15 JUNE SITTING OF THE
'*Vereinbarungsversammlung*'[22]

N.Rh.Z., 18 June 1948

Cologne, 17 June

We told you some days ago:[23] the existence of the revolution has been denied; it will demonstrate its existence by means of a second revolution.

The events of 14 June[24] are only the first flashes of lightning heralding this second revolution, and the Camphausen ministry has already disintegrated. The *Vereinbarungsversammlung* has given the people of Berlin a vote of confidence by placing itself under their protection.[25] This is a retrospective recognition of the March fighters. The Assembly has taken the constitution out of the ministers' hands and is endeavouring to 'make an agreement' with the people, by setting up a commission to examine all petitions and addresses relevant to the constitution. This is a retrospective rejection of its own declaration of incompetence.[26] The Assembly has promised to begin its work of constitution-making by the removal of the foundation-stone of the old building – the feudal relationships which burden the land. This is to promise a night of 4 August.[27]

In short: the Berlin Assembly denied its own past on 15 June,

22. '*Vereinbarungsversammlung*' (literally, 'assembly of agreement') was Marx's ironic term for the Prussian National Assembly, called on 22 May 1848 'to establish the future constitution of the state by agreement (*Vereinbarung*) with the Crown'. On the theory of *Vereinbarung*, see 'The Bourgeoisie and the Counter-Revolution', part III.

23. 'The Debate on the Revolution in Berlin' (14 June 1848), *MEW* 5, pp. 64–6.

24. On 14 June 1848 the people of Berlin carried out a series of spontaneous and unorganized actions (in particular the storming of the arsenal) in response to the National Assembly's refusal to declare that those who had fought in the March revolution 'had served the fatherland well'.

25. By the resolution of 15 June that the Assembly 'does not require the protection of the armed forces and has placed itself under the protection of the Berlin population'.

26. This refers to the resolution of 9 June that the Assembly's 'task was not to give judgements but to work out the constitution by agreement with the Crown'.

27. During the night of 4 August 1789 the French National Assembly proclaimed the abolition of a large number of feudal burdens.

just as it denied the past of the people on 9 June. It has undergone its own 21 March.[28]

But the Bastille has still not been stormed.

Meanwhile, an apostle of revolution is approaching from the East, unstoppable, irresistible. He already stands before the gates of Toruń.[29] He is the *tsar of Russia. The tsar will save the German revolution by forcing its centralization.*

THE PRAGUE RISING

N.Rh.Z., 18 June 1848   Frederick Engels
                                            Cologne, 17 June

A new Posen bloodbath[11] is being prepared in Bohemia. The Austrian soldiery has drowned the possibility of peaceful co-existence between Bohemia and Germany in Czech blood.

Prince Windischgrätz[31] was positioning his cannons against Prague on the Vyšehrad and the Hradčany.[32] Troop concentrations were being built up and a surprise attack was being prepared against the Slav Congress[33] and the Czechs.

The people learned of these military preparations. They swarmed around the prince's residence and demanded weapons. They met with a refusal. Excitement mounted, the armed and unarmed crowds grew in size. Then a shot was fired from an inn opposite the commander's palace; Princess Windischgrätz fell to the ground, mortally wounded. The order to attack was given on the spot; the infantry advanced and the people were pressed back. But every-

28. On 21 March 1848 Frederick William appeared to yield to popular demands he had previously resisted and promised that Prussia would be turned into a constitutional state and merged in a united Germany.

29. A fortress in Posen, on the frontier with the Russian empire.

30. This refers to the bloody suppression by Prussian troops of the Polish rising in the Grand Duchy of Posen and the fierce persecution of Polish revolutionaries which followed in May and June 1848.

31. Alfred, Fürst zu Windischgrätz was an Austrian field-marshal.

32. Vyšehrad and Hradčany are the respective names of the southern and the north-western districts of old Prague.

33. The Slav Congress met in Prague on 2 June 1848. Most of its supporters adopted the theory of Austro-Slavism, that the Austrian state must be maintained so as to preserve the small Slav nationalities (in particular the Czechs) from German domination. However, a strong minority upheld the democratic and revolutionary idea of the destruction of the Austrian state in alliance with the German and Hungarian democrats, and it was their agitation on the streets of Prague which led Windischgrätz to make the preparations mentioned here.

where barricades were set up, halting the advance of the troops. Cannons were moved up, and the barricades were destroyed with grape-shot. The blood flowed in streams. The struggle lasted throughout the night of the 12th–13th and into the next morning. Finally the soldiers managed to take the main streets and force the people back into the more confined parts of the town, where artillery cannot be used.

This is as far as our latest information goes. Moreover, many members of the Slav Congress have been expelled from the town under strong military escort. It would seem then that the military have secured at least a partial victory.

However the rising may end, a war of annihilation of the Germans against the Czechs is now the only possible solution.[34]

In making their revolution, the Germans had to be punished for the sins of their entire past. They were punished for them in Italy. In Posen they have once more been burdened with the curses of all Poland. And now there is Bohemia as well.

Even in places where the French came as enemies,[35] they were able to gain recognition and sympathy. The Germans, however, are recognized nowhere and find sympathy nowhere. Even where they come forward as the magnanimous apostles of liberty they are rejected with bitter sarcasm.

And rightly so. A nation which has allowed itself to be used throughout its history as an instrument for oppressing all other nations, a nation of this kind must first prove that it has really become revolutionary. It must prove this in some other way than through a few semi-revolutions, which have had no other result than to allow the old indecisiveness, weakness and disunity to continue in altered forms; revolutions during which a Radetzky[36] remains in Milan, a Colomb and a Steinäcker in Posen, a Windischgrätz in Prague and a Hüser in Mainz, just as if nothing had happened.[37]

34. This apparently opaque sentence can be explained as follows: Engels considered that with the defeat of the Prague rising the revolutionary and democratic minority among the Czechs had been crushed. The Czech people were therefore now solidly counter-revolutionary, under the control of Windischgrätz, and a revolutionary Germany would have to fight against them.

35. i.e. in the French revolutionary wars of 1792–1814.

36. Count Joseph Radetzky was an Austrian field-marshal, and supreme commander of the Austrian troops in Italy in 1848.

37. Colomb, Steinäcker and Hüser were all Prussian generals.

A revolutionized Germany would have to disown the whole of its past, especially in relation to the neighbouring peoples. It would have to proclaim the freedom of the peoples it had previously oppressed, at the same time as it proclaimed its own freedom.

And what *has* revolutionary Germany done? It has completely ratified the old oppression of Italy, Poland, and now Bohemia too, by the German soldiery. Kaunitz[38] and Metternich have received a complete justification.

After all this, are the Germans really asking the Czechs to trust them?

And are the Czechs at fault for their unwillingness to attach themselves to a nation which oppresses and ill-treats other nations while freeing itself?

Are they at fault for refusing to send representatives to an assembly like our miserable, half-hearted Frankfurt 'National Assembly', which trembles at the prospect of its own sovereignty?[39]

Are they at fault for disowning the impotent Austrian government, whose indecision and paralysis seems to serve neither to prevent nor to organize the dissolution of Austria, but only to confirm it? A government which is too weak to liberate Prague from the cannons and the soldiers of a Windischgrätz?

But it is the brave Czechs themselves who are to be pitied most of all. Whether they win or lose, their downfall is assured. They have been driven into the arms of the Russians by four hundred years of German oppression, of which the street battles in Prague are but a continuation. In the great struggle between the West and the East of Europe, which will break out in a very short time – perhaps in a few weeks – an unhappy destiny has placed the Czechs on the side of the Russians, on the side of despotism against the revolution. The revolution will win, and the Czechs will be the first to be crushed by it.

It is the Germans again who will bear the guilt for the downfall of the Czechs. It is the Germans who have betrayed them to Russia.

38. Wendel Anton, Fürst von Kaunitz, was an Austrian diplomat and protagonist of 'enlightened despotism'.

39. Most German liberals and radicals in 1848 claimed that Bohemia was a part of Germany, and that it should be represented in the Frankfurt National Assembly. However, the leader of the Czech national movement, Palacký, replied to an invitation to join in elections to the Assembly with an outright refusal (8 April), and he was followed in this by the Czech, though not by the German, inhabitants of Bohemia.

THE FALL OF THE CAMPHAUSEN MINISTRY

N.Rh.Z., 23 June 1848

Cologne, 22 June

*Scheint die Sonne noch so schön
Einmal muss sie untergehn,*[40]

and this applies even to the sun of 30 March, reddened with hot Polish blood.[41]

The Camphausen ministry was the liberal-bourgeois garment put on by the counter-revolution. Now the counter-revolution feels strong enough to cast off the burdensome disguise.

Some kind of temporary left-centre cabinet could perhaps follow the ministry of 30 March in a few days' time. However, its real successor will be the *ministry of the Prince of Prussia*.[42] Camphausen has thus had the honour of providing the party of feudal absolutism with its natural chief, and his ministry with this successor.

Was there any need to pamper the bourgeois guardians any longer? Do not the Russians stand at the eastern border, and Prussian troops in the west? Have the Poles not been won over to Russian propaganda by means of shrapnel and caustic? Have not all preparations been made to repeat the bombardment of Prague in almost all the towns of the Rhineland? Has the army not had plenty of time to revert into brutality in the Danish and Polish wars, and in the many small-scale conflicts between the military and the people? Is the bourgeoisie not tired of revolution? And has there not risen up in the middle of the sea the rock on which the counter-revolution will build its church, namely England?

The Camphausen ministry is still trying to grab a few penn'-orths of popularity, still trying to arouse public sympathy, by ensuring that it withdraws from the stage as the *victim of deception*. It is in fact the deceiver deceived. In the service of the big bourgeoisie, it had to try to defraud the revolution of its democratic

40. 'However beautifully the sun shines, it must go down eventually.' From Raimund's play *Das Mädchen aus der Feenwelt oder der Bauer als Millionär* (*The Girl from Fairyland or The Peasant as Millionaire*), II, vi.

41. The Camphausen ministry took office on 30 March 1848, and its period of office coincided with the suppression of the Polish rising in Posen (April–May 1848). Camphausen's ministry came to an end on 20 June 1848.

42. See p. 146, n. 85.

achievements; in the struggle with democracy it had to make an alliance with the aristocratic party and become the instrument of its counter-revolutionary appetites. Now that party is strong enough to be able to throw its protector overboard. *Herr Camphausen sowed reaction in the interests of the big bourgeoisie; he has harvested it in the interests of the feudal party.* The former was his good intention, the latter his bad luck. A penn'orth of popularity for a disappointed man! A penn'orth of popularity!

> *Scheint die Sonne noch so schön*
> *Einmal muss sie untergehn!*

But in the East the sun is rising again.

THE JUNE REVOLUTION

N.Rh.Z., 29 June 1848

The Paris workers have been *overwhelmed* by superior forces; they have not *succumbed* to them. They have been *beaten*, but it is their enemies who have been *vanquished*. The momentary triumph of brutal violence has been purchased with the destruction of all the deceptions and illusions of the February revolution, with the dissolution of the whole of the old republican party, and with the fracturing of the French nation into two nations, the nation of the possessors and the nation of the workers. The tricolour republic now bears only *one colour*, the colour of the defeated, the *colour of blood*. It has become the *red republic*.

There was no republican group of repute on the side of the people, neither that of the *National* nor that of the *Réforme*.[43] Without leaders, without any means other than the insurrection itself, the people withstood the united bourgeoisie and soldiery longer than any French dynasty, with all its military apparatus, ever withstood a fraction of the bourgeoisie united with the people. In order that the people's last illusion should disappear, in order to allow a complete break with the past, it was necessary for the customary poetic accompaniment of a French rising, the enthusiastic youth of the bourgeoisie, the pupils of the École Polytechnique, the three-cornered hats, to take the side of the

43. The two main republican groups in France in 1848 were centred around the newspapers *Le National* and *La Réforme*, characterized elsewhere by Marx as the respective organs of bourgeois and petty-bourgeois republicanism.

oppressors. The pupils of the Faculty of Medicine had to deny the aid of science to the wounded plebeians, who have committed the unspeakable, infernal crime of hazarding their lives for their own existence for once, instead of for Louis Philippe or M. Marrast.[44]

The last official remnant of the February revolution, the Executive Commission,[45] has melted away like an apparition before the seriousness of events. Lamartine's[46] fireworks have turned into Cavaignac's[47] incendiary rockets. '*Fraternité*', the brotherhood of opposing classes, one of which exploits the other, this '*fraternité*' was proclaimed in February and written in capital letters on the brow of Paris, on every prison and every barracks. But its true, genuine, prosaic expression is *civil war* in its most terrible form, the war between labour and capital. This fraternity flamed in front of all the windows of Paris on the evening of 25 June. The Paris of the bourgeoisie was illuminated, while the Paris of the proletariat burned, bled and moaned in its death agony.

Fraternity lasted only as long as there was a fraternity of interests between bourgeoisie and proletariat. Pedants of the old revolutionary traditions of 1793; constructors of socialist systems, who went begging to the bourgeoisie on behalf of the people, and who were allowed to preach long sermons and to compromise themselves as long as the proletarian lion had to be lulled to sleep;[48] republicans, who wanted to keep the whole of the old bourgeois order, but remove the crowned head; supporters of the dynastic opposition,[49] upon whom chance had foisted the fall of a dynasty instead of a change of ministers; Legitimists, who

44. Armand Marrast was the leader of the moderate republicans in the 1840s, the editor of *Le National*, a member of the Provisional Government of February–May 1848, and the chairman of the Constituent National Assembly.

45. The Executive Commission set up by the Constituent Assembly replaced the Provisional Government on 10 May 1848, and lasted until 24 June.

46. Alphonse de Lamartine was a French poet and historian, a moderate republican in politics. He was Foreign Minister in the Provisional Government of 1848, at which time he issued his fiery declarations to the governments of Europe, hence 'fireworks'.

47. Louis-Eugène Cavaignac was a French general and a moderate republican. In May 1848 he was made Minister of War, and in June was given dictatorial powers to suppress the Paris insurrection.

48. See the Communist Manifesto, above, pp. 94–7.

49. The group led by Odilon Barrot before 1848, which supported a moderate reform of the electoral system and the removal of Guizot, hoping thereby not to overthrow the Orleans monarchy but to broaden its base of support.

wanted not to cast aside the livery but to change its cut; all these were the allies with whom the people made its February. What the people instinctively hated in Louis Philippe was not the man himself but the crowned rule of a class, capital on the throne. But, generous as ever, it imagined it had destroyed its enemy when it had only overthrown the enemy of its enemy, the *common* enemy.

The *February revolution* was the *beautiful* revolution, the revolution of universal sympathy, because the conflicts which erupted in the revolution against the monarchy slumbered harmoniously side by side, as yet *undeveloped*, because the social struggle which formed its background had only assumed an airy existence – it existed only as a phrase, only in words. The June revolution is the *ugly* revolution, the repulsive revolution, because realities have taken the place of words, because the republic has uncovered the head of the monster itself by striking aside the protective, concealing crown.

Order! was Guizot's battle cry. *Order!* screamed Sébastiani,[50] Guizot's follower, as Warsaw reverted to Russian rule. *Order!* screams Cavaignac, the brutal echo of the French National Assembly and the republican bourgeoisie.

Order! thundered his grape-shot, as it lacerated the body of the proletariat.

None of the innumerable revolutions of the French bourgeoisie since 1789 was an attack on *order*; for they perpetuated class rule, the slavery of the workers, *bourgeois order*, no matter how frequent the changes in the political form of this rule and this slavery. June has violated this *order*. Woe unto June!

Under the *Provisional Government* it was customary, indeed it was a *necessity*, combining politics and enthusiasm at once, to preach to the generous workers who (as could be read on thousands of official placards) had '*placed three months of misery at the disposal of the republic*', that the February revolution had been made *in their own interests*, and that the February revolution was concerned above all with the *interests of the workers*. But after the opening of the National Assembly everyone came down to earth. What was important now was *to bring back labour to its old*

---

50. Horace, comte Sébastiani was the French Minister of Foreign Affairs from 1830 to 1832. In 1831 he refused to protest against the tsar's suppression of the Polish revolution, and called for a return by both parties to the treaty settlement of 1815. By this the greater part of Poland formed part of the Russian empire, with the tsar as its king.

situation, as Minister Trélat[51] said. In other words, the workers had fought in February in order to be thrown into an industrial crisis.

The task of the National Assembly was to reverse the events of February, at least for the workers, and to throw them back into their old situation. But even that did not happen, because it is no more in the power of an assembly than that of a king to call a halt to an industrial crisis of a general character. The National Assembly, in its brutal eagerness to finish with the tiresome phrases of February, did not even adopt those measures which *were* possible on the basis of the old conditions. It either pressed the Paris workers between the ages of seventeen and twenty-five into the army, or it threw them onto the streets; non-Parisian workers were expelled from Paris and sent to the Sologne, without receiving even the money customarily provided on dismissal; finally, Parisians of full age were given alms, provisionally and in militarily organized factories, on condition that they did not take part in any public meetings, i.e. on condition that they ceased to be republicans. The sentimental post-February rhetoric proved inadequate. So also did the brutal legislation enacted after 15 May.[52] The decision had to be made in fact, in practice. Has the rabble made the February revolution for *itself* or for *us*? In June the bourgeoisie posed the question in such a way that it had to be answered – with grape-shot and barricades.

And yet, as one deputy said on 25 June,[53] the whole National Assembly was stupefied by the rising. As the question and its answer drowned the walls of Paris in blood, it was dazed with astonishment. Some were stunned because their illusions were vanishing in a cloud of gunsmoke; others because they could not understand how the people could dare to come forward *independently* on behalf of its *very own* interests. Russian gold, English gold, the Bonapartist eagle, the *fleur-de-lis*: talismans of all kinds had to be interposed between this remarkable occurrence and their understanding. However, *both sides* of the Assembly felt that they

51. Ulysse Trélat was a doctor and politician, on the editorial board of *Le National* and Minister of Public Works from May to June 1848.

52. On 15 May 1848 Blanqui and his party led their supporters to a number of key points in order to set up a new Provisional Government to replace the National Assembly and the Executive Commission. The latter replied with a number of measures directed against the political life of Paris and the national workshops.

53. Ducoux [Marx].

were separated from the people by an immeasurable chasm. No one dared to speak on behalf of the people.

As soon as the astonishment had passed, there followed an outbreak of rage, and the majority rightly hissed off the stage those miserable utopians and hypocrites who commited the anachronism of continuing to utter the word '*fraternité*'. It was now a matter of abolishing this word and the illusions hiding in its ambiguous bosom. When La Rochejaquelein,[54] the Legitimist, with his enthusiasm for chivalry, inveighed against the infamy of the declaration *Vae victis*,[55] the majority of the Assembly suffered an attack of St Vitus' dance, as if stung by an adder. The Assembly cries 'woe' over the workers in order to conceal that the 'vanquished' is none other than itself. Either it or the republic must now disappear. Hence its frantic howls of 'long live the republic'.

A deep abyss has opened before us. Should it mislead democrats, should it delude us into thinking that struggles over the form of the state are without content, illusory, null and void?

Only weak and cowardly temperaments can bring up this question. The confrontations which arise out of the very conditions of bourgeois society must be fought out, they cannot be imagined away. The best form of state is not that in which social antagonisms are blurred or forcibly shackled, that is to say artificially shackled, shackled only in appearance. It is rather that in which they can freely come into conflict, and thus be solved.

We shall be asked whether we have no tears, no sighs, no words for the victims of the people's rage, for the National Guard, the Mobile Guard, the Republican Guard, the troops of the line.[56]

54. Henri, marquis de La Rochejaquelein was a leading Legitimist, and a deputy in 1848 to the Constituent National Assembly. The reference here is to his speech of 25 June 1848 suggesting that the Assembly should declare an amnesty for insurgents who surrendered.

55. 'Woe to the vanquished.' The expression is supposed to have been used by the Roman Brennus in 390 B.C. on the occasion of the fall of Rome to the Gauls.

56. The National Guard had existed since 1789, with some interruptions. As reorganized by Louis Philippe in 1831 it was limited to property-owning citizens who would, it was thought, maintain the monarchy and the existing social order. In 1848, however, it abandoned the July monarchy and joined the republican forces. It was democratized in February 1848 by the admission of all (male) citizens between the ages of twenty and sixty. The Mobile Guard was set up on 25 February 1848 by the Provisional Government to maintain order in Paris (see 'The Class Struggles in France', in *Surveys from Exile*, pp. 52–3). The Republican Guard was founded in 1800 as the Guard of Paris, and

The reply is this: the state will look after their widows and orphans, decrees will glorify them, solemn funeral processions will inter their remains, the official press will declare them immortal, the European reaction from east to west will pay homage to them.

But the plebeians are tortured with hunger, reviled by the press, abandoned by doctors, abused by honest men as thieves, incendiaries, galley-slaves, their women and children thrown into still deeper misery, their best sons deported overseas: it is the *privilege*, it is the *right of the democratic press* to wind the laurels around their stern and threatening brows.

THE PRUSSIAN PRESS BILL

N.Rh.Z., 20 July 1848

Cologne, 19 July

We were thinking of amusing our readers once more with the debates of the *Vereinbarungsversammlung*, and in particular of presenting a brilliant speech by deputy Baumstark,[57] but events have prevented this.

Charity begins at home. When the existence of the press is threatened, even deputy Baumstark must be left aside.

Herr Hansemann[58] has laid an interim press law before the Assembly. His fatherly concern for the press demands our immediate consideration.

Before 1848, the Code Napoléon[59] was beautified by the addition of the most edifying sections of the Landrecht.[60] After the

---

continued to exist throughout the nineteenth century under various names. As the Municipal Guard of Paris under the July monarchy it put down a number of insurrections with ferocity, and was the object of particular hatred on the part of the people in February 1848. The Provisional Government at first intended to dissolve it, but a paramilitary force of this nature soon turned out to be necessary to suppress opposition from the left, and it was therefore kept in being and in May 1848 given the new name of Republican Guard of Paris (later simply Republican Guard).

57. Eduard Baumstark was a university professor and a Right deputy in the Berlin Assembly.

58. David Justus Hansemann was an industrialist from the Rhineland, and the leader of the liberal movement of the 1840s there; from March to September 1848 he was Prussian Minister of Finance.

59. The French civil law issued in 1807 and imposed on the occupied regions of western Germany. It remained in force in the Rhineland after 1815.

60. The Prussian legal code.

revolution, this has changed; now the Landrecht is enriched with the most fragrant blossoms of the Code and the September laws.[61] Duchâtel[62] is naturally no Bodelschwingh.[63]

We have already given the main details of this press bill.[64] We had only just had the opportunity to show that articles 367 and 368 of the Code Pénal[65] stood in the most glaring contradiction with the freedom of the press (by undergoing an investigation for libel),[66] when Herr Hansemann proposed not only to extend it to the whole of the kingdom, but also to make it three times more severe. In the new bill, we find everything we have grown to know and love through practical experience.

We find it prohibited, on pain of three months' to three years' imprisonment, to accuse anyone of an action which is punishable by law, or which merely 'puts him in public contempt'; we find it prohibited to assert the truth of a fact except on the basis of 'completely valid evidence'; in short, we rediscover the most classic characteristics of Napoleon's despotic rule over the press.

One might well say that Herr Hansemann has fulfilled his promise to give the old Prussian provinces a share in the advantages of the laws of the Rhineland!

These measures are crowned by paragraph 10 of the bill: if the libel was committed against *state officials* in relation to their official business, the normal punishment can be *increased by a half*.

Article 222 of the Code Pénal provides for a period of from one month up to two years' imprisonment when an official has received an insult in words (*outrage par parole*) during the performance of, or incidentally (*à l'occasion*) to, the performance of

61. These were laws sharpening the censorship of the press and restricting the application of the jury system, which were issued in France in September 1835.

62. Charles, comte Duchâtel was a member of De Broglie's ministry of 1834 to 1836 which introduced the September laws.

63. Ernst, Freiherr von Bodelschwingh, a Prussian official who, as Oberpräsident of the Rhine province (1834–42), endeavoured to introduce the Landrecht into the Rhineland. From 1845 to 1848 he was Minister of the Interior.

64. *Neue Rheinische Zeitung*, 17 July 1848 (not written by Marx or Engels).

65. The Napoleonic code of criminal law was extended to the occupied regions of western Germany, and remained in force in the Rhineland after 1815.

66. A libel investigation against the *Neue Rheinische Zeitung* had followed an article on 5 July reporting the arrest of Gottschalk and Anneke, and accusing the police of brutality ('Arrests', *MEW 5*, pp. 166–8). See also *MEW 5*, pp. 198–201.

his office. So far, and despite the benevolent endeavours of public prosecutors, this article did not apply to the press, and for good reasons. In order to remedy this abuse, Herr Hansemann transformed article 222 into the above-mentioned paragraph 10. Firstly, 'incidentally' was changed into the more convenient phrase 'in relation to their official business'; secondly, the tiresome 'in word' was changed into 'in writing'; thirdly, the punishment was increased threefold.

From the day when this law comes into force, the Prussian officials will be able to sleep soundly. If Herr Pfuel[67] burns the hands and ears of the Poles with caustic, and the press publishes this: four and a half months to four and a half years in prison! If citizens are thrown into prison by mistake, although it is known that they are not the guilty ones, and the press points this out: four and a half months to four and a half years in prison! If local officials become travelling salesmen of the reaction and collect signatures for royalist addresses, and the press unmasks those gentlemen: four and a half months to four and a half years in prison!

From the day when this law comes into force, the officials will be able, unpunished, to commit any arbitrary, tyrannical, or illegal action; they will be free to flog and order floggings, to arrest and imprison without trial; the only effective control, the press, will have been made ineffective. On the day when this law comes into force, the bureaucracy will be able to celebrate and rejoice: it will be more powerful, more unhindered, and stronger than before March.

Indeed, what is left of the freedom of the press when the press may no longer hold up to the contempt of the public that which *deserves* the contempt of the public?

According to the existing laws, the press could at least present the facts as proofs of its general assertions and accusations. This situation will now come to an end. The press will no longer *report*, it will only be permitted to engage in general phrasemaking, so that right-thinking people, from Herr Hansemann down to the simple citizen drinking his pale ale will have the right to say, 'The press merely *grumbles*, it never *brings proof*.' It is precisely for that reason that the bringing of proof is being forbidden.

67. Ernst Heinrich von Pfuel was a Prussian general, in charge of the suppression of the Posen rising in April and May 1848.

By the way, we would recommend Herr Hansemann to make an addition to his generous bill. He should declare it a punishable offence to hold up the gentlemen of the bureaucracy, not just to public contempt, but also to public ridicule. This omission will otherwise be painfully felt.

We shall not deal with the paragraphs on obscenity, the regulations relating to confiscation, etc. in any detail. They outdo the cream of the press legislation of the July monarchy and the Restoration.[68] Just one specific point: by paragraph 21, the public prosecutor can demand the confiscation of both the finished publication and the *manuscript handed over for printing*, if the content constitutes a felony or a misdemeanour liable to official prosecution. What broad pastures this opens for philanthropic state prosecutors! What an enjoyable diversion, to go to a newspaper office whenever you wish and have the 'manuscript handed over for printing' presented to you for examination, as it is after all possible that it could constitute a felony or a misdemeanour.

How laughable is the solemn seriousness of that paragraph of the proposed constitution[69] and the 'fundamental rights of the German people' which states that '*the censorship can never be re-established*', when placed beside this bill!

THE BILL FOR THE ABOLITION OF FEUDAL BURDENS[70]

N.Rh.Z., 30 July 1848

Cologne, 29 July

If any Rhinelander has forgotten what he owes to 'foreign domination' and the 'oppression of the Corsican tyrant', he should read the bill for the abolition of various burdens and dues without compensation which Herr Hansemann, in the year of grace 1848, has allowed the *Vereinbarungsversammlung* to see 'for clarification'. Fealty, enfranchisement-money, relief, heriot, protection-money, jurisdiction-tax, village court tax, wardship, sealing-money, cattle-tithe, bee-tithe, etc.[71] – how strange, how

68. The French constitutional monarchy of Louis Philippe (1830–48) and the restored Bourbon monarchy (1814–30).
69. The 'Draft of a Constitutional Law for the Prussian State', issued on 20 May 1848.
70. This bill was laid before the Prussian National Assembly on 11 July 1848, and introduced by Gierke on 18 July.
71. An attempt has been made to give the approximate English feudal equivalent to the German terms in the text. The German terms are, in order

barbaric, is the sound of these preposterous names to our ears which have been civilized by the Code Napoléon, by the French Revolution's destruction of feudal survivals! How incomprehensible to us is this whole jumble of semi-medieval services and dues, this natural history museum of the mouldiest plunder of antediluvian times!

But take off your shoes, German patriot, for you are standing on hallowed ground! These barbarisms are the remnants of the glory of Germanic Christendom, they are the final links of a chain which weaves its way through history and unites you with the majesty of your forefathers, right back to the Cheruskans in their woods. This stink of putrefaction, this feudal slime, found here in its classical purity, is the most genuine product of our fatherland, and he who is a true German must exclaim, with the poet:

> This is truly my native air!
> It touched my cheeks, and they glowed!
> And this is the muck of my fatherland:
> This mud of the country road![72]

When one reads this bill, it appears at first sight that our Minister of Agriculture, Herr Gierke,[73] is making a tremendous 'bold stroke'[74] on the instructions of Herr Hansemann, and abolishing a whole medieval situation with a stroke of the pen, and gratis too of course.

If, however, one looks at the *justification* given for the bill, one finds that it demonstrates right at the beginning that in fact *absolutely no* feudal burdens will be abolished without compensation, with a bold assertion which directly contradicts the 'bold stroke'.

The practical timidity of the honourable minister treads warily and cautiously between these two pieces of audacity. On the left

of appearance, *Lehnsherrlichkeit, Allodifikationszins, Sterbefall, Besthaupt, Kurmede* (both forms of heriot), *Schutzgeld, Jurisdiktionszins, Dreidinggelder, Zuchtgelder, Siegelgelder, Blutzehnt,* and *Bienenzehnt.*

72. Heine, 'Germany: A Winter's Tale', *The Poetry and Prose of Heinrich Heine*, p. 198.

73. Julius Gierke was the town syndic of Stettin, in 1848 a deputy in the Prussian National Assembly (Left Centre), and Prussian Minister of Agriculture from March to September.

74. An ironic reference to Heinrich von Gagern's famous speech of 24 June 1848 in the Frankfurt Assembly in which he proposed what he described as a 'bold stroke': the immediate creation of a provisional central authority for Germany by the Assembly itself.

we have 'the general welfare' and the 'requirements of the spirit of the age', on the right the 'established rights of the landed estates', and in the middle the 'praiseworthy idea of a freer development of relations on the land', embodied in the shame-faced embarrassment of Herr Gierke. What a triptych!

Enough of this. The minister fully recognizes that in general feudal burdens may only be abolished in return for compensation. With this, the most oppressive, widespread and important burdens *remain in existence*, or, in other words, in view of the fact that the peasants had already got rid of them, they *are restored*.

'But', says Herr Gierke,

if nevertheless certain relations, which lack internal justification or whose continued existence cannot be brought into consonance with the requirements of the spirit of the age and the general welfare, have been abolished *without compensation*, the people hit by this should not fail to realize that they are making some sacrifices, not only to the general good, but also in their own properly understood interest, in order to make the relation between those with rights and those with duties peaceful and friendly, and in this way to guarantee to landed property in general the position in the state which is due to it for the common good.

The revolution on the land consisted in the actual removal of all feudal burdens. The 'Ministry of the Deed',[75] which recognized the revolution, now recognizes it in the countryside by liquidating it on the quiet. The old *status quo* cannot be restored in its entirety; even Herr Gierke sees that the peasants would kill their feudal barons without further ado. A spectacular list of insignificant, regionally limited feudal burdens are therefore abolished, and the main feudal burden, summed up in the simple phrase *compulsory labour services*, is restored.

With the abolition of all the rights listed above, the nobility sacrifices less than 50,000 thalers a year, but thereby saves many millions. In this way the nobility will surely be able to reconcile itself with the peasants, as the minister hopes, and in the future even gain their votes at elections. This would indeed be a good bargain, if Herr Gierke has made no mistakes in his calculations.

The objections of the peasants would be removed, and so would those of the nobility, provided it correctly grasped the situation.

75. The usual designation of the Auerswald-Hansemann ministry, which lasted from 26 June to 21 September 1848, and opened with Hansemann's public 'recognition of the revolution' in an attempt to gain the support of the Left in the Assembly.

There remains the Assembly itself and its scruples, which arise from the rigid attachment to logic displayed by jurists and radicals. The distinction between burdens to be abolished and burdens to be retained, which is nothing other than a distinction between fairly valueless and very valuable burdens, must receive an apparent justification in law and economics for the sake of the Assembly. Herr Gierke must prove that the burdens to be abolished 1) lack an adequate inner justification, 2) go against the general welfare, 3) go against the requirements of the spirit of the age, and 4) can be abolished without injuring the rights of private property, without what would be called expropriation without compensation.

In order to demonstrate the insufficiency of the grounds for these dues and services, Herr Gierke immerses himself in the most shadowy regions of feudal law. He conjures up the whole of the 'originally very slow development of the Germanic states in the course of a millennium'. But what use is that to him? The deeper he goes, the more he stirs up the musty sediment of feudal law, the more does it demonstrate to him not the insufficient, but, from the feudal standpoint, the very solid basis of the burdens under consideration; and the unfortunate minister merely exposes himself to general mirth when he spares no pains to get feudal law to give forth oracular judgements appropriate to modern civil law, or to make the feudal baron of the twelfth century think and decide in the same way as the bourgeois of the nineteenth century.

Fortunately, Herr Gierke has inherited von Patow's principle:[76] everything which emanates from specifically feudal qualities and hereditary subjection is to be abolished without compensation, the remainder must be redeemed in cash. But does Herr Gierke believe it requires any great penetration to demonstrate that, on the contrary, all the burdens to be abolished are equally 'emanations of feudal qualities'?

We hardly need to add that, in the interests of overall consistency, Herr Gierke smuggles modern legal concepts in among the feudal legal distinctions, and always appeals to the former in time of need. However, since he measures some of the feudal burdens against the conceptions of modern law, one cannot see why this

76. Erasmus, Freiherr von Patow was a moderate liberal. In 1848 he sat in the Prussian National Assembly, from April to June 1848 he was Minister of Trade, and on 20 June he presented to the Assembly his memorandum on the redemption of feudal burdens, containing the principle mentioned in the text.

does not happen in all cases. But of course, the compulsory labour services would come off badly when measured against the modern freedom of the individual and of property.

It is still worse for Herr Gierke when he introduces the argument of 'the public welfare' and 'the requirements of the spirit of the age'. It is perfectly obvious that if these insignificant burdens are obstacles to the public welfare, and contradict the spirit of the age, then so do the labour services, the *corvées* and the *laudemia*,[77] only to a greater extent. Or does Herr Gierke find that the right to pluck the peasant's *geese* (paragraph 1, section 14) is outdated, while the right to fleece the *peasant* is appropriate to the times?

There follows the demonstration that the abolition in question does not injure the rights of property. This glaring untruth can only appear proven by pretending to the nobility that these rights are of no value to them. The minister now proceeds to enumerate with great enthusiasm all eighteen sections of the first paragraph, but he does not realize that the more worthless the relevant *burdens*, the more worthless the *bill*. Good for him! What a shame it is that we have to snatch him away from his sweet delusions and break into the Archimedean circle of feudalism which he has constructed!

But now one more difficulty! In previous monetary redemptions of the burdens now to be abolished, the peasants have been terribly cheated by corrupt commissions acting in favour of the nobility. Now they are demanding the revision of all redemption agreements concluded under the old government, and they are quite right to do so.

Herr Gierke, however, cannot permit this. 'Formal right and law' stand against this, as against any progress at all, since every new law abolishes an old 'formal right and law'.

The consequences of such an act can be stated with certainty. If, in order to bring advantages to the obligated (the peasants), action is taken in a manner contradicting basic legal principles (revolutions also contradict basic legal principles), untold harm must result for a very great part of the landed property in the state, and consequently (!) for the state itself.

And now Herr Gierke shows with shattering thoroughness that such a proceeding

77. A Roman Law term applied in the Middle Ages to the sum of money paid by the vassal to his lord for the latter's consent to the alienation of the fief.

would put in question the whole legal foundation of landed property, and thereby, in connection with innumerable trials and costs, afflict landed property, the main basis of national prosperity, with a wound only to be healed with difficulty.

He shows further that

it is an attack on the legal validity of contracts, an attack on the most indubitable contractual relationships, and would result in the destruction of all confidence in the stability of the civil law and therefore endanger the whole of commercial intercourse in the most threatening way.

Here too the minister sees an attack on the right of property, which would offend against legal principles. Why then is abolition of the burdens themselves without compensation not an attack on property? It involves not only the most indubitable contractual relationships but also services carried out without objection since time immemorial, whereas the contracts the peasants wanted to revise were by no means undisputed, since the bribes and the frauds were notorious and in many cases demonstrable.

It cannot be denied: insignificant as the suppressed burdens are, Herr Gierke has indeed 'brought advantages to the obligated in a manner contradicting basic legal principles', and 'formal right and law *are* directly opposed to this action'; he is destroying 'the whole legal foundation of landed property', and striking at the roots of the 'most indubitable rights'.

Was it worth it, to commit such terrible sins in order to achieve such miserable results?

Of course the minister is attacking property – that is undeniable – but it is feudal, not modern bourgeois property he is attacking. Bourgeois property, which raises itself on the ruins of feudal property, is *strengthened* by this attack on feudal property. The only reason for Herr Gierke's refusal to revise the redemption contracts is that those contracts have changed feudal property relations into *bourgeois* property relations, and that he cannot therefore revise them without at the same time formally injuring bourgeois property. And bourgeois property is naturally just as holy and untouchable as feudal property is assailable, and, depending on the level of the minister's need and courage, actually assailed.

What, then, is the short meaning of this long law?

It is the most conclusive proof that the German revolution of 1848 is only a parody of the French revolution of 1789.

The French people finished with the feudal burdens in *one day*, the fourth of August 1789, three weeks after the storming of the Bastille.

On 11 July 1848, four months after the March barricades, the feudal burdens finished with the German people, as testified by Gierke and Hansemann.

The French bourgeoisie of 1789 did not leave its allies the peasants in the lurch for one moment. It knew that the basis of its rule was the destruction of feudalism on the land and the establishment of a class of free peasant landowners.

The German bourgeoisie of 1848 does not hesitate to betray the peasants who are its *natural allies*, its own flesh and blood, and without the peasants this bourgeoisie is powerless against the nobility.

The continued existence of feudal rights, their sanctioning in the form of their (illusory) abolition, that then is the result of the German revolution of 1848. The mountain moved and lo! – a mouse emerged.

THE RUSSIAN NOTE

N.Rh.Z., 3 August 1848

Cologne, 1 August

Instead of falling upon Germany with an army, Russian diplomacy has provisionally made do with a note, in the form of a circular sent to all the Russian consulates in Germany. This note was first published in the official organ[78] of the regency in Frankfurt, and soon met with a friendly reception in other official and unofficial papers. It is unusual that Nesselrode, the Russian Minister of Foreign Affairs, should ply his craft in public in this way, and this activity therefore deserves a close examination.

In the happy days before 1848 the German censorship made sure that nothing the Russian government might dislike could be printed, even under the heading 'Greece', or 'Turkey'.

Since the terrible March days this convenient way out has unfortunately been barred. Nesselrode has therefore had to turn journalist.

78. The official organ of the Reichsverwesung was the *Frankfurter Oberpostamts-Zeitung*, and Nesselrode's circular, issued on 6 July, was published therein on 28 July. It is printed in full in *Nouveau Recueil Général de Traités*, vol. XI, Göttingen, 1853, pp. 461–7.

According to him it is the 'German press, whose hatred of Russia seemed to have ended momentarily', which has called forth 'the most unfounded speculations and commentaries' in relation to Russian 'security measures' on the border. After the gentle introduction, a stronger tone is adopted: 'Daily, the German press spreads the most tasteless rumours, the most hateful calumnies against us.' Nesselrode goes on to refer to 'raving declamations', 'madcaps' and 'perfidious malevolence'.

At the next press trial a German state prosecutor may well use the Russian note as a certified basis for his accusations.

And why must the German, and in particular the 'democratic' press be attacked, and if possible destroyed? Because it misunderstands the 'benevolent and disinterested sentiments', the 'open and peaceful intentions' of the Russian tsar.

'When has Germany had any reason to complain of us?' asks Nesselrode in the name of his lord and master. 'During the whole period of the oppressive rule of a conqueror on the Continent, Russia poured out her blood in order to *support Germany in maintaining her integrity and independence.* Although Russian land had already long been liberated, Russia continued to follow its German allies to all the battlefields of Europe and to stand by them.'

In spite of its many well-paid agents, Russia is involved in a serious self-deception if it imagines sympathies can be awakened in the year 1848 by the memory of the so-called wars of liberation. And did Russia really shed its blood for us Germans?

Quite apart from the fact that before 1812 Russia 'supported' Germany's 'integrity and independence' by means of an open alliance and secret negotiations with Napoleon, sufficient compensation for this so-called help was taken later, in the form of robbery and plunder. The tsar's help was given in fact to the princes allied with him, his support, despite the Proclamation of Kalisch,[79] was given to the representatives of absolutism 'by the grace of God' against a ruler who emerged from the French Revolution. The Holy Alliance and its unholy works, the bandit congresses of Karlsbad, Laibach, Verona, etc.,[80] the joint

79. This proclamation was issued by Alexander I and Frederick William III on 25 March 1813, offering freedom and independence to the German people if they would take part in the war against Napoleon.

80. The Russians only attended the Congresses of Troppau-Laibach (October 1820–May 1821) and Verona (October–November 1822). The Karlsbad meeting of August 1819 was limited to the chief member-states of the German Confederation, above all Austria and Prussia.

Russian-German persecution of any liberal utterance, in short the whole policy directed by Russia since 1815, have certainly given us a feeling of deep thankfulness. The house of Romanov and its diplomats need not worry: we shall never forget *this* debt. As far as Russian help in the years 1814 and 1815 is concerned, gratitude for this aid, paid for with English subsidies, is absolutely the last feeling to which we are susceptible.

The reasons for this are quite obvious to anyone with a little insight. If Napoleon had remained victorious in Germany, he would have removed at least three dozen well-loved princelings, adopting his customarily energetic procedure. French legislation and administration would have created a solid foundation for German unity and spared us thirty-three years of shame, as well as the tyranny of the Federal Diet, which Nesselrode naturally praises to the skies. A couple of Napoleonic decrees could have completely destroyed the whole medieval wilderness, those labour services and tithes, those exemptions and privileges, in short that economy of feudalism and patriarchalism with which we are now tortured in all the nooks and crannies of our 'fatherlands'. The rest of Germany would then have long stood at the level reached by the left bank of the Rhine soon after the first French revolution; we should have had neither grandees from Uckermark[81] nor a Pomeranian Vendée,[82] and there would have been no more need to inhale the stagnant air of the 'historic' and 'Teutonic-Christian' swamps.

But Russia is magnanimous. Even without receiving any thanks, the tsar retains his 'benevolent and disinterested attitude' towards us. Yes, 'despite insults and provocations', his 'opinions have undergone no change'.

For the moment, these attitudes are manifested in a 'passive and observational system' which Russia has undeniably brought to a pitch of great virtuosity. The tsar knows how to wait until the appropriate moment. Notwithstanding the immense troop movements which have taken place since March in Russia, Nesselrode is naive enough to pretend that all Russian troops have constantly

81. The northern part of the Mark of Brandenburg, like Pomerania a purely agricultural region of Prussia and a junker stronghold.

82. The counter-revolutionary insurrection led by the nobility and supported by the peasantry which took place in that region of western France in 1793. Marx uses the word in a general sense to cover all counter-revolutionary intrigues and plots.

remained 'motionless in their barracks'. In spite of the classic 'To horse, gentlemen!',[83] in spite of the confidential, frank and venomous outpourings of police chief Abramovicz in Warsaw against the German people, in spite, or rather because, of the success of the threatening notes from St Petersburg, the Russian government is and remains animated by feelings of 'peace and reconciliation'. Russia continues to be 'open, peaceful and defensive'. In Nesselrode's circular, Russia is patience itself and pure innocence, despite many insults and provocations.

Let us set out some of Germany's crimes against Russia, as listed in the note. First: a 'hostile attitude', and second: 'fever for change over the whole of Germany'. So much benevolence from the tsar as opposed to a 'hostile' attitude by Germany! How insulting to the fatherly heart of our dear brother-in-law![84] And this accursed sickness: 'fever for change'! That is actually the main atrocity, although listed here as the second. From time to time Russia presents us with a different illness: the cholera. Never mind! The 'fever for change' referred to here is not only infectious; it often takes on a virulently severe form, so that people of the highest rank are required to make a hurried departure for England.[85] Was the German 'fever for change' perhaps one of the grounds which spoke against Russian intervention in March and April? Germany's third crime: the pre-parliament[86] in Frankfurt presented war against Russia as a necessity of contemporary politics. The same thing occurred in clubs and newspapers, and was the more unforgivable in that according to the stipulations of the Holy Alliance and later treaties between Russia, Austria and Prussia, we Germans should pour out our blood only in the interests of the princes, and not in our own. The fourth: discussions took place in Germany about the restoration of the old

83. Nicholas I is said to have uttered this phrase on hearing of the proclamation of the republic in France in February 1848.

84. Tsar Nicholas I of Russia was the brother-in-law of Frederick William IV of Prussia.

85. William, prince of Prussia (later William I) was the person of the 'highest rank'. He was the leading supporter within the royal family of the clique of Prussian nobles and generals who opposed all concessions to the revolution. He was compelled to flee from Berlin in March 1848 and stayed in London until June.

86. The pre-parliament consisted of a group of notables who met in Frankfurt after the March revolutions and took it upon themselves to convene the German National Assembly.

Poland within its genuine 1772 boundaries. The knout for you Germans, followed by Siberia! But no, when Nesselrode wrote this circular he did not yet know the Frankfurt Assembly's vote on the question of the annexation of Posen.[87] The Assembly has expiated our guilt, and a mild, forgiving smile now appears on the lips of the tsar. Germany's fifth crime: 'its deplorable war against a Nordic monarchy'.[88] Germany presumably deserves a milder punishment than would otherwise be necessary for this, owing to the success of Russia's threatening note, the hurried retreat of the German army (ordered by Potsdam[89]), and the explanation given by the Prussian envoy in Copenhagen of the motive and the aim of the war.[90] Six: 'open advocacy of a defensive and offensive alliance between Germany and France'. Finally, seven: 'the reception given to the Polish refugees, their free journey on the railways, and the insurrection in the Posen district'.

If language did not serve diplomats and similar persons 'as a means of concealing their thoughts', Nesselrode and brother-in-law Nicholas would joyfully embrace us, and give fervent thanks that so many Poles from France, England, Belgium, etc. were enticed to Posen, and given travelling facilities, so that they might be shot down with grape-shot and shrapnel, branded with caustic, slaughtered, sent away with shorn heads and, if possible (as in Cracow[91]), completely wiped out by a treacherous bombardment.

Despite these seven deadly sins committed by Germany, is it true that Russia has remained on the defensive, taken no offensive steps? It is, and that is why the Russian diplomat invites the world to admire the love of peace and the moderation of his tsar.

87. On 27 July the Frankfurt Assembly voted to accept Pfuel's line of demarcation of 4 June between German and Polish Posen and to incorporate the German part into Germany, after a debate in which most speakers rejected the idea of a restoration of the old Poland of 1772. See below, p. 151.

88. The war of April–August 1848 over Schleswig-Holstein between Prussia (acting initially on the intructions of the German Confederation and later, as the Frankfurt Assembly thought, on its own instructions) and Denmark.

89. The seat of the Prussian monarchy, near Berlin.

90. The note of 8 April 1848 from Major Wildenbruch, emissary extraordinary of the king of Prussia, to the Danish Foreign Minister, in which it was pointed out that Prussia was waging war not to snatch the duchies from Denmark but to oppose and crush the 'radical and republican elements from Germany' which were stirring up trouble in the king of Denmark's dominions. Printed in *Nouveau Recueil*, vol. XI, pp. 507–8.

91. Cracow, the centre of the Polish national movement in Austria, was bombarded on 26 April by the Habsburg authorities.

According to Nesselrode, the Russian tsar's rule of procedure 'from which he has not deviated for one moment', is as follows:

Russia will in no way intervene in the internal affairs of those countries which want to change their organization, but will rather leave the peoples completely free, without any obstacle from the Russian side, to accomplish the political and social experiments they want to undertake, and not attack any power which has not itself attacked Russia; however, we are resolved to reject any enroachment on our own internal security, and to make sure that if the territorial equilibrium is destroyed or altered in some respect this will not happen at the expense of our rightful interests.

The sender of the Russian note has forgotten to add illustrative examples. After the July revolution, the tsar assembled an army on his western borders, in order to make a practical demonstration to the French, in alliance with his faithful German servants, of the way in which he intended 'to leave the peoples completely free to accomplish their political and social experiments.' It was not his fault, but that of the Polish revolution of 1830, that this rule of procedure could not be applied, and that his plans had to take another direction.[92] Soon afterwards, the same manoeuvre was seen in relation to Spain and Portugal. The proof is to be found in the tsar's open and secret support for Don Carlos and Dom Miguel.[93] When, at the end of 1842, the king of Prussia wanted to set up a kind of constitution, on the harmless 'historical' basis of the medieval estates, which played such an appropriate role in the Patents of 1847,[94] it was Nicholas, as is well known, who refused

92. Like most European democrats and revolutionaries of the time, Marx took the view that the revolutionary outbreak in Poland on 29 November 1830 prevented an impending Russian attack on France. It now seems more likely (from Nicholas's correspondence with Grand Duke Constantine) that the idea of intervention against France was dropped in August 1830 owing to the failure of the other reactionary powers to cooperate, and that the mobilization of the Russian army was meant to deter the Germans from following the French path and in general to provide backing for the tsar's diplomatic manoeuvres.

93. Don Carlos was the brother of the Spanish king, Ferdinand VII, and the clerical and conservative pretender to the Spanish throne in the early nineteenth century; he was at the centre of the Carlist War of 1833–40. Dom Miguel was similarly a clerical and conservative pretender, who usurped the Portuguese throne in 1828 and was defeated and deposed in 1834.

94. There was in fact only one Patent, issued on 3 February 1847, convoking the first United Diet. Alongside the Patent there were issued three ordinances on the same day, specifying the Diet's mode of organization and procedure.

to tolerate this and cheated us 'Christian Germans' out of many years of patented joy.[95] As Nesselrode says, he did this because Russia never intervenes in the internal organization of another country. We hardly need to mention Cracow. Let us consider merely the latest example of the tsar's 'rule of procedure'. The Wallachians overthrow their old government and provisionally replace it with a new one. They want to transform the whole of the old system and follow the example of civilized peoples. 'In order to allow them to accomplish their political and social experiments completely freely', a Russian army corps invades the country.[96]

After these examples, it should be possible for everyone to find the application of this 'rule of procedure' to Germany. However, the Russian note spares us the need to follow our own logic. It says:

As long as the Confederation, in whatever *new form* it may appear, leaves untouched the neighbouring states and does not seek forcibly to extend its territorial area or jurisdiction outside the *limits* provided for it by the *treaties*, the tsar will also respect its *internal* independence.

The second relevant passage speaks a clearer language:

When Germany really succeeds in solving the problem of its organization, without disadvantage for its internal order, and if the new forms imprinted with its nationality are not such as to endanger order in other states, we shall genuinely offer our congratulations, for the same reasons as those which led us to want a strong and united Germany in its previous political forms.

It is the following passage, however, which has the plainest and most indubitable ring. Here Nesselrode speaks of Russia's ceaseless endeavours to recommend and uphold harmony and unity in Germany:

We are not referring of course to that material unity dreamed of today by a levelling and megalomaniac democracy, which would sooner or later inevitably place Germany in a state of war with all the neighbouring

95. In the summer of 1842 Frederick William IV visited Nicholas in St Petersburg, and the tsar attempted to dissuade him from calling together representatives from the Provincial Diets to form a United Committee in Berlin. He failed, but his opposition, together with that of Metternich and the prince of Prussia, contributed to strengthening Frederick William's hesitations and no doubt delayed the calling of the United Diet.

96. On 10 July 1848 Russian troops invaded Wallachia (the central part of what is now Rumania) in reply to the revolution in Bucharest and the formation of a liberal provisional government.

states if it could realize its ambitious theories as it conceives them; we are referring rather to the *moral unity*, the genuine agreement in views and intentions in all political questions which the German Confederation had to present to the external world. The aim of our policy is only to *maintain this unity*, the bond which attaches the German governments to each other. We still want now what we wanted at that time.

As can be seen from the foregoing, the Russian government is genuinely willing to allow us the *moral* unity of Germany. However, no *material* unity! No supersession of the previous administration of the Federal Diet by a central power based on popular sovereignty, a power real not apparent, a power which acts seriously and capably! What magnanimity!

'We still want now what we wanted then' (i.e. before February 1848). That is the sole phrase in the Russian note that no one will doubt. We would however point out to Herr Nesselrode that the wish and its accomplishment are and remain two separate things.

The Germans now know exactly what they can expect of Russia. As long as the old system lasts, painted over with new modern colours, or if the Germans return obediently to the Russian and 'historical' track deserted in 'momentary inebriation and exaltation', Russia will stand by 'openly and pacifically'.

The situation within Russia – the cholera epidemic, the partial rebellions in some districts, the revolution fomented in St Petersburg but prevented at the last minute, the plot in the Warsaw citadel, the volcanic soil of the Kingdom of Poland;[97] all these circumstances contributed towards the benevolent and 'disinterested attitude' of the tsar towards Germany.

But a much more powerful influence over the 'passive and observational system' of the Russian government was doubtless exercised by the course of events in Germany itself.

Could Nicholas himself have looked after his own interests any better, and fulfilled his intentions any quicker, than the rulers of Berlin-Potsdam, Innsbruck, Vienna, Prague, Frankfurt, Hanover and almost every other cosy corner of our fatherland, now once more replete with moral unity in the Russian style? Have not Pfuel (of the caustic[98]), Colomb and the shrapnel-general[99] in

97. See p. 106, n. 12.
98. General Pfuel gained the nickname 'Pfuel von Höllenstein' from his use of caustic (*Höllenstein*) to brand Polish prisoners in Posen.
99. Nickname of General Hirschfeld, Colomb's second in command in Posen.

Posen, Windischgrätz in Prague, all worked in such a way as to fill the tsar's heart with ecstasy? Did not Windischgrätz receive a dazzling letter of commendation from Nicholas, presented to him in Potsdam by the young Russian envoy, Meyendorf? Has Russia any reason to be dissatisfied with Hansemann, Milde and Schreckenstein in Berlin, and Radowitz, Schmerling and Lichnowsky[1] in Frankfurt? The gullibility of the Frankfurt Assembly must surely be a healing balm for some of the pains of the recent past. Under such conditions, Russian diplomacy has no need of an armed invasion of Germany. The 'passive and observational system' is quite sufficient – and the note we have just discussed.

THE DEBATE ON POLAND IN THE FRANKFURT ASSEMBLY[2]

N.Rh.Z., 20 August 1848   Frederick Engels
                                              Cologne, 19 August

We have made a detailed examination of Stenzel's[3] report, which was the basis of the debate. We have demonstrated how he falsifies the remote as well as the recent history of Poland and of the Germans in Poland, how he distorts the whole question, how the historian Stenzel has rendered himself guilty not only of intentional falsification but also of crude ignorance.[4]

Before we deal with the debate itself, we must glance once more at the Polish question.

Considered in isolation, the question of Posen is entirely lacking in meaning, and impossible to solve. It is a fragment of the Polish question, and can only be solved in conjunction with the latter. The boundary between Germany and Poland can only be determined when Poland again exists.

1. These six men had only a negative quality in common: they were not of the Left. Hansemann, Milde and Schreckenstein were Prussian ministers at the time, Radowitz and Lichnowsky were on the pro-Prussian Right of the Frankfurt Assembly, and Schmerling sat with the Right Centre there and worked for Austria rather than Prussia.
2. This is the third article in a series of nine.
3. Gustav Adolf Stenzel was a liberal historian and a deputy to the Frankfurt National Assembly in 1848, moving from the Left Centre to the Right Centre in the course of the year. He presented the report on the annexation of part of Posen to Germany on 24 July 1848 on behalf of the Assembly's committee on international law.
4. In the first two articles of this series, published on 9 and 12 August (*MEW* 5, pp. 319–31).

But can and will Poland exist again? This was denied in the debate.

A French historian has said: *Il y a des peuples nécessaires*; there are *necessary peoples*. The Polish people belongs unconditionally amongst these necessary peoples in the nineteenth century.

But the national existence of Poland is more necessary for us Germans than for any other people.

What has been the immediate basis of the power of reaction in Europe since 1815, in part, indeed, since the first French revolution? It is the Holy Alliance between Russia, Prussia and Austria. And what holds this Holy Alliance together? The *division of Poland*, which is advantageous to all three allies.

The line of cleavage which the three powers drew through Poland is the band which chains them together; a jointly committed crime has made each responsible for the other.

From the moment when the first rape of Poland was committed, Germany was a dependency of Russia. Russia ordered Prussia and Austria to remain absolute monarchies, and Prussia and Austria had to obey. The endeavours of the Prussian bourgeoisie to conquer power for itself, half-hearted and timid endeavours in any case, were completely shipwrecked on the impossibility of detaching Prussia from Russia, on the backing provided by Russia for the Prussian feudal and absolutist class.

A contributory factor to this situation was that, right from the first attempts made by the Holy Alliance to suppress Poland, the Poles were engaged not only in an insurrectional struggle for their independence but also, and simultaneously, in a revolutionary confrontation with their own internal social conditions.

The partition of Poland was a result of the alliance of the big feudal aristocracy in Poland with the three partitioning powers. It was not a progressive step, as asserted by the ex-poet Herr Jordan,[5] but rather the last remaining means for the big aristocracy to save itself from a revolution. It was completely and utterly reactionary.

Even the first partition resulted in an entirely natural alliance of the other classes, i.e. the gentry, the burghers of the towns and, in part, the peasants, against both the external oppressors of Poland

5. Wilhelm Jordan was a poet and journalist, and a member of the Left in the Frankfurt National Assembly until the Polish debate of July 1848, when his extreme nationalist and anti-Polish opinions led him to move to the Centre.

and the big aristocracy of the country itself. The constitution of 1791[6] shows how well the Poles of that time already understood that their independence *vis-à-vis* foreign powers was inseparable from the overthrow of the aristocracy and agrarian reform within the country.

The vast agricultural lands between the Baltic and the Black Sea can only be freed from patriarchal-feudal barbarism by an agrarian revolution which will transform the serfs and the peasants owing compulsory labour services into free landed proprietors, a revolution which will be identical with the French revolution of 1789 in the country districts. The Polish nation has the merit of having been the first of all the neighbouring agricultural peoples to proclaim this necessity. Their earliest attempt at reform was the constitution of 1791; during the rising of 1830 Lelewel described agrarian revolution as the sole means of saving the country, but his view was adopted too late by the Diet; finally, agrarian revolution was openly proclaimed in the insurrections of 1846 and 1848.

From the day when Poland's oppression began the Poles have played a revolutionary role and thereby riveted their oppressors even more firmly to the counter-revolution. They compelled their oppressors to maintain the patriarchal-feudal situation not just in Poland but in their other possessions. And particularly after the Cracow rising of 1846,[7] the struggle for Polish independence has at the same time been the struggle of *agrarian democracy* – the only kind possible in eastern Europe – against *patriarchal-feudal absolutism*.

As long as we help to oppress Poland, therefore, as long as we chain a part of Poland to Germany, just so long do we remain chained to Russia and Russia's policies, just so long do we remain unable to break thoroughly with our own indigenous patriarchal-

6. The Polish constitution of 3 May 1791 contained a number of important reforms, such as the abolition of the noble's right of veto and the establishment of ministerial responsibility to the Diet, and it made a slight breach in the system of serfdom by giving binding legal force to emancipation contracts between lord and peasant. The reaction of the conservative nobility to the constitution of 1791 was to call in the aid of Catherine II of Russia. After a short war (1792–3) the constitution was abolished and Poland partitioned a second time.

7. The democratic aspect of Polish nationalism, which first came to the fore in the Cracow uprising of 1846, was even stronger in the Posen rising of March–May 1848, which was joined by the Polish peasants and artisans, though still led by the lesser nobility.

feudal absolutism. The creation of a democratic Poland is the first condition for the creation of a democratic Germany.

But it is not simply that the creation of Poland and the regulation of its boundary with Germany is necessary; it is also by far the most soluble of all the political questions which have come to the surface since the revolution in eastern Europe. The independence struggles of the variegated jumble of nationalities to the south of the Carpathians are of an entirely different order of complexity from the Polish struggle for independence and the settling of the border between Germany and Poland, and they will cost far more blood, confusion and civil war.

It is obvious that the issue at stake here is the creation of a state on a viable basis, not the setting up of a sham Poland. Poland must have at least the boundaries of 1772; it must possess not only the regions around its great rivers but also their outlets to the sea, and at the very least an extensive stretch of coastline on the Baltic.

Germany could have guaranteed all this to Poland while still securing its own interests and honour if, after the revolution and in its own interests, it had had the courage to demand, arms in hands, that Russia give up Poland. In view of the German-Polish intermixture in the border regions and particularly on the coast, it was a matter of course that both sides would have had to make mutual concessions, that some Germans would have had to become Polish and vice versa; but this would not have created any difficulty.

After the German semi-revolution, however, no one had the courage to take such a decisive stand. To make spectacular speeches about the liberation of Poland; to receive Poles at railway stations on their way through Germany and offer them the warmest sympathy of the German people (to whom has that not been offered?): all this was perfectly acceptable. But to begin a war with Russia, to call into question the whole European balance of power and, above all, to give back a single fragment of the stolen territory? No, he who asks for this does not know his Germans!

And what was the significance of war with Russia? War with Russia meant the complete, open and real break with the whole of our shameful past, it meant the real liberation and unification of Germany, it meant the erection of democracy on the ruins of feudalism and the bourgeoisie's short dream of domination. War with Russia was the only possible way to save our honour and our interest *vis-à-vis* our Slav neighbours, and in particular the Poles.

But we were philistines, and we remain philistines. We made a couple of dozen large and small revolutions which we ourselves became terrified of even before they had been completed. After a lot of loud talk we did precisely nothing. All problems were dealt with in a spirit of the most faint-hearted, thick-headed, narrow-minded philistinism, and in this way our real interests were naturally again compromised. From the standpoint of this petty philistinism even the great question of the liberation of Poland was reduced to a trifling phrase about the reorganization of a part of the province of Posen, and our enthusiasm for the Poles changed into shrapnel and caustic.[8]

The sole possible solution, the only solution which would have preserved Germany's honour and Germany's interests was, we repeat, war with Russia. The risk of war was not taken, and there followed the unavoidable consequence: the soldiery of reaction, beaten in Berlin, raised their heads again in Posen. Under the cover of saving Germany's honour and nationality they took up the banner of the counter-revolution and suppressed the Polish revolutionaries, our allies. Germany, taken in by this, momentarily applauded its own victorious foes. The new partition of Poland was accomplished and all that was lacking was the sanction of the German National Assembly.

The Frankfurt Assembly had open to it one last way of making reparation: it could have excluded the whole of Posen from the German Confederation and declared the question of the boundary to be open until it was possible to negotiate over it on equal terms with a restored Poland.

But this would have been demanding too much of our Frankfurt professors, lawyers and clerics in the National Assembly! The temptation was too great; they, peaceful citizens who had never fired a gun, had the opportunity, by standing up and sitting down

8. Originally, in March 1848, there was great sympathy among German liberals for the Poles, and the Prussian government was compelled to promise that a commission would be set up to discuss the 'national reorganization of the Grand Duchy of Posen', which was to include the arming of Polish troops, the appointment of Poles to official positions, and the introduction of Polish as the official language. On 14 April, however, this 'reorganization' was limited to the eastern part of the province, and the area in question was further reduced in size by the decree of 26 April. Meanwhile, the Germans of Posen had come into conflict with the Polish National Committee on the spot, a situation which degenerated into a civil war in late April between the Poles and the Prussian troops. This time most German liberals took the Prussian army's side, under the influence of the strong agitation of the German minority there.

again, of conquering an area of five hundred square miles for Germany, of annexing eight hundred thousand *Netzbrüder*, German Poles,[9] Jews and Poles, even if at the cost of Germany's honour and her real, lasting interest. What a temptation! They have succumbed to it, they have confirmed the partition of Poland.

THE CRISIS AND THE COUNTER-REVOLUTION

I *N.Rh.Z.*, 12 September 1848

Cologne, 11 September

Read our reports from Berlin, and you will see whether we did not correctly predict the development of the ministerial crisis there.[10] The old ministers resign; the ministry's plan to maintain itself by dissolving the *Vereinbarungsversammlung*, by using cannons and martial law, does not appear to have met with the approval of the camarilla.[11] The junkers of Uckermark are burning with eagerness for a conflict with the people, for a repetition of the Paris June scenes in the streets of Berlin; however, they will fight only for the MINISTRY OF THE PRINCE OF PRUSSIA and never for the Hansemann ministry. They will call on Radowitz,[12] Vincke[13] and

9. *Netzbrüder*: German-speaking colonists introduced into the Netz district by Frederick II after the first partition of Poland (1772).

German Poles: German-speaking inhabitants of Poland, referred to as German Poles (*Deutschpolen*) by Engels to underline their lack of real historical ties with Germany and their long-standing connection with Poland in previous centuries.

10. The ministerial crisis in Prussia began with the resignation of the Auerswald-Hansemann ministry on 8 September and ended temporarily with the formation of the Pfuel ministry on 22 September. It was set off by the Prussian National Assembly's vote of 7 September in favour of a resolution introduced by deputy Stein calling on the Minister of War to order all officers to abstain from reactionary intrigues and to cooperate in setting up the constitutional state. The resolution was adopted with 219 votes in favour and 143 against. It had in fact already been passed once on 9 August (as the Stein-Schulze army order), but the Minister of War had failed to act on it, and the Assembly was therefore trying again.

11. The clique of reactionary Prussian nobles and officers, headed by Leopold von Gerlach, which gathered around Frederick William IV at Potsdam and had a determining influence on royal policy behind the scenes.

12. Joseph von Radowitz was a Prussian general and politician, one of Frederick William's closest associates. He was a leading member of the pro-Prussian Right in the Frankfurt Assembly.

13. Georg, Freiherr von Vincke was a liberal member of the Westphalian nobility, who sat in the United Diet of 1847 and on the Right in the Frankfurt Assembly in 1848.

reliable people of that type, who stand apart from the Berlin Assembly and are not obliged to it in any way. The cream of the Prussian and Westphalian nobility – associated on the face of it with certain bourgeois innocents of the extreme Right such as Beckerath[14] and his friends, who will take over the prosaic commercial business of the state – that is the Ministry of the prince of Prussia which they intend to bless us with. In the meantime they will throw out hundreds of rumours, possibly call on Waldeck[15] or Rodbertus[16] and mislead public opinion, while at the same time making their military preparations. Finally, when the time is ripe, they will come out openly.

We are approaching a decisive struggle. The counter-revolution is compelled to fight its last battle by the simultaneous crises in Frankfurt and Berlin, and by the latest decisions of the two Assemblies. If in Berlin they take the risk of trampling underfoot the constitutional principle of the rule of the majority, if they put against the 219 votes of the majority twice that number of cannons, if they take the risk of defying the majority both in Berlin and in Frankfurt with a ministry regarded as impossible by both Assemblies – **If in this way they provoke civil war between Prussia and Germany, Democrats will know what to do.**

II *N.Rh.Z.*, 13 September 1848

Cologne, 12 September

In Frankfurt a new Reich ministry is being formed, as we reported yesterday, and as has now been confirmed from other sources. We shall perhaps hear by midday today that it has been definitively constituted. In Berlin the ministerial crisis continues. This crisis is only susceptible of two solutions.

Either a Waldeck ministry, with the recognition of the authority

14. Hermann von Beckerath was a banker in Krefeld and a leading Rhenish liberal. In 1848 he sat with the Right Centre in the Frankfurt Assembly, and was Reich Minister of Finance from August to September 1848. It is not clear why Marx places Beckerath on the 'extreme Right'.

15. Benedict Francis Waldeck was a Prussian state official in Berlin. In 1848 he led the Left in the Berlin Assembly.

16. Johann Karl Rodbertus was a Prussian landowner and economist, who upheld a form of 'state socialism'. In 1848 he led the Left Centre in the Prussian Assembly and was Minister of Religious Affairs in the Auerswald-Hansemann cabinet.

of the German National Assembly, and of the sovereignty of the people.

Or a Radowitz-Vincke ministry, with the dissolution of the Berlin Assembly, the liquidation of the conquests of the revolution and sham constitutionalism, or indeed, the return of the United Diet.

Let us not hide this point from ourselves: the conflict which has broken out in Berlin is a conflict between the Assembly, which has asserted its *constituent* nature for the first time, and the Crown, not between the *Vereinbarer*[17] and the ministers.

Everything turns on whether they have the courage to dissolve the Assembly or not.

But has the Crown the right to dissolve the Assembly?

In constitutional states, of course, the Crown has the right, in case of a conflict, to dissolve legislative chambers called on the basis of the constitution, and to appeal to the people through new elections.

Is the Berlin Assembly a constitutional, legislative chamber?

No. It has been called 'to agree with the Crown on the constitution of the Prussian state', and is founded not on a constitution but on a *revolution*. It in no sense received its mandate from the Crown or its responsible ministers, but solely from its electors and from itself. The Assembly was sovereign as the legitimate expression of the revolution, and the mandate which Camphausen and the United Diet drew up for it, in the electoral law of 8 April, was nothing more than a *pious wish*, the fate of which was to be decided by the Assembly itself.

At the outset the Assembly more or less accepted the theory of *Vereinbarung*. Then it saw how it had been swindled by the ministers and the camarilla. Finally, it performed an act of sovereignty, it momentarily presented itself as a constituent assembly instead of a *Vereinbarungsversammlung*.

As the sovereign assembly for Prussia it had a full right to do this.

However, a sovereign assembly cannot be dissolved by anyone, it is subject to no one's orders.

Even as a mere *Vereinbarungsversammlung*, even according to Camphausen's own theory, it stands beside the Crown as an *equal partner*. Both parties *contract* a state treaty, both parties have an

17. The compromisers or 'agreers', i.e. the members of the *Vereinbarungsversammlung*.

equal share in sovereignty – that is the theory of 8 April, the Camphausen-Hansemann theory, and therefore the *official* theory, recognized by the Crown itself.

If the Assembly is the *equal* of the Crown, *the Crown has no right to dissolve the Assembly*. Otherwise, logically, the Assembly would have the *right to depose the king*.

The dissolution of the Assembly would therefore be a coup d'état. And the way to reply to a coup d'état has already been demonstrated, on 29 July 1830 and 24 February 1848.[18]

It will be said that the Crown could after all appeal again to the same electors. But everyone knows that *today* the electors would elect an entirely different Assembly, an Assembly which would make short work of the Crown.

It is clear that after the dissolution of this Assembly the only appeal possible is to *entirely different electors* from those of 8 April. No other elections are possible than elections held under the tyranny of the sabre.

Let us therefore have no illusions: if the Assembly is victorious, if it enforces a ministry of the Left, the power of the Crown *alongside* the Assembly will be broken, the king will simply be the paid servant of the people, we shall stand again in the morning light of 19 March[19] – provided always that the Waldeck ministry does not betray us as previous ministries have done.

If the Crown is victorious, if it enforces the Ministry of the prince of Prussia, the Assembly will be dissolved, the right of association will be suppressed, the press will be muzzled, an electoral law with property qualifications will be decreed, perhaps indeed the United Diet will be conjured up once again, and all this will occur under the protection of a military dictatorship, of cannons and bayonets.

Which of the two sides gains the victory will depend on the

18. On 26 July 1830 the government of Charles X of France issued four ordinances dissolving the Chamber of Deputies, prescribing new elections on a much narrower franchise, and introducing a stringent censorship. The reply to this royal coup d'état was the 1830 revolution, which culminated in the removal of the Bourbon monarchy on 29 July and its replacement by the Orleans monarchy. On 24 February 1848 the Orleans monarchy was in its turn overthrown.

19. On 19 March 1848, after the bloody street battles of the previous day in Berlin, Frederick William IV issued his proclamation 'To my dear Berliners' promising the withdrawal of the troops from Berlin if the rebels dismantled their barricades.

attitude of the people, and in particular on the attitude of the democratic party. The democrats must choose.

We stand on the threshold of 26 July.[20] Will the Crown take the risk of issuing the ordinances now being devised in Potsdam? Will it provoke the people into making the leap from 26 July to 24 February in *one* day?

The intention is there, certainly, but what is needed is the courage to act.

III *N.Rh.Z.*, 14 September 1848

Cologne, 13 September

The crisis in Berlin has gone a step further: the *conflict with the Crown*, which yesterday we could only describe as unavoidable, *has now really begun.*

Our readers will find the king's answer to the resignation of the ministers in another column.[21] By this letter the Crown itself has entered the foreground, taken sides with the ministers, and placed itself in opposition to the Assembly.

But it has gone further than this: it has formed an extra-parliamentary ministry, it has called on Beckerath, who sits with the extreme Right in Frankfurt and, as everyone knows in advance, will never be able to reckon on a majority in Berlin.

The king's answer is countersigned by Auerswald.[22] Auerswald is responsible for pushing the Crown forward in this way in order to cover his dishonourable retreat, and for his attempt simultaneously to hide behind the constitutional principle and to tread it underfoot, with the result that he has *compromised the Crown and fomented republicanism.*

'The constitutional principle', scream the ministers. 'The constitutional principle', screams the Right. 'The constitutional principle', wheezes the *Kölnische Zeitung*[23] in an empty echo.

20. See p. 159, n. 18.

21. In his message of 10 September 1848 to the Assembly, Frederick William IV declared that its resolution of 7 September 1848 was a violation of the principles of constitutional monarchy, and that the Auerswald-Hansemann ministry had been right to resign in protest against it.

22. Rudolf von Auerswald was a liberal member of the Prussian nobility. He was Prime Minister and Foreign Minister from June to September 1848.

23. A daily newspaper which had appeared in Cologne since 1802. In the 1840s it was the main organ of the moderate Rhineland liberals, and had a standing feud with the *Neue Rheinische Zeitung* throughout the period of the revolution.

'The constitutional principle'! Are these gentlemen really so stupid as to believe that the German people can be led out of the storms of 1848, out of the daily more threatening collapse of all the institutions handed down by history, by means of the worm-eaten doctrine of the separation of powers as put forward by Montesquieu and Delolme,[24] by means of worn out phrases and long exploded fictions?

'The constitutional principle'! But these very gentlemen, who want to save the constitutional principle at any price, must first of all realize that in a provisional situation it can only be saved by energetic action.

'The constitutional principle'! But has it not already been shown, by the vote of the Berlin Assembly, by the conflicts between Potsdam and Frankfurt, by the disturbances, the attempts at reaction, and the provocations of the soldiery, that in spite of all phrases we still *stand on a revolutionary footing*, that the fiction that we are already in a situation of *constituted*, completed constitutional monarchy leads to nothing but conflicts, conflicts which have already brought the 'constitutional principle' to the edge of the abyss?

Every state which finds itself in a provisional situation after a revolution requires a dictator, an energetic dictator at that. We attacked Camphausen from the beginning for failing to act dictatorially, for failing to destroy and remove the remnants of the old institutions immediately. Thus, while Camphausen lulled himself to sleep with constitutional fairy-tales, the defeated party strengthened its positions in the bureaucracy and the army. Here and there, indeed, it even ventured on an open struggle. The Assembly was called in order to negotiate a constitution. It took its place beside the Crown as an equal partner. Two powers with equal rights in a provisional situation! Camphausen sought to 'save freedom' by means of the separation of powers. But precisely this separation of powers had to lead to conflicts in such a situation. Behind the Crown lay hidden the counter-revolutionary camarilla of the nobility, the military and the bureaucracy. Behind the majority of the Assembly stood the bourgeoisie. The

24. Montesquieu's doctrine, as expressed notably in *The Spirit of the Laws* (1748) was that the ideal form of state was a constitutional monarchy, in which the three powers, i.e. the legislature, executive and judiciary, were separate and independent of each other. This doctrine was further developed some fifty years later by the Swiss constitutional lawyer Delolme.

ministry endeavoured to mediate between them. Too weak to represent the interests of the bourgeoisie and the peasants in a decisive fashion, and to overthrow the power of the nobility, the bureaucracy and the army leaders at one stroke, too maladroit to avoid injuring the bourgeoisie on all sides by its financial measures, it achieved nothing apart from making itself impossible for all parties, and bringing about the very collision it wanted to prevent.

It is the *salut public*, public safety, which is of decisive significance in an unconstitutional situation, not this or that principle. The ministry could only avoid a conflict between the Assembly and the Crown by unilaterally recognizing the principle of public safety, even at the risk of a conflict between the ministry itself and the Crown. But it preferred to remain 'presentable' at Potsdam. It never hesitated to apply measures of public safety, i.e. dictatorial measures, against the democrats. What else can one call the application of the old laws regarding political crimes, at a time when Herr Märker[25] himself had already recognized that these paragraphs of the old Prussian Landrecht had to be removed? What else were the mass arrests which took place in all parts of the kingdom?

But the ministry has taken good care not to intervene against the counter-revolution on grounds of public safety!

Owing to this half-heartedness of the ministry when confronted with the daily more threatening counter-revolution, it became necessary for the Assembly *itself to dictate* measures of public safety. If the Crown, as represented by the ministers, was too weak, the Assembly itself had a duty to intervene. This it did by the resolution of 9 August,[26] but only in a very mild manner. The ministers were given a single warning, and they disregarded it.

But how could they possibly have accepted it? The resolution of 9 August tramples on the constitutional principle, it is an infringement by the legislature against the executive, it disturbs the separation of powers and their control by each other which is so necessary in the interests of freedom, it turns the *Vereinbarungsversammlung* into a National Convention.[27]

25. Friedrich August Märker sat with the Centre in the Prussian National Assembly, and from June to September 1848 he was Prussian Minister of Justice.

26. See p. 156, n. 10.

27. A reference to the revolutionary assembly of September 1792–November 1795 in France, which (until the Thermidor reaction of July 1794) exercised dictatorial powers in the interests of the revolution, executed the king, and played a part in initiating the Terror.

And there follows a flood of threats, a thunderous appeal to the fears of the petty bourgeoisie, and a long-term perspective of a terrorist regime with the guillotine, progressive taxation, confiscations and the red flag.

The Berlin Assembly a Convention! What irony!

But the gentlemen who predict this are not entirely mistaken. If the government continues on its present course, we shall have a Convention in the near future, a Convention not just for Prussia but for the whole of Germany, a Convention whose task will be to suppress the insurrection of our twenty Vendées, and to prosecute the unavoidable Russian war by all possible means. Now, of course, we only have a parody of the Constituent Assembly.[28]

But how has the constitutional principle been upheld by the ministerial gentlemen who appeal to it?

On 9 August they calmly allowed the Assembly to adjourn in the belief that the ministers would carry out the resolution. The latter had no intention of announcing their refusal to the Assembly; much less did they intend to lay down their offices.

After a whole month of reflection, and under the threat of numerous interpellations, they abruptly pointed out to the Assembly that there was no question of their carrying out the resolution.

When the Assembly replied by instructing the ministers to carry out the resolution in any case, they hid behind the Crown, produced a split between the Crown and the Assembly, and thereby provoked a tendency towards republicanism. And these gentlemen still speak of the constitutional principle!

Let us sum up. The inevitable conflict between two equal powers in a provisional situation has set in. The ministry did not carry on the business of government energetically enough; it omitted to take measures necessary for public safety. The Assembly was only doing its duty when it called on the ministry to fulfil its obligations. The ministry asserted that this was an attack on the Crown, and compromised the Crown at the very moment of its resignation. Crown and Assembly confront each other. *Vereinbarung* has led to division, to conflict. Perhaps the sword will decide.

He who is most courageous and consistent will gain the victory.

28. The French Constituent Assembly of June 1789–September 1791 laid the foundations of the constitutional monarchy.

IV *N.Rh.Z.*, 16 September 1848

Cologne, 15 September

The ministerial crisis has once more entered a new stage; not through the arrival and vain endeavours of the impossible Herr Beckerath, but through the *military revolt in Potsdam and Nauen.*[29] The conflict between democracy and aristocracy has broken out *in the very bosom of the Guard:* the soldiers see their liberation from the tyranny of the officers in the Assembly's resolution of 7 September; they are issuing addresses of thanks to the Assembly, they are giving it a hearty cheer.

With this the sword has been wrested from the hands of the counter-revolution. Now they are not likely to risk dissolving the Assembly, and if they do not take that step there will be nothing left but to give way, to carry out the resolution of the Assembly, and to call on Waldeck to form a ministry.

The revolt of the Potsdam soldiers has probably spared us the trouble of making a revolution.

REVOLUTION IN VIENNA

N.Rh.Z., 12 October 1848

Cologne, 11 October

In its *first* number (1 June) the *Neue Rheinische Zeitung* had a revolution to report from Vienna (that of 26 May[30]). Today, on the occasion of our *first* reappearance after the interruption brought about by the state of siege in Cologne, we bring news of the much more important Vienna revolution of 6 and 7 October.[31]

29. In Nauen, on 10 September, the Guards refused to obey an order to attack the citizens of the town; in Potsdam, on 13 September, the First and Second Guards Regiments rose in revolt against their officers. The main reason for this was the confiscation of an address of thanks the soldiers intended to send to deputy Stein and the Berlin Assembly for the resolution of 7 September. (See p. 156, n. 10.)

30. The revolutionary *journée* of 26 May in Vienna was the response of the students and workers to the Pillersdorf ministry's proclamation of 25 May dissolving the Academic Legion and closing the University.

31. The Vienna revolution of 6-7 October broke out under the impact of the news that the Habsburg government was about to attack Hungary (on 3 October a state of siege had been proclaimed over Hungary, the Budapest parliament had been dissolved, and Jellačić had been appointed as Supreme Commander).

The detailed reports on the Vienna events have compelled us to leave aside all discussion articles for today. We shall say just a few words, therefore, about the Vienna revolution itself. Our readers will observe from the reports of our correspondent in Vienna[32] that this revolution is in danger, if not of being wrecked, at least of being obstructed in its development, by the bourgeoisie's mistrust of the working class. Even so, its impact on Hungary, Italy and Germany has shattered the whole military strategy of the counter-revolution. The flight of the emperor and the Czech deputies from Vienna[33] compels the Viennese bourgeoisie to continue the struggle or to surrender unconditionally. The Frankfurt Assembly, which is at present engaged in giving us Germans

A NATIONAL HOUSE OF REFORM AND ONE GREAT
WHIP FOR US ALL[34]

is rudely awakened from its dreams by the Vienna events; the Berlin ministry realizes the mistake it is making in relying on the cure-all known as the *state of siege*. Like the revolution, the state of siege has made the grand tour of the world. The attempt was even made to apply the experiment on a large scale to a whole country, Hungary. This precipitated a revolution in Vienna instead of a counter-revolution in Hungary. The state of siege will not recover from this setback. The state of siege has been compromised for ever. It is an irony of fate that Cavaignac, the western hero of the state of siege, simultaneously with Jellačić, its eastern hero,[35] has become the target of attack of all the classes he saved in June with his grape-shot. He can only retain his position for a short while by going over resolutely to the revolution.

32. Eduard von Müller-Tellering. He survived the siege of Vienna and later lived in exile in London.

33. On 7 October the Austrian Emperor Ferdinand fled from Vienna to Olmütz (Olomouc); at the same time most of the Czech deputies to the Reichstag left Vienna for Prague.

34. 'Der Tannhäuser', *The Poetry and Prose of Heinrich Heine*, p. 215.

35. Josip Jellačić, count of Bužim was a Croat and an Austrian general, appointed Ban of Croatia in 1848 as a counterweight to the Hungarians. He took an active part in putting down the revolutions in Austria and in Hungary.

THE 'COLOGNE REVOLUTION'

N.Rh.Z., 13 October 1848

Cologne, 12 October

The *Kölnische Zeitung* tells us that the 'Cologne Revolution' of 25 September was a carnival jest, and the *Kölnische Zeitung* is right. On 26 September the commander of the Cologne garrison played Cavaignac. And the *Kölnische Zeitung* admires the commander for his wisdom and moderation. Which is the pathetic spectacle, however: the workers of 25 September, practising barricade-construction, or the Cavaignac of 26 September, who in all seriousness proclaimed a state of siege, suspended newspapers, disarmed the citizens' militia[36] and banned the societies?

Poor *Kölnische Zeitung*! The Cavaignac of the 'Cologne Revolution' cannot be an inch taller than the 'Cologne Revolution' itself. Poor *Kölnische Zeitung*! It has to take the 'revolution' as a joke and the 'Cavaignac' of this droll revolution in earnest. O tiresome, thankless, self-contradictory subject!

We shall not waste a word on the question of the justification of the Cologne commander's action. D'Ester[37] has exhausted this subject.[38] In any case, we view the Cologne military headquarters as a subordinate instrument. The real authors of this curious tragedy were the 'loyal citizens', the Dumonts[39] and their allies. No wonder, then, that Dumont had his newspapers spread abroad the address against d'Ester, Borchardt and Kyll.[40] What

36. One of the many ways in which the German revolutions of March 1848 drew inspiration from the French example was the well-nigh universal demand for the setting up of a *Bürgerwehr* or citizens' militia on the model of the French National Guard (see p. 133, n. 56). These militias were often, as in Cologne, formed on a voluntary basis, but did not receive official recognition.

37. Karl Ludwig d'Ester was a Cologne doctor, a member of the Cologne branch of the League of Communists, and a leader of the Democratic party in the Prussian National Assembly. Following the breach between Marx and the Cologne district of the League, d'Ester took up a petty-bourgeois democratic position.

38. On 29 September 1848 in the Berlin Assembly d'Ester demanded the raising of the state of siege in Cologne and the disciplining of the Cologne military commander for his illegal actions.

39. Joseph Dumont was a moderate liberal, and the proprietor of the *Kölnische Zeitung*.

40. The Rhineland deputies Borchardt and Kyll had supported d'Ester's demand for the raising of the state of siege. Certain right-wing members of the Cologne bourgeoisie replied to this on 2 October with an address to the Prussian National Assembly attacking the three deputies for their attitude.

these 'loyal men' had to defend was their own action, not the Cologne commander's.

The occurrence at Cologne wandered through the Sahara desert of the German press in the form given to it by the Cologne version of the *Journal des Débats*.[41] This is sufficient reason to return to the question.

Moll, one of the best-loved leaders of the Workers Society, was about to be arrested. Schapper and Becker[42] had already been arrested. The authorities had chosen a Monday to carry out these measures, a day on which, as is well known, most of the workers have no employment. They must therefore have known beforehand that the arrests would call forth great unrest among the workers, and might even provoke violent resistance. Curious coincidence that these arrests took place precisely on a Monday. It was the easier to foresee the disturbance in that at any moment, after Stein's[43] army order, Wrangel's proclamation[44] and Pfuel's appointment as Prime Minister,[45] a decisive counter-revolutionary stroke, and therefore a revolution, was awaited from Berlin. The workers had therefore to regard the arrests as *political* rather than judicial measures. They saw the office of public prosecutor as simply a counter-revolutionary authority. They believed that the intention was to rob them of their leaders on the eve of important events. They decided to get Moll out of jail at any

41. A French daily newspaper founded in 1789, which was the organ of the Orléanists in the 1830s and 1840s. It opposed the revolution of 1848. The 'Cologne version' was presumably the *Kölnische Zeitung*.

42. Hermann Heinrich Becker was a Cologne journalist and judicial official. In 1848 he was a member of the Cologne Democratic Society, the Rhineland District Committee of Democrats, the Cologne Committee of Public Safety and the Workers Society.

43. Julius Stein was a Breslau headmaster and a democratic journalist. In 1848 he sat with the Left in the Prussian National Assembly, and acted as chairman of the Berlin Democratic Club. On the army order see p. 156, n. 10.

44. Friedrich Heinrich, Graf von Wrangel was a Prussian general and a member of the camarilla. In 1848 he was in command of the Third Army Corps in Berlin, and on 13 September was appointed to the newly created post of Commander of all Troops in the Marks (i.e. in the province of Brandenburg, in which Berlin was situated). In this capacity he issued a proclamation on 17 September, declaring that it was his task 'to uphold public order' and attacking 'elements which wanted to seduce the people into illegal actions'.

45. The Pfuel ministry was formed on 21 September, with Pfuel as Prime Minister, Eichmann as Minister of the Interior, and Graf von Dönhoff as Foreign Minister. It was a ministry of Prussian officials and soldiers, and lasted only until 31 October.

price. And they only left the field of battle when they had achieved their aim. The first barricades were set up when the workers, assembled on the Altenmarkt, were informed that the military was advancing to the attack on all sides. They were not in fact attacked; they therefore did not have to defend themselves. In addition, it had become known to them that there was absolutely no important news from Berlin. They therefore withdrew, after they had vainly awaited the enemy for a great part of the night.

There is thus nothing more ridiculous than the accusation of cowardice made against the Cologne workers.

But certain other accusations have been made against them in order to justify the state of siege and to fashion the Cologne events into a June insurrection on a small scale. The actual plan of the workers, it is said, was to plunder the good town of Cologne. This accusation rests on the rumoured plundering of *one* draper's shop. As if every town did not have its contingent of thieves, who naturally make use of days of public disturbance! Or is the plundering in question the plundering of arsenals? In that case, the Cologne prosecutor should be sent to Berlin to draw up the act of accusation against the March revolution. Without the plundering of arsenals we should perhaps never have experienced the pleasure of seeing Herr Hansemann transformed into a bank director and Herr Müller[46] into a state secretary.

We have said enough of the Cologne workers. Now we come to the so-called democrats. What does the *Kölnische Zeitung* reproach them with (along with the *Deutsche Zeitung*,[47] the *Augsburger Allgemeine Zeitung*,[48] and the other 'loyal' papers, whatever their names may be)?

The heroic Brüggemanns,[49] Bassermanns,[50] etc. demanded

46. Friedrich Müller was the Cologne police director before 1848. In 1848 he became a deputy in the Prussian National Assembly, sitting with the Right Centre, and was appointed a junior minister in the Ministry of Justice.

47. A south German liberal newspaper, which favoured the unification of Germany as a constitutional monarchy under Prussian leadership. It appeared from 1847 to September 1848 in Heidelberg with the historian Gervinus as its editor.

48. A newspaper published in Augsburg from 1810 to 1882. It supported the constitutional monarchist Right in the 1848 revolution.

49. Karl Heinrich Brüggemann was an economist and a liberal journalist. He edited the *Kölnische Zeitung* from 1846 to 1855.

50. Friedrich Daniel Bassermann was a Mannheim bookseller and a moderate liberal politician. In 1848 he represented the government of Baden at the Federal Diet, and sat with the Right Centre in the Frankfurt National Assembly.

blood, and the soft-hearted democrats, owing to their *cowardice*, allowed no blood to flow.

The true facts are simply these: the democrats told the workers, in the inn Zum Kranz (on the Altenmarkt), in the Eiser Hall, and on the barricades, that under no circumstances did they want a putsch.[51] At that moment, indeed, when there was no great question impelling the whole population to take part in the struggle, with the result that any uprising was bound to fail, such an action would be senseless, they said, and, still worse, would exhaust the workers *before* the day of decision, since tremendous events were expected in the next few days. The day for the people to venture on revolution would come when the Berlin ministry ventured on counter-revolution. The judicial investigation will confirm our account. The gentlemen of the *Kölnische Zeitung* would have done better to harangue the deluded workers with their words of wisdom from the top of the barricades, instead of standing in front of them in the 'nocturnal gloom' with 'folded arms and stern looks' and 'reflecting on the future of their people'.[52] What use is wisdom after the event?

But the good press played its worst tune of all in connection with the situation of the citizens' militia. The militia refused to sink to the position of abject servant of the police; that was its duty. But it also delivered up its weapons voluntarily; this can only be excused for one reason: the liberal section of the militia knew that the illiberal section would joyfully seize the opportunity of stripping itself of its weapons. A partial resistance would have been pointless.

The 'Cologne revolution' has had *one* result. It has revealed the existence of a phalanx of more than two thousand saints, whose 'satisfied virtue and solvent morality'[53] can only lead a 'free life' in a state of siege. Perhaps there will be an opportunity one day to write an *Acta Sanctorum* – the biographies of these saints. Our readers will then discover how they obtained the 'treasures' which are resistant 'both to moths and to rust', they will learn how the economic background of the 'noble sentiments' was acquired.

51. The Cologne democrats referred to here included, in particular, Marx and his supporters. See Introduction, p. 44.

52. These are quotations from the article 'Die Barrikaden in Köln', published in the *Kölnische Zeitung*, 30 September 1848.

53. *Satte Tugend und zahlungsfähige Moral*, from Heine's poem 'Anno 1829'.

R. – 10

THE PROCLAMATION OF THE DEMOCRATIC CONGRESS
TO THE GERMAN PEOPLE

N.Rh.Z., 3 November 1848

Cologne, 2 November

We reproduce below the proclamation of the 'Democratic Congress':[54]

To the German People

Through long shame-filled years the German people has sighed beneath the yoke of tyranny. The bloody deeds of Vienna and Berlin gave justification to the hope that its freedom and unity would with a single stroke come true. The devilish arts of an accursed reaction opposed this development, in order to cheat the heroic people of the fruits of its magnificent uprising. Vienna, a central bastion of German freedom, stands at this very moment in the greatest peril. Sacrificed to the machinations of a still powerful camarilla,[55] it was to have been delivered over again to the bonds of tyranny. But its noble population rose up as one man, and now stands face to face with the armed hordes of its oppressors, defiant unto death. Vienna's cause is Germany's, it is the cause of freedom. With the fall of Vienna, the old despotism will raise its banner still higher; with the victory of Vienna, it will be annihilated. It is our duty, German brethren, not to allow Vienna's freedom to perish, not to abandon Vienna's freedom to the military victories of barbaric hordes. It is the holiest duty of the German governments to hurry to the aid of this hard-pressed sister-city with all their influence; but it is also the holiest duty of the German people at the same time to make any sacrifice to save Vienna, in the interests of its own freedom, in the interests of its self-preservation. Let the German people never be burdened with the shame of callous indifference where all is at stake. We therefore ask you, brethren, to contribute, each according to his own strength, towards saving Vienna from ruin. What we do for Vienna, we do for Germany. Help yourselves! The men you sent to Frankfurt to

54. The second Democratic Congress was held in Berlin from 26 to 30 October 1848. It was dominated by the conflict between the Cologne Workers Society and petty-bourgeois democrats such as d'Ester and Reichenbach over the programme to be adopted. As the bourgeois democrats were in the majority, the proclamation finally adopted and quoted here was not to the satisfaction of Marx and his followers, for the reasons he gives.

55. The Vienna camarilla, like its Berlin counterpart, was a group of reactionary generals and nobles who gathered around the reigning monarch. In the Austrian case, the camarilla was dominated by three men, Windischgrätz, Schwarzenberg, and Thun, and was in practice the ruling body, owing to the feeble-mindedness of Emperor Ferdinand.

establish liberty have rejected the call to help Vienna with scornful laughter. It is now up to you to act. Insist with a powerful and immutable will that your governments submit to the voice of your majority and save the German cause and the cause of freedom in Vienna. Hurry! You are the power, your will is law! Rise up! Rise up! you men of freedom, in all German lands and wherever else the ideas of freedom and humanity inspire noble hearts. Rise up before it is too late! Save Vienna's freedom, save Germany's freedom. The present will admire you, posterity will reward you with immortal renown!

29 October 1848   THE DEMOCRATIC CONGRESS IN BERLIN

This proclamation makes up for its lack of revolutionary energy with a snivelling pathos reminiscent of a sermon, behind which lies concealed the most utter poverty of thought and emotion.

Some examples!

The proclamation expected that with the Vienna and Berlin revolutions of March, 'the unity and freedom of the German people would *with a single stroke* come true'. In other words, the proclamation dreamed of a '*single stroke*' which would make the '*development*' of the German people towards 'unity and freedom' superfluous.

However, immediately afterwards, the absurd 'single stroke' which replaces the development itself turns into a '*development*' which the reaction *opposed*. A mere phrase, a phrase which cancels itself out!

We take no account of the monotonous repetition of the basic theme: Vienna is in danger, therefore Germany's freedom is in danger; help Vienna, and you will help yourself. This idea is never clothed in flesh and blood; instead the *one* phrase is turned around itself so often that it extends into an oration. We shall only remark that the artificial, untrue sentiment of the proclamation always succumbs to this clumsy rhetoric.

It is our duty, German brethren, not to allow Vienna's freedom to perish, not to abandon Vienna's freedom to the military victories of barbaric hordes.

And how are we to make a start on this task?
First of all, by appealing to the sense of duty of the German governments. This is simply incredible!

It is the holiest duty of the German governments to hurry to the aid of this hard-pressed sister-city with all their influence.

Should the Prussian government send Wrangel, Colomb or the prince of Prussia against Auersperg,[56] Jellačić and Windisch-grätz? Was it permissible for the 'Democratic' Congress to adopt for one moment this childish and conservative attitude towards the German governments? Could it indeed for one moment separate the cause and the 'holiest interests' of the German governments from the cause and the interests of 'Croat order and freedom'?[57] The governments will smile in self-satisfaction at this innocent enthusiasm.

And the people?

The people are in general exhorted 'to make any sacrifice to save Vienna'. Well and good! But the 'people' expect specific demands from the Democratic Congress. He who demands everything demands nothing and receives nothing. The *specific* demand, i.e. the *point*, is this:

Insist with a powerful and immutable will that your governments submit to the voice of your majority and save the German cause and the cause of freedom in Vienna. Hurry! You are the power, your will is law! Rise up!

Let us assume that huge popular demonstrations succeed in persuading the governments to take public steps to save Vienna – we would simply be blessed with a second edition of Stein's army order. They want to use the present 'German governments' as 'saviours of freedom'! As if they were not accomplishing their true mission, their 'holiest duty' as the Gabriels of 'constitutional freedom' in executing the orders of the Reich ministry! The 'Democratic Congress' should either have kept quiet about the German governments, or mercilessly revealed their conspiracy with Olmütz[58] and St Petersburg.

Although the proclamation recommends 'haste', and there is in truth no time to lose, its humanistic phraseology snatches it away, beyond the boundaries of Germany, beyond all geographical

56. Karl, Graf von Auersperg was an Austrian general; he commanded the garrison of Vienna, and actively helped to defeat the October insurrection.

57. The phrase refers ironically to the support given by the Croats under Jellačić to the Austrian government in its attacks on the Hungarian and Viennese revolutions.

58. Olmütz, now Olomouc, was the town in Moravia which formed the temporary residence of the Austrian court during the siege of Vienna.

limits, into the cosmopolitan and misty land of the 'noble heart' in general:

Hurry! Rise up! you men of freedom, in all German lands and *wherever else* the ideas of freedom and humanity inspire noble hearts.

We do not doubt that such 'hearts' exist even in Lapland.

In Germany and *wherever else*! By fizzling out into this empty, indeterminate phrase, this 'proclamation' has managed to express its true nature.

It remains unforgivable that the 'Democratic Congress' should have approved such a document. For this 'the present' will not 'admire' it, nor will 'posterity reward it with immortal renown'.

Let us hope that, despite the 'Proclamation of the Democratic Congress', the people will awake from their lethargy and bring to the Viennese the only help they can still bring them at this moment – by defeating the counter-revolution which is on their own doorstep.

THE VICTORY OF THE COUNTER-REVOLUTION IN VIENNA[59]

N.Rh.Z., 7 November 1848

Cologne, 6 November

Croat freedom and order has conquered and celebrated its victory with arson, rape, plunder and indescribable atrocities. *Vienna is in the hands of Windischgrätz, Jellačić and Auersperg.* Whole hecatombs of human sacrifices have been flung into the grave of the aged traitor Latour.[60]

All the dismal prophecies of our Vienna correspondent have been confirmed, and he himself has perhaps already been slaughtered.[61]

We hoped at one time that Vienna's deliverance would come through the aid of the Hungarians, and we are still in the dark about the movements of the Hungarian army.

59. Vienna fell on 31 October 1848 to the combined armies of Windischgrätz, Jellačić and Auersperg.

60. Theodor, Graf Baillet von Latour, an Austrian general, was Minister of War from July to October 1848. In the course of the revolutionary *journée* of 6 October in Vienna he was put to the sword, after which his corpse was suspended from a lamp-post.

61. See p. 165, n. 32.

Treachery of all kinds has prepared the fall of Vienna. The whole of the history of the Reichstag[62] and the city council since 6 October is nothing but a continuous story of treachery. Who was represented in the Reichstag and the city council?

The *bourgeoisie*.

One part of the Vienna citizens' militia openly sided with the camarilla at the beginning of the October revolution. And at the end of the October revolution we find another part of the militia fighting against the proletariat and the Academic Legion,[63] in collusion with the imperial bandits. To whom do these sections of the citizens' militia belong?

To the *bourgeoisie*.

In France, however, the bourgeoisie took its place at the *head* of the counter-revolution only after it had levelled every barrier which stood in the way of its supremacy as a class. In Germany the bourgeoisie finds itself pressed into the *retinue* of absolute monarchy and feudalism before it has even made sure of the basic conditions for its own freedom and supremacy. In France it stepped forth as a despot, and made its own counter-revolution. In Germany it plays the role of a slave, and makes the counter-revolution required by the despots who rule it. In France it conquered in order to humble the people. In Germany it humbles itself in order to prevent the people from conquering. In the whole of history there is no more ignominious example of abjectness than that provided by the *German bourgeoisie*.

Who flocked out of Vienna and left the surveillance of its abandoned riches to the people's generosity, only to slander the people for standing guard during their flight, and to watch them being slaughtered on its return?

The *bourgeoisie*.

Whose innermost secrets are expressed by that thermometer which fell when the people of Vienna showed signs of life and rose in their death-agony? Who speaks in the Runic language of the stock market quotations?

The *bourgeoisie*.

62. The Constituent Assembly of the hereditary lands of the Austrian Empire (i.e. excluding Hungary), which was elected in July 1848. After the Vienna revolution of 6 October the Czechs withdrew from the Reichstag, and the remaining deputies elected a permanent committee which played the part of a revolutionary government, jointly with the city council, from 7 to 31 October.

63. This consisted of university students, and was the most radical of the military organizations engaged in the defence of Vienna at this time.

The 'German National Assembly' and its 'Central Authority' have betrayed Vienna. Whom do they represent?

First and foremost, the *bourgeoisie*.

The victory of 'Croat freedom and order' in Vienna was conditioned by the victory of the 'respectable' republic in Paris. Who was the victor of the June days?

After the victory of the bourgeoisie in Paris, the European counter-revolution could begin its orgies of celebration.

The power of arms was defeated everywhere in the February and March days. Why? Because it represented nothing but the *governments*. After the June days the power of arms has conquered everywhere, because everywhere the *bourgeoisie* is to be found in collusion with the governments, while, on the other side, it has control of the official leadership of the revolutionary movement, and puts into operation all those half-measures which have their natural outcome in an abortion.

The nationalist fanaticism of the Czechs was the most powerful instrument of the Vienna camarilla. *The allies are already at loggerheads.* Our readers will find printed in this issue the protest of the Prague deputation against the contemptuous rudeness with which they were greeted at Olmütz.[64]

This is *the first symptom of the war which will begin between the Slav party with its hero Jellačić and the party of the pure camarilla with its hero Windischgrätz, which is above all feelings of nationality.* The German country people of Austria are for their part as yet unpacified. Their voice will penetrate shrilly through the caterwauling of the Austrian nationalities. And from a third side, as far as Budapest, there can be heard the voice of that friend of the peoples, the tsar; his executioners are waiting in the Danubian principalities for the decisive word.

Finally, the latest decision of the German National Assembly in Frankfurt, by which German Austria is incorporated into the German Reich,[65] ought itself to have led to a gigantic conflict, if

64. This is in fact a reference to the protest of the Czech deputation to Olmütz against the absolutist tone of the manifesto of 16 October entrusting Windischgrätz with dictatorial powers. The conflict Marx speaks of did not take place because the Court gave way, issuing instead the more conciliatory manifesto of 19 October which promised the immediate recall of the Reichstag.

65. On 27 October the Frankfurt Assembly adopted the 'greater German' solution of the German problem by including German Austria into the German Reich, but excluding the rest of Austria, and thereby calling for the

the German Central Authority and the German National Assembly did not find that their mission was accomplished simply by appearing on the stage, to be hissed off by the European public. Despite their pious resignation, the struggle in Austria will take on dimensions more colossal than any struggle world history has yet seen.

What has just been played in Vienna is the second act of a drama. Its first act was played in Paris under the title '*The June Days*'. In Paris the Mobile Guard, in Vienna the Croats – in both cases the *lazzaroni*, the armed and bought lumpenproletariat, fighting against the working and thinking proletariat. We shall soon experience the third act in Berlin.

If we assume that the counter-revolution lives throughout Europe through *weapons*, it will die throughout Europe through *money*. The fate that will annul the victory of the counter-revolution will be general European *bankruptcy*, the *bankruptcy of the state*. The points of bayonets will break like brittle firewood on the points of economics.

But the course of development will not wait for the payment-day of that promissory note drawn by the European states on European society. The devastating counter-blow to the June defeat will be struck in Paris. With the victory of the 'red republic' in Paris, the *armies* will be vomited forth from the *inside* of the other countries[66] and over the boundaries, and the *real power* of the contending parties will reveal itself in a pure form. Then we shall remember June and October, and we too shall call out: '*Vae victis!*'

The pointless massacres since the June and October days, the tedious sacrificial feast since February and March, the cannibalism of the counter-revolution itself, all these things will convince the peoples that there is only one way of *shortening*, simplifying and concentrating the murderous death-pangs of the old society, the bloody birth-pangs of the new, only *one way – revolutionary terrorism*.

---

dissolution of the Habsburg monarchy. (Article 3 of the Constitution: 'If a German land is under the same sovereign as a non-German land, the relations between the two lands can only be based on the principles of a personal union.')

66. i.e. the Holy Alliance countries.

THE COUNTER-REVOLUTION IN BERLIN

I *N.Rh.Z.*, 12 November 1848

Cologne, 11 November

The *Pfuel ministry* was a 'misunderstanding'; its real meaning is the *Brandenburg ministry*.[67] The Pfuel ministry was an *announcement of the content*, the Brandenburg ministry *is* the content.

Brandenburg in the Assembly and the Assembly in Brandenburg.[68]

SO RUNS THE EPITAPH OF THE HOUSE OF BRANDENBURG!

Emperor Charles V was admired because he arranged his funeral while he was still alive.[69] But to carve a bad joke on your own gravestone! That is to go one better than Charles V, even including his Criminal Court Decrees.[70]

Brandenburg in the Assembly and the Assembly in Brandenburg!

Once upon a time a king of Prussia appeared in the Assembly. He was not the real Brandenburg. The Marquess of Brandenburg,[71] who appeared in the Assembly the day before yesterday, was the real king of Prussia.

The guard-room in the Assembly, the Assembly in the guard-room! That is to say: *Brandenburg in the Assembly, the Assembly in Brandenburg!*

Or will the *Assembly in Brandenburg* – as is well-known, Berlin lies in the province of Brandenburg – attain mastery over . . . the

67. The Pfuel ministry expressed a 'misunderstanding' between the Crown and the people about the significance and extent of the counter-revolution; the Brandenburg ministry cleared up this misunderstanding by expressing the true meaning of the counter-revolution.

Friedrich, Graf von Brandenburg was a Prussian general and the natural son of Frederick William II. He was a military man without previous political experience or ambitions. On 2 November 1848 the king appointed Brandenburg as Prime Minister and Baron Manteuffel as Minister of the Interior; on 9 November the Prussian National Assembly was prorogued and its place of meeting changed from Berlin to the small provincial town of Brandenburg.

68. A reference to Frederick William IV's phrase about the Brandenburg ministry: 'Either Brandenburg in the Chamber or the Chamber in Brandenburg.'

69. According to the legend, Emperor Charles V is said to have made the arrangements for his own funeral shortly before his death.

70. The Constitutio Criminalis Carolina, accepted in 1532 by the Diet of Regensburg. It was notorious for the exceptionally severe punishments it imposed.

71. Count (not Marquess) Brandenburg announced the move from Berlin to Brandenburg himself when he appeared in the Assembly on 9 November.

Brandenburg in the Assembly? Will Brandenburg seek protection in the Assembly just as Capet once did in another Assembly?[72]

BRANDENBURG IN THE ASSEMBLY AND THE ASSEMBLY IN BRANDENBURG is an ambiguous phrase, an equivocal phrase, heavy with destiny.

Clearly, the people find it infinitely easier to deal with *kings* than with *legislative assemblies*. History possesses a whole catalogue of vain popular uprisings against national assemblies. It offers only two great exceptions. The English people, in the person of Cromwell, dispersed the Long Parliament. The French people, in the person of Bonaparte, dispersed the Council of the Five Hundred. But the Long Parliament had already long been a *rump*, the Council of the Five Hundred had long been a *corpse*.

Have *kings* been more fortunate than peoples in *coups directed against legislative assemblies*?

Charles I, James II, Louis XVI and Charles X are not very promising predecessors.

But there are better precedents in Spain and Italy. And most recently in Vienna?

Nevertheless, it should not be forgotten that the parliament sitting in Vienna was a *congress of peoples*,[73] and that the *representatives of the Slav peoples*, with the exception of the Poles, joined the imperial camp with fifes playing and drums beating.

The war of the Vienna camarilla with the Reichstag was at the same time the war of the Slav Reichstag with the German Reichstag. In the Berlin Assembly, on the other hand, there is no Slav schism, only a *slave* schism, and slaves are not a party. They are at most the camp-followers of a party. The withdrawal of the Berlin Right[74] does not strengthen the enemy camp, it infects it rather with a fatal weakness – *treachery*.

In Austria, the Slav party *conquered alongside* the camarilla; it will now *fight against* the camarilla for the spoils of victory. If the Berlin camarilla wins, it will not have to share the victory with the Right and enforce it against the Right; it will give the Right a *tip* – and then *kick it out*.

72. Louis XVI ('Capet') took refuge from the wrath of the people of Paris in the French National Assembly on 10 August 1792.

73. The Austrian Reichstag of 1848 represented most of the Austrian nationalities, and could therefore be described in this way.

74. After the proclamation of 9 November 1848 on the prorogation and transfer of the Assembly, 96 deputies of the Right obediently left the building; the other 263 deputies voted to continue sitting in Berlin, and did so.

The Prussian Crown is *in the right* in so far as it opposes itself to the Assembly as an *absolute Crown*. But the Assembly is in the wrong because it does not oppose itself to the Crown as an *absolute Assembly*. It ought to have had the ministers arrested for *high treason*, as betrayers of the *sovereignty of the people*. It ought to have *outlawed and proscribed* every official who obeyed commands other than its own.

Yet it may well be that the *political* weakness displayed by the National Assembly in *Berlin* will turn into *civil* strength in the *provinces*.

The bourgeoisie would have liked to transform the *feudal kingdom* into a *bourgeois kingdom* in the *amicable* way. After it had torn away from the feudal party the coats-of-arms and titles which offended its bourgeois pride, as well as the revenues pertaining to feudal property and offensive to the bourgeois mode of appropriation, the bourgeoisie would only too willingly have joined the feudal party and enslaved the people in alliance with it. But the old bureaucracy refuses to sink to the level of servant of a bourgeoisie it previously ruled as a despotic schoolmaster. The feudal party refuses to make a bonfire of its honours and interests on the altar of the bourgeoisie. And, finally, the Crown sees its true, indigenous social foundation in the elements of the old feudal society, whose supreme outgrowth it is, whereas it considers the bourgeoisie to be an alien, artificial soil, in which it can only achieve a stunted growth.

The bourgeoisie would transform the intoxicating '*grace of God*' into a sobering *legal title*, the rule of blue blood into the rule of white paper, the royal sun into a bourgeois astral lamp.

The monarchy therefore refused to let the bourgeoisie mislead it. It replied to the bourgeois semi-revolution with a complete counter-revolution. It threw the bourgeoisie back into the *arms of the revolution, of the people*, by making the call: 'Brandenburg in the Assembly and the Assembly in Brandenburg.'

While admitting that we do not expect an appropriate answer to the situation from the bourgeoisie, we should on the other side not omit to remark that the Crown too, in its coup against the National Assembly, had recourse to hypocritical inconsistency, and hid behind apparent constitutionalism at the very moment when it was endeavouring to slough off this burdensome semblance of reality.

It is the German Central Authority which gave the order for

Brandenburg's coup d'état (on Brandenburg's instructions). *The Guards regiments entered Berlin at the command of the Central Authority.* The Berlin counter-revolution is taking place at the orders of the German Central Authority.[75] Brandenburg gave Frankfurt the order to give him this order. Frankfurt denies its own sovereignty in the act of asserting it. Bassermann naturally seized the opportunity of playing the servant as master.[76] But he has the satisfaction of seeing that the master, for his part, is playing the servant.

Whatever the immediate outcome of the struggle in Berlin, the *dilemma* is posed – *king* or *people* – and the people will win, with the slogan 'Brandenburg in the Assembly and the Assembly in Brandenburg'.

We may well yet have a rough schooling to go through, but this will be preparatory training for – THE REVOLUTION AS A WHOLE.

II *N.Rh.Z.*, 12 November 1848, *second edition*
Cologne, 11 November

The *European revolution* is describing a *circular course*. It began in Italy, it assumed a European character in Paris, Vienna felt the first impact of the February revolution, the Berlin revolution was in its turn influenced by the Vienna revolution. It was in Italy – in Naples – that the European counter-revolution struck its first blow, in Paris – the June days – that it assumed a European character, in Vienna that the first impact of the June counter-revolution was felt, and in Berlin that the counter-revolution was completed and compromised. *But it is from Paris that the crowing of the Gallic cock will once more awaken Europe.*[77]

In Berlin the counter-revolution has compromised itself. Everything compromises itself in Berlin, even the counter-revolution.

In Naples, the counter-revolution was the lumpenproletariat allied with the monarchy, against the bourgeoisie.

75. There is no evidence that the Central Authority in Frankfurt gave such an order. However the removal of the Prussian National Assembly was seen by some of Frederick William's advisers as the precondition for an alliance between the king and Frankfurt.

76. On 7 November Bassermann was sent to Berlin by the Reich ministry to mediate between the king and the Assembly.

77. Heine wrote of the French revolution of 1830: 'The Gallic cock has crowed a second time, and now it is daybreak even in Germany.' H. Heine, *Sämmtliche Werke*, vol. 14, Hamburg, 1867–8.

In Paris, it was the greatest historical battle which has ever taken place. The bourgeoisie, allied with the lumpenproletariat, against the working class.

In Vienna, it was a whole swarm of nationalities which imagined the counter-revolution would bring emancipation, as well as secret treachery by the bourgeoisie against the workers and the Academic Legion. In addition to this, conflict within the citizens' militia itself, and finally, the attack from the people which gave the Court an excuse for its own attack.

In Berlin, *nothing of the kind*. The bourgeoisie and the people on one side; the non-commissioned officers on the other.

Wrangel and Brandenburg, two men without heads, without hearts, without a political tendency, with nothing but the pure military moustache – that is the opposition to this querulous, indecisive, too-clever-by-half National Assembly.

The will! – whether it be the will of the donkey, the ox, or the military moustache – this is all that is needed to oppose the will-less grumblers of the March revolution. And the Prussian court, which has no more will than the National Assembly, seeks out the two most stupid men in the kingdom and says to these lions: *represent the will*. Even Pfuel had a few atoms of grey matter. But in face of *absolute stupidity*, the argumentative grumblers who are defending the achievements of March must shrink back.

'The Gods themselves fight in vain against stupidity',[78] exclaims the afflicted National Assembly.

And these Wrangels, these Brandenburgs, these blockheaded numbskulls, who are able to *will* because they lack a will of their own, because they will what they are *ordered* to will, who are too stupid to diverge from orders given to them with trembling voice and quivering lips, these people too are *compromising* themselves in so far as they omit to engage in *skull-bashing*, the sole activity these *bulldozers* are capable of.

Wrangel can do no more than confess that he knows of only one National Assembly, a National Assembly which obeys orders. Brandenburg takes lessons in parliamentary procedure, and after enraging the Chamber with his blunt and repulsive sergeant-major's language, allows 'the tyrant to be tyrannized by others' and obeys the order of the National Assembly, by most humbly *requesting* the right to speak, which he had only shortly before

78. Schiller, *The Maid of Orleans*, III, vi.

wanted to *take*. 'I had rather be a tick in a sheep, than such a valiant ignorance.'[79]

The calm attitude of Berlin *delights* us; in this way the ideals of the Prussian officer corps are being destroyed.

But what of the National Assembly? Why does it not issue an excommunication, why does it not declare Wrangel to be outside the law, why does no deputy step into the midst of Wrangel's bayonets, declare the illegality of the position, and harangue the soldiery?

The Berlin National Assembly should look through the *Moniteur*, the *Moniteur* of 1789 to 1795.[80]

And what shall *we* do on this occasion?

We shall refuse to pay taxes. A Wrangel, a Brandenburg comprehends – for these beings are learning Arabic from the Hyghlans[81] – that he wears a sword and receives a uniform and his pay. He does *not* understand, however, where sword, uniform and pay come from.

There is now only one way left to defeat the monarchy, at least until the epoch of the anti-June revolution in Paris, which will take place in December.[82]

The monarchy is defying the bourgeoisie as well as the people. Let us therefore defeat it in the bourgeois manner.

How does one defeat a monarchy in a bourgeois manner?

By starving it out.

And how does one starve it out?

By refusing to pay the taxes.

Keep this point well in mind! All the princes of Prussia, the Brandenburgs, the Wrangels, produce no *soldiers' rations*. You yourselves produce the rations.

79. Shakespeare, *Troilus and Cressida*, III, iii.

80. *Le Moniteur Universel*, a daily paper, first appeared in Paris in 1789 and published the proceedings and decrees of the revolutionary institutions. It later became, as from 1799, the official organ of the French government.

81. On 3 November the *Kölnische Zeitung* printed an account of an imaginary African tribe called the 'Hyghlans', which contained the words, 'Many of them are learning the Arabian language.'

82. A reference to the election of the French President, which was to take place on 10 December 1848.

III *N.Rh.Z.*, 14 November 1848

Cologne, 13 November

Just as the French National Assembly once found its official meeting-place locked, and had to continue its sittings in an indoor tennis-court, so the Prussian National Assembly must meet in the Berlin shooting-gallery.[83]

The decision taken there, as our Berlin correspondent will report in this morning's special edition, is that *Brandenburg has committed high treason*. The *Kölnische Zeitung* has not reported this.

In the meantime we have just received a letter from a *member of the National Assembly*, containing these words:

> *The National Assembly has unanimously declared (with 242 members present) that Brandenburg has committed high treason by this measure (the dissolution of the militia), and anyone who cooperates actively or passively in the execution of this measure must be considered as a traitor.*[84]

Dumont's credibility is well known.

Now that the National Assembly has declared Brandenburg to be a traitor, the **obligations to pay taxes automatically ceases.** *No taxes are owed to a government of traitors.* Tomorrow we shall explain to our readers in detail how *in England, the oldest constitutional country*, they deal with similar confrontations by using the weapon of tax-refusal.[85] In any case, the treacherous government has itself shown the people the right way by immediately refusing the National Assembly its attendance allowances, and thereby seeking to starve it out.

The above-mentioned deputy also informs us that **the militia will not surrender its weapons.**

The struggle therefore appears to be unavoidable, and it is **the duty of the Rhineland to hurry to the aid of the Berlin National Assembly with men and weapons.**

83. From 11 to 13 November 1848 the Prussian National Assembly met in a shooting-gallery, having been driven from their normal meeting-place on 10 November.

84. The resolution of 11 November, adopted at the ninety-eighth sitting of the National Assembly.

85. The explanation was given in the *Neue Rheinische Zeitung* of 15 November; see also pp. 261–3.

NO MORE TAXES!!!

N.Rh.Z., 17 November 1848 (*Extraordinary Supplement*)

Cologne, 16 November

No newspapers from Berlin have come out, with the exeption of the *Preussischer Staats-Zeitung*, the *Vossische Zeitung*[86] and the *Neue Preussische Zeitung*.[87]

The militia has been disarmed in the district where the state officials live, but not elsewhere. Their battalion is the one which massacred the engineering workers on 31 October.[88] Its disarming is thus in fact a victory for the people's cause.

The National Assembly was once again driven out of its meeting-place, in this case the city hall. It then assembled in the Mielenz Hotel and finally, with all its 226 votes, adopted the following resolution on tax-refusal:

The Brandenburg ministry is not entitled to dispose of the state's money and to raise taxes as long as the National Assembly is unable freely to continue its sittings in Berlin. This resolution enters into force as from 17 November.

National Assembly of 15 November 1848.

All taxes are therefore abolished as from today! The payment of taxes is high treason, the refusal to pay taxes is the first duty of the citizen!

THE FRANKFURT ASSEMBLY

N.Rh.Z., 23 November 1848

Cologne, 22 November

The Frankfurt parliament has annulled the resolution of the Berlin Assembly on tax-refusal on the ground that it is illegal. In doing this it has declared for Brandenburg, for Wrangel, for all

86. A Berlin newspaper, which adopted a moderate liberal attitude in the 1840s.

87. An explicitly reactionary newspaper founded in Berlin in June 1848 by the camarilla and the junkers associated with it (including Bismarck). More commonly known as the *Kreuzzeitung*.

88. On 31 October 1848 a demonstration took place in Berlin, sparked off by the Assembly's rejection of the proposal that the Prussian government be asked to aid Vienna with money and soldiers. In its course the 8th battalion of the militia shot at an unarmed crowd of engineering workers.

that is Prussian. Frankfurt has moved to Berlin, Berlin has moved to Frankfurt. The German parliament is in Berlin, the Prussian parliament is in Frankfurt. The Prussian parliament has become a German parliament, the German parliament has become a Brandenburg-Prussian parliament. Prussia was supposed to merge into Germany,[89] and now the German parliament in Frankfurt wants Germany to merge into Prussia.

The German parliament! How could one speak of a German parliament after the terrible events in Berlin and Vienna? No one thought any longer of the life of the noble Gagern[90] after the death of Robert Blum.[91] No one thought any longer of a Schmerling[92] after the Brandenburg-Manteuffel ministry. The professorial gentlemen who 'made history' for their private satisfaction had to permit the bombardment of Vienna, the murder of Robert Blum, and the barbarisms of Windischgrätz. The gentlemen who were so concerned with the history of German civilization left the practical application of civilization to Jellačić and his Croats. Whilst the professors made the theory of history, history itself went on its own stormy way and worried very little about the history of the professors.

This resolution has destroyed the Frankfurt parliament. It has thrown it into the arms of the traitor Brandenburg. The Frankfurt parliament has made itself guilty of high treason, and it must be judged. When a whole people rises up, in order to protest against an act of royal despotism, when this protest takes the entirely legal form of a refusal to pay taxes, and an assembly of professors – without any authority – declares this refusal of taxes, this uprising of the whole people, to be illegal, then this assembly is outside all the laws, it is an assembly of traitors.

It is the duty of all those members of the Frankfurt Assembly

89. In the royal manifesto of 21 March 1848 Frederick William IV stated: 'Prussia is henceforth merged into Germany.'

90. Heinrich von Gagern was one of the leading figures of south German liberalism, in 1848 a Right-Centre deputy, President of the Frankfurt National Assembly, and from December 1848 to March 1849 President of the Reich ministry.

91. Robert Blum was a journalist from Leipzig and the leader of the Left in the Frankfurt Assembly. He took part in the Vienna revolution of October 1848 and was afterwards court-martialled and shot.

92. Anton, Ritter von Schmerling was an Austrian liberal, in 1848 a member of the Frankfurt Assembly (Right Centre), and Minister of the Interior from July to September 1848, President and Foreign Minister from September to December 1848, in the Reich ministry.

who voted against the resolution to withdraw from this 'deceased Federal Diet'. It is the duty of all democrats to elect these 'Prussians' who have resigned from Frankfurt as members of the German National Assembly in Berlin, as representatives of the departed 'Germans'. The National Assembly in Berlin is not a 'part': it is the whole, for it is capable of making decisions. The Brandenburgian Assembly in Frankfurt will however become a 'part'; for certainly the 150 members who will have to withdraw will be followed by others who have no wish to constitute a Frankfurt Federal Diet. The Frankfurt parliament! It fears a red republic and decrees a *red monarchy*! We do not want a *red* monarchy, we do not want the purple-coloured Crown of Austria to be placed over Prussia, and we therefore declare that the German parliament is guilty of high treason. Yet even this would be to rate it too highly, by ascribing to it a political importance it lost long ago. The severest judgement has already been passed on the Frankfurt Assembly: people have disregarded its resolutions and ... forgotten it.

THE BOURGEOISIE AND THE COUNTER-REVOLUTION

I *N.Rh.Z.*, 10 December 1848

Cologne, 9 December

We have never concealed the fact that we stand on a *revolutionary*, not on a *legal foundation*. Now the government, for its part, has abandoned the hypocrisy of the legal foundation. It has placed itself on the revolutionary foundation, for the counter-revolutionary foundation is also revolutionary.

Paragraph 6 of the law of 6 April 1848[93] lays down:

It is the responsibility of the future representatives of the people in all cases to agree on the laws and on the budget, and to exercise the right to grant supply.

In paragraph 13 of the law of 8 April 1848[94] there is the following passage:

93. 'An Ordinance on Certain Foundations of the Future Prussian Constitution' issued by the Camphausen ministry on 6 April 1848.
94. 'The Electoral Law for the Assembly to be Called to Agree with the King on the Prussian State Constitution', was passed by the second United Diet on 8 April 1848.

The Assembly which meets together on the basis of the present law is authorized to *establish the future constitution of the state* by agreement with the Crown, and to exercise the existing powers of the estates, namely in relation to the grant of supply, for the duration of its session.

The government chases the *Vereinbarungsversammlung* out of existence, dictates a so-called constitution[95] to the country on its own authority, and itself grants the taxes denied to it by the representatives of the people.

The Prussian government has put a sensational end to the Camphausen saga, which was a kind of solemn right-wing saga of Job.[96] In revenge, the inventor of this epic tale, the great Camphausen, calmly continues to sit in Frankfurt as the envoy of that same Prussian government, and continues to intrigue with the Bassermanns in the service of that same Prussian government. This Camphausen, who invented the theory of *Vereinbarung* in order to rescue the legal foundation, i.e. in order to swindle the revolution of the honours owing to it, simultaneously invented the mines which would later explode the legal foundation and the theory of *Vereinbarung* as well.

This man gave us the *indirect* elections which produced an Assembly to which the government could thunder 'too late' at the moment of its momentary resistance. He brought back the prince of Prussia, the head of the counter-revolution, and sank so low as to transform the prince of Prussia's flight into an educational trip, by issuing an official lie.[97] He kept the old Prussian legislation on political crimes in force and the old courts in operation. Under Camphausen the old bureaucracy and the old army won a breathing-space in which to recover from their terror and completely reconstitute themselves. All the chief men of the *ancien régime* remained at their posts undisturbed. The camarilla waged war in Posen while Camphausen himself was waging war in Denmark. The purpose of the Danish war was to provide a diversion for the surplus patriotic energy of the youth of Germany, which was subjected to appropriate disciplinary measures

95. On 5 December 1848 the National Assembly was dissolved and a new constitution was issued setting up two legislative chambers and giving the king an absolute right of veto on all laws.

96. A reference to the satirical poem by Karl Arnold Kortum, *Die Jobsiade. Ein komisches Heldengedicht.* (*The saga of Job. A comical heroic poem.*)

97. In Camphausen's speech of 6 June 1848 to the National Assembly Prince William of Prussia's flight to England in March was presented as an educational trip which had already been arranged before the revolution.

by the police after its return. The war was also supposed to provide General Wrangel and his celebrated Guards regiments with a certain popularity, and to rehabilitate the Prussian soldiery in general. As soon as this aim had been fulfilled, the pseudo-conflict had to be smothered at any cost. This was the reason for the shameful armistice which Camphausen himself brought the German National Assembly to accept.[98] The result of the Danish war was the appointment of the 'Supreme Commander of both Marks',[99] and the return to Berlin of the Guards regiments driven out in March.

And then there is the war which the Potsdam camarilla waged in Posen under Camphausen's auspices!

The war in Posen was more than a war against the Prussian revolution. It spelled the fall of Vienna, the fall of Italy, the defeat of the June heroes. It was the first decisive triumph gained over the European revolution by the Russian tsar. And all this occurred under the auspices of the great Camphausen, 'the thinking friend of history', the knight of the great debate, the hero of mediation.

The counter-revolution had thus taken control of all important positions under Camphausen's ministry and through his agency. It had prepared its army for battle, while the *Vereinbarungsversammlung* debated. Under Hansemann-Pinto,[1] the Minister of the Deed, the old police force was newly accoutred, and the bourgeoisie carried on a war against the people as bitter as it was petty. Under Brandenburg the conclusion was drawn from these premises. All that was needed now was – a military moustache and a sabre instead of a head.

When Camphausen resigned, we made this statement: 'He sowed reaction in the interests of the big bourgeoisie, but he will reap it in the interests of the aristocracy and absolutism.[12]

We do not doubt that his excellency the Prussian envoy Camp-

98. The Armistice of Malmö between Prussia and Denmark, concluded on 26 August, provided for the setting up of a mixed Prussian-Danish administrative commission in Schleswig-Holstein, and thus meant the abandonment of the German Provisional Government for the Duchies at Kiel. The Frankfurt Assembly ratified the decision on 16 September, thus reversing its own vote of 4 September.

99. See p. 167, n. 44.

1. An ironical allusion to the similarity between Hansemann's financial proposals and those of the eighteenth-century Dutch financier Pinto, who saw speculation on the stock-exchange as a means of speeding up the circulation of money.

2. See the article 'The Fall of the Camphausen Ministry', p. 129.

hausen counts himself at this moment as one of the feudal lords, and will have reconciled himself with his 'misunderstanding' in the most peaceful way.

However, no mistake should be made here: one should not ascribe any world-historical initiative to a Camphausen or a Hansemann; these are men of very subordinate importance. They were nothing but the instruments of a class. Their language and activities were merely the official echo of the class which had pushed them into the foreground. They were simply the big bourgeoisie – in the foreground.

It was the representatives of this class who formed the *liberal opposition* at the United Diet, that sweetly sleeping institution momentarily reawakened by Camphausen.

The gentlemen of this liberal opposition have been reproached with being untrue to their principles after the March revolution. This is an error.

The big landowners and capitalists, in other words the money-bags, who alone were represented in the United Diet, had grown in wealth and in general culture. The old divisions between the estates of the realm had lost their material foundation with the development of bourgeois society in Prussia, i.e. with the development of industry, trade and agriculture, and the nobility itself had become fundamentally bourgeoisified. Instead of dealing in devotion, love and piety, it now dealt above all in sugar beet, liquor and wool. Its chosen jousting-ground had become the wool market. Against these forces stood the absolutist state, whose old social foundation had been conjured away from beneath its feet by the course of historical development; it had become a fetter and a hindrance for the new bourgeois society, with its changed mode of production and its changed needs. The bourgeoisie had to lay claim to a share in political power, if only to assert its purely material interests. It alone was capable of bringing its commercial and industrial interests to bear through legislation. It had to take the administration of these its 'holiest interests' out of the hands of an outdated, ignorant and arrogant bureaucracy. It had to assert its control of the resources of the state, resources which it considered to be its own creation. It was also ambitious enough to wish to conquer a political position commensurate with its social position, once it had deprived the bureaucracy of the monopoly of so-called culture, and had become conscious of the extent of its superiority over the bureaucracy in real understanding of the requirements of bourgeois society. In order to attain its goal, it had to allow free discussion of its own interests and views, and of the actions of the government. It called this 'the right of freedom of the press'. It had to be able to *associate* freely. This was called 'the right of freedom of association'. *Religious freedom* and so on had equally to be demanded, as the necessary consequence of *free competition*. And before March 1848 the Prussian bourgeoisie was firmly set on the road to the realization of all its wishes.

The Prussian state was in a condition of financial need. Its credit had dried up. This was the secret of the convocation of the United Diet. It is true that the government struggled against its fate, and that the 'United' was unceremoniously dismissed. But the shortage of money and the absence of credit would infallibly have thrown the government ever further into the arms of the bourgeoisie. Like feudal barons, kings by the grace of God have exchanged their privileges for hard cash from time immemorial. The emancipation of the serfs was the first, the constitutional monarchy the second great act of this world-historical bargain in all the Christian-Germanic states. 'Money has no master', but masters cease to be masters once their money has run out.

The liberal opposition in the United Diet was therefore nothing other than the opposition of the bourgeoisie to a form of government which no longer corresponded to its interests and needs. In order to oppose the Court, they had to pay court to the people.

Perhaps they really imagined that their opposition was *on behalf of* the people.

They could at any rate only claim from the government the rights and freedoms they were striving to attain for themselves under the rubric of the *rights of the people* and the *freedom of the people*.

This opposition was well on the way to success, as we have said, when the *storm of February* burst forth.

II *N.Rh.Z.*, 15 December 1848

Cologne, 11 December

After the March deluge – a deluge in miniature – had subsided, it left behind no monsters on the surface of the Berlin earth, no revolutionary colossi, but rather creatures of the old style, thick-set bourgeois shapes: the liberals of the United Diet, the representatives of the class-conscious Prussian bourgeoisie. The provinces which have the most developed bourgeoisie, the Rhineland and Silesia, provided the greater part of the new ministries. Behind them a whole train of Rhenish lawyers. In the same measure as the bourgeoisie was forced into the background by the feudal party, the Rhineland and Silesia made room in the ministries for the old Prussian provinces. The Brandenburg ministry only retains a connection with the Rhineland through a Tory from Elberfeld. Hansemann and von der Heydt![3] The whole difference between March and December 1848 is contained for the Prussian bourgeoisie in these two names.

The Prussian bourgeoisie was thrown to the highest position in the state, not as it would have liked, through a *peaceful transaction with the Crown*, but through a *revolution*. Against the Crown it had to represent not its own interests but the people's interests, i.e. it had to act against itself, for a *popular movement* had cleared the way for it. However, in the bourgeoisie's eyes the Crown was only the divine umbrella behind which its own profane interests were concealed. The inviolability of *its own* interests and the corresponding political forms had the following meaning when translated into constitutional language: the inviolability of the Crown. Hence the enthusiasm of the German and in particular the Prussian bourgeoisie for *constitutional monarchy*. If therefore the February revolution and its German after-effects were welcomed by the Prussian bourgeoisie because the direction of the state was thereby thrown into its hands, the revolution was also and just as much a disappointment, because it attached to bourgeois rule conditions the bourgeoisie was both unwilling and unable to fulfil.

The bourgeoisie had not moved a muscle. It had allowed the people to fight on its behalf. The power handed over to it was not therefore the power of a general who has defeated his opponents, but rather that of a committee of public safety to which the victorious people has entrusted the maintenance of its own interests.

Camphausen was always aware of the inconveniences involved in this position; the whole weakness of his ministry arose from this awareness and the circumstances which conditioned it. A kind of blush of shame therefore transfigured even the most shameless acts of Camphausen's government. Frank shamelessness and

3. August, Freiherr von der Heydt, a banker from Elberfeld in the Rhineland, was appointed Minister of Trade in the Brandenburg ministry (December 1848).

impertinence were the privilege of the Hansemann government. The tint of red constitutes the only difference between these two painters.

The Prussian March revolution must not be confused either with the English revolution of 1648 or with the French revolution of 1789.

In 1648 the bourgeoisie was in alliance with the modern nobility against the monarchy, the feudal nobility and the established church.

In 1789 the bourgeoisie was in alliance with the people against the monarchy, the nobility and the established church.

The revolution of 1789 was (at least in Europe) only prefigured by the revolution of 1648, which in turn was only prefigured by the rising of the Netherlands against Spain.[4] Both revolutions were approximately a century in advance of their predecessors, not only in time but also in content.

In both revolutions, the bourgeoisie was the class which was *genuinely* to be found at the head of the movement. The proletariat, and the other sections of the town population which did not form a part of the bourgeoisie, either had as yet no interests separate from those of the bourgeoisie, or they did not yet form independently developed classes or groups within classes. Therefore, where they stood in opposition to the bourgeoisie, as for example in 1793 and 1794 in France, they were in fact fighting for the implementation of the interests of the bourgeoisie, although not *in the manner* of the bourgeoisie. The *whole of the French terror* was nothing other than a *plebeian manner* of dealing with the *enemies of the bourgeoisie*, with absolutism, feudalism and parochialism.

The revolutions of 1648 and 1789 were not *English* and *French* revolutions; they were revolutions of a *European* pattern. They were not the victory of a *particular* class of society over the *old political order*; they were the *proclamation of the political order for the new European society*. In these revolutions the bourgeoisie gained the victory; but the *victory of the bourgeoisie* was at that time the *victory of a new social order*, the victory of bourgeois property over feudal property, of nationality over provincialism, of competition over the guild, of the partition of estates over primogeniture, of the owner's mastery of the land over the land's mastery of its owner, of enlightenment over superstition, of the family over the family name, of industry over heroic laziness, of

4. The Dutch war of liberation began in 1572.

civil law over privileges of medieval origin. The revolution of 1648 was the victory of the seventeenth century over the sixteenth century, the revolution of 1789 was the victory of the eighteenth century over the seventeenth century. Still more than expressing the needs of the parts of the world in which they took place, England and France, these revolutions expressed the needs of the whole world, as it existed then.

Nothing of this is to be found in the *Prussian March revolution*. The February revolution had *done away with* the constitutional monarchy in reality and the rule of the bourgeoisie in the mind. The purpose of the Prussian March revolution was to *establish* the constitutional monarchy in the mind and the rule of the bourgeoisie in reality. Far from being a *European revolution* it was merely the stunted echo, in a backward country, of a European revolution. Instead of being in advance of its own age it was behind it by more than half a century. It was *secondary* from the very beginning, but, as is well known, secondary diseases are more difficult to cure, and, at the same time, ravage the body more, than original ones. Here it was not a matter of setting up a new social order, but of the rebirth in Berlin of the society which had expired in Paris. The Prussian March revolution was not even *national* and *German*; it was from its inception *provincial* and *Prussian*. All kinds of provincial uprisings – e.g. those in Vienna, Kassel and Munich – swept along beside it and contested its position as the main German revolution.

Whereas 1648 and 1789 had the infinite self-confidence that springs from standing at the summit of creativity, it was Berlin's ambition in 1848 to form an anachronism. Its light was like the light of those stars which first reaches the earth when the bodies which radiated it have been extinct for a hundred thousand years. The Prussian March revolution was such a star for Europe – only on a small scale, just as it was everything on a small scale. Its light was light from the corpse of a society long since putrefied.

The German bourgeoisie had developed so sluggishly, so pusillanimously and so slowly, that it saw itself threateningly confronted by the proletariat, and all those sections of the urban population related to the proletariat in interests and ideas, at the very moment of its own threatening confrontation with feudalism and absolutism. And as well as having this class *behind* it, it saw *in front of* it the enmity of all Europe. The Prussian bourgeoisie was not, like the French bourgeoisie of 1789, the class which represented the *whole* of modern society in face of the representatives of the old society, the monarchy and the nobility. It had sunk to the level of a type of *estate*, as clearly marked off from the people as from the Crown, happy to oppose either, irresolute against each of its opponents, taken individually, because it always saw the other one in front of it or to the rear; inclined from the outset to treachery against the people and compromise with the crowned representative of the old society, because it itself already belonged to the old society; representing not the interests of a new society against an old but the renewal of its own interests within an obsolete society; at the steering-wheel of the revolution, not because the people stood behind it but because the people pushed it forward; at the head of the movement, not because it represented the initiative of a new social epoch, but only because it represented the malice of an old; a stratum of the old state which had not been able to break through to the earth's surface but had been thrown up by an earthquake; without faith in itself, without faith in the people, grumbling at those above, trembling before those below, egoistic in both directions and conscious of its egoism, revolutionary in relation to the conservatives and conservative in relation to the revolutionaries, mistrustful of its own slogans, which were phrases instead of ideas, intimidated by the storm of world revolution yet exploiting it; with no energy in any respect, plagiaristic in all respects; common because it lacked originality, original in its commonness; making a bargaining-counter of its own wishes, without initiative, without faith in itself, without faith in the people, without a world-historical function; an accursed old man, who found himself condemned to lead and mislead the first youthful impulses of a robust people in his own senile interests – sans teeth, sans eyes, sans taste, sans everything – this was the nature of the *Prussian bourgeoisie* which found itself at the helm of the Prussian state after the March revolution.

III *N.Rh.Z.*, 16 December 1848

Cologne, 15 December

The theory of *Vereinbarung*, which the bourgeoisie, having entered the government in the shape of the Camphausen ministry, immediately proclaimed as the 'broadest' basis of the Prussian *contrat social*, was by no means an empty theory; it had grown on the tree of 'golden' life.

The March revolution by no means subjected the sovereign by the grace of God to the sovereign people. It only compelled the Crown, the absolutist state, to come to terms with the bourgeoisie, to *make an agreement* [*sich vereinbaren*] with its old rival.

The Crown would sacrifice the nobility to the bourgeoisie, the bourgeoisie would sacrifice the people to the Crown. On this condition, the monarchy would become bourgeois and the bourgeoisie would become royal.

After March there existed only these two powers. They did each other mutual service as lightning conductors of the revolution. All this naturally happened on the '*broadest democratic basis*'.

That was the *secret of the theory of Vereinbarung*.

The dealers in oil and wool[5] who formed the first ministry after the March revolution fancied themselves in their role, which was to hide the compromised Crown beneath their plebeian wings. They revelled in the luxury of being presentable at Court, and, reluctantly and out of sheer generosity, they abandoned their raw Roman virtues – the Roman virtues of the United Diet – and bridged the chasm which threatened to swallow up the throne with the corpse of their former popularity. What airs Camphausen gave himself as the *midwife* of the constitutional throne! The good man was openly moved by himself, by his own magnanimity. The Crown and its party unwillingly tolerated this humiliating protectorate; it made the best of a bad job in the expectation of better days.

The half-dissolved army, the bureaucracy shaking for its positions and emoluments, the humiliated feudal estate, whose leader was on a trip abroad to study constitutions,[6] all these people easily deceived the '*bourgeois gentilhomme*' with a few polite words and courtesies.

The Prussian bourgeoisie was *nominally* in possession of power, and it did not doubt for a moment that the forces of the old state had placed themselves unreservedly at its disposal and become transformed into devoted servants of its own omnipotence.

Not just in the ministry, but over the whole extent of the kingdom, the bourgeoisie was intoxicated by this delusion. Did it not find willing and submissive accomplices in the army, the bureau-

5. Camphausen dealt in oil and corn before attaining political prominence, Hansemann began as a wool-merchant.
6. See p. 187, n. 97.

cracy, and even among the feudal nobility, for its only post-March deeds of heroism, namely the often bloody provocations of the militia against the unarmed proletariat? The local representatives of the bourgeoisie, the *municipal councillors* – whose importunately servile baseness was later trampled on in an appropriate fashion by such people as Windischgrätz, Jellačić and Welden[7] – braced themselves for only one kind of endeavour, their patriarchally serious words of warning to the people. And were not these words of warning, the only heroic deeds of the municipal councillors after the March revolution, gazed at in admiration by the district presidents who had been struck dumb and the divisional generals who had withdrawn into themselves? Was there still any room for the Prussian bourgeoisie to doubt that the old resentment of the army, the bureaucracy and the feudal nobility had died away and been replaced by respectful devotion towards itself, the magnanimous victor, the bridle both of anarchy and of its own excessive claims?

The position was clear. The Prussian bourgeoisie had only one more task, that of making its power secure, removing troublesome anarchists, restoring 'law and order' and regaining the profits lost during the March storm. Now it could only be a question of restricting to a minimum the *costs of production* of its rule and of the March revolution which was the condition of that rule. In its struggle with feudal society and the Crown the Prussian bourgeoisie had been compelled to lay claim in the name of the people to a number of weapons, such as the right of association, freedom of the press, etc. Would these weapons not inevitably be destroyed, once they were in the hands of a deluded people which no longer needed to carry them *on behalf of* the bourgeoisie and was demonstrating a regrettable inclination to carry them *against* the bourgeoisie?

There was obviously only one more obstacle in the way of the *agreement* between the bourgeoisie and the Crown, the bargain between the bourgeoisie and the old state now resigned to its fate. The bourgeoisie was convinced of this. And that obstacle was the people, *puer robustus sed malitiosus*[8] as Hobbes put it. The *people*, and the *revolution*!

7. Franz, Freiherr von Welden was an Austrian general, governor of Vienna from November 1848 to April 1849, and supreme commander of the Austrian troops fighting against Hungary, April–June 1849.

8. 'A strong but malicious boy', from the preface to Hobbes's *De Cive*.

The *revolution* was the *legal title of the people*; the people based their vehement claims on the revolution. The revolution was the bill of exchange the people had drawn on the bourgeoisie. The bourgeoisie had come to power through the revolution. The bill of exchange fell due on the first day of bourgeois rule. The bourgeoisie had to dishonour it.

The meaning of the *revolution* in the popular mind was: you bourgeois are the *comité du salut public*, the committee of public safety in whose hands we have placed the power, not so that you may *reach a compromise with* the Crown in your own interests, but so that you may enforce our interests, the interests of the people, *against* the Crown.

The *revolution* was the people's protest against the bourgeoisie's compromise with the Crown. While it compromised with the Crown, therefore, the bourgeoisie *had to protest* against the *revolution*.

And this happened under the great Camphausen. The *March revolution was not recognized*. The representatives of the nation in Berlin constituted themselves as the *representatives of the Prussian bourgeoisie*, as the *Vereinbarungsversammlung*, by rejecting the motion for the recognition of the March revolution.

The Berlin Assembly turned what had happened into a non-event. It openly proclaimed to the Prussian people that it had not compromised with the bourgeoisie in order to make a revolution against the Crown, but that it had made a revolution so that the Crown might make an agreement with the bourgeoisie directed against itself! In this way, the *legal title* of the revolutionary people was annulled and the *legal foundation* of the conservative bourgeoisie was attained.

The *legal foundation*!

Brüggemann, and through him the *Kölnische Zeitung*, have prattled, yarned and whined so much about the 'legal foundation', so often lost and regained it, perforated it, patched it up, tossed it from Berlin to Frankfurt and then back to Berlin, contracted it, extended it, changed it from a simple foundation into an inlaid foundation, from an inlaid foundation into a false floor – the chief instrument of the stage magician – and from a false floor into a trap-door with no floor at all, with the result that our readers have rightly come to view the legal foundation as the foundation of the *Kölnische Zeitung*, they have come to confuse the shibboleth of the Prussian bourgeoisie with the private shibboleth of Joseph Dumont, a necessary idea of the world history of Prussia with an arbitrary hobby-horse of the *Kölnische Zeitung*, and to see in the legal foundation only the soil in which the *Kölnische Zeitung* grows.

The *legal foundation*, and, what is more, the *Prussian legal foundation*!

The *legal foundation*, upon which, *after* March, there danced the knight of the grand debate, Camphausen, the reawakened spectre of the United Diet, and the *Vereinbarungsversammlung*! Was this the Constitutional Law of 1815,[9] the Diet Law of 1820,[10] the Patent of 1847, or the law of 8 April 1848 for the election of an assembly to make an agreement with the king on a constitution?

It was none of these.

The 'legal foundation' meant simply that the revolution had not gained its foundation, and the old society had not lost its foundation, that the March revolution was merely an 'occurrence', which had given the 'impulse' to an 'agreement' between the throne and the bourgeoisie. This 'agreement' had long been under preparation within the old Prussian state, the Crown itself had already expressed the need for it in earlier royal decrees, although before March it had not considered the matter to be '*urgent*'. The 'legal foundation', to put it briefly, meant that the bourgeoisie wished to negotiate with the Crown on the same footing *after* March as *before* March, as if no revolution had taken place and the United Diet would have achieved its goal without the revolution. The 'legal foundation' meant that the legal title of the people, the *revolution*, did not exist in the social contract between the government and the bourgeoisie. *The bourgeoisie derived its claims from the old Prussian legislation, in order to prevent the people from deriving any claims from the new Prussian revolution.*

It is obvious that the *ideological half-wits* retained by the bourgeoisie, their newspapermen and the like, had to present this veneer of bourgeois interest as the actual interest of the bourgeoisie, and to persuade themselves and others of this. In the head of

9. The 'Ordinance Concerning the Creation of a Representation of the People' of 22 May 1815; a promise to call a general Prussian parliament which was not fulfilled.

10. The 'Ordinance Concerning the Future Organization of the State Debt', 17 January 1820. This promised that any future loans would require the consent of a Diet.

a Brüggemann, the phrase of the legal foundation became transformed into a real substance.

The Camphausen ministry had accomplished its task, a task of *mediation* and *transition*. That is to say, it formed the *mediating link* between the bourgeoisie which had been raised up on the shoulders of the people and the bourgeoisie which no longer needed the shoulders of the people; between the bourgeoisie which, in appearance, represented the people against the Crown, and the bourgeoisie which, in reality, represented the Crown against the people; between the bourgeoisie which had peeled itself off from the revolution and the bourgeoisie which, as the kernel of the revolution, had itself been peeled.

In accordance with its role, the Camphausen ministry limited itself with virginal modesty to *passive resistance* to the revolution.

Admittedly, it rejected it in theory. But in practice it only *fought* against its forms of appearance and merely *tolerated* the reconstitution of the old powers in the state.

In the meantime the bourgeoisie believed it had arrived at the point where *passive resistance* must go over to *active attack*. The Camphausen ministry resigned, not because it had committed this or that blunder, but for the simple reason that it was the *first* ministry after the March revolution, it was the ministry *of* the March revolution, and, true to its origins, still had to conceal its representation of the bourgeoisie beneath the dictatorship of the people. The equivocal origin and ambiguous character of the Camphausen ministry continued to impose on it certain proprieties, certain reservations and allowances towards the sovereign people, which the bourgeoisie began to find irksome. A second ministry, chosen directly from the Assembly, would no longer have to observe these proprieties.

Camphausen's resignation was therefore a puzzle for the coffee-house politicians. The Ministry of the Deed, the *Hansemann ministry*, followed after Camphausen because the bourgeoisie had decided to go over from the period of passive betrayal of the people to the Crown to the period of *active* subjection of the people to its own rule, as agreed on with the Crown. The Ministry of the Deed was the *second* ministry *after* the March revolution. That was its whole secret.

IV *N.Rh.Z.*, 31 December 1848

Cologne, 29 December

Gentlemen! In matters of money, there is no room for soft-hearted-ness![11]

Hansemann summed up the whole of the liberalism of the United Diet in these few words. This man was the necessary head of the ministry which emerged from the *Vereinbarungsversammlung* itself, the ministry which was to change *passive resistance* against the people into an *active attack* on the people, the Ministry of the Deed.

In no Prussian ministry have there been so many *middle-class* names! Hansemann, Milde, Märker, Kühlwetter,[12] Gierke! Even the ministry's presentable master of ceremonies, von Auerswald, belonged to the liberal nobility, i.e. the Königsberg opposition, which had espoused the bourgeois cause.[13] Among this rabble, only Roth von Schreckenstein[14] represented the old, bureau-cratized, Prussian feudal nobility. *Roth von Schreckenstein!* Surviving title of a lost historical novel by the late Hildebrandt![15] But Roth von Schreckenstein was only the feudal mounting of the bourgeois jewel. Roth von Schreckenstein, placed in the middle of a bourgeois ministry, signified, in gigantic letters: the feudality, the army, the bureaucracy of Prussia follow the newly risen star of the Prussian bourgeoisie. These magnates have put themselves at its disposal, and it has planted them in front of its throne, just as bears were planted in front of monarchs on old heraldic emblems. Roth von Schreckenstein is only supposed to be the bear of the bourgeois ministry.

On 26 June the Hansemann ministry presented itself to the

11. A phrase from Hansemann's speech of 8 June 1847 to the United Diet, in which he opposed the granting of a loan to the king to build the Berlin-Königsberg railway.

12. Friedrich von Kühlwetter was Minister of the Interior in Prussia from June to September 1848.

13. The Königsberg (now Kaliningrad) Provincial Diet had been an impor-tant centre of opposition in the 1840s, under the leadership of liberal members of the local nobility, such as Count Schwerin and the brothers Auerswald. The East Prussian representatives in the United Diet of 1847 cooperated with the Rhenish liberals in their opposition to the king's policy.

14. Ludwig, Freiherr von Roth von Schreckenstein was a Prussian general, and Minister of War from June to September 1848.

15. A reference to the historical novel *Kuno von Schreckenstein, oder die weissagende Traumgestalt* (*Kuno von Schreckenstein, or the Prophetic Vision*) by C. Hildebrandt, Quedlinburg, 1821.

National Assembly. Its serious existence first began in July. The *June revolution* was the background of the Ministry of the Deed, just as the *February revolution* was the background of the Ministry of Mediation.[16]

As the Prussian crown exploited the bloody victory of the Croats over the Viennese bourgeoisie, so the Prussian bourgeoisie, in its fight against the people, exploited the bloody victory of the Paris bourgeoisie over the Paris proletariat. The agony of the Prussian bourgeoisie after the Austrian November[17] is *retribution* for the agony of the Prussian people after the French June. The German philistines, in their short-sighted narrow-mindedness, confused themselves with the French bourgeoisie. They had overthrown neither the throne nor feudal society, much less removed its last remnants. They did not have to maintain a society they had created. In their inborn egoism and craftiness they believed after June (as after February, indeed, ever since the beginning of the sixteenth century) that they could draw three quarters of the profit from the labour of others. They did not realize that the Austrian November lay in wait behind the French June, and the Prussian December behind the Austrian November. They did not realize that if in France the bourgeoisie, having smashed the throne, only saw one enemy before it, the proletariat, the situation was reversed in Prussia. There the bourgeoisie possessed only one ally in its struggle with the Crown – the people. Not that the bourgeoisie and the people had no interests which brought them into opposition as enemies. But one *identical* interest cemented them together against a third power which oppressed both of them simultaneously.

The Hansemann ministry saw itself as a *ministry of the June revolution*. And in every Prussian town the philistines changed into 'honest republicans' in face of the 'red brigands' – although they did not cease to be honest royalists, and occasionally overlooked that their 'reds' bore – the black and white cockade.[18]

In the speech from the throne on 26 June, Hansemann made

16. The Camphausen ministry.

17. i.e. the repressive measures taken by the Habsburg authorities against the population of Vienna after the defeat of the revolution on 31 October, and the definitive assumption of power by the counter-revolution, signalized by the formation of Prince Schwarzenberg's ministry of 21 November.

18. The meaning of this sentence is unclear. Black and white were the colours of the Prussian state flag, and Marx thus seems to be alluding to the limited, 'Prussian' character of the alleged revolutionaries of the time.

short work of Camphausen's mysterious and nebulous 'monarchy on the *broadest democratic basis*'.

'*Constitutional monarchy on the basis of the bicameral system* and the joint exercise of the legislative power by both Chambers and the Crown' – this is the dry formula to which he reduced the prophetic declaration of his enthusiastic predecessor. 'Alteration where necessary of a situation which cannot be brought into consonance with the new constitution of the state, liberation of property from the fetters which restrict its *advantageous utilization* in a large part of the kingdom, reorganization of the administration of justice, reform of tax laws, in particular *removal of tax exemptions* etc.', and above all 'the *strengthening of the state power*, which is necessary for the protection of the *freedom* gained' (by the bourgeoisie) 'against reaction' (exploitation of freedom in the interests of the feudal nobility) 'and anarchy' (exploitation of freedom in the interests of the people), 'and for the *restoration of the confidence which has been disturbed*.' This was the ministerial programme, this was the programme of the ministry of the Prussian bourgeoisie, whose classical representative is Hansemann.

In the United Diet, Hansemann was the bitterest and most cynical opponent of confidence, for '*there is no room for soft-heartedness in matters of money*'. In the ministry, Hansemann proclaimed that the '*restoration of the confidence which has been disturbed*' was the main necessity, for – and this time his remarks were directed to the *people*, not, as before, to the *throne* – '*there is no room for soft-heartedness in matters of money*'.

Then it was a question of the confidence which *gives* money, now it is a question of the confidence which *makes* money; there it was *feudal* confidence, loyal confidence in God, King, and Fatherland, here it is *bourgeois* confidence, confidence in trade and traffic, in the interest on capital, in the solvency of business associates, in short, commercial confidence; not faith, hope and charity, but *credit*.

'*Restoration of the confidence which has been disturbed*': Hansemann expressed with these words the *idée fixe* of the Prussian bourgeoisie.

Credit depends on the certainty that the exploitation of wage labour by capital, of the proletariat by the bourgeoisie, and of the small citizen by the great citizen, will continue in its customary manner. Consequently, every political stirring of the proletariat, whatever its nature, even if it has occurred directly at the behest of the bourgeoisie, disturbs confidence, i.e. credit. When Hansemann spoke of the 'restoration of the confidence which has been disturbed', his real meaning, therefore, was the *suppression of any political stirring by the proletariat* and those sections of society whose interests do not directly coincide with the interests of the class which considers itself to be at the helm of the state.

Hansemann therefore placed the '*strengthening of the state power*' close beside the 'restoration of the confidence which has been disturbed'. He was mistaken only in the nature of this 'state power'. He believed he was strengthening that state power which is worthy of credit, of bourgeois confidence, but he only strengthened the state power which simply insists on confidence, and, where necessary, obtains it with grape-shot because it possesses no credit. He wanted to be niggardly with the costs of production of bourgeois rule, and as a result he burdened the bourgeoisie with the exorbitant millions which were the cost of the restoration of feudal rule in Prussia.

With the workers Hansemann was very convincing. He had, he said, just the medicine for them in his pocket. But before he could take it out, it was above all necessary to restore 'confidence'. This could be done if the working class put a stop to its political agitation and intervention in the affairs of the state, and returned to its old habits. If it followed his advice, confidence would be restored, and the secret medicine would already be effective precisely because it was no longer necessary or applicable, for in this case the malady, i.e. the disturbance of bourgeois order, would have been removed. What need is there of a medicine where there is no illness? But if the people remained obstinate, he would '*strengthen the state power*', the police, the army, the courts, the bureaucracy, he would set his dogs at the people's throat, for 'confidence' has become a 'matter of money', and:

Gentleman! In matters of money, there is no room for soft-heartedness!

However much Hansemann might smile about this now, his programme was in fact an *honourable*, a well-meant programme.

He wanted to strengthen the state power not only against anarchy, i.e. the people, but also against the reaction, i.e. against the Crown and the feudal interests, in so far as they might attempt to oppose the money-bags, and the 'most necessary', i.e. the most modest political pretensions of the bourgeoisie.

The Ministry of the Deed, in its very composition, was a protest against this 'reaction'.

It was distinguished from all earlier Prussian ministries by the fact that its real Prime Minister was the Minister of Finance. For centuries, the Prussian state had very carefully concealed the subordination of war, internal affairs, external affairs, church and school affairs, even the royal household, faith, hope and charity, to the profane matter of the *finances*. The Ministry of the Deed made this tiresome, bourgeois truth its motto, by placing at its head Hansemann, the man whose ministerial programme, like his opposition programme, could be summed up in the following words:

Gentlemen! In matters of money, there is no room for soft-heartedness!

The monarchy had become a 'matter of money' in Prussia.

Let us now go over from the programme of the Ministry of the Deed to its deeds.

A serious attempt was made to carry out the threat of 'strengthening the state power' against 'anarchy', i.e. against the working class and all those sections of the bourgeoisie which did not stick to Hansemann's programme. It can indeed be said that with the exception of the increase of the beet tax and the brandy tax, this *reaction* against so-called *anarchy*, i.e. against the revolutionary movement, was the sole serious deed of the Ministry of the Deed.

A mass of press trials on the basis of the Landrecht, or, in default of that, the Code Pénal, numerous arrests on the same 'adequate basis' (von Auerswald's formula), the introduction of a constabulary in Berlin[19] with a proportion of one constable to two houses, police attacks on the freedom of association, letting loose the militia on proletarians who became uppish, examples of a state of siege, all these brave deeds from the Olympian days of Hansemann are still fresh in our memory. There is no need to give details.

Kühlwetter summed up this side of the endeavours of the Ministry of the Deed in the following utterance: 'A state which wishes to be absolutely free must have an absolutely immense supply of policemen as its executive power,' and Hansemann

19. The Auerswald-Hansemann ministry introduced a detachment of armed special constables in addition to the ordinary police force.

himself murmured the gloss which became a fixed system under his ministry: 'This would make an important contribution to the *establishment of confidence*, and to the *resuscitation of the trading activities which are at present languishing.*'[20]

Under the Ministry of the Deed the old Prussian police, the state prosecutor's office, the bureaucracy in general and the army were all 'strengthened' because, in Hansemann's deluded view, since they were in the *pay* of the bourgeoisie, they were therefore at its *service*. The important thing is that they were 'strengthened'.

On the other side, the attitude of the proletariat and of the bourgeois democrats can be characterized by *one* event. Because some reactionaries had mishandled certain democrats in Charlottenburg, the people stormed the Prime Minister's residence in Berlin. The Ministry of the Deed had become as popular as that. The next day Hansemann proposed a law against riots and public assemblies.[21] This is the clever way in which he intrigued against the reaction.

The real, palpable, popular action of the Ministry of the Deed was therefore purely a *police* action. In the eyes of the proletariat and the *urban* democrats, the ministry and the *Vereinbarungsversammlung*, whose majority was represented in the ministry, as well as the Prussian bourgeoisie, whose majority in turn formed the majority in the *Vereinbarungsversammlung*, constituted nothing other than a part of the *old*, and now revived, *state of policemen and officials*. Their hostility to the bourgeoisie was increased by the fact that the bourgeoisie was in power and had formed itself into an integral part of the police by means of the citizen's militia.

In the people's eyes, this was the 'conquest of March': the liberal gentlemen of the bourgeoisie also took over the functions of the *police*. A double police force, in other words!

It emerges, not from the deeds of the ministry, but from its proposal for organic laws, that it '*strengthened*' the police, the ultimate expression of the old state, and urged it on to deeds of valour, exclusively in the interests of the bourgeoisie.

20. Extracts from speeches made on 7 August to the National Assembly by Kühlwetter and Hansemann.

21. Members of a democratic club were attacked in Charlottenburg on 20 August; the next day there were demonstrations in Berlin against the residence of the Minister of the Interior (Kühlwetter) and against Auerswald's residence. On 22 August Hansemann introduced his bill forbidding unauthorized public assemblies and gatherings, passed by a large majority on 24 August.

In the Hansemann ministry's proposals on local government, juries and the militia, it is *ownership* in one form or another which determines the section of the population that is brought within the constitution. Admittedly, the most servile concessions are made in all these proposals to the power of the king, for the bourgeois ministry believed that it possessed in the king an ally who was now harmless. However, in compensation for this, the rule of capital over labour emerges all the more mercilessly.

The militia law which the *Vereinbarungsversammlung* accepted has now been turned against the bourgeoisie and has provided the legal pretext for its disarmament. Of course the bourgeoisie imagined that the militia law would only become effective after the municipal regulations had been issued and the constitution had been promulgated, i.e. after its own rule had been consolidated. The experiences the Prussian bourgeoisie has undergone in connection with the militia law should contribute towards its enlightenment; it ought to learn from this that, for the present, when it thinks it is acting against the people, it is only acting against itself.

For the people, therefore, the Hansemann ministry was summed up *in practice* in old-fashioned Prussian police measures, and *in theory* in offensive distinctions of the Belgian type between bourgeois and non-bourgeois citizens.[22]

Let us now go over to the other part of the ministerial programme, to its support of *anarchy against the reaction.*

In this direction the ministry has more pious wishes to show for itself than deeds.

The division of the Crown domains and their sale to private owners, the opening up of banking to free competition, the transformation of the Seehandlung[23] into a private body, all these measures come into the category of pious *bourgeois* wishes.

The Ministry of the Deed suffered the misfortune that all its economic attacks on the feudal party took place under the aegis of

22. The Belgian constitution of 1831 made this distinction by establishing a high property qualification for electors, reduced but not abolished by the liberal ministry of Rogier in 1848.

23. The full title of this body was the Preussische Seehandlungsgesellschaft (Prussian Company for Maritime Affairs). It was founded in 1772 as a private credit company, and was made the Prussian state's own finance house in 1820, as a means of circumventing the Diet Law of that year by providing a secret source of loans.

the *forced loan*, and that its reforming measures in general therefore appeared to the people to be merely financial expedients to
fill the coffers of the strengthened 'state power'. The result was
that Hansemann reaped the hatred of one party without gaining
the favour of the other. And it cannot be denied that he only
risked a serious attack on feudal privileges where he was confronted with the problem which touched him most closely, the
money problem, the *money problem as interpreted by the Ministry
of Finance*. It was in this narrow sense that he called out to the
feudal party:

Gentlemen! In matters of money, there is no room for soft-heartedness!

His positive bourgeois endeavours to combat the feudal party
thus bore the same colouring as his negative measures for the
'*resuscitation of trading activities*' – they appeared to be police
interventions. In political economy, *police* means *treasury*. The
increases in the beet tax and the brandy tax, which Hansemann
pushed through the National Assembly and raised to the level of
laws, enraged the money-bags 'with God for King and Fatherland'[24] in Silesia, Brandenburg, Saxony, East and West Prussia,
etc. However, while these measures brought down the wrath of
the industrial landowners in the old Prussian provinces, they did
not stir up any less dissatisfaction amongst the bourgeois brandy
manufacturers of the Rhineland, who saw that they had been
placed in still more unfavourable conditions for competing with
the old Prussian provinces. And, filling the cup to overflowing,
they embittered the workers of the old provinces, for whom they
meant, and could mean, nothing other than *an increase in the
price of an essential foodstuff*. The only positive result of these
measures, then, was the replenishment of the coffers of the
'strengthened state power'. And this example is sufficient, for it
is the only anti-feudal deed of the Ministry of the Deed, the only
deed which was *genuinely* carried out, the only bill with this intention which actually became law.

Hansemann's 'proposals' for the abolition of *tax exemptions on
landed property and on certain classes of people*, as also his projected income tax, called forth fits of rage among the landed
enthusiasts for 'God, King and Fatherland'. They decried him as a

24. The words at the mast-head of every issue of the *Kreuzzeitung*.

communist and even now the Knight of the Prussian Cross crosses himself three times whenever he hears the name of Hansemann.[25] It sounds to him like Fra Diavolo.[26] The abolition of the land tax exemption, the only significant measure proposed by a Prussian minister during the magnificent reign of the *Vereinbarungsversammlung*, came to grief through the *principled obtuseness of the Left*, for which Hansemann himself had provided the justification. Should the Left open up new sources of financial assistance for the ministry of the 'strengthened state power' before the constitution had been constructed and sworn in?

The bourgeois ministry *par excellence* was unfortunate enough to see its most radical measures paralysed by the radical members of the *Vereinbarungsversammlung*. It was so petty that its whole crusade against feudalism culminated in a *tax increase* equally hateful to all classes, while its financial wizardry resulted in the abortion of the *forced loan*: two measures which in the end only provided *subsidies for the campaign of the counter-revolution against the bourgeoisie itself*. The *feudal party*, however, had become convinced of the 'malevolent' intentions of the *bourgeois* ministry. And so Hansemann's original slogan proved its accuracy in the financial struggle of the Prussian bourgeoisie against feudalism, since in its condition of powerless unpopularity it could only exact *money which would be used against it*!

The bourgeois ministry had succeeded in arousing the equally bitter enmity of the urban proletariat, the bourgeois democrats and the feudal party; then, with the eager support of the *Vereinbarungsversammlung*, it managed to alienate even the peasant class, subjected as that class was to the yoke of feudalism. It should by no means be forgotten that for half its life this Assembly saw the Hansemann ministry as a suitable representative and that the bourgeois martyrs of today are Hansemann's henchmen of yesterday.

The proposal for emancipation from feudal burdens, laid before the Assembly by Patow on 20 June, was criticized by us at the

25. Knight of the Prussian Cross: an allusion to the title of the *Kreuzzeitung* (literally: newspaper of the cross). In November 1848 it published a number of articles attacking Hansemann as a 'leader of the extreme Left', discussed in detail by Marx in the 17 November issue of the *Neue Rheinische Zeitung* (*MEW* 6, pp. 24–8).

26. The nickname of Michele Pezza, the leader of a south Italian robber band which fought against the occupying French forces from 1798 to 1806.

time.[27] It was a most miserable concoction, combining the power-less bourgeois desire to remove feudal privileges because they were 'incompatible with the new constitution of the state' with the bourgeois fear of laying one's hands in a revolutionary fashion on any kind of property. Lamentable, cowardly, narrow-minded egoism deluded the Prussian bourgeoisie to such an extent that it pushed aside its *necessary ally* – the *peasant class*.

On 3 June 1848 deputy Hanow[28] put the motion

that all negotiations in progress for the purpose of settling relations between landowners and peasants, and for the redemption of services, be stopped at once on the application of either party, until a new law can be issued on this matter, based on fair principles.

And only *at the end of September*, four months later, under the Pfuel ministry did the *Vereinbarungsversammlung* accept the bill for the cessation of pending negotiations between landowners and peasants, after it had rejected all liberal amendments and retained clauses for the 'reservation of provisional assessments of current services' and the 'recovery of disputed taxes and outstanding debts'.

In *August*, if we are not mistaken, the *Vereinbarungsversammlung* decided that Nenstiel's motion for 'the *immediate abolition of compulsory labour services*' was *not urgent*.[29] How then could the peasants regard it as an urgent matter to fight for that Assembly, when it had thrown them back behind the actual situation they themselves had conquered in March?

The French bourgeoisie began with the liberation of the peasants. With the peasants it conquered Europe. The Prussian bourgeoisie was so caught up in its own most immediate, *narrowest* interests that it forfeited even this ally and made it into an instrument in the hands of the feudal counter-revolution.

The *official* history of the dissolution of the bourgeois ministry is well known.

The 'state power' was so far 'strengthened' under its protective wings, the energy of the people so far suppressed, that the Dios-

27. In a number of articles in the *Neue Rheinische Zeitung*, of which 'The Bill for the Abolition of Feudal Burdens' is printed above. For the others see *MEW* 5, pp. 106–7 and 309–14.

28. Friedrich Hanow was the director of an orphanage in Brandenburg. In 1848 he sat with the Left Centre in the Prussian National Assembly.

29. Johann Nenstiel was a Silesian merchant, who sat with the Centre in the Prussian Assembly. It was on 1 September 1848, in fact, that the Assembly voted that Nenstiel's motion was not urgent and could be added to the ordinary agenda of business.

curi,[30] Kühlwetter and Hansemann, had already on 15 July to issue a warning to all the provincial presidents of the kingdom about the reactionary machinations of the administration's officials, especially the district presidents. Later on, an 'Assembly of the Nobility and the Possessors of Large Estates for Protection' – i.e. of their privileges[31] – was able to sit in Berlin alongside the *Vereinbarungsversammlung*, and finally, on 4 September 1848, a 'Communal Diet for the Maintenance of the Threatened Property Rights of Landownership', clearly handed down from the Middle Ages, was able to assemble in Oberlausitz in opposition to the so-called Berlin National Assembly.

The energy displayed by the government and the so-called National Assembly against these ever more threatening symptoms of counter-revolution found its appropriate expression in paper admonitions. The Citizen Ministry[32] only had bayonets, bullets, prisons and bailiffs for the people, '*for the restoration of the confidence which has been disturbed and the resuscitation of trading activities*'.

The Schweidnitz affair, in which the soldiery directly massacred the bourgeoisie in the militia,[33] at last awakened the National Assembly from its apathy. On 9 August it braced itself for a deed of heroism, the Stein-Schultze army order, which used the tactfulness of the Prussian officer as the ultimate instrument of compulsion. What a coercive measure! Did not the honour of the royalist forbid the officers to consider the honour of the citizen?

On 7 September, a month after the *Vereinbarungsversammlung* had adopted the Stein-Schulze army order, it decided once again that its decision had been a genuine decision and must be implemented by the ministers. Hansemann refused, and on 11 September resigned, having previously had himself appointed as a bank director at an annual salary of 6000 thalers – for *there is no room for soft-heartedness in matters of money*.

Finally, on 25 September, the *Vereinbarungsversammlung* gratefully accepted a wholly watered-down formula of recognition from Pfuel. In the meantime, the Stein-Schultze army order had

30. Castor and Pollux, the twin sons of Leda in Greek myth.
31. A reference to the General-Versammlung zur Wahrung der materiellen Interessen aller Klassen des preussischen Volks, also called the Junkerparlament, a congress of big landowners which met in Berlin on 18 August 1848.
32. The Auerswald-Hansemann ministry.
33. On 31 July the troops of the garrison of Schweidnitz fired on the citizens' militia, killing fourteen people.

sunk to the level of a *bad joke* owing to the concentration of masses of troops around Berlin, and the fact that the Wrangel army order ran parallel to it.[34]

It is only necessary to skim over the dates given above and the history of the Stein-Schultze army order to be convinced that this order was not the *real* reason for Hansemann's resignation. Would Hansemann, who did not shrink from recognizing the revolution, have shrunk from that paper proclamation? Would Hansemann, who managed to recapture his ministerial portfolio every time it slipped from his hands, on this occasion have left it lying on the ministerial bench for all comers out of sheer honest irritation? No, our Hansemann is no dreamer! He was simply duped, just as he represented the duped bourgeoisie as a whole. He was led to believe that the Crown would not let him go in any circumstances. He was permitted to lose the last appearance of popularity, so that he could then be sacrificed to the rancour of the backwoods junkers, while the Crown freed itself from bourgeois tutelage. Moreover, the plan of campaign agreed on with Russia and Austria required a general of the camarilla, outside the *Vereinbarungsversammlung*, at the head of the cabinet. Under the Citizen Ministry the old 'state power' had been sufficiently 'strengthened' to be able to risk this coup.

Pfuel did not come up to expectations. The victory of the Croats in Vienna made even a Brandenburg a suitable instrument.

The *Vereinbarungsversammlung* was ignominiously dispersed, hoaxed, ridiculed, humiliated and persecuted under the Brandenburg ministry, and the *people* remained *indifferent* at the decisive moment. Its *defeat* was the *defeat of the Prussian bourgeoisie*, of the *constitutionalists*, and therefore a victory for the *democratic party*, however dearly the latter had to pay for this victory.

But what of the *octroi* of a constitution?[35]

It used to be said that a 'piece of paper' would never force itself between the king and *his* people.[36] Now it is said: *only a piece*

34. See p. 167, n. 44.

35. The term *octroi* was used widely in nineteenth-century Europe to refer to a solemn act done by a king out of the plenitude of his power, usually, as in this case, the grant of a constitution. The constitution in question is that issued by Frederick William IV on 5 December 1848.

36. In his speech at the opening of the first United Diet (11 April 1847), Frederick William IV said that he would never allow a piece of paper to be inserted between the Lord God in heaven and this land, as a second providence, so to speak.

of paper shall force itself between the king and *his* people. Prussia's *real* constitution is the *state of siege*. The dictated French constitution contained only one paragraph 14, providing for its abolition.[37] Every paragraph of the dictated Prussian constitution is a paragraph 14.

By this constitution, the Crown grants privileges – but only to itself.

It grants itself the freedom to dissolve the Chambers for an indefinite period. It grants the ministers the freedom to issue appropriate laws in the interval (even laws on property, etc.). It grants the deputies the freedom to impeach the ministers for this, at the risk of being declared 'internal enemies' in a state of siege. Finally, it grants itself the freedom to replace this dangling 'piece of paper', when the shares of counter-revolution are buoyant in the spring, with a Christian-Germanic Magna Carta *organically* emerging from the medieval differentiation of estates, or indeed to give up the constitutional game altogether. Even in the last instance, the conservative part of the bourgeoisie would fold its hands and pray: *'The Lord giveth, the Lord taketh away, blessed be the name of the Lord.'*

The history of the Prussian bourgeoisie demonstrates, as indeed does that of the whole German bourgeoisie from March to December, that a purely *bourgeois revolution*, along with the establishment of *bourgeois hegemony* in the form of a *constitutional monarchy*, is impossible in Germany. What *is* possible is either the feudal and absolutist counter-revolution or the *social-republican revolution*.

However, we have a guarantee that the more active part of the bourgeoisie will have to awaken again from its apathy, in the shape of the *monstrous bill* with which the counter-revolution will surprise the bourgeoisie in the spring. As our friend Hansemann so sensibly said:

Gentlemen! In matters of money, there is no room for soft-heartedness!

37. Paragraph 14 of the French constitutional charter of 1815 (another *octroi*) provided that the king could issue ordinances without the consent of parliament in case of necessity.

THE MAGYAR STRUGGLE[38]

N.Rh.Z., 13 January 1849   Frederick Engels
                                         Cologne, January 1849

Whereas in Italy the revolution's first rejoinder to the counter-revolution of last summer and autumn has already begun,[39] on the Hungarian plains the last fight to suppress the movement which proceeded directly out of the February revolution is coming to an end. The new Italian movement is the prelude of the movement of 1849, the war against the Magyars is the sequel of the movement of 1848. This sequel will probably stretch out into the new drama which is silently being prepared.

The sequel is heroic, as was the first rapid kaleidoscope of the tragedy of the 1848 revolution, or the fall of Paris and Vienna, comfortingly heroic indeed after the feeble and petty interlude between June and October. The last act of 1848 is joined to the first act of 1849 by means of *terrorism*.

For the first time in the revolutionary movement of 1848, for the first time since 1793, a nation encircled by a numerically superior counter-revolution has dared to oppose craven counter-revolutionary fury with revolutionary passion, to oppose white terror with red terror. For the first time for a long while we come upon a really revolutionary character, a man who has dared to pick up the gauntlet to fight a last-ditch struggle in the name of his people, a man who for his nation is Danton and Carnot rolled into one – Louis Kossuth.[40]

The odds are terrible. The whole of Austria, headed by sixteen million fanaticized Slavs, against four million Magyars.

The *levée en masse*, the national manufacture of weapons, the *assignats*, short shrift for anyone who obstructs the revolutionary movement, the revolution in permanence, in short all the chief characteristics of the glorious year 1793 are to be seen again in

38. The political and constitutional conflict between the Magyars and the Austrian government finally developed into open war in December 1848 with the advance of Windischgrätz's troops into Hungary.

39. The Italian revolution flared up again in November 1848, with the victory of the radical republicans in Rome and the flight of the Pope to Gaeta, and repeated disturbances in Florence directed against the Grand Duke.

40. Lajos Kossuth was a Magyar nationalist and revolutionary who dominated the Hungarian Diet in 1848, and led Magyar resistance against the Habsburgs. After the defeat of Hungary in 1849 he lived in exile.

Hungary as armed, organized and galvanized by Kossuth. Vienna lacked this revolutionary organization, which must be set up within twenty-four hours so to speak, on pain of destruction, otherwise Windischgrätz would never have entered the city. We shall see whether he can penetrate into Hungary in spite of this revolutionary organization.

Let us look more closely at the struggle and the parties engaged in it.

The Austrian monarchy emerged out of the attempt to unite Germany into a single kingdom in the way that the French kings up to Louis XI had accomplished this in France. The attempt came to grief on the wretched locally oriented narrow-mindedness of both Germans and Austrians, and the correspondingly petti-fogging spirit of the House of Habsburg. Instead of the whole of Germany, the Habsburgs obtained only those south German districts which were in direct conflict with isolated Slav tribes or in which a German feudal nobility and German burghers[41] jointly ruled over subjugated Slav tribes. In both cases the Germans of each province needed support from outside. They obtained this support by associating against the Slavs, and this association was in fact the result of the unification of the provinces in question under the Habsburg sceptre.

This was the origin of German Austria. One only needs to look up in the nearest available textbook how the Austrian monarchy came into existence, how it split up and then again united, and all this in the course of the struggle against the Slavs, in order to see the correctness of this account.

Hungary is attached to German Austria. The Magyars waged the same struggle in Hungary as the Germans in German Austria. The Archduchy of Austria and Styria, a German wedge thrust forward between Slav barbarians, held out its hand across the Leitha[42] to the Magyar wedge, similarly thrust forward between Slav barbarians. Just as the German nobility dominated and germanized the Slav tribes to the south and north, in Bohemia, Moravia, Carinthia and Carniola, and thereby drew them into the movement of Europe as a whole, so also did the Magyar

41. 'Burghers' is a rendering of '*Bürgerschaft*' (strictly 'burgherdom'), Engels's term for the urban proprietors of pre-capitalist times.

42. A tributary of the Danube, which formed the historic boundary between the hereditary lands of the Austrian emperor (Cisleithania) and the lands of the Crown of St Stephen (Transleithania, or Hungary).

nobility dominate the Slav tribes of Croatia, Slavonia and the Carpathian lands. Their interests were the same, and their enemies were natural allies. The alliance of the Magyars and the Austrian Germans was a necessity. All that was lacking was one great event, a fierce attack on both of them, in order to make this alliance indissoluble. This development occurred with the conquest of the Byzantine empire by the Turks. The Turks threatened Hungary and in the second instance Vienna, and for centuries Hungary was riveted indissolubly to the House of Habsburg.

But the common enemies of both gradually lost their strength. The Turkish empire declined into impotence, and the Slavs lost the power to make insurrections against the Magyars and the Germans. Indeed, in the Slav lands a section of the ruling German and Magyar nobility assumed a Slav nationality, and with this the Slav nations themselves gained an interest in the preservation of a monarchy which had increasingly to protect the nobility against the developing German and Magyar bourgeoisie. The national antagonisms vanished and the House of Habsburg adopted a different policy. The same House of Habsburg that had swung itself into the throne of the German empire on the shoulders of the German burghers became, more emphatically than any other dynasty, the representative of the feudal nobility against the burghers.

It was in accordance with this policy that Austria took part in the partition of Poland. The grand Galician *starosts* and *voivods*,[43] the Potockis, Lubomirskis and Czartoryskis, betrayed Poland to Austria and became the most loyal supporters of the House of Habsburg, which, in return, guaranteed their possessions against the attacks of the lesser nobility and the burghers.

But the burghers of the towns gained more and more wealth and influence, and agriculture, as it progressed alongside industry, put the peasants in a different position in relation to the owners of the land. The movement of these bourgeois and their peasant allies against the nobility became ever more threatening. And since the movement of the peasants, who are always the bearers of national and local narrow-mindedness, is necessarily a local and national movement, the old national conflicts re-emerged at the same time.

This was the state of affairs when Metternich played his master stroke. He deprived the nobility, with the exception of the most

43. *Starost, voivod*: administrative divisions of the old kingdom of Poland and, by extension, the great nobles in charge of them.

powerful feudal barons, of all influence on the direction of state policy. He deprived the bourgeoisie of its power, while winning over the most powerful financial barons – the state of the finances compelled him to do this. In this way, resting on high feudality and high finance, as also on the bureaucracy and the army, he attained the ideal of absolute monarchy more completely than all his rivals. The bourgeoisie and peasants of each nation were restrained by the nobility of that nation and the peasants of every other nation, whilst the nobility of each nation was restrained by their fear of the bourgeoisie and peasants of their own nation. The different class interests, limited national attitudes and local prejudices, in all their complexity, held each group in a position of total reciprocal stalemate, and allowed that old rogue Metternich complete freedom of movement. The Galician massacres[44] show how far he had succeeded in inflaming the peoples against each other. In that instance, Metternich suppressed the democratic Polish movement, which had been begun in the interests of the peasants, by using the religious[45] and national fanaticism of the Ruthenian peasants themselves.

At first the year 1848 brought the most frightful confusion to Austria, by momentarily freeing all these different peoples who had hitherto been in thrall to each other through Metternich's agency. Germans, Magyars, Czechs, Poles, Moravians,[46] Slovaks, Croats, Ruthenes, Rumanians, Illyrians[47] and Serbs all came into conflict, whilst the individual classes within each of these nations also fought each other. But order soon came into this confusion. The disputants divided into two huge armed camps: on one side, the side of revolution, were the Germans, Poles and Magyars; on the other side, the side of counter-revolution, were the others, i.e.

44. In February 1846 a Polish nationalist rising broke out in Galicia and Cracow. At the same time the Ruthenian peasants rose against the Polish nationalist nobles, with the encouragement and aid of the Austrian authorities, and massacred large numbers of them.

45. The Ruthenes mostly adhered to the Uniate Church, which had Orthodox rites although it recognized the supremacy of the Pope; this made for conflict with the Roman Catholic Poles.

46. There was no separate Moravian nationality in the nineteenth century; the word 'Moravian' refers here to the Czech inhabitants of Moravia.

47. There has never been an Illyrian nationality; Illyria was the area on the east coast of the Adriatic inhabited in the nineteenth century by Slovenes, Croats and Serbs. The poet Ljudevit Gaj invented the 'Illyrian nationality' in the 1830s in order to give the south Slavs a sense of unity. In view of later developments, 'Yugoslav' would be a reasonable but anachronistic translation.

all the Slavs with the exception of the Poles, plus the Rumanians and the Saxons of Transylvania.

What is the origin of this line of separation according to nationality? On what facts is it based?

It corresponds to the whole previous history of the peoples in question. It is the beginning of the decision on whether all these great and small nations will live or die.

The whole previous history of Austria up to the present day is a demonstration of this, and the year 1848 has confirmed it. Amongst all the nations and nationalities of Austria there are only three bearers of progress, which have actively intervened in history and are still capable of independent life: Germans, Poles and Magyars. They are therefore revolutionary now.

The chief mission of all the other great and small nationalities and peoples is to perish in the universal revolutionary storm. They are therefore now counter-revolutionary.

As far as the Poles are concerned, we refer the reader to our articles on the Frankfurt debate on Poland.[48] In order to tame their revolutionary spirit Metternich had already appealed to the Ruthenes, a nationality distinguished from the Poles by a somewhat different dialect and in particular by the Greek religion, who had belonged to Poland from time immemorial and first learned by the agency of Metternich that the Poles were their oppressors. As if the Poles themselves had not been oppressed just as much as the Ruthenes in the old Poland, and as if Metternich were not their common oppressor under Austrian rule!

This is enough on the subject of the Poles and Ruthenes, who are in any case so clearly divided from Austria proper by history and by geographical position that we had to deal with them first of all before we could settle accounts with the rest of the jumble of peoples.

However, let us point out that the Poles are displaying great political insight and a truly revolutionary attitude in fighting, as they do now, in alliance with their old enemies the Germans and Magyars, against the pan-Slav counter-revolution. A Slav people to which freedom is dearer than Slavdom has demonstrated its viability by that very decision, and has in this way already made certain of its future.

And now we come to Austria proper.

48. *MEW* 5, pp. 319–63. The third article, which is particularly relevant in this context, is printed above.

In the early Middle Ages, Austria south of the Sudeten and Carpathian Mountains, i.e. the regions of the upper Elbe valley and the middle Danube, was a land inhabited exclusively by Slavs. These Slavs belonged in language and customs to the same stock as the Slavs of Turkey, the Serbs, Bosnians, Bulgars, Thracian and Macedonian Slavs – that of the South Slavs, so called to distinguish them from the Poles and the Russians. Apart from these related Slav tribes, the immense area which stretches from the Black Sea to the Bohemian Forest and the Tyrolese Alps was inhabited only by a few Greeks (in the south of the Balkan peninsula) and scattered Wallachians speaking a Romance language (in the lower Danube region).

From the west, the Germans thrust themselves like a wedge between this compact Slavic mass; the Magyars did the same from the east. The German element conquered the western part of Bohemia and penetrated on both sides of the Danube beyond the Leitha. The Archduchy of Austria, part of Moravia and most of Styria were all germanized, and the Czechs and Moravians were thus separated from the Carinthians and Carniolans. In the same way the Magyars entirely cleared out the Slavs from Transylvania and central Hungary as far as the German border and occupied the area, thus separating the Slovaks and some Ruthenian districts (in the north) from the Serbs, Croats and Slavonians, and subjecting all these peoples to themselves. Finally the Turks, following in the footsteps of the Byzantines, subjugated the Slavs living south of the Danube and the Save. The historical role of the South Slavs had thus come to an end for all time.

The last attempt of the South Slavs to intervene independently in history was the Hussite War, a Czech nationalist peasant war fought under a religious flag against the German nobility and German imperial suzerainty. The attempt failed and since then the Czechs have remained continuously in tow to the German Reich.

The victorious Germans and Magyars then took over the historical initiative in the Danube region. The South Slavs would have become Turkish without the Germans and, in particular, without the Magyars; a part of them actually did become Turkish, indeed Mohammedan, as the Slav Bosnians still are today. And that is a service for which the Austrian South Slavs have not paid too dearly even by exchanging their nationality for that of the Germans or Magyars.

The Turkish invasion of the fifteenth and sixteenth centuries was the second edition of the Arabian invasion of the eighth century. The victory of Charles Martel was repeated again and again under the walls of Vienna and on the Hungarian plains. The whole development of Europe was threatened again at Wahlstatt[49] by the Mongolian invasion, just as it had been at Poitiers.[50] And where it was a matter of saving this development, could the decision indeed have depended on a few long-decayed and impotent nationalities, such as the Austrian Slavs, which received their own salvation into the bargain?

As in external affairs, so too internally. The class which provided the driving force, the bearer of further development, the burgher class, was everywhere German or Magyar. The Slavs experienced difficulties in producing a national class of burghers. The South Slavs could only manage this occasionally. And with the burghers, industrial power, capital, was in German or Magyar hands, German culture advanced, and the Slavs came under German domination intellectually as well, right down as far as Croatia. The same thing happened, only later and therefore to a lesser degree, in Hungary, where the Magyars took over intellectual and commercial leadership together with the Germans. The Hungarian Germans, however, have become true Magyars in sentiment, character and customs, despite their retention of the German language. The only exceptions are the newly introduced peasant colonists,[51] the Jews, and the Saxons of Transylvania, who persist in retaining an absurd nationality in the middle of a foreign country.

And if the Magyars remained somewhat behind the German Austrians in civilization, they have made up for this brilliantly by their political activity of more recent times. From 1830 to 1848 there existed in Hungary alone more political life than in the whole of Germany, the feudal forms of the old Hungarian constitution were better exploited in the interests of democracy than the modern forms of the south German constitutions. And who stood

49. At the battle of Wahlstatt (Silesia) in 1241 the Mongols were defeated by German and Slav armies, and their westward penetration was halted.

50. The victory of Charles Martel over the Arabs took place in 732 at Poitiers.

51. German peasant colonists were introduced into Hungary in the late eighteenth century.

at the head of this movement? The Magyars. Who supported the Austrian reaction? The Croats and Slavonians.[52]

The Austrian Slavs founded a separatist movement in opposition to this Magyar movement as well as to the reawakening political movement in Germany: *pan-Slavism*.

Pan-Slavism arose in Prague and Zagreb, not in Russia or Poland. Pan-Slavism is an alliance of all the small Slav nations and nationalities of Austria and secondarily of Turkey, for the purpose of fighting against the Austrian Germans, the Magyars and ultimately the Turks. The Turks are only involved in this accidentally and can remain entirely outside our discussion, being a similarly decayed nation. Pan-Slavism is fundamentally directed against the revolutionary elements in Austria and is therefore reactionary from the outset.

Pan-Slavism immediately demonstrated this reactionary tendency with a double betrayal: it sacrificed the sole Slav nation to have played a revolutionary role so far, the Poles, to its petty nationalist narrow-mindedness, and it *sold* itself and Poland *to the Russian tsar*.

Pan-Slavism leads directly to the establishment of a Slav empire under Russian domination, from the Erzgebirge and the Carpathians to the Black, Aegean and Adriatic Seas, an empire which would include about a dozen Slav languages and chief dialects, in addition to German, Italian, Magyar, Wallachian, Turkish, Greek and Albanian. The whole thing would be held together not by the elements which have so far held together and developed Austria, but by the abstract characteristic of Slavdom and the so-called Slav language, which is of course supposed to be common to the majority of the inhabitants. But where does this Slavdom exist except in the heads of a few ideologists, where does the 'Slav language' exist except in the imagination of Herr Palacký,[53] Herr Gaj and their confederates, and, roughly speaking, in the Old Slav litany of the Russian church, which no Slav understands any more? In reality all these peoples have the most varied levels of civilization, from Bohemia's modern industry and culture, which has been developed (by Germans) to a relatively high degree,

52. Inhabitants of Slavonia, a province attached to the kingdom of Croatia. They were largely Croat in nationality.
53. František Palacký was a Czech historian and liberal politician, the proponent of 'Austro-Slavism' and the leader of the Czech national movement in the mid nineteenth century.

down to the well-nigh nomadic barbarism of the Croats and the Bulgars; these nations therefore really have the most opposed interests. In reality, the Slav language of these ten or twelve nations is composed of so many dialects, for the most part mutually incomprehensible; although these can be reduced to a number of main branches (Czech, Illyrian, Serbian and Bulgarian), they have turned into mere patois owing to the complete neglect of all literature and the crudeness of most of the peoples, who, with few exceptions, have always used a *foreign* non-Slavic language as their written language. The unity of pan-Slavism is therefore either a mere fantasy or ... *the Russian knout*.

And which nations are supposed to head this great Slav empire? Precisely those which have been scattered and split up for a thousand years, for which elements capable of life and development had *forcibly* to be imported by other, non-Slavic peoples, and which were saved from succumbing to Turkish barbarism by the victorious arms of non-Slavic peoples. Small, powerless nationalities ranging in number from a few thousands to not quite two millions, everywhere separated from each other and robbed of their national strength! So weak have they become that, for example, the people which were most powerful and most terrifying in the Middle Ages, the Bulgars, now have a reputation in Turkey for their meekness and faint-heartedness and regard it as an honour to be called *dobre chrisztian*, good Christian! Does a single one of these peoples, Czechs and Serbs not excepted, possess a national historical tradition which lives in the minds of the people and transcends the pettiest local conflicts?

The time for pan-Slavism was the eighth and ninth centuries, when the South Slavs still controlled the whole of Hungary and Austria and threatened Byzantium. If they could not resist the German and Magyar invasion then, if they could not win their independence and form a stable empire at a time when their two enemies, the Magyars and the Germans, were tearing each other to pieces, how will they do this now, after a thousand years of subjection and de-nationalization?

There is no country in Europe that does not possess, in some remote corner, at least one remnant-people, left over from an earlier population, forced back and subjugated by the nation which later became the repository of historical development. These remnants of a nation, mercilessly crushed, as Hegel said, by the course of history, this *national refuse*, is always the fanatical representative of the counter-revolution and remains so until it is completely exterminated or de-nationalized, as its whole existence is in itself a protest against a great historical revolution.

In Scotland, for example, the Gaels, supporters of the Stuarts from 1640 to 1745.

In France the Bretons, supporters of the Bourbons from 1792 to 1800.

In Spain the Basques, supporters of Don Carlos.

In Austria the pan-Slav South Slavs, who are nothing more than the *national refuse* of a thousand years of immensely confused development. It is the most natural thing in the world that this national refuse, itself as entangled as the development which brought it into existence, sees its salvation solely in a reversal of the entire development of Europe, which according to it must proceed not from west to east but from east to west, and that its weapon of liberation, its unifying bond, is the *Russian knout*.

The South Slavs had already shown their reactionary character before 1848. The year of revolution itself exposed this quite openly.

Who made the Austrian revolution when the February storm broke loose? Vienna or Prague? Budapest or Zagreb? The Germans and Magyars or the Slavs?

It is true that a small democratic party existed among the more educated South Slavs, who, while not wishing to give up their nationality, nevertheless wished to place it at the disposal of freedom. Owing to this illusion, the movement succeeded in awakening the sympathies of the democrats of western Europe as well, sympathies which were entirely justified as long as the Slav democrats fought together with them against the common foe; but the illusion was destroyed by the bombardment of Prague. From this event onwards, all the South Slav peoples placed themselves at the disposal of the Austrian reaction, following the precedent set by the Croats. Those leaders of the South Slav movement who are still spinning yarns about national equality and a democratic Austria are either blockheaded dreamers, as for example many of the journalists, or scoundrels like Jellačić. Their democratic assurances mean no more than the democratic assurances of the official Austrian counter-revolution. Suffice it to say that in practice the re-establishment of South Slav nationality begins with the most furious brutality against the Austrian and Magyar revolutions, with the first of many great services to be performed for the Russian tsar.

Apart from the high nobility, the bureaucracy and the soldiery, the Austrian camarilla only found support among the Slavs. The Slavs caused the fall of Italy, the Slavs stormed Vienna, and it is the Slavs who are now falling upon the Magyars from all sides. They are led by two peoples: the Czechs, under Palacký, wielding the pen; and the Croats, under Jellačić, wielding the sword.

This is the thanks for the general sympathy displayed by the German democratic press in June for the Czech democrats when they were shot down with grape-shot by the same man, Windischgrätz, who is now their hero.

To sum up: in Austria, leaving aside the Poles and the Italians, the Germans and the Magyars have assumed the historical initiative, in the year 1848 as in the previous thousand years. They represent the *revolution*.

The South Slavs, who have trailed behind the Germans and Magyars for a thousand years, only rose up to establish their national independence in 1848 in order to suppress the German-Magyar revolution at the same time. They represent the *counter-revolution*. Two similarly decayed nations, entirely lacking in active historical forces, have attached themselves to the South Slavs: the Saxons and Rumanians of Transylvania.

The House of Habsburg, which founded its strength on the union of Germans and Magyars in the fight against the South Slavs, is now eking out the last moments of its existence by uniting the South Slavs in the fight against the Germans and Magyars.

That is the political side of the question. Now for the military side.

The area exclusively inhabited by Magyars does not even comprise a third of Hungary and Transylvania taken together. From Bratislava onwards, to the north of the Danube and the Tisza, up to the crest of the Carpathians, there live several million Slovaks and a number of Ruthenes. In the south, between the Save, the Danube and the Drave, there live Croats and Slavonians; further east, along the Danube, there is a Serbian colony of over half a million. These two Slav belts are joined together by the Wallachians and Saxons of Transylvania.

The Magyars are therefore surrounded on three sides by natural enemies. The Slovaks who hold the mountain passes would be dangerous opponents, in view of the terrain, which is perfect for partisan warfare, if they were less lethargic in character.

In the north, then, the Magyars have merely to fend off the attacks of armies which have broken through from Galicia and Moravia. However, in the east the Rumanians and Saxons rose up *en masse* and joined the local Austrian army corps. Their position is excellent, partly owing to the mountainous nature of the country, partly because they control most of the towns and fortresses.

Finally, in the south, the Serbs of the Banat, supported by German colonists, Wallachians and, like the Rumanians, by an Austrian army corps, are covered by the immense morass of Alibunar and are almost unassailable.

The Croats are covered by the Drave and the Danube, and as they have at their disposal a strong Austrian army with all its resources, they had already pushed forward onto Magyar territory before October[54] and they are now holding their line of defence on the lower Drave with ease.

From the fourth side, from Austria, Windischgrätz and Jellačić are advancing in close columns. The Magyars are surrounded on all sides, surrounded by an enemy with an enormous numerical superiority.

The struggle is reminiscent of the struggle against France in the year 1793. There is only the difference that the thinly populated and only semi-civilized land of the Magyars has far fewer resources than the French republic had in those days.

Weapons and munitions manufactured in Hungary must necessarily be of very bad quality; in particular it is impossible to manufacture artillery quickly. The country is much smaller than France, and every inch of land lost is a correspondingly greater blow. The Magyars have nothing left but their revolutionary enthusiasm, their courage, and the energetic, fast moving organization Kossuth was able to give them.

Nevertheless, Austria has not yet won.

If we do not beat the emperor's troops on the Leitha, we shall beat them on the Répce; if not on the Répce, we shall beat them at Pest; if not at Pest, we shall beat them on the Tisza – but, at all events, we shall beat them.[55]

54. Jellačić invaded Hungary on 11 September 1848, acting on his own initiative, although the Habsburg court did not disavow him. Croat forces were advancing on Budapest in October when they were recalled to take part in the siege of Vienna.

55. Quoted from Kossuth's speech on 9 November 1848 to the Hungarian parliament.

So said Kossuth, and he is doing his best to keep his word. Even with the fall of Budapest[56] the Magyars still have the huge heath of lower Hungary, an area made, as it were, for partisan warfare on horseback, which offers numerous almost impregnable positions between the swamps where the Magyars can establish themselves. And, since they almost all have mounts, they possess all the qualifications for waging such a war. If the imperial army ventures into this desolate district, it will have to import all its provisions from Galicia or Austria, because it will find nothing there, absolutely nothing, and it cannot be foreseen how it will maintain itself. It will accomplish nothing in close formation, and if it is divided up into flying squads it will be lost. Its unwieldiness would irretrievably deliver it into the hands of the fast-moving bands of Magyar horsemen, and even in case of victory there would be no possibility of pursuit; while each imperial straggler would meet with the deathly enmity of every peasant and every shepherd. The war in these steppes would be similar to the Algerian war,[57] and the ungainly Austrian army would need years to bring it to an end. And the Magyars will be saved if they only hold out for a couple of months.

The Magyar cause therefore stands far better than the paid enthusiasts for black and yellow[58] would have us believe. They have not yet been defeated. However, if they do fall, they fall with honour as the last heroes of the 1848 revolution, and only for a short time. Then the Slav counter-revolution, with all its barbarism, will momentarily overwhelm the Austrian monarchy and the camarilla will see what kind of ally it has. But at the first victorious uprising of the French proletariat, which Louis Napoleon is doing his best to conjure up, the Austrian Germans and the Magyars will gain their freedom and take a bloody revenge on the Slav barbarians. The general war which will then break out will scatter this Slav Sonderbund,[59] and annihilate all these small pig-headed nations even to their very names.

The next world war will not only cause reactionary classes and

56. On 5 January 1849.

57. The French conquest of Algeria occupied in all a period of seventeen years, from the first expedition in 1830 to the final surrender in 1847.

58. The Austrian imperial colours.

59. Literally, 'separate league', from the alliance formed by the seven Catholic cantons of Switzerland in defence of the Jesuits and clerical privilege against the centralizing, democratic and anti-clerical tendencies of the majority. It was defeated in the Sonderbund War of November 1847.

dynasties to disappear from the face of the earth, but also entire reactionary peoples. And that too is an advance.

DEMOCRATIC PAN-SLAVISM

I *N.Rh.Z.*, 15 February 1849 Frederick Engels
Cologne, 14 February

We have pointed out often enough that the sweet dreams which came to the surface after the February and March revolutions, the fantasies of universal brotherhood between peoples, of a European federal republic and of everlasting world peace, were fundamentally nothing more than a cover for the helplessness and the inactivity of the spokesmen of that time. They did not see, or did not want to see, what had to be done to make the revolution secure; they could not implement, or did not want to implement any really revolutionary measures. The narrowness of one side, the counter-revolutionary intrigues of the other side, produced a tacit agreement that the people should merely be given sentimental phrases instead of revolutionary deeds. The magniloquent scoundrel Lamartine was the classic *hero* of this epoch of betrayal of the people concealed beneath the flowers of poetry and the frippery of rhetoric.

The peoples which have passed through the revolution know how dearly they have had to pay for the fact that at that time, in their generosity, they believed the fine words and the haughty assurances of their spokesmen. Instead of the securing of the revolution, they were everywhere given the undermining of the revolution by reactionary parliaments; instead of the implementation of the promises given on the barricades, they were given the counter-revolutions of Naples, Paris, Vienna and Berlin, the fall of Milan and the war against Hungary; instead of the brotherhood of peoples, they were given the renewal of the Holy Alliance on the broadest basis under the patronage of England and Russia. And the same men who were in April and May still applauding the bombastic phrases of the epoch, now only redden when they think of how they let themselves be cheated by idiots and scoundrels.

We have learnt through painful experience that the 'European brotherhood of peoples' will come to pass not through mere phrases and pious wishes but only as a result of thorough revolutions and bloody struggles; that it is not a matter of fraternization between all European peoples underneath a republican flag, but of the alliance of revolutionary peoples against counter-revolutionary peoples, an alliance which does not happen on *paper* but on the *field of battle*.

All over western Europe these bitter but necessary experiences have robbed Lamartine's phrases of all credit. In the east however there still exist parties, supposedly democratic, revolutionary parties, which never weary of echoing these phrases and sentimentalities and preaching the gospel of the European brotherhood of peoples.

These parties (leaving out of consideration certain ignorant German enthusiasts such as Herr A. Ruge, etc.) are the *democratic pan-Slavists* of the various Slav peoples.

The programme of democratic pan-Slavism lies before us in a pamphlet entitléd: '*Proclamation to the Slavs*. By a Russian patriot, Michael Bakunin, Member of the Slav Congress in Prague' (Köthen, 1848).

Bakunin is our friend. That will not prevent us from subjecting his pamphlet to criticism.

Listen how, right at the beginning of his proclamation, Bakunin harks back to the illusions of March and April last:

The revolution's very first sign of life was a cry of hatred against the old oppression, a cry of sympathy and love for all oppressed nationalities. The peoples ... finally felt the shame with which the old diplomacy had laden mankind, and recognized that the welfare of nations will never be secure as long as a single people in Europe lives under oppression ... Away with the oppressors, was the cry which resounded as from a single mouth. Hail to the oppressed, the Poles, the Italians and all! No more wars of conquest, but just the one last war, fought out to the end, the good fight of the revolution for the final liberation of all peoples! Down with the artificial barriers which have been forcibly erected by congresses of despots in accordance with so-called historical, geographical, commercial and strategic necessities! Let there be no other boundaries but those which correspond to nature, boundaries drawn justly and in a democratic sense, boundaries which the sovereign will of the peoples itself prescribes on the basis of its national qualities. This is the call which issues forth from all peoples (pp. 6–7).

Already in this passage we meet again all the visionary enthusiasm of the first months after the revolution. There is no mention here of the obstacles which are really in the way of such a general liberation, of the utterly different levels of civilization of the individual peoples and the equally different political needs conditioned by those levels. The word 'freedom' replaces all of this. Of reality itself there is either no discussion at all, or, in so far as it does come into consideration, it is portrayed as something absolutely abominable, the arbitrary creation of 'congresses of despots' and 'diplomats'. The supposed will of the people confronts this bad reality with its categorical imperative, with its absolute demand for plain and simple 'freedom'.

We have seen who was the stronger. The supposed will of the people was duped so outrageously precisely because it accepted such an imaginary abstraction from the relations which actually existed at the time.

Out of the plenitude of its own power, the revolution proclaimed the dissolution of the despotic states, the dissolution of the Prussian kingdom . . . Austria . . . the Turkish empire . . . finally the dissolution of the last consolation of the despots, the Russian empire . . . and as the ultimate aim of all this – the general federation of European republics (p. 8).

In actual fact it must appear peculiar to us here in the west that all these fine plans, after the failure of the *first* attempt to carry them out, can still be counted as something of great merit. That was indeed precisely the worst feature of the revolution, that it 'proclaimed the dissolution of the despotic states out of the plenitude of its own power', but at the same time did not move a muscle 'out of the plenitude of its own power' to execute its decree.

The Slav Congress was called at that time. It completely adopted the standpoint of these illusions. Listen to this:

Keenly feeling the common bond of history (?) and blood, we swear never to let our destinies be separated again. Execrating politics, of which we have so long been the victims, *we ourselves stood up* for our right to complete *independence* and *made the vow* that this would henceforth be *common to all Slav peoples*. We recognized the independence of Bohemia and Moravia ... we held out our fraternal hand to the German people, to democratic Germany. In the name of those of us who lived in Hungary, we offered a fraternal alliance ... to the Magyars, the furious foes of our race. In our alliance of liberation we also did not forget those of our brothers who sigh beneath the Turkish yoke. We solemnly condemned that criminal policy which thrice tore Poland apart ... All this we said, and we demanded with all the democrats of all peoples (?): liberty, equality and the fraternity of all nations (p. 10).

Democratic pan-Slavism is still making these demands today:

Then we felt certain of our cause ... *justice* and *humanity* were entirely on our side, and on the side of our foes was nothing but illegality and barbarism. These were *no empty dreams* which we devoted ourselves to, but rather the ideas of the *only true and necessary policy*, the policy of *revolution*.

'Justice', 'humanity', 'liberty', 'equality', 'fraternity', 'independence' – so far we have found nothing more in the pan-Slav manifesto than these more or less moral categories, which admittedly sound very fine, but *prove absolutely nothing* in historical and political matters. 'Justice', 'humanity', 'liberty', etc., may demand this or that a thousand times over; but if the cause is an impossible one, nothing will happen and it will remain, despite everything, 'an empty dream'. The pan-Slavists could have learned something about their illusions from the role the mass of the Slavs has played since the Prague Congress, they could have realized that there is nothing to be achieved against iron reality with all the pious wishes and beautiful dreams in the world, and that their policy was as little a 'policy of revolution' as that of the French Second Republic. And yet they come to us now, in January 1849, with the same old phrases about whose content western Europe was disillusioned by a most bloody counter-revolution!

Just one word about 'the universal brotherhood of peoples' and the drawing of 'boundaries, which the sovereign will of the peoples itself prescribes on the basis of its national qualities'. The United States and Mexico are two republics; the people are sovereign in both of them.

How did it happen that a war broke out over Texas[60] between these two republics, which are supposed to be 'united' and 'federated' according to the *moral theory*, how did it happen that the 'sovereign will' of the American people, supported by the courage of the American volunteers, moved the naturally drawn boundaries some hundreds of miles further south for reasons of 'geographical, commercial and strategic necessity'? And will Bakunin reproach the Americans with this 'war of conquest', which admittedly gives a hard knock to his theory based on

60. The war of 1845–7 between Mexico and the United States, after which large areas of Mexico were ceded to the U.S. (February 1848).

'justice and humanity', but which was waged simply and solely in the interests of civilization? Or is it perhaps a misfortune that magnificent California was snatched from the lazy Mexicans, who did not know what to do with it? Or that the energetic Yankees are increasing the means of circulation by the rapid exploitation of the Californian gold-mines, have concentrated a thick population and extensive commerce on the most suitable stretch of the Pacific coast within a few years, are building big cities, opening steamship communications, laying a railway from New York to San Francisco, opening the Pacific for the first time to actual civilization, and are about to give world trade a new direction for the third time in history? The 'independence' of a few Spanish Californians and Texans may suffer by this, 'justice' and other moral principles may be infringed here and there; but what does that matter against such world-historical events?

Let us remark in passing that the editors of the *Neue Rheinische Zeitung* were fighting long before the revolution against this theory of the universal brotherhood of peoples, which is aimed at nothing but a random fraternization without regard for the historical position or the social level of development of the individual peoples, and that we had indeed to fight against our best friends, the English and French democrats. The proofs of this are contained in the English, French and Belgian democratic newspapers of that time.[61]

As far as pan-Slavism specifically is concerned, we have developed the point in Number 194 of the *Neue Rheinische Zeitung*[62] that, leaving aside the well meant self-deceptions of the democratic pan-Slavists, it has in reality no other aim than to give a point of support to the fragmented Austrian Slavs, who are at present dependent on the Germans and the Magyars for their history, literature, politics, commerce and industry. On one side this was to be provided by Russia, on the other side by the Austrian monarchy, dominated by its Slav majority and dependent on Russia. We have explained how such small nations, dragged along for centuries by history against their will, must necessarily be counter-revolutionary, and how their whole position in the 1848 revolution was in truth counter-revolutionary. In dealing with this manifesto of democratic pan-Slavism, which

61. See for example Marx and Engels's 'Speeches on Poland', above, also *MEW* 2, pp. 611–24, and *MEW* 4, pp. 426–8, 432–8 and 444–58.
62. See 'The Magyar Struggle', above.

demands independence for all Slavs without differentiation, we must return to this point.

By the way, one must admit that the political romanticism and sentimentality of the democrats at the Slav Congress was highly excusable. With the exception of the Poles – and the Poles are not pan-Slavists, for obvious reasons – they all belong to nationalities which are either, as in the case of the South Slavs, necessarily counter-revolutionary owing to their whole historical position, or, as in the case of the Russians, still far removed from a revolution and therefore at least at present still counter-revolutionary. These parties, having become democratic through receiving an education abroad, endeavoured to harmonize their democratic convictions with their feeling of nationalism, which is very pronounced among the Slavs, as is well known; and since the positive world, the real situation of their country, offered no points of contact for this reconciliation, or only simulated ones, there was nothing left to them but the other-worldly 'kingdom of the dream',[63] the realm of pious wishes, the politics of delirium. How wonderful it would be, if Croats, Pandours[64] and Cossacks formed the vanguard of European democracy, if the ambassador of the Siberian republic could present his credentials in Paris! A pleasant prospect indeed; but the most enthusiastic pan-Slavist will not demand that European democracy should await its realization – and at present it is precisely the nations whose particular independence is demanded by the manifesto that are the particular enemies of democracy.

We repeat: apart from the Poles, the Russians, and at most the Slavs of Turkey, no Slav people has a future, for the simple reason that all the other Slavs lack the primary historical, geographical, political and industrial conditions for a viable independence.

Peoples which have never had a history of their own, which come under foreign domination the moment they have achieved the first, crudest level of civilization, or are *forced onto* the first level of civilization by the yoke of the foreigner, have no capacity for survival and will never be able to attain any kind of independence.

And that has been the fate of the Austrian Slavs. The Czechs,

63. H. Heine, 'Germany: A Winter's Tale,' *The Poetry and Prose of Heinrich Heine*, ed. F. Ewen, ch. 7.

64. A force of brutal soldiery of South Slav origin, raised and enrolled under the Habsburg banner in the mid eighteenth century.

amongst whom we ourselves should like to count the Moravians and the Slovaks, although they are linguistically and historically distinct, never had a history. Since Charlemagne Bohemia has been bound to Germany. The Czech nation emancipated itself for one moment and formed the Great Moravian Empire, but was immediately subjugated again and tossed back and forth like a football for five hundred years between Germany, Hungary and Poland. Then Bohemia and Moravia became definitively attached to Germany, and the Slovak areas remained with Hungary. Is this 'nation', with absolutely no historical existence, actually making a claim for independence?

It is the same with the so-called South Slavs proper. Where is the history of the Illyrian Slovenes, the Dalmatians,[65] the Croats and the Schokazen?[66] They lost the last trace of political independence after the eleventh century, and since then have been partly under German, partly under Venetian and partly under Magyar rule. Is it really intended to botch together a powerful, independent and viable nation out of these tattered rags?

But there is worse to come. If the Austrian Slavs formed a compact mass like the Poles, Magyars or Italians, if they were in a position to gather from twelve to twenty million people in a state, their claims would have a serious character despite everything. But the actual situation is the precise opposite of this. The Germans and the Magyars have inserted themselves between the Slavs like a broad wedge up to the outermost ends of the Carpathians, and separated the Czechs, Moravians and Slovaks from the South Slavs by a zone some sixty to eighty miles wide. Five and a half million Slavs live to the north of this zone; five and a half million Slavs live to the south of it. They are divided by a compact mass of ten to eleven million Germans and Magyars, who are allies by history and by necessity.

But why shouldn't the five and a half million Czechs, Moravians and Slovaks be able to form a state? And the five and a half million South Slavs, together with the Turkish Slavs?

Inspect the distribution of the Czechs and their linguistically related neighbours on the first linguistic map you find. They are inserted into Germany like a wedge, but they are gnawed at and

65. Inhabitants of the Austrian crownland of Dalmatia, of mainly Croat nationality, with some Serbs in the south.
66. A small South Slav national group which in the seventeenth century fled from the advance of the Turks into Bosnia to settle in southern Hungary.

forced back on both sides by the German element. A third of Bohemia speaks German; there are seventeen Germans to every twenty-four Czechs in Bohemia. And it is precisely the Czechs who are to form the nucleus of the intended Slav state; for the Moravians are just as heavily mixed with Germans, the Slovaks with Germans and Magyars, and moreover they are entirely demoralized as far as nationality is concerned. What a Slav state, which would be ultimately *dominated by the German bourgeoisie of the towns*!

The same is true of the South Slavs. The Slovenes and Croats cut off Germany and Hungary from the Adriatic; and Germany and Hungary *cannot* allow themselves to be cut off from the Adriatic, owing to 'geographical and commercial necessities' which are admittedly no obstacle for Bakunin's imagination, but which exist all the same and are just as much matters of life and death for Germany and Hungary as the Baltic coast from Danzig to Riga is for Poland. And where the existence of great nations and the free development of their resources is at stake, nothing will be decided by such sentimental factors as deference to a few dispersed Germans or Slavs. Not to mention the fact that these South Slavs are similarly mixed up with German, Magyar and Italian elements, that here too the projected South Slav state breaks up into disconnected fragments with the first glance at the language map, and that, at best, the whole state would be delivered into the hands of the Italian bourgeoisie of Trieste, Fiume and Zara, and the German bourgeoisie of Agram, Laibach, Karlstadt, Semlin, Pancsova and Weisskirchen.

But couldn't the Austrian South Slavs link up with the Serbs, Bosniaks,[67] Morlaks[68] and Bulgars? Certainly, if, apart from the difficulties already mentioned, the age-old hatred of the people of the Austrian borderlands for the Turkish Slavs beyond the Save and the Unna did not exist; but these people have related to each other for centuries as rogues and bandits, and, despite all their racial affinities, their mutual hatred is infinitely greater than that between Slavs and Magyars.

In actuality the Germans and Magyars would be in an *extremely* pleasant situation if the Austrian Slavs were put in possession of their so-called 'rights'. An independent Bohemian-Moravian

67. The Mohammedan inhabitants of Bosnia, usually Serb in nationality.
68. A national group descended from the old romanized population of Illyria, Serb in language, and living in north Dalmatia and south Istria.

state wedged in between Silesia and Austria, Austria and Styria cut off by the 'South Slav republic' from the Adriatic and the Mediterranean, their natural trade outlets, eastern Germany torn to pieces like a loaf gnawed by rats! And all this would be out of gratitude for the pains the Germans have taken to civilize the obstinate Czechs and Slovenes, and to introduce amongst them trade, industry, a tolerable agriculture and education!

But it is precisely this yoke forced upon the Slavs under the pretext of civilization which constitutes one of the greatest crimes committed by the Germans, as also by the Magyars! Listen to this:

You were right to boil with anger, and right to pant for revenge against that *execrable German policy*, which was directed at nothing other than your ruin, which *has enslaved you for centuries* (p. 5) . . . The Magyars, the *furious enemies* of our race, who, though they numbered hardly four millions, had the presumption to impose their yoke on eight million Slavs (p. 9) . . .

What the Magyars have done against our Slav brothers, what crimes they have committed against our nationality, how they have trampled our language and our independence underfoot, all this I know (p.30).

What then are the immense and terrible crimes of the Germans and the Magyars against the Slav nation? We are not referring here to the partition of Poland, which does not belong in this context, but to the 'centuries of injustice' that are supposed to have been perpetrated against the Slavs.

In the north the Germans have conquered back from the Slavs the region between the Elbe and the Warta, which was previously German and later became Slav; this conquest was conditioned by the 'geographical and strategic necessities' which emerged from the division of the Carolingian empire. These Slav districts have been completely germanized; the thing is done and cannot be redressed, even if the pan-Slavists were to rediscover the lost languages of the Sorbs, Wends and Obotrians[69] and impose them on the people of Leipzig, Berlin and Stettin. Up to now it has not been denied that this conquest was in the interests of civilization.

In the south the Germans found that the Slav peoples had

69. Three West Slav peoples, which settled between the Elbe and the Oder after the fifth century, and were later forcibly germanized, with the partial exception of the Sorbs of Lausitz, who still survive in the G.D.R. as a distinct national group.

already been scattered. The non-Slav Avars[70] had taken care of this when they occupied the region later seized by the Magyars. The Germans made these Slavs their tributaries and waged a number of wars against them. They also fought against the Avars and the Magyars, and deprived them of the whole country between the Ems and the Leitha. Whereas here they germanized forcibly, the germanization of the Slav lands proceeded on a much more peaceful footing, through migration and the influence of the more developed nation on the undeveloped nation. German industry, German trade, German education automatically brought the German language into the country. As far as 'oppression' is concerned, the Slavs were no more oppressed by the Germans than the mass of the Germans themselves were.

If we look at Hungary, we find that there are many Germans there too, yet the Magyars have never had cause to complain of an 'execrable German policy', even though there were 'hardly four million' of them. And if the 'eight million Slavs' had to allow the four million Magyars to impose their yoke on them for *eight centuries*, this alone is sufficient proof that the few Magyars had more vitality and energy than the many Slavs.

But of course the greatest 'crime' of the Germans and the Magyars was that they prevented these twelve million Slavs from becoming Turkish! What would have happened to these small and fragmented nationalities, which have played such a wretched role in history, if the Magyars and Germans had not held them together and led them against the armies of Mohammed and Suleiman, if their so-called 'oppressors' had not fought the decisive battles in defence of these weak semi-nations? Does not the fate of the 'twelve million Slavs, Wallachians and Greeks' who have been 'trodden underfoot by seven hundred thousand Ottomans' (p. 8) right up to the present day speak loudly enough?

And finally was it not a 'crime', was it not an 'execrable policy' that, at the time when great monarchies were a 'historical necessity' throughout Europe, the Germans and the Magyars united all these small, crippled, powerless nationalities into a great empire and enabled them to take part in an historical development which would have been entirely foreign to them had they been left to themselves? Naturally, that kind of thing cannot be

70. A Tartar people which settled in the Balkans from the sixth to the ninth century. They were finally defeated by Germans, Slavs, Turks and Magyars, and disappeared from the historical record.

accomplished without forcibly crushing the occasional sensitive specimen of national plant life. But nothing is accomplished in history without force and pitiless ruthlessness, and what indeed would have happened to history if Alexander, Caesar and Napoleon had had the same quality of compassion now appealed to by pan-Slavism on behalf of its decayed clients! And are the Persians, the Celts and the Germanic Christians[71] not worth the Czechs, the Oguliner[72] and the Sereschaner.[73]

Now, however, as a result of the immense progress in industry, trade and communications, political centralization has become a far more urgent need than it was in the fifteenth and sixteenth centuries. Anything which has yet to be centralized is being centralized now. And *now* the pan-Slavists come to us and demand that we should let these half-germanized Slavs 'go free', that we should abolish a centralization which is forced on these Slavs by all their material interests!

It appears, in short, that these 'crimes' of the Germans and the Magyars against the Slavs in question are some of the best and most commendable of the deeds we and the Magyar people can pride ourselves on in the course of our history.

By the way, we should add that the Magyars have been too forbearing and too weak towards the arrogant Croats, especially since the revolution. It is notorious that Kossuth conceded everything possible to them, except that their deputies might speak Croat at the Diet. And this forbearance towards a naturally counter-revolutionary nation is the only thing the Magyars can be reproached with.

II *N.Rh.Z.*, 16 February 1849   Frederick Engels
                                                  Cologne, 15 February

We finished yesterday by showing that the Austrian Slavs have never had a history of their own, that they are dependent on the

71. *Christliche Germanen*, a simultaneous reference to the defeat of Prussian resistance by Napoleon in the 1800s, and the insistence of the romantic reaction, and Frederick William IV in particular, on the 'Christian' and 'Germanic' character of Prussia.
72. Oguliner: the members of a detachment of infantry on the military border of Croatia, created in 1746, and stationed at Ogulin.
73. Sereschaner: the members of a special cavalry detachment attached to Austrian border regiments from 1700 onwards for purposes of reconnaissance and minor skirmishes with the Turks.

Germans and Magyars for their history, literature, politics, commerce and industry, that they are already partially germanized, magyarized or italianized, that if they set up independent states those states will be ruled not by them but by the German and Italian bourgeoisie of their towns, and finally, that neither Hungary nor Germany can tolerate the forcible detachment and independent establishment of such small and unviable inter-mediate states.

However, all that would not in itself be decisive. If the Slavs had begun a *new revolutionary history* at any time within the period of their oppression, they would have proved their capacity for independent existence by that very act. The revolution would have had an interest in their liberation from that moment onwards, and the particular interest of the Germans and Magyars would vanish in face of the greater interest of the European revolution.

But that did not happen at any time. The Slavs – let us recall again that we exclude the Poles from all this – were always precisely the *chief tools of the counter-revolutionaries*. Being oppressed at home, they were the *oppressors of all revolutionary nations* abroad, as far as the influence of the Slavs extended.

Let no one reply to this that we are acting in the interest of German nationalist prejudices. There are proofs available in German, French, Belgian and English newspapers that it was precisely the editors of the *Neue Rheinische Zeitung* who were attacking all German nationalist stupidity in the most decisive fashion long *before* the revolution.[74] Admittedly they did not, like some other people, scold the Germans in a wildly exaggerated way and on the basis of mere hearsay; instead of this they merci-lessly laid bare, with historical proofs, the shabby role Germany has played in history thanks to its nobility and its burghers, and, of course, to its stunted industrial development; they have always recognized the justified position of the great historical nations of the west, of the English and the French, in contrast to the back-ward Germans. But precisely on account of that, we must be permitted not to share the enthusiastic illusions of the Slavs and to judge other peoples just as strictly as we have judged our own nation.

It has always been said that the Germans were the shock troops of despotism throughout Europe. We are far from denying the

74. See 'Speeches on Poland', above; also *MEW* 2, pp. 564–84, and *MEW* 4, pp. 207–47, 514–18 and 526–7.

shameful role of the Germans in the shameful wars against the French revolution from 1792 to 1815, in the oppression of Italy since 1815 and of Poland since 1772; but who stood behind the Germans, who used them as their mercenaries or their vanguard? England and Russia. Indeed, the Russians have boasted up to the present day that they decided the overthrow of Napoleon with their innumerable armies, and this of course is largely correct. One thing at least is certain, and that is that three quarters of the armies which by their numerical superiority forced Napoleon back from the Oder to Paris were composed of Slavs, either Russian or Austrian.

And what about the oppression of the Italians and Poles by the Germans? A wholly Slav and a half Slav power rivalled each other in partitioning Poland; the armies which overwhelmed Kościuszko[75] contained a majority of *Slavs*; the armies of Diebitsch and Paskievitch[76] were exclusively *Slav* armies. In Italy, the *tedeschi*[77] have for long years borne alone the disgrace of counting as oppressors; but, once again, what was the composition of the armies which could best be used for the suppression of the Italian revolutions and whose brutalities could be laid at the door of the Germans? They were composed of Slavs. Go to Italy and ask who suppressed the revolution in Milan. They will no longer say '*i tedeschi*' – since the *tedeschi* made a revolution in Vienna they are not hated any more – but rather '*i croati*'. That is how the Italians now sum up the whole Austrian army, i.e. everything for which they have the deepest hatred: *i croati*.

And yet these accusations would be irrelevant and unjustified if the Slavs had taken a serious part anywhere in the movement of 1848, if they had hastened to enter the ranks of the revolutionary peoples. One single courageous attempt at a democratic revolution, even if it is stifled, will expunge whole centuries of infamy and cowardice from the memory of other peoples and will instantly rehabilitate a nation, however deeply it may have been despised. The Germans discovered that last year. But while the French, the

75. Tadeusz Kościuszko was a Polish general and patriot who took part in the war of 1791–2 and led the insurrection of 1794.

76. Count Hans Diebitsch and Ivan Fedorovich Paskievitch were both Russian field-marshals. Diebitsch commanded the war against the Poles in 1831, and on his death was replaced by Paskievitch, who served as viceroy of Poland from 1832 to 1856. In 1849 Paskievitch commanded the Russian troops against Hungary.

77. Germans.

Germans, the Italians, the Poles and the Magyars were raising the banner of revolution, the Slavs fell in as *one* man under the banner of *counter-revolution*. In the van the South Slavs, who had already defended their own particular counter-revolutionary wishes against the Magyars for many years; then the Czechs; and behind them, armed for battle and ready to appear on the field at the decisive moment . . . the Russians.

It is known that in Italy the Magyar hussars went over in great numbers to the Italians, just as in Hungary whole Italian battalions placed themselves at the disposal of the Magyar revolutionary government and are still fighting under the Magyar flag; it is known that in Vienna the German regiments sided with the people, and were absolutely unreliable even in Galicia; it is known that Austrian and non-Austrian Poles fought in their masses in Italy, in Vienna and in Hungary against the Austrian armies, and are still fighting in the Carpathians; but has anyone ever heard of Czech or South Slav troops rebelling against the black and yellow flag?

On the contrary, so far we know only that an Austria shaken to its very foundation was kept in being and momentarily secured by the enthusiasm of the Slavs for black and yellow; that it was precisely the Croats, Slovenes, Dalmatians, Czechs, Moravians and Ruthenes who provided such men as Windischgrätz and Jellačić with their contingents for the suppression of the revolution in Vienna, Cracow, Lvov and Hungary, and, as we have now learnt from Bakunin, that the Slav Congress in Prague was not dispersed by Germans but by Galician, Czech and Slovak Slavs and '*nothing but Slavs*' (p. 33).

The revolution of 1848 compelled all the European peoples to declare for it or against it. In one month all the peoples which were ripe for revolution had made their revolution, all the unripe peoples had formed an alliance against the revolution. At that time, it was necessary to disentangle eastern Europe's confused ravel of peoples. Everything depended on which nation seized the revolutionary initiative, which nation developed the greatest revolutionary energy and thereby secured its future. The Slavs remained dumb, the Germans and the Magyars, true to their previous historical position, placed themselves in the forefront. And in this way the Slavs were thrown completely into the arms of the counter-revolution.

But the Slav Congress at Prague?

We repeat: the so-called democrats among the Austrian Slavs are either rogues or visionaries, and the visionaries, who can find no basis in their own people for these ideas introduced from abroad, have been continuously led around by the nose by the rogues. At the Prague Slav Congress the visionaries had the upper hand. As soon as their fantasies appeared to threaten the *aristocratic* pan-Slavists, Count Thun,[78] Palacký and their associates, they betrayed the visionaries to Windischgrätz and the black and yellow counter-revolution. Is there not a bitter, striking irony in the fact that this congress of enthusiasts, defended by the enthusiastic youth of Prague, was dispersed by soldiers of their own nation, that the visionary Slav Congress was so to speak confronted with a military Slav Congress! The Austrian army, the conqueror of Prague, Vienna, Lvov, Cracow, Milan and Budapest: that is the real, the active Slav Congress!

The unprincipled and unclear nature of the fantasies of the Slav Congress is shown by its fruits. The bombardment of a town like Prague would have filled any other nation with an inextinguishable hatred of the oppressors. What did the Czechs do? They kissed the rod which had chastised them till the blood came, they enthusiastically took the oath to the flag beneath which their brothers had been massacred and their women violated. The battle in the streets of Prague was the turning point for the Austrian democratic pan-Slavists. In return for the promise of their miserable 'national autonomy' they betrayed democracy and revolution to the Austrian monarchy, to 'the centre', 'the systematic realization of despotism in the heart of Europe', as Bakunin himself says on p. 29. And one day we shall take a bloody revenge on the Slavs for this cowardly and base betrayal of the revolution.

It has finally become clear to these traitors that, despite their treason, they have been taken in by the counter-revolution, that there is no intention of creating either a 'Slav Austria' or a 'federal state on the basis of national equality', least of all of setting up democratic institutions for the Austrian Slavs. Jellačić, who is no greater scoundrel than most of the democratic Austrian Slavs, bitterly regrets having been exploited; and Stratimiro-

78. Leo, Graf von Thun was a member of that section of the high Bohemian nobility which was allied with the Czech nationalists (later described as the 'feudals'). In 1848 he was Governor of Bohemia, from 1849 to 1860 he was Minister of Religious Affairs.

vić[79] has openly rebelled against Austria in order to avoid being exploited any further. Once more the Slovanská Lípa unions[80] are everywhere coming up against the government and daily undergoing painful experiences which show them the trap they allowed themselves to be enticed into. But now it is too late; in their own homeland they are powerless against the Austrian soldiery they themselves reorganized, they are rebuffed by the Germans and Magyars they betrayed, they are rebuffed by revolutionary Europe, and they will have to endure the same military despotism they helped to impose on the Viennese and the Magyars. 'Be submissive to the emperor, so that the imperial troops don't treat you as if you were rebellious Magyars.' With these words Patriarch Rajačić[81] showed what they must expect now.

How differently the Poles have behaved! Oppressed, enslaved, bled dry for eighty years, they have always placed themselves on the side of the revolution, they have declared that the independence of Poland is inseparable from the revolutionizing of Poland. The Poles have joined in the fight in Paris, Vienna, Berlin, Italy and Hungary, in all the revolutions and revolutionary wars, without worrying whether they were fighting against Germans, Slavs, Magyars, or even against Poles. The Poles are the only Slav nation which is free from all tendencies towards pan-Slavism. But they have very good reasons for this: they have mainly been subjugated by *their own* so-called *Slav brothers*, and among the Poles hatred for the Russians precedes hatred for the Germans, quite justifiably. For this reason, then, because the liberation of Poland is inseparable from the revolution, because Pole and revolutionary have become identical words, the Poles can be as certain of the sympathy of the whole of Europe and the restora-

79. Džordže Stratimirović was an Austrian general of Serbian extraction. In 1848 he led the Serbian national movement and was president of the Provisional Government of the Voivodina (May–August 1848). He was then made supreme commander of all Serbian troops in the Voivodina, and took part in the campaign against Hungary.

80. 'Slav Linden': Czech nationalist society, founded in April 1848, with branches all over Bohemia. The Prague centre was in the hands of moderate liberals, who went over to the reaction after June 1848, but the provincial unions were often led by radical nationalists, who continued to agitate against the Austrian government up to the middle of 1849.

81. Josif Rajačić was appointed Patriarch of the Austrian Serbs in 1848. He strongly upheld Habsburg authority and fiercely opposed the Hungarian revolution. In 1849 he was appointed Regent of the Voivodina.

tion of their nationality as the Czechs, the Croats and the Russians can be certain of the hatred of the whole of Europe and the bloodiest revolutionary war of the whole West against them.

The Austrian pan-Slavists ought to realize that all their wishes are fulfilled, in so far as they can be fulfilled at all, in the restoration of the 'united Austrian monarchy'[82] under Russian protection. If Austria collapses, they have in store for them the revolutionary terrorism of the Germans and the Magyars, but not, as they imagine, the liberation of all the nations enslaved under the Austrian sceptre. They are therefore bound to want Austria to remain united, indeed, to want Galicia to remain part of Austria so that the Slavs may retain their majority in the state. In this respect the interests of pan-Slavism are *directly opposed* to the restoration of Poland; for a Poland without Galicia, a Poland which does not stretch from the Baltic to the Carpathians, is no Poland. It follows however that a 'Slav Austria' will similarly remain a mere dream; for without the supremacy of the Germans and the Magyars, without the two centres of Vienna and Budapest, Austria falls to pieces again, as proved by its whole history up to the last few months. The realization of pan-Slavism would therefore have to be limited to a Russian protectorate over Austria. The openly reactionary pan-Slavists were therefore quite right to cling to the maintenance of the whole monarchy; it was the only way to save anything. The so-called democratic pan-Slavists were in a difficult dilemma: either abandonment of the revolution and at least partial salvation of their nationality by the Austrian monarchy, or abandonment of their nationality and salvation of the revolution by the collapse of that monarchy. At that time the fate of revolution in eastern Europe depended on the attitude of the Czechs and the South Slavs; we shall not forget that at the decisive moment they betrayed the revolution to St Petersburg and Olmütz for the sake of their petty nationalist aspirations.

What would be said if the democratic party in Germany placed at the head of their programme the demand for the return of Alsace, Lorraine, and also Belgium, which belongs in every respect to France, on the pretext that the majority of the population there is Germanic? How ridiculous the German democrats would make themselves if they wanted to set up a pan-German

82. Engels made an ironical use here of the official Austrian expression for the monarchy as a whole (österreichische Gesamtmonarchie), including both the hereditary Austrian lands and the kingdom of Hungary.

alliance of Germans, Danes, Swedes, Englishmen and Dutchmen, for the 'liberation' of all German-speaking lands! Luckily German democracy has advanced beyond these fantasies. The German students of 1817 and 1830 nursed similar reactionary fantasies and are now evaluated throughout Germany according to their deserts. The German revolution first came into existence, the German nation first began to be something, when people had entirely freed themselves from these futilities.

But pan-Slavism is just as childish and reactionary as pan-Germanism. If one re-reads the history of the pan-Slav movement in Prague last spring, one has the feeling of being carried back thirty years: tricolour ribbons, Old Frankish costume, Old Slav masses, a complete restoration of the era and the customs of the primeval forest, the Svornost – a complete copy of the Burschenschaft,[83] the Slav Congress – a new edition of the Wartburg Festival,[84] the same phrases, the same wild enthusiasm, the same lamentations afterwards: 'We a stately edifice had built,'[85] etc. Anyone who wants to see this famous song translated into Slav prose should read Bakunin's pamphlet.

Just as, in the long run, there emerged from the German Burschenschaften the most emphatically counter-revolutionary attitude, the most furious hatred of the French and the most narrow-minded nationalism, just as they later all became traitors to the cause for which they had pretended to enthuse, precisely in the same way, only more quickly, because the year 1848 was a year of revolution, did the democratic appearance of the democratic pan-Slavists dissolve into fanatical hatred of the Germans and Magyars, indirect opposition to the restoration of Poland (Lubomirsky),[86] and direct attachment to the counter-revolution.

And if a few upright Slav democrats now called on the Austrian

83. Svornost: Czech nationalist student organization, set up in Bohemia in March 1848. Burschenschaften: German student organizations, set up in the 1810s, which agitated for German unification.

84. The Wartburg Festival was a celebration of the three-hundredth anniversary of the Reformation, held on 18 October 1817, at which the students demonstrated against Metternich and in favour of German unification.

85. *Wir hatten gebauet ein staatliches Haus*; the title of a song by August Daniel Binzer mourning the dissolution of the Jena Burschenschaft in 1819.

86. Jerzy, Prince Lubomirsky was a reactionary and pan-Slavist Polish magnate who took part in the Slav Congress and later in 1848 sat in the Austrian Reichstag.

Slavs to join the revolution, to look on the Austrian monarchy as their main enemy, and indeed to side with the Magyars in the interests of the revolution, this reminds one of the hen which runs around at the edge of the pond in despair over the young ducks it has itself incubated, which now suddenly escape into an environment utterly foreign to it, where it cannot follow them.

Let us in any case have no illusions about this. With all pan-Slavists, nationality, i.e. imaginary, general Slav nationality, *comes before the revolution.* The pan-Slavists want to join the revolution on condition that they are permitted to constitute all Slavs without exception, and without regard for the most vital necessities, into independent Slav states. We Germans would have gone far in March if we had wanted to lay down the same absurd conditions! However, the revolution does not allow conditions to be dictated to it. Either one is a revolutionary and accepts the consequences of the revolution, whatever they may be, or one is thrown into the arms of the counter-revolution and is one morning to be found arm in arm with Nicholas and Windischgrätz, perhaps entirely unknowingly and unwillingly.

The Magyars and ourselves should guarantee the Austrian Slavs their independence – this is what Bakunin demands, and people of the calibre of a Ruge are actually capable of making him such promises in secret. They are demanding of us and the other revolutionary nations of Europe that we should guarantee an existence without let or hindrance to the centres of counter-revolution situated close by our door, a right freely to conspire and bear arms against the revolution; that we should constitute a counter-revolutionary Czech state right in the heart of Germany, that we should break the power of the German, Polish and Magyar revolutions by thrusting between them Russian advance posts on the Elbe, in the Carpathians and on the Danube!

We would not even think of it. We reply to the sentimental phrases about brotherhood which are offered to us here in the name of the most counter-revolutionary nations in Europe that hatred of the Russians was, and still is, the *first revolutionary passion* of the Germans; that since the revolution a hatred of the Czechs and the Croats has been added to this, and that, in common with the Poles and the Magyars, we can only secure the revolution against these Slav peoples by the most decisive acts of terrorism. We now know where the enemies of the revolution are concentrated: in Russia and in the Slav lands of Austria; and no phrases, no references to an indefinite democratic future of these lands will prevent us from treating our enemies as enemies.

And if Bakunin finally proclaims the following:

Truly, the Slav must not *lose* anything, he must *gain*! Truly, he must live! And we *shall* live. *As long as the smallest part* of our rights is contested, as long as *a single member is divided off from our general body or kept torn away* from it, just so long will we fight *to the utmost,* an implacable, life-and-death struggle, until finally Slavdom is great and free and stands in the world independently –

if revolutionary pan-Slavism means this passage seriously, and leaves the revolution entirely out of the picture where it is a question of the imaginary Slav nationality, then we too know what we have to do.

Then we shall fight 'an implacable life-and-death struggle' with Slavdom, which has betrayed the revolution; a war of annihilation and ruthless terrorism, not in the interests of Germany but in the interests of the revolution!

THE TRIAL OF THE RHINELAND DISTRICT COMMITTEE OF DEMOCRATS. SPEECH BY KARL MARX IN HIS OWN DEFENCE[87]

N.Rh.Z., 25 February 1849

Gentlemen of the jury!

If the action now in progress had been brought *before* 5 December, I should have understood the charge made by the public prosecutor. Now, *after* 5 December, I do not understand how the public prosecutor still dares to call on laws which the Crown itself has trodden underfoot.

On what has the ministry based its criticism of the National Assembly, of the decision to refuse to pay taxes? On the laws of 6 April and 8 April 1848. And what did the government do on 5 December 1848, when it unilaterally promulgated a constitution and imposed a new electoral law on the country? It thereby tore up the laws of 6 April and 8 April. These laws no longer exist for

87. The trial of the Rhineland District Committee of Democrats took place on 8 February 1849. Marx, Karl Schapper, and the lawyer Karl Schneider II were accused in connection with the Proclamation of 18 November 1848, signed by the three men, calling on citizens to forcibly resist attempts to collect taxes (printed in *MEW* 6, p. 33). They were all acquitted by the jury.

the supporters of the government. Should they continue to exist
for its opponents? On 5 December, the government put itself on a
revolutionary footing, namely the footing of *counter-revolution.* In
this situation there are only accomplices and revolutionaries. The
government itself changed the mass of citizens into rebels, in so
far as they based themselves on existing laws and defended those
laws against the government's breach of them. *Before* 5 December
it was possible to disagree about the meaning of the National
Assembly's transfer to Brandenburg, its dissolution, and the state
of siege in Berlin. *After* 5 December it became an authentic fact
that these measures formed the introduction to the counter-
revolution, that any modes of action were permissible against a
party which itself no longer recognized the conditions under
which it *was* the government, and therefore could no longer be
recognized by the country as the government. Gentlemen! The
Crown could at least have saved the appearance of legality; it has
disdained even to do this. It could have dispersed the National
Assembly and then had its ministry appear before the country and
say: 'We have ventured on a coup d'état. The situation forced us
to do this. Formally speaking, we have disregarded the law, but
there are moments of crisis when the very existence of the state is
at risk. There is only *one* inviolable law on such occasions, the law
of the state's own preservation. When we dissolved the Assembly,
no constitution existed. Therefore, we could not have broken the
constitution. However, two organic laws do exist, those of 6
April and 8 April 1848. In point of fact only *a single* organic law
exists, the *electoral law.* We invite the country to participate in
new elections in accordance with *this* law. We, the *responsible
ministry,* will appear before the Assembly which emerges from
these elections. We expect this Assembly to recognize the coup
d'état as a *deed of deliverance* necessitated by the circumstances. It
will give its retrospective sanction to the coup. It will say that we
have infringed against a legal formula in order to save the fatherland. Let the Assembly decide our fate!'

If the ministry had acted in this way, it could have brought us
before its tribunal with some *apparent* justification. The Crown
would have saved the appearance of legality. It was not able to do
this, nor did it *wish* to.

In the eyes of the Crown, the March revolution was a brute fact.
One brute fact can only be extirpated by another. In annulling the
new elections due to be held on the basis of the law of April 1848,

the ministry *denied* its *responsibility, annulled the very court it was responsible to.* In this way it transformed the National Assembly's appeal to the people from the outset into mere appearance, fiction, an imposture. In inventing a Chamber resting on a property qualification as an integral part of the legislative assembly, the ministry tore up the organic laws, abandoned the legal foundation, falsified the elections and denied the people any possibility of judging the Crown's 'deed of deliverance'.

It follows, gentlemen, that one fact cannot be denied, and no later historian will deny it: the Crown has made a revolution, it has thrown the existing legal situation overboard, and it cannot appeal to the laws it has so shamefully invalidated. After the successful conclusion of a revolution, one can hang one's opponents but not condemn them. One can clear them out of the way as defeated foes, but not judge them as criminals. After a successful revolution or counter-revolution one cannot apply the laws one had invalidated against the *defenders* of those same laws. This is a cowardly semblance of legality, which you, gentlemen of the jury, will not sanction by your final judgement.

I have told you, gentlemen, that the government has falsified the judgement of the people on the Crown's 'deed of deliverance'. Nevertheless, the people have already decided *against* the Crown and *for* the National Assembly. The elections to the Second Chamber are the only legally valid elections, because they alone took place on the basis of the law of 8 April 1848. And almost all the tax-refusers have been re-elected to the Second Chamber, many of them two or three times over. The deputy for Cologne, Schneider II,[88] is in fact one of the accused in this trial. The question of the right of the National Assembly to resolve to refuse to pay taxes has therefore already been confirmed in practice by the people.

Leaving aside this supreme judgement, you will all concede, gentlemen, that you are not confronted here with a crime in the ordinary sense, that there is here absolutely no conflict with the laws, such as is relevant to this forum. In normal circumstances, the public power executes the existing laws; the criminal is he who breaks those laws or violently opposes the public power in its

88. Karl Schneider II was a Cologne lawyer and sat as a Radical-Democrat in the Prussian National Assembly. He was chairman of the Cologne Democratic Society, and a member of the Cologne Committee of Public Safety formed during the September crisis as the nucleus of a revolutionary government.

execution of those laws. In our case, one public power has broken the law, and the other public power, it is unimportant which one, has upheld it. A conflict between two state powers does not lie within the jurisdiction of either private law or criminal law. The question as to who is in the right, the Crown or the National Assembly, is a historical question. All the juries, all the courts of Prussia, cannot decide this question. There is only one power which can decide it: history. I do not understand, therefore, how we can be accused on the basis of the Code Pénal.

We are dealing here with a struggle between two powers, and only superior power can decide between two powers. This has been pointed out equally by the revolutionary and by the counter-revolutionary press, gentlemen. An organ of the government itself proclaimed the same fact shortly before the decisive phase of the struggle. The *Neue Preussische Zeitung*, the organ of the present ministry, saw this point very clearly. A few days before the crisis, it made approximately the following statement: this is no longer a matter of law, but of force, and we shall see whether the old kingdom by the grace of God still has the force. The *Neue Preussische Zeitung* grasped the situation correctly. Force versus force. A physical victory had to decide the issue. The counter-revolution has won, but this only concludes the first act of the drama. In England, the struggle lasted for more than twenty years. After repeated victories, Charles I finally mounted the scaffold. And what guarantee can there be, gentlemen, that the present ministry and the officials who have made themselves into its instruments will not be condemned as traitors by the present Chamber or by its successors?

Gentlemen! The public prosecutor has sought to base his accusation on the laws of 6 and 8 April. I was therefore compelled to demonstrate that those very laws speak against a conviction. But I shall not conceal the fact that I do not recognize these laws, and will never recognize them. They were never even valid for the deputies who emerged from the popular elections; still less could they prescribe a path for the March revolution to follow.

How did the laws of 6 April and 8 April arise? Through an agreement reached between the government and the United Diet. In this way they hoped to establish continuity with the old legal situation and suppress the revolution which had swept away this situation. Men like Camphausen, etc. considered it important to preserve the appearance of lawful progress. And how did they do this? By a series of obvious and inept contradictions. Let us dwell for a moment on the old legal position, gentlemen. Was not the very existence of Prime Minister Camphausen a breach of the law, since he was a *responsible minister*, a minister without a previous official career in the Prussian administration? Camphausen's position as a *responsible Prime Minister* was illegal. This *legally* non-existent official recalled the United Diet in order to have it pass laws it was not *legally* entitled to pass. And this self-condemning formalistic game was described as progress through the law, as the maintenance of the legal foundation!

But let us disregard the formal aspect, gentlemen. What was the United Diet? The representative of old, decayed social relations. The revolution had taken place in opposition to these relations. The representative of the defeated society was then presented with organic laws which were supposed to recognize, regulate and organize the revolution against that old society. What an absurd contradiction! The Diet had collapsed with the old monarchy.

Now, gentlemen, let us look squarely at the so-called *legal foundation*. I am all the more compelled to discuss this point because we are rightly considered to be the foes of the legal foundation, apart from the fact that the laws of 6 April and 8 April owe their existence merely to the formal recognition of the legal foundation.

First and foremost, the Diet represented big landed property. Big landed property was in reality the basis of the medieval, *feudal society*. In contrast to this, *our* society, *modern bourgeois society*, rests on industry and trade. Landed property itself has lost all the previous conditions of its existence, it has become dependent on trade and industry. Agriculture is consequently now carried on in an industrial fashion, and the old feudal lords have sunk to the position of manufacturers of cattle, wool, corn, sugar beet, schnapps and so on, in other words to people who engage in trade with the products of their industries, just like any other tradesman! However much they might hold fast to their old prejudices, they have in practice become members of the bourgeoisie, who produce as much as possible as cheaply as possible, who buy where they can get the best bargain and sell at the highest possible price. These gentlemen's mode of life, of production and of appropriation therefore gives the lie to their inherited and grandiloquent delusions. Landed property requires *medieval modes of production and commercial intercourse* to be the dominating element in society. The United Diet represented this medieval mode of production and intercourse, which had long ceased to exist, and whose representatives in equal measure held onto their old privileges and joined in the enjoyment and exploitation of the advantages of the new society. The new bourgeois society, which rests on entirely different foundations and on a changed mode of production, had to seize political power for itself; it had to snatch this power from the hands of those who represented the interests of the foundering society, and whose political power, in its entire organization, had proceeded from entirely different material relations of society. *Hence the revolution.* The revolution was directed against the *absolute monarchy*, the highest political expression of the old society. But it was directed just as much against the *representation of the estates*, a social order long since destroyed by modern industry, or, at the most, existing in the form of a few pretentious remnants daily further outstripped by bourgeois society and driven into the background in a state of dissolution. Why then was the view taken that the new society which asserted its rights in the revolution should allow the United Diet, the representative of the old society, to dictate laws to it?

In order to maintain the *legal foundation*, it is alleged. But what do you understand by the maintenance of the legal foundation, gentlemen? The maintenance of laws which belong to a bygone social epoch, which were made by the representatives of extinct or declining social interests, and which therefore also convert interests contradictory to the general need into laws. However, society does not depend on the law. That is a legal fiction. The law depends rather on society, it must be the expression of society's communal interests and needs, arising from the existing material mode of production, and not the arbitrary expression of the will of the single individual. I have here in my hands the Code Napoléon, but it is not the Code which created modern bourgeois society. Instead, it is bourgeois society, as it originated in the eighteenth century and underwent further development in the nineteenth century, which finds its merely legal expression in the Code. As soon as the Code ceases to correspond to social relations, it is no more than a bundle of paper. Social relations cannot make old laws the foundation of the new development of society; nor could these old laws have created the old social circumstances.

These laws emerged from these old circumstances, and they

must perish with them. They must necessarily alter in line with changes in the condition of life. The defence of old laws against the new needs and claims of social development is fundamentally nothing but a hypocritical defence of outdated particular interests against the contemporary interest of the whole. This *attempt to maintain the legal foundation* involves treating particular interests as *dominant* when they are in fact *no longer dominant*; it involves the imposition on a society of laws which are themselves condemned by that society's conditions of life, its mode of appropriation, its trade and its material production; it involves the prolongation of the activities of legislators who only serve particular interests; it involves the misuse of the state power in order to forcibly subordinate the interests of the majority to the interests of the minority. At every moment, therefore, this attempt comes into conflict with existing needs, hinders trade and industry, and sets the stage for *social crises* which come to a head in *political revolutions*.

This is the true meaning of this attachment to the legal foundation, of maintenance of the legal foundation. And this phrase 'the legal foundation', involving either conscious deception or unconscious self-deception, was used to support the recall of the United Diet, and the fabrication by it of organic laws for the National Assembly made necessary by the revolution and created by it. And these laws are supposed to provide the guidelines for the National Assembly!

The National Assembly represented modern bourgeois society as opposed to the feudal society represented in the United Diet. It was elected by the people in order independently to establish a constitution which would correspond to the conditions of life which had come into conflict with the previous political organization and the previous laws. It was therefore sovereign from the outset, a constituent assembly. If it nevertheless condescended to adopt the standpoint of compromise and negotiation, this was a purely formal act of politeness towards the Crown, a mere ceremony. It is not necessary here for me to examine the question whether the Assembly had the right to act on behalf of the people in becoming the *Vereinbarungsversammlung*. In the judgement of the Assembly, a conflict with the Crown could be avoided with the good will of both parties.

This much however is certain: the laws of 6 and 8 April, negotiated with the United Diet, were formally invalid. Materially, they were only significant in so far as they expressed and laid down the conditions under which the National Assembly could be a real expression of popular sovereignty. The 'United Diet legislation' was only a form of words which spared the Crown the humiliation of proclaiming: *I have been defeated.*

N.Rh.Z., 27 February 1849

Gentlemen of the jury,

I shall now proceed to the closer elucidation of the prosecution's case.

The public prosecutor said:

The Crown has alienated a part of the power which lay entirely in its hands. Even in private life, an act of renunciation does not go beyond the clear words in which the renunciation is made. But the law of 8 April 1848 does not concede to the National Assembly the right to refuse to pay taxes, nor does it fix on Berlin as the National Assembly's necessary place of residence.

Gentlemen! The power in the hands of the Crown had been *smashed to pieces*; it surrendered power to save what fragments it could. You will recall, gentlemen, how shortly after his accession to the throne, the king gave a formal pledge in Königsberg and Berlin that he would concede a constitution. You will recall how the king swore high and low, in 1847, at the opening of the United Diet, that he would permit no piece of paper to come between him and *his* people. After March 1848, the king himself, through the medium of the constitution he promulgated, proclaimed that he was a *constitutional* king. He inserted this abstract piece of foreign frippery, this piece of paper, between his people and himself. Will the public prosecutor dare to assert that the king voluntarily contradicted his solemn promises in such a striking way, that he voluntarily rendered himself guilty before all Europe of the intolerable inconsistency of consenting to negotiate with the Assembly or to issue a constitution? The king made the concessions *enforced* on him by the revolution. No more, no less!

The prosecution's vulgar comparison unfortunately proves nothing. Of course, if I renounce something, I renounce nothing more than I renounce *expressly*. If I present you with a gift, it would be sheer impudence if you endeavoured to extract further favours on the basis of my deed of gift. But after March it was the people who gave, the Crown which received the gift. It is obviously true that the gift must be interpreted in the sense given it by the giver and not the receiver, by the people and not by the Crown.

The Crown's absolute power had been broken. The people had won the victory. The two sides concluded an armistice, and the people were deceived. The public prosecutor has himself taken pains to demonstrate thoroughly to you, gentlemen, that the people were deceived. In order to contest the National Assembly's right to refuse to pay taxes, the public prosecutor pointed out in detailed fashion that if something of the kind was contained in the law of 6 April, it is no longer to be found in the law of 8 April. The intervening period was therefore used for the purpose of removing from the representatives of the people the rights conceded to them two days before. Could the public prosecutor possibly have compromised the Crown's *reputation for honesty* more strikingly? Could there be any more irrefutable proof that the intention was to *deceive* the people?

The public prosecutor continued: 'The right to *transfer* and *prorogue* the National Assembly emanates from the executive power, and is recognized in all constitutional countries.'

As far as the *executive power's* right to *transfer* the legislative chambers is concerned, I would invite the public prosecutor to indicate a single law or example in favour of this assertion. In England, for example, the king had an old-established historical right to call Parliament together wherever he pleased. There is no law which lays down that London is the English Parliament's place of meeting. You know, gentlemen, that in general in England the main political freedoms are sanctioned by common law, not by written law. An example is the freedom of the press. But if an English ministry had the idea of transferring Parliament from London to Windsor or Richmond ... it is sufficient merely to formulate this for its impossibility to be recognized.

In constitutional countries the Crown has of course the right to *prorogue* parliament. However, do not forget that on the other side all constitutions specify the *length of time* during which parliament may be prorogued and the point at which they must be recalled. No constitution exists in Prussia, this is yet to be established; there is no legal time-limit for the recall of a prorogued parliament, but for that reason there is also no royal right of prorogation. Otherwise the Crown could have prorogued the Chambers for ten days, or for ten years, or for ever. Wherein lay the guarantee that the Chambers would ever be called, or, once called, remain in session? The continued existence of the Chambers side by side with the Crown was left to the Crown's own discretion. The legislative power, if indeed one is entitled to speak here of a legislative power, had become a fiction.

Gentlemen! Here, on the basis of a single example, you can see the result of the attempt to compare the conflict between the Prussian crown and the Prussian National Assembly with the situation in constitutional countries. It leads to the *defence of monarchical absolutism*. On the one hand the public prosecutor vindicates the Crown's rights as the rights of a constitutional executive; but on the other hand there exists no law, no custom, no organic institution, to impose on the Crown the limitations proper to a constitutional executive. This is the demand put to the people's representatives: that they should play the role of a *constitutional* parliament *vis-à-vis* an *absolute* monarch!

Does it still need to be shown that the case we are dealing with is not one of an executive and a legislature confronting one another, and that the doctrine of the constitutional separation of powers cannot be applied to the Prussian National Assembly and the Prussian crown? Disregard the revolution, stick merely to the official *theory of Vereinbarung*. Even according to this theory, two sovereign powers confronted each other. One of these powers had to destroy the other, there is no doubt about that. Two sovereign powers cannot function simultaneously, side by side, *in one state*. This would be a self-contradiction, like squaring the circle. Material force had to decide between the two sovereignties. But we ourselves are not required to investigate here the possibility or the impossibility of *Vereinbarung*. Enough of that! Two powers enter into relations in order to conclude a treaty. Camphausen himself implied there was a possibility that the treaty would not come into existence. Speaking from the ministerial bench itself to the *Vereinbarungsversammlung*, he indicated the imminent danger to the country if the compromise did not materialize. The danger lay in the original relationship betwen the compromising National Assembly and the Crown, and now, after the event, the intention is to make the National Assembly responsible for this danger, by denying this original relationship and presenting the Assembly as a *constitutional body*. To solve the difficulty by passing straight over it!

I believe I have proved to you, gentlemen, that the Crown had neither the right to transfer the Assembly nor the right to prorogue it.

But the public prosecutor did not confine himself to investigating the *legality* of the Crown's transfer of the National Assembly; he endeavoured to demonstrate the *expediency* of this action. 'Would it not have been expedient', he said, 'if the National Assembly had obeyed the Crown and moved to Brandenburg?' The public prosecutor bases this expediency on the situation of the Chamber itself. It was not free in Berlin, etc.

Was not the Crown's intention in making this transfer as clear as day? Has it not stripped all the reasons given officially for the transfer of their apparent justification? It was not a matter of freedom of deliberation, but of the choice between sending the Assembly home and arbitrarily issuing a new constitution, and creating a sham representation by choosing docile deputies. When a quorum of deputies unexpectedly turned up in Brandenburg, hypocrisy was abandoned and the dissolution of the National Assembly was proclaimed.

It is clear in any case that the Crown did not have the right to declare the National Assembly free or unfree. No one but the Assembly itself could decide whether it enjoyed or did not enjoy the freedom necessary for its deliberations. There was nothing more convenient for the Crown than to be able to declare the National Assembly unfree and not accountable for its actions whenever it took a decision obnoxious to the Crown, and then to place it under an interdict.

The public prosecutor has also spoken of the government's duty to protect the dignity of the National Assembly against the terrorism of the Berlin population.

This argument sounds like a satire on the government itself. I do not wish to speak of its behaviour towards individual persons: these persons were after all the elected representatives of the people. The government sought to humiliate them in every way. It persecuted them in the most infamous manner, and set on foot a kind of ferocious hunt against them. Let us leave aside personalities, and ask how it preserved the dignity of the National Assembly in its *work*. Its archives – the documents of the committees, the royal embassies, the legislative proposals, the preliminary drafts – have been abandoned to the soldiery, who have turned them into pipe-lighters, heated stoves with them, and trodden them underfoot.

Even the forms of judicial process were not observed; the archives were simply seized without any inventory being taken.

The plan was to destroy this work which had cost the people so much, in order to be able to slander the National Assembly more effectively, and to remove from view those plans for reform which were hateful to the government and the aristocrats. After all this, is it not well-nigh ridiculous to assert that the government transferred the National Assembly from Berlin to Brandenburg out of tender care for its dignity?

I come now to the public prosecutor's arguments on the question of the *formal validity* of the resolution against the payment of taxes.

This resolution could only have attained formal validity, says the prosecution, if the Assembly had obtained for it the *sanction of the Crown*.

But, gentlemen, the Crown confronted the Assembly in the person of the Brandenburg ministry, not in its own person. This then is the nonsensical act the public prosecutor demands of the Assembly: it should have reached an agreement with the Brandenburg ministry to proclaim it guilty of treason and to refuse to grant it any taxes! What does this suggestion mean other than that the National Assembly should have decided on unconditional submission to every demand made by the Brandenburg ministry?

The resolution against the payment of taxes was formally invalid for another reason, says the public prosecutor, for a bill can only become law on the *second reading*.

On the one hand the government ignored the *essential* forms it was bound to observe towards the National Assembly; on the other hand it expects the National Assembly to observe the most inessential *formalities*. Nothing could be simpler! A proposal objectionable to the Crown passes its first reading; the second reading is prevented by the use of armed force. The law is and remains invalid because it lacks a second reading. The public prosecutor has overlooked the exceptional situation which prevailed when the representatives of the people passed that resolution, while threatened by bayonets in their place of meeting. The government has committed outrage after outrage. It has recklessly broken very important laws, including the Habeas Corpus Act[89]

89. On 28 August 1848 the Berlin Assembly passed a form of Habeas Corpus Act, entitled 'A Law for the Protection of Personal Freedom'.

and the law on the militia.[90] It has arbitrarily introduced an unrestricted military despotism, in the form of the state of siege. The people's representatives have been chased from pillar to post. And while *all the laws* are shamelessly broken, they demand that a mere *rule of procedure* should be observed to the letter.

I do not know, gentlemen, whether it is a case of intentional falsification (far be it from me to suppose the public prosecutor would do this) or merely ignorance, when he says that 'the National Assembly never wanted any compromise, it never sought any compromise'.

If the people have any reproach to make of the Berlin National Assembly, it is precisely its lust for compromise. If the members of the Assembly themselves have any regrets, these are regrets over its mania for compromise. It was the mania for compromise which gradually alienated the people, which led to the loss of all its positions of strength, and which finally exposed it to the attacks of the Crown without the defence of a nation behind it. When it wanted at last to assert its will, it stood there isolated and powerless, precisely because it failed to have a will and to assert it at the proper time. It first announced its mania for compromise when it denied the revolution and sanctioned the theory of *Vereinbarung*, when it degraded itself from a revolutionary National Assembly to an ambiguous association of compromisers. It carried its weakness for compromise to an extreme when it accepted von Pfuel's apparent recognition of Stein's army order at its face value. The announcement of this army order had by then become a farce, as it could only be seen as the comic echo of Wrangel's army order. And yet instead of ignoring it, the Assembly eagerly grabbed hold of the Pfuel ministry's toned-down version, which reduced the original to complete meaninglessness. In order to avoid any serious conflict with the Crown it accepted the shadow of a demonstration against the old, reactionary army as a real demonstration. It affected to consider something which was no longer even an apparent solution to the conflict as the real solution. So little desirous of struggle, so much inclined towards compromise, was this Assembly, though presented by the public prosecutor as quarrelsome and mischievous.

Should I point out yet another symptom of the Chamber's

90. On 13 October 1848 the Assembly passed the 'Law on the Creation of a Citizens' Militia'. The militia was dissolved on 11 November after Wrangel's troops entered Berlin.

conciliatory character? Cast your minds back, gentlemen, to the agreement reached by the National Assembly with Pfuel over the law for the cessation of redemption negotiations. If the Assembly was unable to crush the enemy represented by the army, it was of vital importance to win over the friend represented by the peasantry. But the Assembly renounced this friendship. It was more concerned to avoid a conflict with the Crown, to avoid a conflict under all circumstances, to compromise. It considered it to be more important to compromise than to act in the interests of its own self-preservation. And now they reproach this Assembly with not wanting any compromise, with not trying to achieve one!

Even when the conflict had broken out, the Assembly still sought a compromise. Gentlemen, you know the pamphlet produced by Unruh,[91] a man of the Centre. You will have learned from it how many attempts were made to avoid a break, how deputations were sent to the Crown and not allowed an audience, how individual deputies tried to prevail upon ministers who thrust them aside with aristocratic pride, how concessions were made and laughed to scorn. The Assembly wanted to make peace at a time when the only suitable thing was to prepare for war. And the public prosecutor accuses this Assembly of not having wanted a compromise, of not having tried to achieve one!

The Berlin National Assembly clearly abandoned itself to a gigantic illusion, it showed its failure to understand its own position and its own conditions of existence, when it held an amicable understanding, a compromise with the Crown to be possible, and endeavoured to put this into effect, both *before* and *during* the conflict.

The Crown did not want a compromise. It could not. Let us make no mistake, gentlemen of the jury, about the nature of the struggle which erupted in March and was later waged between the National Assembly and the Crown. Here it was not a matter of an ordinary conflict between a ministry and a parliamentary opposition, a conflict between people who were ministers and people who wanted to become ministers, a battle between two political parties in a legislative chamber. Members of the National

91. Hans von Unruh, *Skizzen aus Preussens neuester Geschichte* (Sketches from Prussia's Most Recent History), Madgeburg, 1849. Unruh was a Prussian engineer and moderate liberal politician. In 1848 he led the Left Centre in the Prussian Assembly, from October 1848 he was its chairman. In 1849 he was elected to the Second Chamber.

Assembly, belonging either to the minority or the majority, may well have imagined this to be so. It is the real historical position of the National Assembly, as it emerged from the European revolution and from the March revolution conditioned by the latter, which is the sole decisive factor, and not the opinion of the *Vereinbarungsversammlung*. This was not a case of a political conflict between two parties standing on the ground of *one* society, it was a *conflict between two societies*, a *social* conflict which had taken on a political form, *it was the struggle of modern bourgeois society with the old feudal-bureaucratic society*, the struggle between the society of *free competition* and the society of *guild organization*, between the society of industry and the society of landownership, between the society of knowledge and the society of belief. The Crown by the grace of God, the paternalistic bureaucracy, the independent army, all these institutions formed the appropriate *political* expression of the old society. The appropriate *social* foundation of this old political power was formed by the privileged landowning nobility with its peasants in a state of serfdom or semi-serfdom, small-scale industry organized in a patriarchal or corporate fashion, the mutually exclusive estates, the brutal contrast between town and country, and above all the domination of the country over the town. The old political power – composed of the Crown by the grace of God, the paternalistic bureaucracy, the independent army – saw its actual material foundation vanish from beneath its feet as soon as attacks were made on the privileged estates of the nobility, on the nobility itself, on the domination of country over town, on the subjection of the country people, and on the legislation which corresponded to all these conditions of life, such as the municipal regulations, the criminal law, etc.; in short, on the foundations of the old society.

It was the National Assembly which committed these criminal attacks. And the old society saw that political power had been snatched from its hands when the Crown, the bureaucracy and the army lost their feudal privileges. The National Assembly wanted to abolish these privileges. No wonder, then, that the army, the bureaucracy, and the nobility jointly pressed the Crown to make a coup d'état. No wonder that the Crown, knowing the intimate connection between its own interests and those of the old feudal-bureaucratic society, allowed itself to succumb to this pressure. The Crown was precisely the representative of the feudal and aristocratic society; the National Assembly was the representative of modern bourgeois society. It was a condition of existence for the latter that it should demote the bureaucracy and the army from the position of masters of trade and industry to that of their instruments, that it should *make* them into mere organs of bourgeois commerce. It cannot allow agriculture to be restricted by feudal privileges, or industry by bureaucratic tutelage. This would contradict its fundamental principle of free competition. It cannot allow external trade relations to be regulated by considerations of international dynastic politics instead of by the interests of national production. It must subordinate the organization of finance to the needs of production, whereas the old state had to subordinate production to the needs of the Crown by the grace of God, in particular the need to patch up the royal ramparts, the social supports of the Crown. Just as modern industry is in fact a leveller, so must modern society tear down all legal and political barriers between town and country. In modern society there still exist *classes*, but not *estates*. Its development consists in the struggle between these classes, but the classes are united against the estates and their monarchy by the grace of God.

The monarchy by the grace of God, the highest political expression, the highest political representative of the old feudal-bureaucratic society, can therefore make no *genuine* concessions to modern bourgeois society. Its drive for self-preservation, and the society which stands behind it and on which it rests, will force it again and again to take back the concessions which have been made, to reassert its feudal character, to risk a counter-revolution. After a revolution, counter-revolution is the Crown's constantly self-renewing condition of existence.

On the other side, modern society cannot rest until it has destroyed and removed the official state power inherited from past ages, with which the old society still violently maintains itself. The hegemony of the Crown by the grace of God is precisely the hegemony of the obsolete social elements.

There can therefore be no peace between these two societies. Their material interests and needs require a life-and-death struggle in which one society must win, the other go under. That is the only possible relationship between them. It follows that there can be no peace between the Crown and the popular assembly, the highest political representatives of these two societies. The National Assembly had the choice of either giving way to the old society or stepping forth as an independent power in relation to the Crown.

Gentlemen! The public prosecutor has described the *refusal to pay taxes* as an action 'which shatters the innermost *citadels of society*'. It has nothing to do with the citadels of society.

Why do taxes play such an important part in the history of constitutionalism, gentlemen? This can be explained very simply. Just as the serfs purchased their privileges from the feudal barons with hard cash, so did whole peoples purchase their privileges from the feudal kings. The kings needed money for their wars with foreign nations and also, in particular, for their struggles with the feudal lords. The more trade and industry developed, the more money they required. To the same degree, however, the third estate, the burghers, grew and developed, and came to possess more and more financial resources. The third estate then bought progressively increasing liberties from the kings by means of taxes. In order to make sure of these liberties it reserved for itself the right to renew the grants of money at specific intervals – known as the right to grant and to refuse supply. In English history, in particular, this process can be traced in all its details.

In medieval society, then, taxes were the only bond between the emergent bourgeois society and the ruling feudal state. They formed the bond through which the feudal state was compelled to make concessions to the development of bourgeois society, and to adapt itself to the latter's requirements. In modern states the right to grant and refuse supply has changed into a form of surveillance exercised by bourgeois society over that committee to administer its general interests which is the government.

You will therefore find that a *partial refusal to pay taxes* is an integral part of any constitutional mechanism. This kind of tax-refusal occurs as often as the *budget* is thrown out. The current budget is only granted for a definite period of time; moreover, parliament must be recalled after only a very short interval has elapsed from its prorogation. It is therefore impossible for the Crown to make itself independent. By the rejection of a budget supply is definitively *refused*, unless the new parliament brings the ministry a majority, or the Crown appoints a new ministry in line with the wishes of the new parliament. The rejection of the budget is therefore a *refusal to pay taxes which takes a parliamentary form*. In the present conflict this form was not applicable, because the constitution did not yet exist and was still to be created.

But a refusal to pay taxes such as we have in the present case, which not only rejects the new budget but also forbids the payment of the current taxes, is by no means unheard of. This was a very frequent occurrence in the Middle Ages. Even the old German Diet and the old feudal Estates of Brandenburg made decisions to refuse to pay taxes. And there is no lack of examples in modern constitutional countries. In 1832 in England the refusal to pay taxes led to the fall of the Wellington cabinet.[92] And bear in mind, gentlemen, that it was not the English Parliament which decided on a refusal to pay taxes, it was the people who proclaimed this and accomplished it on their own authority. And England is the historic land of constitutionalism.

The English revolution, which brought Charles I to the scaffold, began with a refusal of supply. The North American revolution, which ended with the Declaration of Independence from England, began with a refusal of supply. In Prussia, too, the refusal to pay taxes may be the harbinger of very terrible things. However, it was not John Hampden who brought Charles I to the scaffold but rather Charles I's own obstinacy, his dependence on the feudal estate, his arrogance in wishing to put down with violence the imperative demands of the newly emerging society. The refusal of supply is only a symptom of the conflict between Crown and people, only a proof that the conflict between the government and the people has reached a high and threatening level. It does not itself produce this conflict and this dissension, but only expresses the existence of such a situation. In the worst case, there follows the fall of the existing government, of the given form of the state. This does not touch the innermost citadels of society. Indeed, in the present case, the refusal to pay taxes was society's act of self-defence against a government which threatened its innermost citadels.

Finally, the public prosecutor accuses us of having gone further than the National Assembly itself, in the incriminating appeal: 'In the first place, the National Assembly did not publish its resolution.' Do I seriously have to reply to this, gentlemen, that the resolution to refuse to pay taxes was not even published in the statute-book?

---

92. The Grey Cabinet resigned in 1832 after the king's refusal to create enough peers to carry through the Reform Bill; for a few days Wellington attempted to form a cabinet, but the threat of a tax-strike (put into effect in some places) was sufficient to compel the return of Grey and the passing of the Reform Bill.

Moreover, it is said, the National Assembly did not call for violence, did not place itself on a revolutionary footing, as we did, but rather wanted to remain on legal ground.

Previously, the public prosecutor had presented the National Assembly as illegal. Now he presented it as legal. In each case the aim was to present us as criminals. If the collection of taxes is declared to be illegal, must I not violently resist the violent accomplishment of this illegality? Even from this point of view, we should be justified in driving out force with force. Anyway, it is absolutely true that the National Assembly wished to remain on purely legal ground, on the ground of passive resistance. There were two courses open to it: the revolutionary course – which it did not adopt, as the gentlemen did not want to risk their necks – and the course of refusing to pay taxes, which remained at the level of passive resistance. It chose the latter course. But in order to carry out this decision the people had to place themselves on revolutionary ground. The attitude of the National Assembly was by no means authoritative for the people. The National Assembly has no rights for itself, it only has the rights handed over by the people for it to maintain. If it fails to execute its mandate, it is extinguished. The people themselves then enter the stage in their own right, and act out of the plenitude of their power. If for example a National Assembly sold itself to a treasonable government, the people would have to drive away both the government and the National Assembly. If the Crown makes a counter-revolution, the people have the right to reply with a revolution. They do not need the permission of any National Assembly. But in fact the Prussian National Assembly has itself stated that the Prussian government attempted a treasonable and criminal act.

I shall briefly sum up, gentlemen of the jury. The public prosecutor cannot apply the laws of 6 and 8 April 1848 against us, after the Crown itself has torn them up. These laws are not decisive in any case, since they were arbitrarily concocted by the United Diet. The National Assembly's resolution against the payment of taxes was formally and materially valid. In our Proclamation we went further than the National Assembly. This was our right and our duty.

Finally, I repeat that only the first act of the drama has come to an end. The struggle between two societies, medieval and bourgeois, will be fought anew in political forms. The same conflicts will return as soon as the Assembly meets again. The organ of the ministry, the *Neue Preussische Zeitung*, has already prophesied this: the same people have been re-elected, it will be necessary to drive away the Assembly a second time.

However, whatever new course the new National Assembly may adopt, the necessary result can be nothing other than this: *complete victory for the counter-revolution* or a *new and victorious revolution*. The victory of the revolution will perhaps first become possible only after the completion of the counter-revolution.

TO THE WORKERS OF COLOGNE

N.Rh.Z., 19 May 1849[93]

At this final moment we warn you against attempting any putsch in Cologne. Owing to Cologne's military situation you would be hopelessly defeated. You have seen in Elberfeld how the bourgeoisie sends the workers into the firing-line and afterwards betrays them in the basest manner.[94] A state of siege in Cologne would demoralize the whole Rhine province, and a state of siege would be the necessary consequence of any uprising from your side at this time. The Prussians will despair at your calm attitude.

The editors of the *Neue Rheinische Zeitung* give you their parting thanks for the concern you have shown for them. Their last word, always and everywhere, will be: *the emancipation of the working class.*

The Editorial Board of the *Neue Rheinische Zeitung*

93. This final issue of the *Neue Rheinische Zeitung* was printed in red.

94. There was a rising of workers and petty bourgeois at Elberfeld against the dissolution of the Second Chamber, which had been elected under the constitution of 5 December 1848, but passed a vote of no confidence in the Brandenburg ministry. The rising lasted from 9 to 14 May 1849, and ended with the heroes' welcome given to the invading Prussian troops by the respectable bourgeois of the town.

Reviews from the *Neue Rheinische Zeitung Revue*[1]

REVIEW: JANUARY–FEBRUARY 1850

Karl Marx and Frederick Engels

'*A tout seigneur, tout honneur.*'[2] Let us begin with Prussia.

The king of Prussia is doing his best to provoke a crisis out of the present period of lukewarm agreements and unsatisfactory compromises. He grants a constitution, then after a little unpleasantness[3] he creates two Chambers which revise this constitution. To ensure that the constitution is acceptable to the Crown, whatever the cost, the Chambers erase every article to which the king might in any way take exception; now, they believe, he will immediately take an oath to this constitution. But on the contrary: in order to give the Chamber proof of his 'royal zeal', Frederick William issues a proclamation in which he makes new suggestions to improve the constitution, the acceptance of which would rob this document of the last semblance of even the least, so-called constitutional, bourgeois guarantees. The king hopes the Chambers will reject these suggestions. Far from it. Though the Chambers may have been mistaken in the Crown, they have now taken care that the Crown will not be mistaken in them. They have accepted everything, but everything: an Upper Chamber, an emergency

1. These three reviews, for January–February, March–April and May–October 1850, first appeared in the *Neue Rheinische Zeitung. Politisch-Ökonomische Revue*, which Marx and Engels edited from London and which was published in Hamburg and New York, in issues 2 (February), 4 (April) and 5–6 (May–October) respectively, the latter double number being the final issue of the *Revue*. They are translated here from the texts printed in *MEW* 7.

2. To every lord the honour he is due.

3. The elections of January 1849 to the Second Chamber, held on the basis of universal suffrage, resulted in a victory for the liberal opposition. Frederick William IV therefore dissolved the Second Chamber in April 1849 and ordered new elections on the basis of the electoral law of 30 May 1849, which laid down a high property qualification as well as unequal representation for different social groups. In this way he secured a Second Chamber consisting largely of big landowners and high state officials, which was prepared to do his will.

court, a veteran reserve and entailed estates[4] – merely so as not to be sent home, merely in order to force the king into finally taking a 'solemn and holy' oath. This is the way the Prussian constitutional bourgeoisie revenges itself.

It will be difficult for the king to invent a humiliation that these Chambers would find too severe. In the end he will feel obliged to declare that 'the more sacred he holds the vow which he is to swear, the more sensible does his soul become of the duties with which God has entrusted him in the interests of the beloved Fatherland',[5] and the less his 'royal zeal' will allow him to swear an oath to a constitution which offers him everything, but his country nothing.

What the gentlemen of the late lamented United Diet, now reunited in the Chambers, are so afraid of, is being driven back to their old position before 18 March;[6] this would mean that the revolution still lay before them, and this time their rewards would be few. Furthermore, in 1847 they were able to refuse the loan supposedly intended for the Eastern Railway,[7] whereas in 1849 they actually voted the government the loan in question first, and made representations afterwards for the theoretical right to grant money.

Meanwhile, outside the Chambers, the bourgeoisie sitting on the juries is taking pleasure in aquitting those accused of political crimes, thereby demonstrating its opposition to the government. In these trials the government is regularly compromising itself, but so are the representatives of democracy – the accused and those in the public gallery. We call to mind the trial of Waldeck, the 'unfailing constitutionalist', the trial in Trier,[8] etc.

4. The constitution as finally accepted by the Chambers and issued by Frederick William on 31 January 1850 retained the following elements of the old pre-revolutionary system: the Upper Chamber, the right to set up emergency courts for high treason trials, the universal obligation to do military service (*Landsturm*), and the entailed and inalienable estates (*Fideikommiss*).

5. Words from Frederick William's message of 7 January 1850 to the Chambers.

6. 18 March 1848: the outbreak of the revolution in Berlin.

7. The loan for the Ostbahn from Berlin to Königsberg (now Kaliningrad) was rejected by the United Diet on 9 June 1847 on the ground that the king had 'totally ignored the rights of the Diet'.

8. Benedict Waldeck was a Left deputy in the Prussian National Assembly, and later in the Second Chamber. He was tried in Berlin in December 1849 for his political activity, but, instead of firmly defending his views, he insisted on his loyalty to the Prussian crown. Karl Grün, the former 'true socialist', behaved similarly at his trial in Trier.

In reply to the question of old Ernst Moritz Arndt,[9] 'Where is the German's fatherland?', Frederick William IV replied: 'Erfurt.'[10] It was not so difficult to parody the *Iliad* in the *Batrachomyomachia*, but no one up till now ever ventured to conceive of a parody of this parody. The Erfurt plan, however, manages to travesty even the *Batrachomyomachia* of the Paulskirche.[11] It is of course completely immaterial whether this incredible assembly convenes in Erfurt or whether the Orthodox tsar forbids it, just as immaterial as the protest against its competency which Herr Vogt will doubtless agree to issue with Herr Venedey.[12] The whole scheme is only of interest to those profound politicians for whom the 'great German' versus 'little German' question[13] was a source of material for their leading articles as productive as it was indispensable, and to the Prussian bourgeoisie, who live in the blissful belief that the king of Prussia, having rejected everything in Berlin,[14] will grant everything in Erfurt.

If the Frankfurt 'National Assembly' will be more or less accurately reflected in Erfurt, the old Federal Diet is reborn in the 'Interim'[15] and reduced to its simplest expression in the

9. In the struggle against Napoleon, nationalist German intellectuals such as Arndt had looked to Prussia as 'the German's fatherland' and to Frederick William III as the national saviour.

10. The Erfurt 'parliament' of March to April 1850 consisted of a number of representatives of the Right in the Frankfurt National Assembly (dissolved the previous year) who supported the Prussian plan to create a 'little German' federal state headed by Prussia, from which Austria would be excluded. Frederick William IV was compelled to abandon this plan almost immediately by joint Russian-Austrian pressure.

11. The *Batrachomyomachia* (Battle of Frogs and Mice), by an unknown author, was a parody of Homer's *Iliad*. The Paulskirche was the meeting-place of the Frankfurt Assembly of 1848–9.

12. Karl Vogt was a natural scientist and a Radical-Democrat deputy in the Frankfurt National Assembly. In 1849 he emigrated to Switzerland and became a professor in Geneva.

13. The problem of whether to exclude Austria from Germany (thus forming a 'little Germany' or *Kleindeutschland*, or to include Austria in part or as a whole, thus forming a 'great Germany' or *Grossdeutschland*, considerably exercised the Frankfurt Assembly in 1849, after it seemed certain to the majority that Germany could only be unified by agreement with either Prussia or Austria.

14. On 3 April 1849 Frederick William IV refused the crown of Germany offered to him by a deputation from Frankfurt.

15. The treaty of 30 September 1849 between Prussia and Austria which provisionally settled the administration of the affairs of Germany, on the basis of the 'maintenance of the German Confederation'.

form of an Austro-Prussian Federal Commission. The 'Interim' has already intervened in Wurtemberg and will soon intervene in Mecklenburg and Schleswig-Holstein.[16]

While Prussia has long been barely scraping its budget together out of issues of paper money, surreptitious loans from the 'Seehandlung'[17] banking house and the remains of the exchequer, and has only now been forced to resort to loans, Austria is in the full flower of national bankruptcy. A deficit of 155 million Austrian florins in the first nine months of the year 1849, which must have risen to 210 or 220 million by the end of December; the complete ruin of government credit at home and abroad following the spectacularly abortive attempt to raise a new loan; the total exhaustion of domestic financial resources – conventional taxes, fire insurance premiums, issues of paper money; the necessity of imposing, on a land already sucked dry, new taxes born of desperation, which will probably never be paid – these are the main characteristics of Austria's financial debility. At the same time the Austrian body politic is decaying more and more rapidly. The government's attempts to resist this process by frantic centralization are in vain; the decomposition has already reached the body politic's outer extremities. Austria is becoming intolerable in the eyes of the most barbarian of its peoples, the mainstays of old Austria – the South Slavs in Dalmatia, Croatia and Banat – intolerable even for the 'loyal' border people.[18] Only an act of desperation still holds out a slight chance of salvation: a foreign war. This foreign war, towards which Austria is being irresistibly propelled, cannot but bring about its rapid and complete disintegration.

Nor has Russia been wealthy enough to pay for its glory, which, moreover, it has had to finance with ready money. Despite the much vaunted gold mines in the Urals and Altai, despite the inexhaustible treasures in the vaults of Petropavlovsk, despite the purchase of government bonds in London and Paris – allegedly motivated by a sheer surplus of money – the Orthodox tsar finds himself obliged to withdraw 5 million silver roubles, under all sorts of false pretexts, from the cash reserves deposited in Petro-

16. See the Review of May–October 1850, below, p. 312.
17. See p. 206, n. 23.
18. 'Border people' (*Grenzer*): the inhabitants of the historic military border districts of Austria, who did military service on the border in return for the right to farm the land.

pavlovsk, in order to cover the paper issue, and he is obliged to have his government bonds sold on the Paris Bourse. Not only this, he also finds it necessary to approach the unbelieving City of London for an advance of 30 million silver roubles.

As a result of the movements of 1848 and 1849 Russia has become so deeply entangled in European politics that it must now urgently execute its old plans with regard to Turkey and Constantinople, 'the key to its house',[19] if they are not to become impracticable for ever. The progress of the counter-revolution, the strength of the revolutionary party in western Europe, which is increasing daily, the internal situation in Russia and the unfavourable state of its finances – all this is forcing it to act rapidly. We recently witnessed the diplomatic prelude to this new and heroic oriental drama.[20] In a few months we shall see the drama itself.

The war against Turkey will necessarily be a European war. This is all the better for Holy Russia, which thereby gains an opportunity of setting a firm foot in Germany, of completing the counter-revolution with the utmost vigour, of helping the Prussians to capture Neuchâtel,[21] and finally, of marching on the centre of the revolution, Paris.

In such a European war England cannot remain neutral. It must take sides against Russia and, for Russia, England is the most dangerous adversary of all. Even if the continental armies must inevitably suffer from overextension as they penetrate further into Russia, and even if they must come to a virtual standstill after crossing the eastern borders of the old Poland – with the risk of the punishment of 1812 being repeated – England nevertheless has the means of striking Russia where it is most vulnerable. Apart

19. Alexander I's description of Constantinople, in a conversation with the French Ambassador Caulaincourt in 1808.

20. In August 1849 the Russian and Austrian governments jointly demanded from the Turkish government the extradition of Hungarians and Poles who had fled to Turkey after the defeat of Hungary.

21. Neuchâtel (Neuenburg), the town and canton of northern Switzerland, was the object of especial Prussian hatred, first because it had thrown off the sovereignty of the king of Prussia and made itself independent in 1848, second because it was the refuge of the revolutionary democrats of south-west Germany after the defeat of the campaign of May and June 1849 in defence of the constitution of the German Reich. In September 1849 the Prince of Prussia told a French agent that the further presence of these elements in Switzerland was intolerable, but that it would take too many troops to recapture Neuchâtel.

from the fact that it can force the Swedes to reconquer Finland, St Petersburg and Odessa have no protection against its fleet. The Russian fleet, as is well known, is the worst in the world, and Kronstadt and Schlüsselberg are just as vulnerable as Saint Jean d'Acre[22] and San Juan de Ulua.[23] But without St Petersburg and Odessa Russia is a giant with severed hands. Furthermore, it cannot do without England even for six months, either for the sale of its raw materials or for the purchase of industrial goods; this became evident even at the time of Napoleon's continental blockade, and is even more the case today. Severance from the English market would drive Russia into the most violent convulsions within a few months. England, on the other hand, can not only do without the Russian market for some time, but can obtain all Russian raw materials from other markets. It is evident that the dreaded might of Russia is by no means as dangerous as is thought. It must nevertheless assume a fearsome form for the German bourgeois, because he rightly suspects that the barbarian hordes from Russia will shortly flood into Germany and play there, as it were, a messianic role.

Switzerland is behaving towards the Holy Alliance in general as the Prussian Chambers behave towards their king in particular. But Switzerland has at least a scapegoat to fall back on, to whom it can pass on two or three times over the blows it receives from the Holy Alliance – a scapegoat, into the bargain, defenceless and at the mercy of its favour and disfavour – the German refugees. It is true that a section of the 'Radical' Swiss in Geneva, Vaud and Berne protested against the cowardly policy of the Federal Council – cowardly both towards the Holy Alliance and towards the refugees; equally true, however, was the Federal Council's assertion that its policy was 'that of the vast majority of the Swiss people'. Meanwhile, on the domestic front, the central government quietly continues to carry out minor bourgeois reforms: the centralization of the customs, coinage, posts, weights and measures – reforms which ensure the applause of the petty bourgeoisie. Of course it has not dared to implement the decision to suspend the

22. A fortress on the Syrian coast, which was taken by Egyptian troops in 1832, and retaken by the English, Austrian, and Turkish fleets jointly in 1840.
23. The fortress of Veracruz on the east coast of Mexico. It was the last fortress to remain in Spanish hands and was finally taken by the Mexicans in 1825.

military treaties[24] and the inhabitants of the founding cantons[25] are still going in droves to Como to sign up for the Neapolitan military service. But for all its humility and complaisance towards the Holy Alliance, Switzerland is threatened by a disastrous storm. In their initial over-confidence after the Sonderbund War,[26] and then completely after the February revolution, the Swiss, who are otherwise so timid, allowed themselves to be seduced into an act of imprudence. They dared something monstrous by wanting to be independent for once; they gave themselves a new constitution in place of that guaranteed by the great powers in 1814, and they recognized the independence of Neuchâtel in spite of the treaties. For this they will be chastised regardless of all their obeisances, favours and police services. And once it is involved in the European war Switzerland's is not the most pleasant of situations. It may have insulted the Holy Alliance; on the other hand, it has also betrayed the revolution.

The suppression of the revolution is being carried out most shamelessly and brutally in France, where the bourgeoisie is leading the forces of reaction in its own interests, and where the republican form of government is allowing these forces to develop with the greatest freedom and consistency. In the short space of a month the reimposition of the wine tax – which immediately and completely ruined half the rural population – was followed in rapid succession by d'Hautpoul's circular, which appoints the police to spy even on civil servants; the law on schoolteachers, which declares that all primary teachers are subject to arbitrary dismissal by the prefects; the education law, which places the schools in the hands of the priests; the transportation law, in which the bourgeoisie vents all its unexpiated desire for revenge upon the June insurgents and, for want of another executioner, delivers them up to the deadliest climate in the whole of Algeria. We shall not mention the innumerable deportations of even the most innocent foreigners, which have continued without a break since 13 June.[27]

24. These treaties (*Militärkapitulationen*) obliged the Swiss cantons to furnish mercenary troops for various foreign powers; article 11 of the Constitution of 1848 forbade the cantons to make such treaties.

25. The three cantons (*Urkantonen*) which founded the Swiss Confederation in the fourteenth century (Schwyz, Uri, and Unterwalden) and took the side of the Sonderbund in the war of 1847.

26. See p. 103, n. 3.

27. On the French events referred to here see 'The Class Struggles in France', Chapter III, in *Surveys from Exile*.

The object of this violent bourgeois reaction is, of course, the restoration of the monarchy. But a considerable obstacle is put in the way of a monarchist restoration by the different pretenders themselves and their parties inside the country. The Legitimists and Orleanists, the two strongest monarchist parties, more or less balance each other out. The third party, the Bonapartists, are by far the weakest. In spite of his seven million votes, Louis Napoleon does not even have a real party, but only a coterie. Always supported by the majority of the Chamber in the general exercise of reactionary rule, he finds himself deserted as soon as his own particular interests as a pretender come into view – deserted not just by the majority in the Chamber but even by his own ministers, who first leave him in the lurch and then force him to declare the next day in writing that – in spite of everything – they enjoy his confidence. Serious though the consequences of these disagreements may be, until now they have only been comic episodes, in which the President of the Republic always comes off the loser. Meanwhile, it can be taken for granted that each monarchist group is conspiring on its own account with the Holy Alliance. The National Assembly has the effrontery to threaten the people openly with the Russians, while there is already enough evidence to prove that Louis Napoleon is plotting with Tsar Nicholas.

To the same extent that the forces of reaction advance the strength of the revolutionary party naturally grows. Ruined by the fragmentation of landownership, by the tax burden and the narrow governmental character of most of the taxes, which are detrimental even from the point of view of the bourgeoisie; disappointed by the promises of Louis Napoleon and the reactionary deputies, the mass of the rural population has embraced the revolutionary party and professes a form of socialism, albeit still very crude and bourgeois. How strong the revolutionary mood is even in the Legitimist departments is demonstrated by the last election in the department of Gard, the centre of royalism and the 1815 'white terror', where a red deputy was elected. Under pressure from big capital, which in the world of commerce and politics has assumed the very same position it had under Louis Philippe, the petty bourgeoisie has followed the lead of the rural population. The situation has changed so radically that even the traitor Marrast and the journal of the *épiciers*,[28] *Le Siècle*, has had

28. Literally 'grocers', a derogatory term for the small shopkeepers. In 'The Class Struggles in France' Marx refers to *Le Siècle* as the 'literary represent-

to come out in favour of the socialists. The position of the different classes towards each other – for which the opposition of the political parties is only another expression – is almost identical with that of 22 February 1848,[29] except that other issues are at stake: the workers have a deeper consciousness of their strength and the peasants, hitherto a politically moribund class, have been swept up into the movement and won over for the revolution.

It is for this reason that the ruling bourgeoisie must attempt to abolish universal suffrage as quickly as possible. In this necessity, on the other hand, lies the certainty of an imminent victory for the revolution, whatever the situation abroad.

The dramatic nature of the situation as a whole is revealed in the strange legislative proposal of deputy Pradié, who in some 200 clauses attempts to prevent coups d'état and revolutions by a decree of the National Assembly. The lack of trust with which high finance regards the apparent restoration of 'order' – here as well as in other capitals – can be seen in the fact that a few months ago the various branches of the House of Rothschild extended their partnership agreement for only *one year* – a period of unprecedented brevity in the annals of commerce.

While the Continent has been occupied for the last two years with revolution and counter-revolution, and the inevitable torrent of words which has accompanied these events, industrial England has been busy with quite another commodity: prosperity. Here, the commercial crisis which broke out *in due course*[30] in the autumn of 1845 was twice interrupted – at the beginning of 1846 by the free trade legislation,[31] and at the beginning of 1848 by the February revolution. Between these two events, a large proportion of the commodities which had been flooding markets abroad gradually found new market outlets, and the February revolution then removed the competition of continental industry in these markets, while English industry did not lose much more from the disruption of the continental market than it would have lost without the revolution from a continuation of the crisis. The

---

ative of the constitutional-monarchist petty bourgeoisie'; *Surveys from Exile*, p. 104.

29. The first day of the disturbances in Paris which led up to the February revolution. At this time the parties were all united on the objective of removing Guizot, though divided on further objectives.

30. In English in the original.

31. i.e. the repeal of the Corn Laws.

February revolution, by temporarily bringing continental industry almost to a standstill, helped the English to weather a crisis year quite tolerably; it contributed substantially to clearing accumulated stocks on the overseas markets and made a new industrial boom possible in the spring of 1849. This boom which, moreover, has extended to a large part of continental industry, has reached such a level in the last three months that the manufacturers claim that they have never known such good times – a claim which is always made on the eve of a crisis. The factories are overwhelmed with orders and are operating at an accelerated rate; they are resorting to every possible means to circumvent the Ten Hours Act and to increase working hours; scores of new factories are being built throughout the industrial districts, and old ones are being extended. Ready money is being loaded onto the market, idle capital is striving to take advantage of this period of general profit; the discount rate is giving rise to speculation and quick investments in manufacturing or in trade in raw materials; almost all articles are rising absolutely in price; all prices are rising relatively.

In short, England is enjoying the full bloom of 'prosperity'. The only question is how long this intoxication will last. Not very long, at any rate. Many of the larger markets – particularly the East Indies – are already almost saturated. Even now exports are being directed less to the really large markets than to the entrepots of world trade, from where goods can be directed to the more favourable markets. As a result of the colossal productive forces which English industry added in the years 1846, 1847 and particularly 1849 to those which already existed in the period 1843–45, and which it still continues to add to, the remaining markets, particularly in North and South America and Australia, will be likewise saturated; and with the first news of their saturation '*panic*'[32] will ensue in speculation and in production simultaneously – perhaps as early as the end of spring, at the latest in July or August. However, as this crisis will inevitably coincide with great clashes on the Continent, it will bear fruit of a very different type from all preceding crises. Whereas hitherto every crisis has been the signal for further progress, for new victories by the industrial bourgeoisie over the landowners and financial bourgeoisie, this crisis will mark the beginning of the modern

32. In English in the original.

English revolution, a revolution in which Cobden will assume the role of Necker.[33]

Now we come to America. The most important thing which has happened here, still more important than the February revolution, is the discovery of the Californian gold mines. Even now, after scarcely eighteen months, it can be predicted that this discovery will have much greater consequences than the discovery of America itself. For three hundred and thirty years all trade from Europe to the Pacific Ocean has been conducted with a touching, long-suffering patience around the Cape of Good Hope or Cape Horn. All proposals to cut through the Isthmus of Panama have come to grief because of the narrow-minded jealousy of the trading nations. The Californian gold mines were only discovered eighteen months ago and the Yankees have already set about building a railway, a great overland road and a canal from the Gulf of Mexico, steamships are already sailing regularly from New York to Chagres, from Panama to San Francisco, Pacific trade is already concentrating in Panama and the journey around Cape Horn has become obsolete. A coastline which stretches across thirty degrees of latitude, one of the most beautiful and fertile in the world and hitherto more or less un-populated, is now being visibly transformed into a rich, civilized land thickly populated by men of all races, from the Yankee to the Chinese, from the Negro to the Indian and Malay, from the Creole and Mestizo to the European. Californian gold is pouring in torrents over America and the Asiatic coast of the Pacific and is drawing the reluctant barbarian peoples into world trade, into the civilized world. For the second time world trade has found a new direction. What Tyre, Carthage and Alexandria were in antiquity, Genoa and Venice in the Middle Ages, what London and Liverpool have been hitherto, the emporia of world trade – this is what New York, San Francisco, San Juan del Norte, Léon, Chagres and Panama will now become. The focal point of international traffic – in the Middle Ages, Italy; in modern times, England – is now the southern half of the North American peninsula: industry and

33. The financial reforms of the banker Jacques Necker in the 1780s were both a contributory factor to the outbreak of the first French revolution and an attempt to prevent it. Richard Cobden, along with John Bright, was the leader of the Anti-Corn-Law League of the 1840s, and the political leader of the industrial bourgeoisie generally. He subsequently became a Liberal minister. For Marx's views on English political development, see the Introduction to *Surveys from Exile*, pp. 18–24.

commerce in the Old World must make tremendous efforts if they are to avoid falling into the same state of decline as the industry and commerce of Italy since the sixteenth century, if England and France are not to become what Venice, Genoa and Holland are today. In a few years we shall have a regular steam-packet line from England to Chagres, from Chagres and San Francisco to Sydney, Canton and Singapore. Thanks to the Californian gold and the untiring energy of the Yankees both coastlines of the Pacific Ocean will be just as populated, just as open to trade, and just as industrialized as is the coast from Boston to New Orleans at present. Then the Pacific Ocean will perform the same role as the Atlantic does now and the Mediterranean did in antiquity and the Middle Ages – the great sea-route for international traffic – and the Atlantic Ocean will decline to a mere inland lake, such as the Mediterranean is today. The only chance for the civilized countries of Europe to avoid falling into the same industrial, commercial and political dependence which characterizes Italy, Spain and Portugal today, lies in a social revolution which, so long as there is still time, will transform the mode of production and exchange according to those requirements of production which arise from the modern productive forces; which will thus make possible the generation of new productive forces which will guarantee the superiority of European industry and so compensate for the disadvantages of Europe's geographical location.

In conclusion a characteristic curiosity from China, which the well-known German missionary, Gützlaff, has brought back with him. The slowly but steadily increasing over-population of the country has long made social conditions in China very oppressive for the great majority of the nation. When the English came they won for themselves the right to conduct free trade with five ports. Thousands of English and American ships sailed to China and within a short time the country was saturated with cheap products manufactured in Britain and America. Chinese industry based on handicraft succumbed to the competition of the machine. The unshakeable Middle Kingdom underwent a social crisis. Taxes could no longer be collected, the state came to the brink of bankruptcy, the population sank into poverty, erupted in rebellion, and scorned, mistreated and killed the emperor's mandarins and bonzes. The country is on the verge of ruin and is threatened by a mighty revolution. But even worse, among the rebellious plebs people appeared who pointed to the poverty of some and the wealth of others, who demanded and still demand a different distribution of property – indeed the total abolition of private property. When Herr Gützlaff came back among civilized people and Europeans after twenty years' absence, he heard talk of socialism and asked what it was. When he was told, he exclaimed in alarm: 'Am I nowhere to escape this ruinous doctrine? Precisely the same thing has been preached for some time in China by many people from the mob.'

Chinese socialism may, of course, bear the same relation to European socialism as Chinese to Hegelian philosophy. But it is still amusing to note that the oldest and most unshakeable empire on earth has, within eight years, been brought to the brink of a social revolution by the cotton bales of the English bourgeoisie; in any event, such a revolution cannot help but have the most important consequences for the civilized world. When our European reactionaries, in the course of their imminent flight through Asia, finally arrive at the Great Wall of China, at the gates which lead to the home of primal reaction and primal conservatism, who knows if they will not find written thereon the legend:

République chinoise
Liberté, Egalité, Fraternité

London, 31 January 1850

*

The wishes of the Prussian bourgeoisie have been fulfilled: the 'man of honour' has taken an oath to the constitution, on condition that it is 'made possible for him to rule with this constitution'.[34] And the bourgeois in the Chambers have already satisfied this desire completely in the few days which have passed since 6 February. Before 6 February they said: 'We must make concessions so that the constitution is ratified on oath; once the oath has been given we can proceed quite differently.' After 6 February they say: 'The king has sworn an oath to the constitution; we have all the guarantees possible; we can safely make concessions.' Eighteen millions have been approved for armaments, without debate, without opposition and almost unanimously for the

34. On 6 February 1850, Frederick William IV took the oath to the constitution of 31 January 1850, and the words quoted are from his speech on that occasion.

mobilization of 500,000 men against an enemy who is still unknown; the budget has been passed in four days, and all government bills pass through the Chambers in less than no time. It is
clear that the German bourgeoisie, as always, lacks nothing in
cowardice and in pretexts for cowardice.

These compliant Chambers have given the king of Prussia
ample opportunity to recognize the advantages of the constitutional system over the absolutist system, not only for the subjects
but also for the rulers. If we think back to the financial troubles of
1842–8, to the abortive attempts to borrow money through the
Seehandlung and the Bank, to Rothschild's dismissive replies, to
the loan refused by the United Diet, to the exhaustion of the
exchequer and public funds, and if we compare all this with the
financial surplus of 1850 – three budgets with a deficit of seventy
millions covered by consent of the Chambers, the mass circulation
of loan certificates and treasury bills, the safer financial footing
provided for the state by the Bank of Prussia, as against the
Seehandlung, and over and above all this, a reserve of thirty-four
millions in approved loans – what a contrast!

According to statements made by the War Minister, the Prussian government regards as probable certain eventualities which
might force it to mobilize its whole army in the interests of European 'peace and order'. Prussia has proclaimed its renewed
membership of the Holy Alliance loudly and clearly enough with
this declaration. It is also evident what enemy this new crusade is
directed against. The centre of anarchy and revolution, the Gallic
Babel is to be destroyed. Whether France is to be attacked directly
or whether this attack is to be preceded by diversionary campaigns
against Switzerland and Turkey, will depend entirely upon how
the situation develops in Paris. At all events the Prussian government now has the means to increase its 180,000 soldiers to 500,000
within two months; 400,000 Russian troops have been marshalled
in Poland, Volhynia and Bessarabia; Austria has at least 650,000
men at the ready. Merely in order to feed these colossal forces
Russia and Austria must begin a war of invasion this year. And on
the question of the initial direction to be taken by this invasion, a
remarkable document has just reached the public.

In one of its latest issues the *Schweizerische Nationalzeitung* has
published a memorandum attributed to the Austrian general
Schönhals, which contains a complete plan to invade Switzerland.
The principal elements of this plan are as follows:

Prussia concentrates around 60,000 men on the Main near the railways; an army corps from Hesse, Bavaria and Wurtemberg concentrates partly near Rottweil and Tuttling and partly near Kempten and Memmingen. Austria draws up 50,000 men in Vorarlberg and in the region of Innsbruck and forms a second corps in Italy between Sesto-Calende and Lecco. In the meantime, Switzerland is delayed by diplomatic negotiations. When the moment comes to attack, the Prussians speed by rail to Lörrach, and the smaller German contingents to Donaueschingen; the Austrians concentrate at Bregenz and Feldkirch, and position their Italian army at Como and Lecco. One brigade stops at Varese and threatens Bellinzona. The ambassadors hand over an ultimatum and depart. Operations begin: the main pretext for the invasion is to restore the federal constitution of 1814 and the freedom of the Sonderbund cantons. The attack itself takes place in a concentric formation against Lucerne. The Prussians advance via Basle towards the River Aar, the Austrians via St Gallen and Zurich towards the River Limmet. The former take up positions from Solothurn to Zurzach, the latter from Zurzach through Zurich as far as Uznach. At the same time a detachment of 15,000 Austrians advances via Chur to the Splügen Pass and combines with the Italian corps, whereupon both advance along the upper Rhine valley towards the St Gotthard Pass; here they join forces with the corps which has moved through Varese and Bellinzona and incite the founding cantons to rebellion. Meanwhile these cantons are cut off from the west of Switzerland by the advance of the main armies, which the smaller contingents make contact with via Schaffhausen, and by the capture of Lucerne; thus the sheep are separated from the goats. At the same time France, which is committed by the 'secret treaty of 30 January' to muster 60,000 men at Lyons and Colmar, occupies Geneva and the Jura under the same pretext which it used to occupy Rome. Thus Berne becomes untenable and the 'revolutionary' government is forced either to capitulate immediately or to starve with its troops in the Bernese Alps.

As can be seen, the project is not bad. It takes into account the lie of the land and proposes taking the flatter and more fertile north of Switzerland first and capturing the only tenable position in the north, that behind the rivers Aar and Limmet, with the combined main forces. It has the advantage of cutting off the Swiss army's main granary and of leaving it for the time being the most difficult mountain terrain. Thus the plan can be put into operation as early as the beginning of spring, and the earlier it is executed the more difficult is the position of the Swiss, who will be forced back into the mountains.

It is extremely difficult on the basis of internal evidence to determine whether the document was published against the will of its authors, or whether it was deliberately composed to find its way into the hands of a Swiss newspaper and be published. Should the latter be the case, its intention could only be to cause the Swiss to exhaust their finances by a rapid and large-scale mobilization of troops – thus producing greater Swiss compliance towards the Holy Alliance – and to confuse public opinion in general as to the intentions of the allies. This would be supported by the ostentatious sabre-rattling accompanying the mobilization of Russia and Prussia and the war plans against Switzerland, and, in addition, by a sentence in the memorandum itself, which recommends the greatest rapidity in the execution of all operations, so that as large an area as possible can be taken before the contingents have concentrated again and moved out. On the other hand there are just as many internal considerations which argue in favour of the memorandum's genuine character as a real proposal to invade Switzerland.

This much is certain: the Holy Alliance will march this year, whether first of all against Switzerland or Turkey, or directly against France; in both cases the Swiss Federal Council can pack its bags. Whether the Holy Alliance or the revolution reach Berne first, it has brought about its own ruin by its craven neutrality. The counter-revolution cannot be satisfied with the Federal Council's concessions, because its very origins are more or less revolutionary; the revolution cannot for one moment tolerate such a treacherous and cowardly government in the heart of Europe between the three nations most closely involved in the movement. The behaviour of the Swiss Federal Council offers the most blatant and, we hope, the last example of what the alleged 'independence' and 'autonomy' of small states between the modern great nations really means.

As far as recent events in France are concerned we refer the reader to the section of the article '1848–1849' contained in this number.[35] In the next number we shall publish a special

35. Chapter II of 'The Class Struggles in France' in *Surveys from Exile*.

article on the virtual abolition of the Ten Hours Act in England.[36]

REVIEW: MARCH–APRIL 1850

Karl Marx and Frederick Engels

(In our previous number the monthly review had to be omitted due to lack of space. We now publish from this review only the part which has reference to England.)

Shortly before the anniversary of the February revolution, when Carlier had the liberty trees cut down, *Punch* published a cartoon of a liberty tree which had bayonets for leaves and bombs for fruit; opposite the French liberty tree, bristling with bayonets, a song is printed in praise of the English liberty tree, which bears the only fruit of reliable quantity: pounds, shillings and pence. But this irritating attempt at wit pales beside the immoderate fits of rage in which *The Times* has been slandering the triumphs of 'anarchy' since 10 March. The reactionary party in England, as in all countries, feels the blow struck in Paris as if it had been actually dealt the blow itself.[37]

But at the moment the greatest threat to 'order' in England does not lie in the dangers emanating from Paris but is a direct consequence of this order itself, a fruit from the English liberty tree: a *commercial crisis*.

We already pointed out in our review for January that a crisis was approaching. It has been precipitated by several factors. Before the last crisis in 1845 surplus capital found an outlet in railway speculation. However, overproduction and excess speculation reached such a pitch that the railway market did not even recover during the prosperity of 1848–9, and even the shares of the most respectable firms in this sector of business are still quoted at extremely low prices. Nor did the low prices for corn and the harvest prospects for 1850 offer any opportunity for the investment of capital, and the various government bonds were subject to too extreme a risk to form the object of large-scale speculation. Thus the surplus capital of the period of prosperity found its usual outlets blocked. For the speculators there remained only the possibility

36. Engels's article 'The English Ten Hours Bill' is translated in *A O B*, pp. 96–108.

37. See 'The Class Struggles in France', in *Surveys from Exile*, pp. 123–8.

of unloading all their capital either into industrial production, or into speculative ventures in colonial foodstuffs and the key industrial raw materials, cotton and wool. With the direct influx of such huge amounts of capital – normally employed in other ways – industrial production naturally grew with extraordinary speed, and as a result the markets became saturated. Thus the outbreak of the crisis was significantly accelerated. Even now the first symptoms of the crisis are becoming evident in the most important sections of industry and speculation. For four weeks the situation in the key industry, cotton, has been completely depressed and within this industry it is the main branches – in particular the spinning and weaving of coarse fabrics – which are suffering most. Cotton yarn and coarse calico have already fallen in price far more than raw cotton. Production is being cut back, and almost without exception the factories are working short time. A temporary revival of industrial activity is hoped for as a result of the spring orders from the Continent; but while the orders already placed for the domestic market, the East Indies, China and the Levant are largely being cancelled again, the continental orders, which always provided work for two months, are hardly coming in at all because of the unsettled political situation. In the woollen industry there are symptoms here and there which indicate that the still more or less 'healthy' state of this business is about to come to an end. Iron production is suffering likewise. Manufacturers think it inevitable that prices will soon fall and they are attempting to prevent too rapid a fall by means of mergers. So much for the state of industry. Let us now turn our attention to speculation. The prices of cotton are falling, partly as a result of new increases in supply, partly as a result of the slump in the industry itself. The same is true of colonial foodstuffs. Supplies are increasing, consumption on the home market is dropping. In the last two months twenty-five shiploads of tea alone have arrived in Liverpool. The consumption of colonial produce, which was held back even during the period of prosperity as a result of the distressed state in the agricultural districts, is all the more subject to the similar pressure which is now making itself felt in the industrial districts. One of the most important colonial traders in Liverpool has already succumbed to this adverse turn of events.

The results of the commercial crisis now impending will be more serious than ever before. It coincides with the agricultural crisis which began with the abolition of corn tariffs in England and has increased as a result of the recent good harvests. For the first time England is experiencing *at the same time* an *industrial* and an *agricultural* crisis. This dual crisis in England will be accelerated, widened in scope and made even more explosive by the convulsions which are now simultaneously imminent on the Continent; and the continental revolution will take on an unprecedentedly socialist character as a result of the repercussions of the English crisis on the world market. It is a known fact that no European country will be hit so directly, to such an extent and with such intensity as Germany. The reason is simple: Germany represents England's biggest continental market, and the main German exports, wool and grain, have by far their most important outlet in England. History is most happily summed up in this epigram addressed to the apostles of order: while inadequate consumption drives the working classes to revolt, overproduction drives the upper classes to bankruptcy.

The Whigs will naturally be the first victims of the crisis. As in the past, they will abandon the helm of state as soon as the threatening storm breaks. And this time they will say farewell for ever to the offices of Downing Street. A short-lived Tory ministry may follow them at first, but the ground will quake under their feet; all the parties of the opposition will unite against them, with the industrialists at their head. The Tories have no popular universal panacea for the crisis, such as the repeal of the Corn Laws. They will be forced at least to carry out a parliamentary reform. This means that they cannot avoid assuming power under conditions which will open the doors of Parliament to the proletariat, place its demands on the agenda of the House of Commons and pitch England into the European revolution.

*

We have little to add to these notes written one month ago on the subject of the impending commercial crisis. The temporary upward trend in business which regularly occurs in spring has finally appeared this year, too, but on a much smaller scale than usual. French industry has particularly profited from this, as it supplies excellent summer fabrics, but in Manchester, Glasgow and the West Riding increased orders have also been received. This temporary revival in industry, it must be remembered, occurs every year and will only delay the development of the crisis a little.

There has been a temporary upward trend in business in the East Indies. The more favourable market situation in England has allowed merchants to sell off their supplies below earlier prices and the situation on the Bombay market has eased a little as a result. These temporary and local improvements in trade are also typical of the episodic movements which occur from time to time, particularly at the beginning of every crisis, and which have only an insignificant effect on its general course.

News has just arrived from America describing the market situation there as completely depressed. America, however, is the most important market; the saturation of this market, the stagnation of business and the drop in prices there mark the actual beginning of the crisis, which will have direct, rapid and inevitable repercussions on England. We need only call to mind the crisis of 1837. Only one article continues to rise in value in America: U.S. Bonds, the only government bonds which offer a safe refuge for the capital of our European apostles of order.

After America's involvement in the downward movement caused by overproduction, we can expect the crisis to develop more rapidly than hitherto in the months to come. Political events on the Continent are likewise daily forcing matters to a head, and the coincidence of economic crisis and revolution, which has already been mentioned several times in this *Revue*, will become more and more inescapable. *Que les destins s'accomplissent!*[38]

London, 18 April 1850

REVIEW: MAY–OCTOBER 1850

Karl Marx and Frederick Engels

The political activity of the last six months has been essentially different from that which preceded it. The revolutionary party has everywhere been driven from the field, and the victors – the various fractions of the bourgeoisie in France, the various princes in Germany – are squabbling over the fruits of their victory. The quarrel is being conducted with a great deal of noise; and it might seem inevitable that there will be an open rupture, and that a decision can only be reached by force of arms. Yet the swords are doomed to remain in their sheaths, and the indeterminacy of

38. Let destiny take its course.

the situation will be repeatedly concealed behind peace treaties, while ever new preparations are made for a phoney war.

Let us first consider the basic *reality* underlying this superficial turbulence.

The years 1843–5 were years of industrial and commercial prosperity, a necessary sequel to the almost uninterrupted industrial depression of 1837–42. As is always the case, prosperity very rapidly encouraged speculation. Speculation regularly occurs in periods when overproduction is already in full swing. It provides overproduction with temporary market outlets, while for this very reason precipitating the outbreak of the crisis and increasing its force. The crisis itself first breaks out in the area of speculation; only later does it hit production. What appears to the superficial observer to be the cause of the crisis is not overproduction but excess speculation, but this is itself only a symptom of overproduction. The subsequent disruption of production does not appear as a consequence of its own previous exuberance but merely as a setback caused by the collapse of speculation. However, as we cannot at this moment give a complete history of the post-1845 crisis, we shall enumerate only the most significant of these *symptoms* of overproduction.

In the years of prosperity from 1843 to 1845, speculation was concentrated principally in railways, where it was based upon a real demand, in corn, as a result of the price rise of 1845 and the potato blight, in cotton, following the bad crop of 1846, and in the East Indian and Chinese trade, where it followed hard on the heels of the opening up of the Chinese market by England.

The extension of the English railway system had already begun in 1844 but did not get fully under way until 1845. In this year alone the number of bills presented for the formation of railway companies amounted to 1,035. In February 1846, even after countless of these projects had been abandoned, the money to be deposited with the government for the remainder still amounted to the enormous sum of £14 million and even in 1847 the total amount of the payments called up in England was over £42 million of which over £36 million was for English railways, and £5½ million for foreign ones. The heyday of this speculation was the summer and autumn of 1845. Stock prices rose continuously, and the speculators' profits soon sucked all social classes into the whirlpool. Dukes and earls competed with merchants and manufacturers for the lucrative honour of sitting on the boards of directors of the various companies; members of the House of Commons, the legal profession and the clergy were also represented in large numbers. Anyone who had saved a penny, anyone who had the least credit at his disposal, speculated in railway stocks. The number of railway journals rose from three to twenty. The large daily papers often each earned £14,000 per week from railway advertisements and prospectuses. Not enough engineers could be found, and they were paid enormous salaries. Printers, lithographers, bookbinders, paper-merchants and others, who were mobilized to produce prospectuses, plans, maps, etc; furnishing manufacturers who fitted out the mushrooming offices of the countless railway boards and provisional committees – all were paid splendid sums. On the basis of the actual extension of the English and continental railway system and the speculation which accompanied it, there gradually arose in this period a superstructure of fraud reminiscent of the time of Law and the South Sea Company.[39] Hundreds of companies were promoted without the least chance of success, companies whose promoters themselves never intended any real execution of the schemes, companies whose sole reason for existence was the directors' consumption of the funds deposited and the fraudulent profits obtained from the sale of stocks.

In October 1848 a reaction ensued, soon becoming a total panic. Even before February 1848, when deposits had to be paid to the government, the most unsound projects had gone bankrupt. In April 1846 the setback had already begun to affect the continental stock markets; in Paris, Hamburg, Frankfurt and Amsterdam there were compulsory sales at considerably reduced prices, which resulted in the bankruptcy of bankers and brokers. The railway crisis lasted into the autumn of 1848, prolonged by the successive bankruptcies of less unsound schemes as they were gradually affected by the general pressure and as demands for payment were made. This crisis was also aggravated by developments in other areas of speculation, and in commerce and industry; the prices of the older, better-established stocks were gradually forced down, until in October 1848 they reached their lowest level.

In August 1845 public attention first turned to the potato blight, which appeared not only in England and Ireland but also

39. John Law, the economist and financier, was one of the key figures associated with the 'South Sea Bubble' which burst in 1720.

on the Continent – the first symptom that the roots of existing society were rotten. At the same time reports were received which no longer left people in any doubt about the huge loss in the corn harvest that had already been expected. These two factors caused corn prices, to rise considerably on all European markets. In Ireland total famine broke out, obliging the English government to give the province a loan of £8 million – exactly £1 for each Irishman. In France, where the calamity was increased by the floods, which caused about £4 million worth of damage, the crop failure was of the utmost gravity. It was no less so in Holland and Belgium. The crop failure of 1845 was followed by an even worse one in 1846, and the potato blight appeared again too, although this time it was not as widespread. Speculation in corn thus had a real basis; it flourished all the more since the rich harvests of 1842–4 had long held it back almost completely. From 1845 to 1847 more corn was imported than ever before. Corn prices rose continuously until spring 1847, when, because of the changing news from various countries about the coming harvest, and because of the measures taken by various governments (the opening of ports to the free import of corn, etc.), a period of fluctuation began. Finally in May 1847 prices reached their highest point. In this month the average price of a quarter of wheat in England rose as high as 102s. 6d. and on single days as high as 115s. and 124s. But considerably more favourable reports soon came in about the weather and the growing crops; prices fell, and in the middle of July the average price stood at only 74s. Unfavourable weather drove prices up again somewhat, until finally, in the middle of August, it was certain that the 1847 harvest would produce an above average yield. The fall in prices could now no longer be stopped; supplies to England increased beyond all expectation, and on 18 September the average price had fallen to 49s. 6d. In the course of sixteen weeks, therefore, the average price had varied by no less than 53s.

During this whole period, not only had the railway crisis continued but, on top of all this, the whole credit system collapsed at the very moment when the corn prices were at their highest, in April and May 1847, and the money market was completely ruined. The corn speculators nevertheless held out through the fall in prices until 2 August. On this day the Bank raised its lowest discount rate to 5 per cent and, for all bills of exchange over more than two months, to 6 per cent. Immediately a series of most spectacular bankruptcies ensued on the Corn Exchange, headed by that of Mr Robinson, Governor of the Bank of England. In London alone, eight great corn merchants went bankrupt, their total liabilities amounting to more than £1½ million. The provincial corn exchanges were totally paralysed; bankruptcies followed one after another at a similar rate, especially in Liverpool. Corresponding bankruptcies took place sooner or later on the Continent according to the distance from London. However, by 18 September, when the price of corn fell to its lowest point, the corn crisis can be regarded as being over in England.

We now come to the commercial crisis proper, the monetary crisis. In the first four months of 1847 the general state of trade and industry still seemed to be satisfactory, with the exception of iron production and the cotton industry. Iron production, given an enormous boost by the railway bubble of 1845, suffered proportionately as this outlet for the excess supply of iron contracted. The cotton industry, the main branch of industry for the East Indian and Chinese markets, had been overproducing for these markets as early as 1845, and very soon a relative recession began. The bad cotton crop of 1846, the rise in prices for both raw material and finished commodity, and the consequent reduction in consumption, all increased pressure on the industry. In the first few months of 1847 production was cut back considerably throughout Lancashire, and the cotton workers were hit by the crisis.

On 15 April 1847 the Bank of England raised its lowest discount rate for short-term bills to 5 per cent, and set a limit to the total amount of discountable bills irrespective of the character of the drawee houses. It also made a peremptory announcement to its customers that, contrary to previous practice, it would no longer renew advances made when these fell due, but would demand repayment. Two days later the publication of its weekly balance sheet showed that the reserves of the Banking Department had dropped to £2½ million. The Bank had therefore taken the above measures to stop the drain of gold from its vaults and to replenish its cash reserves.

The drain of gold and silver from the Bank had various causes. Rising consumption and the considerably higher prices of almost all articles required added means of circulation, particularly gold and silver for retail trade. Further, the continuous payment of instalments for railway construction, which in April alone amounted to £4,314,000, had led to a mass withdrawal of deposits from the Bank. That part of the money called up which was intended for foreign railways, flowed directly abroad. The considerable excess import of sugar, coffee and other colonial produce (consumption and prices having risen even more as a result of speculation), of cotton (following the speculative purchases made since it had become clear that the crop would be scarce), and, in particular, of corn (as a result of repeated harvest failures), had to be paid for mostly in ready cash or bullion, and in this way, too, a considerable amount of gold and silver flowed abroad. This drain of precious metals from England, it may be added, continued until the end of August, despite the Bank's measures mentioned above.

The Bank's decisions, and the news of the low level of its reserves, immediately produced pressure on the money market and a panic throughout English commerce matched in intensity only by that of 1845. In the last week of April and the first four days of May almost all credit transactions were paralysed. However no unusual bankruptcies occurred; trading houses kept their heads above water with enormous interest payments and by the forced sale of supplies, government stocks, etc. at ruinous prices. A whole series of well-established firms saved themselves in this way during the first act of the crisis only by paving the way for their subsequent collapse. But the fact that the first and most threatening danger had been overcome contributed to the raising of confidence; after 5 May pressure on the money market noticeably eased, and towards the end of May the alarm was more or less over.

A few months later, however, at the beginning of August, the bankruptcies mentioned above occurred in the corn trade. Lasting until September, they were hardly over when the general commercial crisis broke out with concentrated force, particularly in the East Indian, West Indian and Mauritian trade. The crisis broke simultaneously in London, Liverpool, Manchester and Glasgow. During September twenty concerns were ruined in London alone, their total liabilities amounting to between £9 and £10 million. 'There were uprootings of commercial dynasties in England not less striking than the fall of those political houses of which we have lately heard so much,' said Disraeli on 30 August 1848 in the House of Commons. The epidemic of bankruptcies in the East Indian trade raged incessantly until the end of the year and was resumed in the first months of 1848 when news arrived of the bankruptcy of the corresponding concerns in Calcutta, Bombay, Madras and Mauritius.

This series of bankruptcies, unprecedented in the history of commerce, was caused by general over-speculation and the resulting excess import of colonial produce. The prices of this produce, which had been kept at an artificially high level for a long time, dropped somewhat before the panic in April 1847, but were subject to a general and steep drop only *after* this panic, when the whole credit system collapsed and one house after the other was forced to sell on a mass scale. This fall was so considerable, particularly from June and July until November, that even the oldest and most reputable concerns were ruined.

The bankruptcies in September were still limited exclusively to *actual merchant houses*. On 1 October the Bank raised its lowest discount rate for short-term bills to 5½ per cent, and declared at the same time that it would henceforth make no more advances against government stocks of any kind. The *joint stock banks* and *private bankers* were now no longer able to withstand the pressure. The Royal Bank of Liverpool, the Liverpool Banking Company, the North and South Wales Bank, the Newcastle Union Joint Stock Bank and others were ruined, one after the other, within a few days. At the same time declarations of insolvency were issued by a large number of smaller private bankers throughout the English provinces.

A considerable number of stock-jobbers, stockbrokers, bill-brokers, shipping agents, tea and cotton brokers, iron manu-facturers and iron merchants, cotton and wool spinners, calico printers, etc. in Liverpool, Manchester, Oldham, Halifax, Glasgow and elsewhere went bankrupt following the general suspension of payments by the banks which characterized the month of October. According to Mr Tooke,[40] these bankruptcies were without precedent in the history of English commerce, both in their number and in the amount of capital involved, and the crisis far exceeded that of 1825. The crisis reached its peak between 22 and 25 October, when all commercial transactions had come to a standstill. A deputation from the City then brought about a suspension of the Bank Act of 1844, which had been the fruit of

40. Thomas Tooke, the economist, was the author of *A History of Prices*..., London, 1848, from which Marx made numerous extracts, and which he drew on extensively for this review.

the deceased Sir Robert Peel's sagacity. With this suspension, the division of the Bank of England into two completely independent departments with separate cash reserves instantly came to an end; another few days of the old arrangement and the Banking Department would have been forced into bankruptcy while £6 million in gold lay stored in the Issue Department.

As early as October the crisis caused the first setback on the Continent. Serious bankruptcies occurred simultaneously in Brussels, Hamburg, Bremen, Elberfeld, Genoa, Livorno, Courtrai, St Petersburg, Lisbon and Venice. While the crisis eased in England, it increased in intensity on the Continent, affecting places hitherto untouched. During the worst period, the exchange rate was favourable for England, and from November on England continuously attracted imports of gold and silver, not only from Russia and the Continent, but also from America. The immediate result was that as the money market eased in England, it tightened in the rest of the commercial world and the crisis grew. Thus the number of bankruptcies outside England rose in November; equally important bankruptcies now occurred in New York, Rotterdam, Amsterdam, Le Havre, Bayonne, Antwerp, Mons, Trieste, Madrid and Stockholm. In December the crisis broke in Marseilles and Algiers and took on a new severity in Germany.

We have now arrived at the point where the February revolution broke out in France. If one looks at the list of bankruptcies which Mr D. M. Evans appends to his *Commercial Crisis of 1847–48* (London, 1848), one finds that in England *not a single concern of any importance* was ruined as a result of this revolution. The only bankruptcies connected with it occurred in stock-jobbing, as a result of the sudden devaluation of all government stocks on the Continent. There were, of course, similar stock-jobbing bankruptcies in Amsterdam, Hamburg, etc. English consols fell by 6 per cent, whereas they had fallen by 3 per cent after the July revolution. Thus, as far as stock-jobbers were concerned, the February republic was only twice as dangerous as the July monarchy.

The panic which broke out in Paris after February, and swept across the whole Continent together with the revolution, was very similar in the course it took to the London panic of April 1847. Credit disappeared suddenly and business transactions came almost to a standstill; in Paris, Brussels and Amsterdam everyone

hurried to the bank to change notes for gold. On the whole, however, very few bankruptcies ensued outside the field of stock-
jobbing, and it cannot easily be proved that these few cases were
necessarily the result of the February revolution. The suspensions
of payment by the Paris brokers, most only temporary, were only
partly connected with stock-jobbing; some were precautionary
measures, by no means caused by insolvency, the rest were
attributable to pure chicanery, aimed at making difficulties for
the Provisional Government in order to force concessions from it.
As far as the banking and commercial bankruptcies in other parts
of the Continent were concerned it is impossible to determine to
what extent they resulted from the duration and gradual spread
of the commercial crisis, how far the situation at the time was
used by already unsound firms to make a judicious exit, and how
far they were really the result of losses caused by the panic
atmosphere of the revolution. At any rate, it is certain that the
commercial crisis contributed far more to the revolution of 1848
than the revolution to the commercial crisis. Between March and
May England enjoyed direct advantages from the revolution,
which supplied her with a great deal of continental capital. From
this moment on the crisis can be regarded as over in England;
there was an improvement in all branches of business and the new
industrial cycle began with a decided movement towards prosperity. How little the continental revolution held back the industrial
and commercial boom in England can be seen from the fact that
the amount of cotton manufactured here rose from 475 million
lb. in 1847 to 713 million lb. in 1848.

In England this renewed prosperity developed visibly during
1848, 1849 and 1850. For the eight months January–August,
England's total exports amounted to £31,633,214 in 1848;
£39,263,322 in 1849 and £43,851,568 in 1850. In addition to this
considerable improvement, manifest in all branches of business
with the exception of iron production, rich harvests were gathered
everywhere during these three years. The average price of wheat in
1848–50 was 36s. per quarter in England, 32s. in France. This
period of prosperity is characterized by the fact that three major
outlets for speculation were blocked. Railway production had
been reduced to the slow development of a normal branch of
industry, corn offered no opportunities due to a series of good
harvests, and, as a result of the revolution, government stocks had
lost the reliable character without which large speculative trans-

actions in securities are not possible. During every period of prosperity capital accumulates. On the one hand increased production generates new capital; on the other, capital which was available but idle during the crisis is released from its inactivity and unloaded onto the market. With the lack of speculative outlets this *additional* capital was forced during these years to flow into actual industry, thus increasing production even more rapidly. How apparent this is in England, without anyone being able to explain it, is demonstrated by this naive statement in the *Economist* of 19 October 1850:

It is remarked that the present prosperity differs from that of former periods within recollection, in all of which there was some baseless speculation exciting hopes that were destined not to be realized. At one time it was foreign mines, at another more railways than could be conveniently made in half a century. Even when such speculations were well founded, they contemplated a realization of income, from raising metals or creating new conveniences, at the end of a considerable period, and afforded no immediate reward. But at present our prosperity is founded on the production of things immediately useful, and that go into consumption nearly as fast as they are brought to market, returning to the producers a fair remuneration and stimulating more production.

Cotton manufacturing, the dominant branch of industry, provides the most striking proof of the extent to which industrial production has increased in 1848 and 1849. The United States cotton crop of 1849 produced a higher yield than in any previous year, amounting to $2\frac{3}{4}$ million bales, or about 1,200 million lb. The expansion of the cotton industry has kept pace with this increase in imports to such an extent that at the end of 1849 stocks were lower than ever before, even after the years of the crop failures. In 1849 over 775 million lb. of cotton were spun, as against 721 million lb. in 1845, the year of the greatest prosperity hitherto. The expansion of the cotton industry is further shown by the great rise in cotton prices (55 per cent) resulting from a relatively minor loss in the 1850 crop. At least the same progress can be seen in all other branches, such as the spinning and weaving of silk, shoddy and linen. Exports in these industries have risen so considerably, particularly in 1850, that they have produced a large increase in the total export figures for the first eight months of this year (£12 million above the corresponding figure for 1848, £4 million above that for 1849), even though in 1850 the export of cotton products has dropped noticeably as a result of the bad cotton crop. In spite of the considerable increase in wool prices, which seems to have been caused by speculation in 1849, but which has now levelled out, the woollen industry has expanded continuously, and new looms are continually being brought into operation. The export of linen textiles in 1844, the highest previously, amounted to 91 million yards, at a value of over £2,800,000, while in 1849 it reached 107 million yards at a value of over £3,000,000.

Another proof of the growth of English industry is the continuously rising consumption of basic colonial produce, particularly coffee, sugar and tea, at continuously rising prices – at least for the first two articles. This increase in consumption is a direct result of the expansion of industry, the more so, as the exceptional market situation created since 1845 by the extraordinary railway investments has long since been reduced to its normal scale, and as the low corn prices of the last few years have not allowed any increase in consumption in the agricultural areas.

In the last few months the broad expansion of the cotton industry has led to renewed attempts to saturate the East Indian and Chinese markets. But the quantity of old stocks still awaiting sale in these areas soon again obstructed these attempts. At the same time, in view of the rising consumption of raw materials and colonial produce, an attempt was made to speculate in these commodities, but a stop was very quickly put to this by the temporary increase in imports, and by the memory of the wounds sustained in 1847, which are still too fresh.

Industrial prosperity will be further increased by the recent opening up of the Dutch colonies, by the impending establishment of trading routes across the Pacific Ocean (to which we shall return) and by the great industrial exhibition of 1851. This exhibition was announced by the English bourgeoisie already in 1849, with the most impressive cold-bloodedness, at a time when the whole Continent was still dreaming of revolution. For this exhibition they have summoned all their vassals from France to China to a great examination, in which they are to demonstrate how they have been using their time; and even the omnipotent tsar of Russia feels obliged to order his subjects to appear in large numbers at this great examination. This great world congress of products and producers is quite different in its significance from the absolutist Congresses of

Bregenz and Warsaw,[41] which have caused our narrow-minded continental democrats so much sweat; different also from the European democratic congresses which the various provisional governments *in partibus infidelium*[42] repeatedly project for the salvation of the world. This exhibition is a striking proof of the concentrated power with which modern large-scale industry is everywhere demolishing national barriers and increasingly blurring local peculiarities of production, society and national character among all peoples. By putting on show the massed resources of modern industry in a small concentrated space, just at a time when modern bourgeois society is being undermined from all sides, it is also displaying materials which have been produced, and are still being produced day after day in these turbulent times, for the construction of a new society. With this exhibition, the bourgeoisie of the world has erected in the modern Rome its Pantheon, where, with self-satisfied pride, it exhibits the gods which it has made for itself. It thus gives a practical proof of the fact that the 'impotence and vexation of the citizen', which German ideologists preach about year in year out, is only these gentlemen's own impotent failure to understand the modern movement, and their own vexation at this impotence. The bourgeoisie is celebrating this, its greatest festival, at a moment when the collapse of its social order in all its splendour is imminent, a collapse which will demonstrate more forcefully than ever how the forces which it has created have outgrown its control. In a future exhibition the bourgeoisie will perhaps no longer figure as the owners of these productive forces but only as their ciceroni.

The loss of the cotton crop has been spreading general alarm among the bourgeoisie since the beginning of the year, just as the potato blight did in 1845 and 1846. This alarm has increased considerably since it became clear that the cotton crop of 1851,

41. The Bregenz meeting of 11–12 October 1850 between the rulers of Austria, Bavaria and Wurtemberg resulted in the signature of the treaty of 12 October by which the three states agreed to oppose Prussia's attempts to gain the headship of the German Confederation. At the Warsaw meeting of 28 October 1850 between Nicholas I, Francis Joseph and Count Brandenburg, the last-named, as Prussia's representative, was put under considerable pressure, and compelled to make concessions to Austria.

42. 'In the lands of the infidels': a favoured expression of Marx's, taken from the title of Catholic bishops appointed to non-Christian territories where they could not reside, and applied here to the impotent governments-in-exile formed after the defeat of the revolutions of 1848, generally by democratic refugees.

too, will not turn out to be much richer than that of 1850. The loss, which would have been insignificant in earlier periods, now represents a very serious threat to the present expansion of the cotton industry, and it has already impeded production considerably. The bourgeoisie, having scarcely recovered from the shattering discovery that one of the central pillars of its social order – the potato – was endangered, now sees the second pillar – cotton – threatened. If just a moderate loss in one year's cotton crop and the prospect of a second has been enough to excite serious alarm amidst the rejoicing over prosperity, a few consecutive years in which the cotton crop really does fail are bound to reduce the whole of civilized society to a temporary state of barbarism. The golden age and the iron age are long past; it was reserved for the nineteenth century, with its intelligence, world markets and colossal productive resources, to usher in the *cotton age*. At the same time, the English bourgeoisie has felt more forcefully than ever the power which the United States exercises over it, as a result of its hitherto unbroken monopoly of cotton production. It has immediately applied itself to the task of breaking this monopoly. Not only in the East Indies, but also in Natal, the northern region of Australia and all parts of the world where climate and conditions allow cotton to be grown, it is to be encouraged in every way. At the same time, that section of the English bourgeoisie kindly disposed towards the Negro has made the following discovery: 'That the prosperity of Manchester is dependent on the treatment of slaves in Texas, Alabama and Louisiana is as curious as it is alarming.' (*Economist*, 21 September 1850). That the decisive branch of English industry is based upon the existence of slavery in the southern states of the American union, that a Negro revolt in these areas could ruin the whole system of production as it exists today is, of course, an extremely depressing fact for the people who spent £20 million[43] a few years ago on Negro emancipation in their own colonies. However, this fact leads to the only realistic solution of the slave question, which has recently again been the cause of such long and violent debate in the American Congress. American cotton production is based on slavery. As soon as the industry reaches a point where it cannot tolerate the United States' cotton monopoly any longer, cotton

43. This was the sum of money voted by Parliament in 1833 to be paid to the plantation-owners in compensation for the abolition of slavery in the West Indies and other British colonies.

will be successfully mass-produced in other countries, and it is hardly possible to achieve this anywhere today except with *free workers*. But as soon as the free labour of other countries can deliver sufficient supplies of cotton to industry more cheaply than the slave labour of the United States, then American slavery will be broken together with the American cotton monopoly and the slaves will be emancipated, because they will have become useless as slaves. Wage labour will be abolished in Europe in just the same way, as soon as it becomes not only unnecessary for production, but in fact a hindrance to it.

If the new cycle of industrial development which began in 1848 takes the same course as that of 1843–7, the crisis will break out in 1852. As a symptom that the excess speculation which is caused by overproduction, and which precedes each crisis, will not be long in coming, we can quote the fact that the discount rate of the Bank of England has not risen above 3 per cent for two years. But when the Bank of England keeps its interest rates down in times of prosperity, the other money dealers have to reduce their rates even more, just as in times of crisis when the Bank raises the rate considerably, they have to raise their rates above the Bank's. The additional capital which, as we have seen above, is always unloaded onto the bond market in times of prosperity, is enough by itself to force down the interest rate, as a result of the laws of competition; but the interest rate is reduced to a much larger extent by the enormous expansion of credit produced by general prosperity, which lowers the demand for capital. In these periods a government is in a position to reduce the interest rate on its funded debts, and the landowner is able to renew his mortgage on more favourable terms. The capitalists with investments in loan capital thus see their income reduced by a third or more, at a time when the income of all other classes is rising. The longer this situation lasts, the more they will be under pressure to look for more profitable capital investments. Overproduction gives rise to numerous new projects, and the success of a few of them is sufficient to attract a whole mass of capital in the same direction, until gradually the bubble becomes general. But, as we have seen, speculation has at this point of time only two outlets: cotton growing and the new world market routes created by the development of California and Australia. It is evident that this time the scope for speculation will assume far greater dimensions than in any earlier period of prosperity.

Let us take a look at the situation in the English agricultural districts. The general pressure produced by the repeal of the Corn Laws and the simultaneous rich harvests has here become chronic, although it has been alleviated somewhat by the considerable increase in consumption caused by prosperity. In addition, with low corn prices the agricultural workers at least are in a relatively better position, although the improvement in England has been more limited than in other countries, where land parcelling is the rule. Under these circumstances the agitation of the Protectionists[44] for the reimposition of corn duties continues in the agricultural areas, although less shrilly and overtly than before. It is evident that this agitation will remain quite insignificant so long as the relatively tolerable position of the agricultural workers continues. But as soon as the crisis breaks, with repercussions in the farming areas, the agricultural depression on the land will provoke considerable unrest. The industrial and commercial crisis will then coincide with the agricultural crisis for the first time, and in all issues which give rise to conflict between town and country, manufacturers and landowners, the two parties will be supported by two great armies: the manufacturers by the mass of the industrial workers, and the landowners by the mass of the agricultural workers.

We now come to the United States of America. The crisis of 1836, which broke out there first and raged most violently, lasted almost without interruption until 1842 and led to a complete transformation of the American credit system. The commerce of the United States recovered on this more solid foundation, if at first very slowly, until from 1842 to 1845 prosperity significantly increased there, too. The rise in prices and the revolution in Europe only brought benefits for America. From 1845 to 1847 it profited from the enormous export of grain and from the 1846 rise in cotton prices. In 1849 it produced the largest cotton crop to date, and in 1850 it made about $20 million from the loss in the cotton crop, which coincided with the new boom in the European cotton industry. The revolutions of 1848 caused a large-scale flow of European capital to the United States, which arrived partly with the immigrants themselves and was partly attributable to European investments in American treasury bonds. This increase in

44. When the Tory party split in 1846 over the repeal of the Corn Laws, the majority group adopted the name 'Protectionist'.

demand for American bonds has forced up their price to such an extent that recently in New York speculators have been seizing on them quite feverishly. Thus, despite all assertions to the contrary in the reactionary bourgeois press, we still maintain that the only form of state to enjoy the confidence of our European capitalists is the *bourgeois republic*. There is only one expression of bourgeois confidence in any form of state: *its quotation on the stock exchange*.

However, the prosperity of the United States increased even more for other reasons. The populated area, the *home market* of the North American union, extended with surprising rapidity in two directions. The population increase, due both to reproduction within America and to the continuing increase in immigration, led to the settlement of whole states and territories. Wisconsin and Iowa were comparatively densely populated within a few years, and there was a significant increase in immigrants to all states in the upper Mississippi region. The exploitation of the mines on Lake Superior and the rising grain production in the whole area around the Great Lakes produced a new boom in commerce and shipping on this system of great inland waterways, which will expand further as a result of an act passed during the last session of Congress, by which trade with Canada and Nova Scotia has been greatly facilitated. While the north-western states have thus gained a new importance, Oregon has been colonized within a few years, Texas and New Mexico annexed and California conquered. The discovery of the Californian gold mines has set the cap on American prosperity. In the second number of this *Revue* – before any other European journal – we drew attention to the importance of this discovery and its necessary consequences for the whole of world trade.[45] This importance does not lie in the increased supply of gold from the newly discovered mines, although this increase in the means of exchange was bound to have consequences for commerce in general. It lies rather in the spur given to investment on the world market by the mineral wealth of California, in the activity into which the whole west coast of America and the eastern coast of Asia has been plunged, in the new market outlets created in California and in all the other countries affected by California. Even taken by itself the Californian market is very important; a year ago there were 100,000 people there; now there are at least 300,000 people, who are producing almost nothing but

45. 'Review: January–February 1850', above, pp. 275–6.

gold, and who are exchanging this gold for their basic living requirements from foreign markets. But the Californian market itself is unimportant compared to the continual expansion of all the markets on the Pacific coast, compared to the striking increase in trade with Chile and Peru, western Mexico and the Sandwich Islands, and compared to the traffic which has suddenly arisen between Asia, Australia and California. Because of California, completely new international routes have become necessary, routes which will inevitably soon surpass all others in importance. The main trading route to the Pacific Ocean – which has really only now been opened up, and which will become the most important ocean in the world – will, from now on, go across the Isthmus of Panama. The establishment of links across the Isthmus by highways, railways and canals is now the most urgent requirement of world trade and has already been tackled in places. The railway from Chagres to Panama is already being built. An American company is having the river basin of San Juan del Norte surveyed with a view to connecting the two oceans, first of all by an overland route and then by a canal. Other routes – across the Isthmus of Darien, the Atrato route in New Granada, across the Isthmus of Tehuantepec – are being discussed in English and American journals. The ignorance in the whole civilized world about the conditions of the terrain in Central America, which has now suddenly been exposed, makes it impossible to determine which route is the most advantageous for a great canal; according to the little information available, the Atrato route and the way across Panama seem to offer the best opportunities. The rapid expansion of the ocean steamer lines has become equally urgent, in order to connect up with the lines of communication across the Isthmus. Steamers are already sailing between Southampton and Chagres, New York and Chagres, Valparaiso, Lima, Panama, Acapulco and San Francisco; but these few lines, with their small number of steamers, are by no means adequate. The increase in steamer lines between Europe and Chagres becomes daily more urgent, and the growing traffic between Asia, Australia and America requires great new steamship lines from Panama and San Francisco to Canton, Singapore, Sydney, New Zealand and the most important station in the Pacific, the Sandwich Islands. Of all the areas in the Pacific Australia and New Zealand in particular have expanded most, as a result of both the rapid progress of colonization and the influence of California, and they do not want to be divided from the civilized world a moment longer by a four to six-month sea voyage. The total population of the Australian colonies (excluding New Zealand) rose from 170,676 in 1839 to 333,764 in 1848; that is, it increased in nine years by 95½ per cent. England itself cannot leave these colonies without steamship links; and the government is negotiating at this moment for a line connecting with the Indian overland post. Whether this line comes about or not, the sheer necessity of a steamship connection with America, and particularly California, where 3,500 people from Australia emigrated to last year, will itself produce a solution. It may be said that the world has only become round since the necessity has arisen for this global steam shipping.

This imminent expansion in steam shipping will be increased further by the opening up of the Dutch colonies already mentioned and by the increase in screw steamers, with which – as is becoming increasingly clear – emigrants can be transported more rapidly, relatively cheaper and more profitably than with sailing ships. Apart from the screw steamers which already sail from Glasgow and Liverpool to New York, new ones are to be employed on this line and a shipping line is to be established between Rotterdam and New York. How universal is the present tendency for capital to flow into oceanic steam shipping is proved by the continuous increase in the number of steamers competing between Liverpool and New York, the establishment of entirely new lines from England to the Cape and from New York to Le Havre, and a whole series of similar schemes which are being hawked around New York.

With the investment of capital in oceanic steam shipping and the building of canals across the American isthmus the ground has already been laid for excess speculation in this area. The centre of this speculation is necessarily New York, which receives the great mass of Californian gold. It has already taken control of the main trade with California and in general performs the same function for the whole of America as London does for Europe. New York is already the centre of all transatlantic steam shipping. All the Pacific steam ships belong to New York companies, and almost all new projects in this branch of industry start in New York. Speculation in foreign steamship lines has already begun in these, and the Nicaragua Company, which was launched in New York, similarly represents the beginning of speculation in the isthmus canals. Over-speculation will soon develop, and even though English capital is flowing *en masse* into all such undertakings, even though the London Stock Exchange will be inundated with all sorts of similar schemes, New York will still remain the centre of the whole bubble, this time as in 1836, and will be the first to experience its collapse. Innumerable schemes will be ruined, but as with the English railway system in 1845, at least the *outline* of a universal shipping system will this time emerge from this over-speculation. No matter how many companies go bankrupt, the steamships – which are doubling the Atlantic traffic, opening up the Pacific, connecting up Australia, New Zealand, Singapore and China with America and are reducing the journey around the world to four months – the steamships will remain.

The prosperity in England and America soon made itself felt on the European continent. As early as summer 1849 the factories in Germany, particularly in the Rhine province, were quite busy again, and since the end of 1849 there has been a general recovery of business. This renewed prosperity, which our German bourgeois naively attribute to the restoration of stability and order, is based in reality only upon the renewed prosperity in England and upon the increased demand for industrial products on the American and tropical markets. In 1850 industry and trade have recovered even further. Just as in England, there has been a temporary surplus of capital and an extraordinary easing of the money market, and the reports of the Frankfurt and Leipzig autumn fairs have reportedly been extremely satisfactory for the bourgeoisie taking part. The troubles in Schleswig-Holstein and Electoral Hesse,[46] the quarrels within the Prussian Union and the threatening notes exchanged between Austria and Prussia have

46. The first war in Schleswig-Holstein had closed with the armistice of Malmö (August 1848); but war broke out again in April 1849, and lasted until July. Prussia finally concluded a peace treaty with Denmark on 2 July 1850 by which all Prussian troops were to be withdrawn from the duchies; the local army of Schleswig-Holstein endeavoured to resist the Danish army, but was defeated at the Battle of Idstedt (5 July 1850). In Electoral Hesse a conflict broke out in September 1850 between the Elector and his parliament; the Elector appealed for help not to Prussia but to Austria and the Federal Diet. Since Hesse was a member of the Erfurt Union, Frederick William replied by occupying Kassel; this was the reason for the threatening exchange of notes between September and November 1850. However the whole affair ended with Prussia's complete submission to the Austrians, the so-called humiliation of Olmütz (29 November 1850). See also below, pp. 310–14.)

not been able to hold back the development of all these symptoms of prosperity for a moment, as even the *Economist* noted, with mocking cockney smugness. . .[47]

We now turn to the political events of the last six months.

In England periods of economic prosperity are always periods of political prosperity for Whiggery – aptly embodied in the person of the smallest man in the kingdom, Lord John Russell.[48] The ministry brings before Parliament little pettifogging reforms which it knows will fail to pass the House of Lords, or which it itself withdraws at the end of the session under the pretext of lack of time. The lack of time is always induced by the previous excess of boredom and empty talk, which the Speaker only brings to an end as late as possible, with the remark that there is no question before the House. At such times the struggle between Free Traders[49] and Protectionists degenerates into pure humbug. The majority of the Free Traders are too preoccupied with the material exploitation of free trade to have the time or inclination to fight further for its logical political extensions; faced with the boom in urban industry, the Protectionists resort to burlesque jeremiads and threats. The parties continue the struggle merely for propriety's sake, in order not to forget each other's existence. Before the last session the industrial bourgeoisie created a huge fuss about financial reform; in Parliament itself they confined themselves to theoretical expostulations. Before the session, Mr Cobden repeated his declaration of war on the tsar on the occasion of the Russian loan, and he almost ran short of sarcasm, so much

47. The passage omitted here forms the opening five paragraphs of Chapter IV of 'The Class Struggles in France', in *Surveys from Exile*, pp. 128–31. In this passage Marx brings his economic analysis to the extremely important conclusion, 'While this general prosperity lasts, enabling the productive forces of bourgeois society to develop to the full extent possible within the bourgeois system, there can be no question of a real revolution. Such a revolution is only possible at a time when *two factors* come into *conflict*: the *modern productive forces* and the *bourgeois forms of production* . . . *A new revolution is only possible as a result of a new crisis; but it will come, just as surely as the crisis itself.*'

48. Lord John Russell was the leader of the Whig party, and Prime Minister in 1846–52 and 1865–6. For Marx's opinion of him, see *AOB*, pp. 245–61.

49. The free trade majority in the House of Commons was composed of Whigs and Peelites as well as the relatively small party led by Cobden that Marx described as 'Free Traders, *par excellence*' (*Surveys from Exile*, pp. 256, 262–4).

did he heap upon the great pauper of St Petersburg. Six months later he was reduced to taking part in the scandalous Peace Congress farce,[50] whose only outcome was that an Ojibway Indian handed a pipe of peace to Herr Jaup[51] – to the great horror of Herr Haynau[52] on the platform – and that the Yankee temperance swindler, Elihu Burrit,[53] went to Schleswig-Holstein and Copenhagen in order to assure the governments concerned of his good intentions. As if the whole Schleswig-Holstein war could ever take a serious turn so long as Herr von Gagern takes part in it and Herr Venedey does not![54]

The great political issue of the past session was actually the *Greek debate*.[55] All the forces of absolutist reaction on the Continent had formed a coalition with the English Tories to overthrow Palmerston.[56] Louis Napoleon had even recalled the French ambassador from London, as much to flatter Tsar Nicholas as French national pride. The whole French National Assembly fanatically applauded this bold break with the traditional English alliance. The affair gave Mr Palmerston the opportunity to present himself in the Commons as the *champion*[57] of civil liberty throughout Europe; he received a majority of forty-six votes, and the result of the coalition, which was as impotent as it was silly, was the non-renewal of the Aliens Bill.[11]

50. In August 1850 an international congress of pacifists met in Frankfurt-am-Main. It was attended by prominent free-traders, philanthropists, and Quakers.

51. Heinrich Jaup was the liberal Prime Minister of Hesse-Darmstadt from 1848 to 1850, and presided over the Frankfurt peace congress.

52. Julius Jakob, Freiherr von Haynau was the Austrian field-marshal notorious for his cruel reprisals against the Hungarians after their defeat in 1849.

53. Elihu Burrit was an American bourgeois philanthropist and pacifist, who organized the Frankfurt peace congress and numerous others.

54. Marx is presumably making a dig here at Venedey's inflated idea of his own importance.

55. The debates of June 1850 on Greece are known in English history as the Don Pacifico debates, since the affair stemmed from Palmerston's handling of Don Pacifico's claim for compensation from the Greek government for damage done to his house by an anti-semitic Greek mob.

56. Viscount Palmerston was at this time Foreign Secretary, and later became Prime Minister (1855–65).

57. In English in the original.

58. The Aliens Bill, first carried in 1793 and sporadically renewed, had empowered the government to expel foreign nationals at its discretion. During the latter half of the nineteenth century the British government did not enjoy this power.

If in his demonstration over Greece and his speeches in Parliament Palmerston confronted European reactionaries as a bourgeois liberal, the English people used the presence of Herr Haynau in London to give a striking demonstration of *its* foreign policy.[59]

While Austria's military representative was chased through the streets of London by the people, Prussia, in the person of its diplomatic representative, suffered a misfortune equally appropriate to its position. It will be recalled how the most ridiculous figure in England, the garrulous man of letters Lord Brougham, ejected the man of letters Bunsen from the gallery of the House of Lords on account of his tactless and offensive behaviour[60] – to the general accompaniment of laughter from all the ladies present. Herr Bunsen, in the spirit of the great power which he represents, calmly put up with this humiliation. He will simply not leave the country, whatever happens to him. He is tied to England by all his private interests; he will continue to exploit his diplomatic post in order to speculate in English religion, to find a place for his sons in the Church of England and for his daughters on one of the social rungs of the English gentry.

The death of Sir Robert Peel has contributed considerably to the accelerated disintegration of the old parties. The party which had formed his main support since 1845, the so-called Peelites, has subsequently disintegrated.[61] Since his death Peel himself has been apotheosized in the most exaggerated fashion by almost all parties as England's greatest statesman. One thing at least distinguished him from the European 'statesmen' – he was no mere careerist. Beyond this, the statesmanship of this son of the bourgeoisie who rose to be leader of the aristocracy consisted in the view that there is today only one real aristocracy: the bourgeoisie. In the light of this belief he continually used his leadership of the landed aristocracy to wring concessions from it for the bourgeoisie. This became evident in the question of Catholic emancipation and the reform of the police, by means of which he increased the bourgeoisie's political power; in the Bank Acts of

59. Haynau visited London in September 1850, and was recognized by some draymen, who attacked him.

60. Henry, Lord Brougham was a former Whig Lord Chancellor; Christian von Bunsen was the Prussian ambassador in London; the exact circumstances of the incident alluded to here are not clear.

61. Sir Robert Peel, leader of the liberal wing of the Tory party, and Prime Minister in 1834–5 and 1841–6, split his party by repealing the Corn Laws in 1846 with Whig and Free Trade support.

1818 and 1844, which strengthened the financial aristocracy; in the tariff reform of 1842 and the free trade legislation of 1846, with which the aristocracy was nothing short of sacrificed to the industrial bourgeoisie. The second supporting pillar of the aristocracy, the 'Iron Duke', the hero of Waterloo,[62] stood faithfully beside the cotton knight Peel, a disappointed Don Quixote. Since 1845 Peel had been treated as a traitor by the Tory party. His power over the House of Commons was based upon the extraordinary *plausibility of his eloquence.* If one reads his most famous speeches, one finds that they consist of a massive accumulation of commonplaces, skilfully interspersed with a large amount of statistical data. Almost all the towns in England want to erect a monument to the man who repealed the Corn Laws. A Chartist journal has remarked, referring to the police trained by Peel in 1829: 'What do we want with these monuments to Peel? Every police officer in England and Ireland is a living monument to Peel.'[63]

The most recent event to cause a controversy in England is the elevation of Mr Wiseman to the position of Cardinal Archbishop of Westminster and the Pope's division of England into thirteen Catholic dioceses.[64] This step taken by the Vicar of Christ, which has been a great surprise for the Church of England, proves once again the illusions to which European reactionaries are subject; as if, after the victories which they have recently won in the service of the bourgeoisie, the restoration of the whole feudal, absolutist order, with all its religious trappings, must now automatically follow. In England Catholicism has its few supporters in the two extremes of society, the aristocracy and the lumpenproletariat. The lumpenproletariat, the mob, which is either Irish or of Irish ancestry, is Catholic by descent. The aristocracy conducted its fashionable flirtation with Puseyism until conversion to Catholicism finally began to become the fashion.[65] At a time when the English aristocracy was being forced in the course of its struggle with the advancing bourgeoisie to flaunt ever more brazenly

62. The Duke of Wellington became a Tory politician, and was Prime Minister in 1828–30.

63. From the article entitled 'The Peel Monument', in the Chartist *Red Republican*, 17 August 1850.

64. On 29 September 1850 the Pope re-established the Roman Catholic hierarchy in England, setting up an archbishopric and twelve bishoprics.

65. After E. B. Pusey; the Oxford movement as it is now known. J. H. Newman, the original leader of this Anglo-Catholic movement, was converted to Rome in 1845.

the religious ideologues of the aristocracy, the orthodox theologians of the High Church were also being forced in their struggle with the theologians of the bourgeois dissenters to recognize more and more the logical consequences of their semi-Catholic dogma and ritual. Indeed the conversion of individual reactionary Anglicans to the original Church, with its monopoly on grace, inevitably also increased in frequency. These insignificant phenomena produced in the minds of the English Catholic clergy the most sanguine hopes for the imminent conversion of all England. The new papal bull, which once again treated England as a Roman province, and which was intended to give a new impetus to this trend towards conversion, is now producing the opposite effect. The Puseyites, suddenly confronted with the serious consequences of their medieval dabbling, are recoiling in horror, and the Puseyite Bishop of London has lost no time in issuing a declaration in which he recants all his errors and declares a war to the death on the Pope. The whole comedy is of interest to the bourgeoisie only in so far as it presents them with an opportunity for new attacks on the High Church and its universities. The commission which is to report on the state of the universities will give rise to furious debates in the next session. The mass of the people is naturally not interested, and is neither for nor against Cardinal Wiseman. With the present dearth of news the papers are presented with welcome material for long articles and vehement diatribes against Pius IX. *The Times* even demands that the government should incite an insurrection in the Papal States and unleash Mazzini and the Italian refugees against the Pope to punish his interference. The *Globe*, Palmerston's press organ, drew an extremely witty parallel between the papal bull and Mazzini's latest manifesto.[66] The Pope, it says, claims spiritual supremacy over England and names bishops *in partibus infidelium*.[67] Here in London an Italian government sits *in partibus infidelium*, headed by the anti-pope, Mr Mazzini. The supremacy which Mr Mazzini does not only claim but actually exercises in the Papal States is at the moment equally of a purely spiritual nature. Like the papal bulls, Mazzini's manifestoes are also purely religious in content. They preach a religion, they make an appeal to faith,

66. Guiseppe Mazzini was the ideological leader of the Italian national movement. In 1849 he led the Provisional Government of the Roman republic, and subsequently lived in exile in England.

67. In the lands of the infidels; see p. 295, n. 42.

they bear the motto: *Dio ed il popolo*, God and the people. We wonder whether there is any difference between the claims made by each, other than that – in contrast to the Pope – Mr Mazzini at least represents the religion of the majority of the people to whom he speaks – for there is scarcely any religion in Italy any longer except that of *Dio ed il popolo*. Moreover, Mazzini has used this opportunity to go a step further. In London, together with the other members of the Italian National Committee he has floated a loan of 10 million francs – approved by the Roman Constituent Assembly[68] – in the form of shares of 100 francs each and, what is more, for the sole purpose of buying weapons and war materials. It cannot be denied that this loan has more chance of succeeding than the abortive voluntary loan of the Austrian government in Lombardy.[69]

England recently delivered Rome and Austria a really serious blow by its trade agreement with Piedmont-Sardinia. This treaty destroys the Austrian scheme for an Italian customs union and secures a considerable area of operation for English trade and the policies of the English bourgeoisie in northern Italy.

The existing organization of the Chartist party is also dis-integrating. Those petty bourgeois who are still in the party, allied with the labour aristocracy, form a purely democratic tendency, whose programme is limited to the People's Charter and a few other petty-bourgeois reforms.[70] The mass of the workers living in really proletarian conditions belong to the revolutionary Chartist tendency. At the head of the first group is Feargus O'Connor; at the head of the second, Julian Harney and Ernest Jones. Old O'Connor, an Irish squire and supposedly a descendant of the old kings of Munster, is, in spite of his ancestry and his political standpoint, a genuine representative of Old England. He is essentially conservative, and feels a highly determined hatred not only for industrial progress but also for the revolution. His

68. The Roman Constituent Assembly was elected in January 1849; after the fall of the Roman republic in July 1849 many of its deputies went into exile in England, and it was there that it granted the loan referred to.

69. The Austrian government of Lombardy and Venetia asked for a 'voluntary loan' in the spring of 1850, which turned into a forced loan when it became clear that the inhabitants were unwilling to subscribe to it.

70. The six points of the People's Charter were manhood suffrage, the ballot, equal electoral districts, payment of M.P.s, abolition of property qualifications, and annual parliaments. Cf. 'The Chartists', *Surveys from Exile*, p. 264.

ideals are patriarchal and petty-bourgeois through and through. He unites in his person an inexhaustible number of contradictions, which find their fulfilment and harmony in a certain blunt *common sense*,[71] and which enable him year in year out to write his interminable weekly letters in the *Northern Star*, each successive letter always in open conflict with the previous one. For this very reason O'Connor claims to be the most consistent man in Great Britain and to have prophesied everything that has happened during the last twenty years. His shoulders, his roaring voice, his great pugilistic skill, with which he is said to have defended Nottingham Market against 20,000 people – all this is an essential part of the representative of Old England. It is clear that a man like O'Connor is bound to be a great obstacle in a revolutionary movement; but such people serve a useful purpose, in that the many old, ingrained prejudices which they embody and propagate disappear with them – with the result that the movement, once it has rid itself of these people, can free itself from these prejudices once and for all. O'Connor will come to grief in the movement; but for that reason he will possess an even stronger claim to the title of 'a martyr in a good cause', like Lamartine and Marrast.

The main point of conflict between the two Chartist tendencies is the land question. O'Connor and his followers want to use the Charter to settle part of the working-class on smallholdings, and eventually to make smallholding property universal in England. It is well known how he failed in his attempt to establish smallholding property on a small scale through a joint-stock company. The tendency of every bourgeois revolution to destroy large-scale landed property might make this division into smallholdings appear to the English workers for a while as something very revolutionary, although it is regularly accompanied by the unfailing tendency of small property to become concentrated and to meet with economic ruin in the face of large-scale agriculture. The revolutionary Chartist tendency opposes this demand for division of the land with a demand for the confiscation of all landed property. The land is not to be distributed but to remain national property.

Despite this split and the emergence of more extreme demands, the Chartists, remembering the circumstances under which the Corn Laws were repealed, still suspect that in the next crisis they will once again have to form an alliance with the industrial

71. In English in the original.

bourgeoisie, the Financial Reformers,[72] and that they will have to help them defeat their enemies, forcing concessions from them in return. This will certainly be the position of the Chartists in the next crisis. The actual revolutionary movement in England can only begin when the Charter has been won, just as the June battle in France was possible only when the republic had been won...[73]

In Germany the political events of the last six months are epitomized in the spectacle of Prussia duping the liberals and Austria duping Prussia.

In 1849 Prussia's hegemony in Germany seemed to be the issue, in 1850 the division of power between Austria and Prussia. In 1851 all that is still in question is the form in which Prussia submits to Austria and returns as a repentant sinner to the bosom of the completely restored Federal Diet. The 'little Germany' which the king of Prussia hoped to obtain in compensation for his unfortunate imperial procession through Berlin on 21 March 1848[74] has transformed itself into 'little Prussia'. Prussia has had to bear every humiliation patiently, and has disappeared from the ranks of the great powers. The perfidious narrowness of its policies has again reduced even the modest dream of the Union[75] to nothing. It falsely ascribed to the Union a liberal character and thus duped the wise men of the Gotha party[76] with constitutional phantas-

72. i.e. the National Association for Parliamentary and Financial Reform, founded in 1849 by Cobden and Bright. This body campaigned on the basis of the so-called 'Little Charter' whose demands included household suffrage, triennial parliaments and the ballot.

73. The passage omitted here forms the bulk of Chapter IV of Engels's edition of 'The Class Struggles in France', in *Surveys from Exile*, from 'Let us now return to France' (p. 131) to the end.

74. See p. 125, n. 28.

75. The Union of Three Kings (i.e. of Prussia, Saxony, and Hanover) was the first fruit of Radowitz's policy of uniting Germany under Prussian headship on a federal basis (26 May 1849). During 1849 it extended rapidly to cover a total of twenty-eight states; however, in 1850 the larger states began to desert Prussia, leaving the smaller states in the Erfurt Union (April 1850), which received a constitution, but had in its turn to be dissolved under Austrian pressure (November 1850).

76. The Gotha party was founded in June 1849 by some prominent members of the monarchist Right in the Frankfurt National Assembly (such as Dahlmann, Bassermann, the brokers Gagern and Brüggemann), after Frederick William IV's refusal to accept the German crown from the Assembly. Its aim was the union of Germany without Austria under a Prussia transformed into a constitutional monarchy.

magoria which were never seriously meant; yet Prussia had become so bourgeois as a result of its whole industrial development, its permanent deficit and its national debt that, twist and turn as it might, it fell even more irredeemably a victim of constitutionalism. While the wise men of Gotha finally discovered how shamefully Prussia had dealt with their dignity and prudence, while even Gagern and Brüggeman finally turned their backs in noble outrage on a government which played such outrageous games with the freedom and unity of the fatherland, Prussia was having just as little joy in the chickens which it had gathered under its protective wings in the shape of the petty princes. Only in their moment of direst distress and defencelessness had they delivered themselves into the claws of the Prussian eagle – claws eager for annexation – and they had to pay dearly for the return of their subjects to their old obedience to the state as a result of Prussian intervention, threats and demonstrations. They had to pay with oppressive military treaties, expensive billeting and the prospect of being mediatized by the Union constitution. But Prussia itself had seen to it that they were to escape this new predicament. Prussia had restored the rule of the forces of reaction everywhere and the more these forces re-established themselves the more the petty princes deserted Prussia to throw themselves into the arms of Austria. Now that they could again rule as they had done before March, absolutist Austria was closer to them than a power whose ability to be absolutist was no greater than its desire to be liberal. Furthermore, Austrian policy did not lead to the mediatization of small states but, on the contrary, to their protection as integral components of the Federal Diet which was to be revived. Thus Prussia watched as Saxony, which a few months earlier had been saved by Prussian troops, deserted her, as did Hanover and Electoral Hesse. Now Baden has followed the rest despite its Prussian garrison. Prussia can see quite clearly from events in the two Hesses that its support of the reactionary forces in Mecklenburg, Hamburg and Dessau was not to its own but to Austria's advantage. Thus the unsuccessful German kaiser has come to realize that he is indeed living in an age of perfidy. But even though he must now stand by while 'his right arm, the Union', is taken from him, the fact is that this arm had already withered away some time before. Thus Austria has already brought the whole of southern Germany under its hegemony and even in north Germany the most important states oppose Prussia.

Austria had finally made such progress that, supported by Russia, it was able to oppose Prussia openly. It did this over two issues: Schleswig-Holstein and Electoral Hesse.

In Schleswig-Holstein 'Germany's sword'[77] has concluded a genuine Prussian separate peace[78] and delivered its allies up to the hands of the hostile superior force. England, Russia and France decided to put an end to the independence of the duchies and recorded this intention in a treaty which Austria also signed. Austria and the other governments, in accordance with the London Treaty, have argued in the restored Federal Diet for a Federal intervention in Holstein in favour of Denmark. Meanwhile Prussia has sought to continue its policy of procrastination by urging the parties to submit to a Federal court of arbitration, which is not yet defined nor in existence and which has been rejected by most of the major governments. It has achieved nothing with all its manoeuvring other than that the major powers have come to suspect it of revolutionary machinations and that it has received a series of threatening notes, which will soon mar its pleasure in an 'independent' foreign policy. The people of Schleswig-Holstein will soon have their father and sovereign restored to them. A people which allows itself to be governed by Herr Beseler and Herr Reventlow,[79] despite having the whole army on its side, shows that it still needs the Danish whip for its upbringing.

The movement in Electoral Hesse gives us an inimitable example of what an 'uprising' in a small German state can lead to. The virtuous bourgeois resistance to the double-dealer, Hassenpflug,[80] had produced everything that could be demanded of such a spectacle. The Chamber was unanimous, the country was unanimous, the civil servants and the army were on the side of the

77. A reference to Frederick William IV's speech of 3 April 1849 in reply to the German National Assembly's offer of the imperial Crown: 'If the Prussian shield and sword is needed against internal or external enemies, I shall not be found missing.'
78. The Prussians were famous for making this move both in the course of the eighteenth century and at the time of the Napoleonic Wars.
79. Wilhelm Beseler was the head of the provisional government of Schleswig-Holstein set up in Kiel in 1848, and a Right Centre deputy at Frankfurt; Graf Friedrich von Reventlow was a reactionary Prussian noble and a member of the provisional government of Schleswig-Holstein.
80. Hans Daniel Hassenpflug was a supporter of the despotic rule of the Elector of Hesse before and after 1848; he was Prime Minister of Electoral Hesse from 1850 to 1855.

citizens; all opposing forces had been removed, the demand 'Out with the prince' had been fulfilled spontaneously, the double-dealer Hassenpflug had disappeared with his whole ministry; everything was going smoothly, all parties kept strictly within the bounds of the law, all excesses were avoided and the opposition had achieved the finest victory in the annals without lifting a finger. And now that the bourgeoisie had all the power in their hands, now that their Committee of Estates met not the least resistance anywhere, now they were for the first time really needed. Now they saw that, instead of Electoral troops, foreign troops were standing at their borders, ready to march in to put an end to this splendid show of bourgeois power within twenty-four hours. Only now did the helplessness and disgrace begin. Whereas earlier the bourgeoisie had not been able to retreat, now they were not able to advance. The refusal to pay taxes in Electoral Hesse proves more strikingly than any earlier event how all clashes within small states end in pure farce. They only result in foreign intervention, and the conflict is brought to an end not only by the removal of the prince but also of the constitution. It proves how ludicrous all these momentous struggles are, in which the petty bourgeoisie of the petty states seeks with patriotic loyalty to save every little achievement left over from the March days from its inevitable destruction.

In Electoral Hesse, in a state of the Union which had to be torn away from the Prussian embrace, Austria was involved in a direct confrontation with its rival. It was Austria who more or less incited the Elector into his attack on the constitution and then placed him under the protection of the Federal Diet. In order to add weight to this protective relationship, to use the business in Electoral Hesse to break Prussian resistance to Austrian hegemony, and to coerce Prussia into rejoining the Federal Diet, Austrian and south German troops have now been marshalled in Franconia and Bohemia. Prussia is also mobilizing its forces. The newspapers are bursting with reports of marches and counter-marches by the army corps. All this noise will lead to nothing, just like the quarrel between the French party of Order and Bonaparte. Neither the king of Prussia nor the emperor of Austria is his own master – only the Russian tsar is. At the tsar's command rebellious Prussia will finally give way without a drop of blood being spilt. The parties will meet peacefully seated in the Federal Diet, without any interruption in the petty jealousy which exists between them, in their conflict with their subjects, or in their vexation at Russian supremacy.

We now come to the abstract country, the European nation, the nation of the *exiles*. We shall not mention the individual groups of exiles, the Germans, French, Hungarians, etc; their *haute politique* is limited to pure *chronique scandaleuse*. But Europe and the people as a whole have recently been given a provisional government in the form of the European Central Committee,[81] consisting of Joseph Mazzini, Ledru-Rollin, Albert Darasz (the Pole)[82] and – Arnold Ruge, who modestly justifies his presence by writing 'member of the Frankfurt National Assembly' after his name. Although it is impossible to say which democratic council has called these four evangelists to office, their manifesto undeniably contains the creed of the broad mass of the exiles and summarizes in fitting form the intellectual achievements which this mass owes to the recent revolution.

The manifesto begins with a pompous enumeration of the strengths of democracy.

What does democracy lack for the achievement of its victory? ... Organization ... We have sects but no church, incomplete and contradictory philosophies but no religion, no collective belief which can assemble the believers under a single sign and harmonize their work ... The day on which we find ourselves all united, marching together under the eyes of the best among us ... will be the eve of the struggle. On this day we shall have counted our numbers, we shall know who we are, we shall be conscious of our power.

Why has the revolution not yet succeeded? Because the organization of revolutionary power has been weak. This is the first decree of the exiles' provisional government.

This state of affairs is to be remedied by the organization of an army of believers, and the founding of a religion.

But to achieve this two great obstacles must be surmounted, two great errors overcome: the exaggeration of the rights of individuality,

81. The Central Committee of European Democracy was set up in June 1850 in London on the initiative of Mazzini, but only lasted until March 1852 owing to ideological differences between its various members. Its manifesto, 'To the Peoples', was published in the Committee's journal, *Le Proscrit*, on 6 August 1850. The italics in Marx's quotations are his own.
82. Albert Darasz took part in the Polish rising of 1830, and after its defeat went into exile, becoming an important figure in a number of Polish exile nationalist organizations. Alexandre Ledru-Rollin had been editor of *La Reforme* (see p. 97, n. 31).

the narrow-minded exclusiveness of theory . . . We must not say 'I': we must learn to say 'we' . . . those who follow their individual susceptibilities refuse to make the small sacrifices demanded by organization and discipline and deny the total body of beliefs which they preach, as a result of the habits of the past . . . Exclusiveness in theory is the negation of our basic dogma. He who says, 'I have discovered a political truth,' and who makes the acceptance of his system into a condition of acceptance into the fraternal association, disavows the people – the only progressive interpreter of the world law – merely in order to assert his own ego. He who maintains that he is able today to discover a definitive solution to the problems which activate the masses, by means of the isolated labour of his intellect, however powerful it may be, condemns himself to the error of incompleteness by abandoning one of the eternal sources of truth: the collective intuition of the people in action. The definitive solution is the secret of our victory . . . For the most part our systems can be nothing but a dissection of corpses, a discovery of evil and an analysis of death, incapable of perceiving or comprehending life. Life is the people in movement, the instinct of the masses raised to an extraordinary power by common contact, by the prophetic feeling of great things to be achieved, by spontaneous, sudden, electric association in the street. It is action, exciting to their highest pitch all the latent powers of hope, devotion, love and enthusiasm which are now dormant, revealing man in the unity of his nature, in the full vigour of his potency. The handshake of a worker at one of those historic moments which begin an epoch will teach us more about the organization of the future than can be taught today by the cold and heartless labour of reason or by knowledge of the illustrious dead of the last two millenia – of the old society.

So, in the end, all this highfalutin nonsense amounts to the highly vulgar and philistine view that the revolution failed because of the jealous ambition of the individual leaders, and because of the conflicting opinions of the various popular teachers.

The struggles of the different classes and fractions of classes with one another, which in their development through specific phases is precisely what constitutes the revolution, are, for our evangelists, only the unhappy consequence of divergent systems. However, the divergent systems are in reality the result of the existence of class struggles. It becomes clear even from this that the authors of the manifesto deny the existence of the class struggle. Under the pretext of fighting the doctrinaire they dispense with all specific realities of the situation, all specific partisan views. They forbid the individual classes to formulate their interests and demands in the face of other classes. They expect the classes to forget their

conflicting interests and to reconcile themselves under the banner
of something hollow and brazenly vague, which, in the guise of
reconciling the interests of all parties, only conceals the domination by one party and its interests – the party of the bourgeoisie.
After what these gentlemen must have experienced in France,
Germany and Italy during the last two years it cannot even be said
that the hypocrisy by means of which they wrap bourgeois
interests in a Lamartinian rhetoric of brotherhood is unconscious.
How much the gentlemen know about 'systems' is shown, moreover, by the fact that they imagine each of these systems to be
merely a fragment of the wisdom compiled in the manifesto, and
to be based solely on one of the rhetorical phrases assembled here:
freedom, equality, etc. Their notions of social organization are
highly striking: a riot in the street, a brawl, a shake of the hand,
and that is that! For them the whole revolution consists merely in
the overthrow of the existing governments; once this aim has
been achieved, 'victory' will have been won. The movement, the
development, the struggle then comes to an end, and under the
aegis of the then ruling European Central Committee the golden
age of the European Republic and the permanent rule of the night-
cap can begin. Just as they hate development and struggle, these
gentlemen hate thought, callous thought – as if any thinker,
including Hegel and Ricardo, would ever have achieved that degree
of callousness with which this mealy-mouthed swill is poured over
the heads of the public. The people are not to worry about the
morrow, they must empty their heads of ideas. When the great
day of decision comes, they will be electrified by mere physical
contact and the riddle of the future will be solved for the people
by a miracle. This summons to empty-headedness is a direct
attempt to swindle precisely those classes who are most oppressed.
One member of the European Central Committee asks,

In saying this, do we mean that we are to march on without a banner;
do we mean that we wish to inscribe a negation on our banner? Such a
suspicion cannot be directed at us. As men of the people, who have been
part of the struggle for many years, we do not for one moment consider
leading them into an *empty future*.

On the contrary, to prove the *fullness* of their *future* these
gentlemen present a record – worthy of Leporello[83] himself – of

83. In Mozart's opera *Don Juan*, the hero's servant and chronicler of his
sexual achievements.

eternal truths and achievements from the whole course of history. This record is put forward as the common ground of 'democracy' in our day and age and is summed up in the following edifying paternoster:

We believe in the progressive development of human ability and strength towards the moral law which has been imposed upon us. We believe in association as the only means to achieve this end. We believe that the interpretation of this moral law and the law of progress can be entrusted to the charge of neither a caste nor an individual, but to the people, enlightened by national education, led by those from its midst whom virtue and the people's genius show to be the best. We believe in the sacredness of both individuality and society, which should never exclude nor conflict with each other, but should harmonize for the betterment of all by all. We believe in freedom, without which all human responsibility disappears; in equality, without which freedom is only an illusion; in brotherhood, without which freedom and equality would be means without an end; in association, without which brotherhood would be an unrealizable programme; in *family, community, state* and *fatherland* as equally progressive spheres which man must successively grow into, in the knowledge and application of freedom, equality, brotherhood and association. We believe in the sanctity of work and in *property* which arises from work as its symbol and fruit; we believe in the duty of society to provide the means for material work through credit and the means for mental work through education . . . to sum up, we believe in a social condition which has God and His law as its apex, and the people as its base . . .

So: progress – association – moral law – freedom – equality – brotherhood – association – family, community, state – sanctity of property – credit – education – God and the people – *Dio e popolo*. These phrases figure in all the manifestoes of the 1848 revolutions, from the French to the Wallachian, and it is precisely for that reason that they figure here as the common basis of the new revolution. In none of these revolutions was the sanctity of property, here sanctified as the product of work, forgotten. Eighty years before their time Adam Smith knew much better than our revolutionary pioneers the precise extent to which bourgeois property is 'the fruit and symbol of work'. As for the socialist concession that society shall grant everyone the material means for work through credit, every manufacturer is accustomed to give his worker credit for as much material as he can process in a week. The credit system is as widely extended nowadays as is compatible with the inviolability of property, and credit itself is after all only a form of bourgeois property.

Summarized, this gospel teaches a social order in which God forms the apex and the people – or, as is said later, *humanity* – the base. That is, they believe in society as it exists, in which, as is well known, God is at the apex and the mob at the base. Although Mazzini's creed, God and the people, *Dio e popolo*, may have a meaning in Italy, where the Pope is equated with God and the princes with the people, it is a bit much to offer this plagiarism of Johannes Ronge,[84] the most insipid swill of the German pseudo-Enlightenment, as the key which will solve the riddle of the century. Furthermore, how easily the members of this school accustom themselves to the small sacrifices which organization and discipline demand, how willingly they give up the narrow exclusiveness of theory is demonstrated by our friend, Arnold Winkelried Ruge, who, to Leo's great joy, has this time been able to recognize the difference between divinity and humanity.[85]

The manifesto ends with the words:

What is needed is a constitution for European democracy, and the foundation of a people's budget or exchequer. What is needed is the organization of an army of initiators.

In order to be one of the first initiators of the people's budget Ruge has turned to '*de demokratische Jantjes van Amsterdam*'[86] – the democratic citizens of Amsterdam – to explain to them their special vocation and duty to provide money. Holland is in distress!

London, 1 November 1850

84. Johannes Ronge was a German priest, the founder of the 'German Catholic' movement of the 1840s, which was an attempt to purge the Roman Catholic church of superstition and bring it into harmony with the modern age.
85. A reference to Ruge's controversy with the reactionary clericalist historian Heinrich Leo at the end of the 1830s. Leo asserted in his pamphlet *Die Hegelingen* (Halle, 1838) that the Young Hegelians were atheists because they were unable to recognize the difference between divinity and humanity.
86. Jantjes: nickname for the Dutch.

Address of the Central Committee to the Communist League (March 1850)[1]

Karl Marx and Frederick Engels

THE CENTRAL COMMITTEE TO THE LEAGUE

Brothers,

In the two revolutionary years of 1848–9 the League proved itself in two ways. First, its members everywhere involved themselves energetically in the movement and stood in the front ranks of the only decisively revolutionary class, the proletariat, in the press, on the barricades and on the battlefields. The League further proved itself in that its understanding of the movement, as expressed in the circulars issued by the Congresses and the Central Committee of 1847[2] and in the *Manifesto of the Communist Party*, has been shown to be the only correct one, and the expectations expressed in these documents have been completely fulfilled. This understanding of the conditions of modern society, which was previously only propagated by the League in secret, is now on everyone's lips and is preached openly in the market place. At the same time, however, the formerly strong organization of the League has been considerably weakened. A large number of members who were directly involved in the movement thought that the time for secret societies was over and that public action alone was sufficient. The individual districts and communes[3]

1. This Address was printed in London and clandestinely distributed within the Communist League network in Germany, then published in the German press after its seizure consequent on the arrest of the Cologne Central Committee of the Communist League in April 1851. It is translated here from the version published by Engels as an appendix to the 1885 edition of Marx's book *The Cologne Communist Trial*, as printed in *MEW* 7.

2. Some of these documents are printed in D. Riyazanov (ed.), *The Communist Manifesto*, Martin Lawrence, 1930.

3. The basic group of the Communist League was the 'commune' (*Gemeinde*), consisting of between three and twenty members. A 'district' (*Kreis*) was formed by between two and ten communes falling within a specified geographical area, its committee (*Kreisbehörde*) being an aggregate of the elected commune committees. The Central Committee (*Zentralbehörde*) appointed certain districts as 'central districts' (*leitende Kreise*), their committees being

allowed their connections with the Central Committee to weaken and gradually become dormant. So, while the democratic party, the party of the petty bourgeoisie, has become more and more organized in Germany, the workers' party has lost its only firm foothold, remaining organized at best in individual localities for local purposes; within the general movement it has consequently come under the complete domination and leadership of the petty-bourgeois democrats. This situation cannot be allowed to continue; the independence of the workers must be restored. The Central Committee recognized this necessity and it therefore sent an emissary, Joseph Moll, to Germany in the winter of 1848–9 to reorganize the League. Moll's mission, however, failed to produce any lasting effect, partly because the German workers at that time had not had enough experience and partly because it was interrupted by the insurrection last May.[4] Moll himself took up arms, joined the Baden-Palatinate army and fell on 29 June in the battle of the River Murg. The League lost in him one of its oldest, most active and most reliable members, who had been involved in all the Congresses and Central Committees and had earlier conducted a series of missions with great success. Since the defeat of the German and French revolutionary parties in July 1849,[5] almost all the members of the Central Committee have re-assembled in London: they have replenished their numbers with new revolutionary forces and set about reorganizing the League with renewed zeal.

This reorganization can only be achieved by an emissary, and the Central Committee considers it most important to dispatch the emissary at this very moment, when a new revolution is imminent, that is, when the workers' party must go into battle with the maximum degree of organization, unity and independence, so that it is not exploited and taken in tow by the bourgeoisie as in 1848.

We told you already in 1848, brothers, that the German liberal bourgeoisie would soon come to power and would immediately

---

charged with the common affairs of a group of districts. See the Statutes of the Communist League, *MEW* 4, pp. 596–601.

4. This refers to the Reich Constitution Campaign; see Introduction, pp. 47–8.

5. For the French side see 'The Class Struggles in France', *Surveys from Exile*, pp. 92–101.

turn its newly won power against the workers. You have seen how this forecast came true. It was indeed the bourgeoisie which took possession of the state authority in the wake of the March movement of 1848 and used this power to drive the workers, its allies in the struggle, back into their former oppressed position. Although the bourgeoisie could accomplish this only by entering into an alliance with the feudal party, which had been defeated in March, and eventually even had to surrender power once more to this feudal absolutist party, it has nevertheless secured favourable conditions for itself. In view of the government's[6] financial difficulties, these conditions would ensure that power would in the long run fall into its hands again and that all its interests would be secured, if it were possible for the revolutionary movement to assume from now on a so-called peaceful course of development. In order to guarantee its power the bourgeoisie would not even need to arouse hatred by taking violent measures against the people, as all of these violent measures have already been carried out by the feudal counter-revolution. But events will not take this peaceful course. On the contrary, the revolution which will accelerate the course of events is imminent, whether it is initiated by an independent rising of the French proletariat or by an invasion of the revolutionary Babel[7] by the Holy Alliance.

The treacherous role that the German liberal bourgeoisie played against the people in 1848 will be assumed in the coming revolution by the democratic petty bourgeoisie, which now occupies the same position in the opposition as the liberal bourgeoisie did before 1848. This democratic party, which is far more dangerous for the workers than were the liberals earlier, is composed of three elements: 1) The most progressive elements of the big bourgeoisie, who pursue the goal of the immediate and complete overthrow of feudalism and absolutism. This fraction is represented by the former Berlin *Vereinbarer*, the tax-resisters;[8] 2) The constitutional-democratic petty bourgeois, whose main aim during the previous movement was the formation of a more or less demo-

6. Marx seems to be referring to the Prussian government, but the same reasoning would presumably apply to other German governments.

7. i.e. France.

8. The *Vereinbarer* were the members of the Prussian National Assembly, which Marx nicknamed the *Vereinbarungsversammlung* (assembly of agreement); see p. 124, n. 22. After the royal coup d'état of November 1848, the left wing of the prorogued Prussian Assembly called on citizens to refuse taxes. The tax-resisters were thus only a section of the *Vereinbarer*.

cratic federal state; this is what their representatives, the Left in the Frankfurt Assembly and later the Stuttgart parliament, worked for, as they themselves did in the Reich Constitution Campaign;[9] 3) The republican petty bourgeois, whose ideal is a German federal republic similar to that in Switzerland and who now call themselves 'red' and 'social-democratic' because they cherish the pious wish to abolish the pressure exerted by big capital on small capital, by the big bourgeoisie on the petty bourgeoisie. The representatives of this fraction were the members of the democratic congresses and committees, the leaders of the democratic associations and the editors of the democratic newspapers.

After their defeat all these fractions claim to be 'republicans' or 'reds', just as at the present time members of the republican petty bourgeoisie in France call themselves 'socialists'. Where, as in Wurtemberg, Bavaria, etc., they still find a chance to pursue their ends by constitutional means, they seize the opportunity to retain their old phrases and prove by their actions that they have not changed in the least. Furthermore, it goes without saying that the changed name of this party does not alter in the least its relationship to the workers but merely proves that it is now obliged to form a front against the bourgeoisie, which has united with absolutism, and to seek the support of the proletariat.

The petty-bourgeois democratic party in Germany is very powerful. It not only embraces the great majority of the urban middle class, the small industrial merchants and master craftsmen; it also includes among its followers the peasants and rural proletariat in so far as the latter has not yet found support among the independent proletariat of the towns.

The relationship of the revolutionary workers' party to the petty-bourgeois democrats is this: it cooperates with them against the party which they aim to overthrow; it opposes them wherever they wish to secure their own position.

The democratic petty bourgeois, far from wanting to transform the whole of society in the interests of the revolutionary proletarians, only aspire to a change in social conditions which will make the existing society as tolerable and comfortable for them-

9. In May 1849 the German National Assembly had to flee Frankfurt after inaugurating the Reich Constitution Campaign. On 6 June about one hundred members of its left wing reconvened in Stuttgart, but on 18 June they were finally dispersed by Prussian troops.

selves as possible. They therefore demand above all else a reduction in government spending through a restriction of the bureaucracy and the transference of the major tax burden onto the large landowners and bourgeoisie. They further demand the removal of the pressure exerted by big capital on small capital through the establishment of public credit institutions and the passing of laws against usury, whereby it would be possible for themselves and the peasants to receive advances on favourable terms from the state instead of from capitalists; also, the introduction of bourgeois property relationships on the land through the complete abolition of feudalism. In order to achieve all this they require a democratic form of government, either constitutional or republican, which would give them and their peasant allies the majority; they also require a democratic system of local government to give them direct control over municipal property and over a series of political offices at present in the hands of the bureaucrats.

The rule of capital and its rapid accumulation is to be further counteracted, partly by a curtailment of the right of inheritance, and partly by the transference of as much employment as possible to the state. As far as the workers are concerned one thing, above all, is definite: they are to remain wage labourers as before. However, the democratic petty bourgeois want better wages and security for the workers, and hope to achieve this by an extension of state employment and by welfare measures; in short, they hope to bribe the workers with a more or less disguised form of alms and to break their revolutionary strength by temporarily rendering their situation tolerable. The demands of petty-bourgeois democracy summarized here are not expressed by all sections of it at once, and in their totality they are the explicit goal of only a very few of its followers. The further particular individuals or fractions of the petty bourgeoisie advance, the more of these demands they will explicitly adopt, and the few who recognize their own programme in what has been mentioned above might well believe they have put forward the maximum that can be demanded from the revolution. But these demands can in no way satisfy the party of the proletariat. While the democratic petty bourgeois want to bring the revolution to an end as quickly as possible, achieving at most the aims already mentioned, it is our interest and our task to make the revolution permanent until all the more or less propertied classes have been driven from their ruling positions, until the

proletariat has conquered state power and until the association of
the proletarians has progressed sufficiently far – not only in one
country but in all the leading countries of the world – that competition between the proletarians of these countries ceases and at
least the decisive forces of production are concentrated in the
hands of the workers. Our concern cannot simply be to modify
private property, but to abolish it, not to hush up class antagonisms but to abolish classes, not to improve the existing society but
to found a new one. There is no doubt that during the further
course of the revolution in Germany, the petty-bourgeois democrats will for the moment acquire a predominant influence. The
question is, therefore, what is to be the attitude of the proletariat,
and in particular of the League towards them: 1) While present
conditions continue, in which the petty-bourgeois democrats are
also oppressed; 2) In the coming revolutionary struggle, which will
put them in a dominant position; 3) After this struggle, during the
period of petty-bourgeois predominance over the classes which
have been overthrown and over the proletariat.

1. At the moment, while the democratic petty bourgeois are
everywhere oppressed, they preach to the proletariat general unity
and reconciliation; they extend the hand of friendship, and seek to
found a great opposition party which will embrace all shades of
democratic opinion; that is, they seek to ensnare the workers in
a party organization in which general social-democratic phrases
prevail, while their particular interests are kept hidden behind,
and in which, for the sake of preserving the peace, the specific
demands of the proletariat may not be presented. Such a unity
would be to their advantage alone and to the complete disadvantage of the proletariat. The proletariat would lose all its
hard-won independent position and be reduced once more to a
mere appendage of official bourgeois democracy. This unity must
therefore be resisted in the most decisive manner. Instead of
lowering themselves to the level of an applauding chorus, the
workers, and above all the League, must work for the creation of
an independent organization of the workers' party, both secret
and open, alongside the official democrats, and the League must
aim to make every one of its communes a centre and nucleus of
workers' associations in which the position and interests of the
proletariat can be discussed free from bourgeois influence. How
serious the bourgeois democrats are about an alliance in which
the proletariat has equal power and equal rights is demonstrated

by the Breslau democrats, who are conducting a furious campaign in their organ, the *Neue Oder-Zeitung*,[10] against independently organized workers, whom they call 'socialists'. In the event of a struggle against a common enemy a special alliance is unnecessary. As soon as such an enemy has to be fought directly, the interests of both parties will coincide for the moment and an association of momentary expedience will arise spontaneously in the future, as it has in the past. It goes without saying that in the bloody conflicts to come, as in all others, it will be the workers, with their courage, resolution and self-sacrifice, who will be chiefly responsible for achieving victory. As in the past, so in the coming struggle also, the petty bourgeoisie, to a man, will hesitate as long as possible and remain fearful, irresolute and inactive; but when victory is certain it will claim it for itself and will call upon the workers to behave in an orderly fashion, to return to work and to prevent so-called excesses, and it will exclude the proletariat from the fruits of victory. It does not lie within the power of the workers to prevent the petty-bourgeois democrats from doing this; but it does lie within their power to make it as difficult as possible for the petty bourgeoisie to use its power against the armed proletariat, and to dictate such conditions to them that the rule of the bourgeois democrats, from the very first, will carry within it the seeds of its own destruction, and its subsequent displacement by the proletariat will be made considerably easier. Above all, during and immediately after the struggle the workers, as far as it is at all possible, must oppose bourgeois attempts at pacification and force the democrats to carry out their terroristic phrases. They must work to ensure that the immediate revolutionary excitement is not suddenly suppressed after the victory. On the contrary, it must be sustained as long as possible. Far from opposing so-called excesses – instances of popular vengeance against hated individuals or against public buildings with which hateful memories are associated – the workers' party must not only tolerate these actions but must even give them direction. During and after the struggle the workers must at every opportunity put forward their own demands against those of the bourgeois democrats. They must demand guarantees for the workers as soon as the democratic bourgeoisie sets about taking over the

10. Founded in 1849, the *Neue Oder-Zeitung* passed in the 1850s as the most radical newspaper published in Germany. Marx contributed to this paper in 1855, the last year of its existence, though basically for economic reasons.

government. They must achieve these guarantees by force if necessary, and generally make sure that the new rulers commit themselves to all possible concessions and promises – the surest means of compromising them. They must check in every way and as far as is possible the victory euphoria and enthusiasm for the new situation which follow every successful street battle, with a cool and cold-blooded analysis of the situation and with undisguised mistrust of the new government. Alongside the new official governments they must simultaneously establish their own revolutionary workers' governments, either in the form of local executive committees and councils or through workers' clubs or committees, so that the bourgeois-democratic governments not only immediately lose the support of the workers but find themselves from the very beginning supervised and threatened by authorities behind which stand the whole mass of the workers. In a word, from the very moment of victory the workers' suspicion must be directed no longer against the defeated reactionary party but against their former ally, against the party which intends to exploit the common victory for itself.

2. To be able forcefully and threateningly to oppose this party, whose betrayal of the workers will begin with the very first hour of victory, the workers must be armed and organized. The whole proletariat must be armed at once with muskets, rifles, cannon and ammunition, and the revival of the old-style citizens' militia,[11] directed against the workers, must be opposed. Where the formation of this militia cannot be prevented, the workers must try to organize themselves independently as a proletarian guard, with elected leaders and with their own elected general staff; they must try to place themselves not under the orders of the state authority but of the revolutionary local councils set up by the workers. Where the workers are employed by the state, they must arm and organize themselves into special corps with elected leaders, or as a part of the proletarian guard. Under no pretext should arms and ammunition be surrendered; any attempt to disarm the workers must be frustrated, by force if necessary. The destruction of the bourgeois democrats' influence over the workers, and the enforcement of conditions which will compromise the rule of bourgeois democracy, which is for the moment inevitable, and make it as difficult as possible – these are the main points which the

11. See p. 166, n. 36.

proletariat and therefore the League must keep in mind during and after the approaching uprising.

3. As soon as the new governments have established themselves, their struggle against the workers will begin. If the workers are to be able to forcibly oppose the democratic petty bourgeois it is essential above all for them to be independently organized and centralized in clubs. At the soonest possible moment after the overthrow of the present governments the Central Committee will come to Germany and will immediately convene a Congress, submitting to it the necessary proposals for the centralization of the workers' clubs under a directorate established at the movement's centre of operations. The speedy organization of at least provincial connections between the workers' clubs is one of the prime requirements for the strengthening and development of the workers' party; the immediate result of the overthrow of the existing governments will be the election of a national representative body. Here the proletariat must take care: 1) that by sharp practices local authorities and government commissioners do not, under any pretext whatsoever, exclude any section of workers; 2) that workers' candidates are nominated everywhere in opposition to bourgeois-democratic candidates. As far as possible they should be League members and their election should be pursued by all possible means. Even where there is no prospect of achieving their election the workers must put up their own candidates to preserve their independence, to gauge their own strength and to bring their revolutionary position and party standpoint to public attention. They must not be led astray by the empty phrases of the democrats, who will maintain that the workers' candidates will split the democratic party and offer the forces of reaction the chance of victory. All such talk means, in the final analysis, that the proletariat is to be swindled. The progress which the proletarian party will make by operating independently in this way is infinitely more important than the disadvantages resulting from the presence of a few reactionaries in the representative body. If the forces of democracy take decisive, terroristic action against the reaction from the very beginning, the reactionary influence in the election will already have been destroyed.

The first point over which the bourgeois democrats will come into conflict with the workers will be the abolition of feudalism; as in the first French revolution, the petty bourgeoisie will want to give the feudal lands to the peasants as free property; that is, they will try to perpetuate the existence of the rural proletariat, and to form a petty-bourgeois peasant class which will be subject to the same cycle of impoverishment and debt which still afflicts the French peasant. The workers must oppose this plan both in the interest of the rural proletariat and in their own interest. They must demand that the confiscated feudal property remain state property and be used for workers' colonies, cultivated collectively by the rural proletariat with all the advantages of large-scale farming and where the principle of common property will immediately achieve a sound basis in the midst of the shaky system of bourgeois property relations. Just as the democrats ally themselves with the peasants, the workers must ally themselves with the rural proletariat.

The democrats will either work directly towards a federated republic, or at least, if they cannot avoid the one and indivisible republic they will attempt to paralyse the central government by granting the municipalities[12] and provinces the greatest possible autonomy and independence. In opposition to this plan the workers must not only strive for the one and indivisible German republic, but also, within this republic, for the most decisive centralization of power in the hands of the state authority. They should not let themselves be led astray by empty democratic talk about the freedom of the municipalities, self-government, etc. In a country like Germany, where so many remnants of the Middle Ages are still to be abolished, where so much local and provincial obstinacy has to be broken down, it cannot under any circumstances be tolerated that each village, each town and each province may put new obstacles in the way of revolutionary activity, which can only be developed with full efficiency from a central point. A renewal of the present situation, in which the Germans have to wage a separate struggle in each town and province for the same degree of progress, can also not be tolerated. Least of all can a so-called free system of local government be allowed to perpetuate a form of property which is more backward than modern private property and which is everywhere and inevitably being transformed into private property; namely communal property, with its consequent disputes between poor and rich communities. Nor can this so-called free system of local government be allowed to

12. The German *Gemeinde* (literally commune or community) here refers equally to an urban municipality or a rural district.

perpetuate, side by side with the state civil law, the existence of communal civil law with its sharp practices directed against the workers. As in France in 1793, it is the task of the genuinely revolutionary party in Germany to carry through the strictest centralization.[13]

We have seen how the next upsurge will bring the democrats to power and how they will be forced to propose more or less socialistic measures. It will be asked what measures the workers are to propose in reply. At the beginning, of course, the workers cannot propose any directly communist measures. But the following courses of action are possible:

1. They can force the democrats to make inroads into as many areas of the existing social order as possible, so as to disturb its regular functioning and so that the petty-bourgeois democrats compromise themselves; furthermore, the workers can force the concentration of as many productive forces as possible – means of transport, factories, railways, etc. – in the hands of the state.

2. They must drive the proposals of the democrats to their logical extreme (the democrats will in any case act in a reformist and not a revolutionary manner) and transform these proposals into direct attacks on private property. If, for instance, the petty bourgeoisie propose the purchase of the railways and factories, the workers must demand that these railways and factories simply be confiscated by the state without compensation as the property

13. It must be noted today that this passage is based on a misunderstanding. At that time, thanks to Bonapartist and liberal falsifiers of history, it was considered an established fact that the centralized administrative machine in France was introduced by the Great Revolution and was used, particularly by the Convention, as an independent and decisive weapon with which to defeat the royalist and federalist forces of reaction as well as the enemy abroad. However, it is now known that during the entire revolution, up to 18 Brumaire, the whole administration of the departments, districts and municipalities consisted of authorities elected by the local population, and that the authorities acted with complete freedom within the limits of the general state legislation. This provincial and local self-government, resembling the American, indeed became the strongest instrument of the revolution, so much so that immediately after the coup d'état of 18 Brumaire Napoleon hurried to replace it by the prefectural rule which still exists and which was thus, from its very beginning, simply a tool of reaction. But just as local and provincial self-government does not necessarily contradict political and national centralization, no more is it bound up with that narrow cantonal or municipal selfishness which we encounter in such a repugnant form in Switzerland and which all south German federal republicans wanted to make the rule in Germany in 1849. [Note by Engels to the 1885 edition.]

of reactionaries. If the democrats propose a proportional tax, then the workers must demand a progressive tax; if the democrats themselves propose a moderate progressive tax, then the workers must insist on a tax whose rates rise so steeply that big capital is ruined by it; if the democrats demand the regulation of the state debt, then the workers must demand national bankruptcy. The demands of the workers will thus have to be adjusted according to the measures and concessions of the democrats.

Although the German workers cannot come to power and achieve the realization of their class interests without passing through a protracted revolutionary development, this time they can at least be certain that the first act of the approaching revolutionary drama will coincide with the direct victory of their own class in France and will thereby be accelerated.

But they themselves must contribute most to their final victory, by informing themselves of their own class interests, by taking up their independent political position as soon as possible, by not allowing themselves to be misled by the hypocritical phrases of the democratic petty bourgeoisie into doubting for one minute the necessity of an independently organized party of the proletariat. Their battle-cry must be: The Permanent Revolution.

London, March 1850

Address of the Central Committee to the Communist League (June 1850)[1]

Karl Marx and Frederick Engels

THE CENTRAL COMMITTEE TO THE LEAGUE

Brothers,

In our last circular, delivered to you by the League's emissary,[2] we discussed the position of the workers' party and, in particular, of the League, both at the present moment and in the event of revolution.

The main purpose of this letter is to present a report on the state of the League.

For a while, following the defeats sustained by the revolutionary party last summer, the League's organization almost completely disintegrated. The most active League members involved in the various movements were dispersed, contacts were broken off and addresses could no longer be used; because of this and because of the danger of letters being opened, correspondence became temporarily impossible. The Central Committee was thus condemned to complete inactivity until around the end of last year.

As the immediate after-effects of our defeats gradually passed, it became clear that the revolutionary party needed a strong secret organization throughout Germany. The need for this organization, which led the Central Committee to decide to send an emissary to Germany and Switzerland, also led to an attempt to establish a new secret association in Switzerland, and to an attempt by the Cologne commune to organize the League in Germany itself.

Around the beginning of the year several more or less well-known refugees from the various movements formed an organization[3] in Switzerland which intended to overthrow the governments

1. The June Address was first published in the same circumstances as the March Address, and is translated from the same source.

2. This refers to the March Address. The emissary was Heinrich Bauer.

3. The organization in question was known as Revolutionary Centralization. Former League members in it included Karl d'Ester.

at the right moment and to keep men at the ready to take over the leadership of the movement and even the government itself. This association did not possess any particular party character; the motley elements which it comprised made this impossible. The members consisted of people from all groups within the movement, from resolute Communists and even former League members to the most faint-hearted petty-bourgeois democrats and former members of the Palatinate government.[4]

In the eyes of the Baden-Palatinate careerists and lesser ambitious figures who were so numerous in Switzerland at this time, this association presented an ideal opportunity for them to advance themselves.

The instructions which this association sent to its agents – and which the Central Committee has in its possession – give just as little cause for confidence. The lack of a definite party standpoint and the attempt to bring all available opposition elements together in a sham association is only badly disguised by a mass of detailed questions concerning the industrial, agricultural, political and military situations in each locality. Numerically, too, the association was extremely weak; according to the complete list of members which we possess, the whole society in Switzerland consisted, at the height of its strength, of barely thirty members. It is significant that workers are hardly represented at all among the membership. From its very beginning, it was an army of officers and N.C.O.'s without any soldiers. Its members include A. Fries and Greiner from the Palatinate, Körner from Elberfeld, Sigel, etc.[5]

They sent two agents to Germany. The first agent, Bruhn,[6] a member of the League, managed by false pretences to persuade certain League members and communes to join the new association for the time being, as they believed it to be the resurrected League. While reporting on the League to the Swiss Central Committee in Zurich, he simultaneously sent us reports on the Swiss association. He cannot have been content with his role as an in-

4. i.e. the provisional revolutionary government of the Palatinate formed during the Reich Constitution Campaign of May–July 1849.

5. A. Fries and Theodor Greiner had been members of the Palatinate provisional revolutionary government; Hermann Körner had organized the Elberfeld insurrection of May 1849 (see p. 264, n. 94); Franz Sigel had been commander-in-chief of the Baden revolutionary army.

6. Karl von Bruhn, a journalist, had participated in the 1848 revolution, and was to edit in the 1860s the Lassallean paper *Nordstern*.

former, for while he was still corresponding with us, he wrote outright slanders to the people in Frankfurt, who had been won over to the Swiss association, and he ordered them not to enter into any contacts whatsoever with London. For this he was immediately expelled from the League. Matters in Frankfurt were settled by an emissary from the League. It may be added that Bruhn's activities on behalf of the Swiss Central Committee remained fruitless. The second agent, the student Schurz[7] from Bonn, achieved nothing because, as he wrote to Zurich, he found that all the people of any use were already in the hands of the League. He then suddenly left Germany and is now hanging around Brussels and Paris, where he is being watched by the League. The Central Committee does not see this new association as a danger, particularly as a completely reliable member of the League[8] is on its committee, with instructions to observe and report on the actions and plans of these people, in so far as they operate against the League. Furthermore, we have sent an emissary[9] to Switzerland in order to recruit the people who will be of value to the League, with the help of the aforementioned League member, and in order to organize the League in Switzerland in general. This information is based on fully authentic documents.

Another attempt of a similar nature had already been made earlier by Struve, Sigel and others, at the time that they joined forces in Geneva. These people had no compunction about claiming quite flatly that the association they were attempting to found was the League, nor about using the names of League members for precisely this end. Of course, they deceived nobody with this lie. Their attempt was so fruitless in every respect that the few members of this abortive association who stayed in Switzerland eventually had to join the organization previously mentioned. But the more impotent this coterie became, the more it showed off with pretentious titles like the 'Central Committee of European Democracy'[10] etc. Struve, together with a few other

7. Karl Schurz had fought in the Baden-Palatinate insurrection; he emigrated to the U.S.A. in 1852, and later became a diplomat, senator, and Secretary of the Interior.
8. Wilhelm Wolff.
9. Ernst Dronke, a collaborator of Marx and Engels on the *Neue Rheinische Zeitung*.
10. Marx and Engels discussed the 'Central Committee of European Democracy' in their Review of May–October 1850, above, pp. 314–18.

disappointed great men, has continued these attempts here in London.[11] Manifestoes and appeals to join the 'Central Bureau of German Refugees' and the 'Central Committee of European Democracy' have been sent to all parts of Germany, but this time, too, without the least success.

The contacts which this coterie claims to have made with French and other non-German revolutionaries do not exist. Their whole activity is limited to a few petty intrigues among the German refugees here in London, which do not affect the League directly and which are harmless and easy to keep under surveillance. All these attempts have either the same purpose as the League, namely the revolutionary organization of the workers' party, in which case they are undermining the centralization and strength of the party by fragmenting it and are therefore of a decidedly harmful, separatist character, or else they can only serve to misuse the workers' party for purposes which are foreign or straightforwardly hostile to it. Under certain circumstances the workers' party can profitably use other parties and groups for its own purposes, but it must not subordinate itself to any other party. Those people who were in government during the last movement,[12] and used their position only to betray the movement and to crush the workers' party where it tried to operate independently, must be kept at a distance at all costs.

The following is a report on the state of the League:

i. Belgium

The League's organization among the Belgian workers, as it existed in 1846 and 1847,[13] has naturally come to an end, since the leading members were arrested in 1848 and condemned to death, having their sentences commuted to life imprisonment with hard labour. In general, the League in Belgium has lost strength since

11. Gustav Struve, a member of the Baden revolutionary committee of May 1849, was later one of the leaders of the German democratic emigration in London. He founded the 'Central Bureau of All-German Refugees' in conjunction with other petty-bourgeois democrats, including Marx's one-time collaborator Arnold Ruge, in opposition to Marx and Engels's 'Social-Democratic Refugee Committee'.

12. i.e. the Reich Constitution Campaign.

13. The Belgian organization of the League had been set up by Marx himself during his Belgian exile (see Introduction, p. 28).

the February revolution and since most of the members of the German Workers Association were driven out of Brussels. The police measures which have been introduced have prevented its reorganization. Nevertheless one commune in Brussels has carried on throughout; it is still in existence today and is functioning to the best of its ability.

ii. Germany

In this circular the Central Committee intended to submit a special report on the state of the League in Germany. However, this report can not be made at the present time, as the Prussian police are even now investigating an extensive network of contacts in the revolutionary party. This circular, which will reach Germany safely but which, of course, may here and there fall into the hands of the police while being distributed within Germany, must therefore be written so that its contents do not provide them with weapons which could be used against the League. The Central Committee will therefore confine itself, for the time being, to the following remarks:

In Germany the League has its main centres in Cologne, Frankfurt am Main, Hanau, Mainz, Wiesbaden, Hamburg, Schwerin, Berlin, Breslau, Liegnitz, Glogau, Leipzig, Nuremberg, Munich, Bamberg, Würzburg, Stuttgart and Baden.

The following towns have been chosen as central districts: Hamburg for Schleswig-Holstein; Schwerin for Mecklenburg; Breslau for Silesia; Leipzig for Saxony and Berlin; Nuremberg for Bavaria, Cologne for the Rhineland and Westphalia.

The communes in Göttingen, Stuttgart and Brussels will remain in direct contact with the Central Committee for the time being, until they have succeeded in widening their influence to the extent necessary to form new central districts.

A decision will not be made on the position of the League in Baden until the report has been received from the emissary sent there and to Switzerland.

Wherever peasant and agricultural workers' associations exist, as in Schleswig-Holstein and Mecklenburg, members of the League have succeeded in exercising a direct influence upon them and, in some cases, in gaining complete control. For the most part, the workers and agricultural workers' associations in Saxony, Franconia, Hesse and Nassau are also under the leadership of the

League. The most influential members of the Workers Brotherhood[14] also belong to the League. The Central Committee wishes to point out to all communes and League members that it is of the utmost importance to win influence in the workers', sports, peasants' and agricultural workers' associations, etc. everywhere. It requests the central districts and the communes corresponding directly with the Central Committee to give a special report in their subsequent letters on what has been achieved in this connection.

The emissary to Germany, who has received a vote of commendation from the Central Committee for his activities, has everywhere recruited only the most reliable people into the League and left the expansion of the League to their greater local knowledge. It will depend upon the local situation whether convinced revolutionaries can be enlisted. Where this is not possible a second class of League members must be created for those people who are reliable and make useful revolutionaries but who do not yet understand the full communist implications of the present movement. This second class, to whom the association must be represented as a merely local or regional affair, must remain under the continuous leadership of actual League members and committees. With the help of these further contacts the League's influence on the peasants' and sports associations in particular can be very firmly organized. Detailed arrangements are left to the central districts; the Central Committee hopes to receive their reports on these matters, too, as soon as possible.

One commune has proposed to the Central Committee that a Congress of the League be convened, indeed in Germany itself. The communes and districts will certainly appreciate that under the present circumstances even regional congresses of the central districts are not everywhere advisable, and that a general Congress of the League at this moment is a sheer impossibility. However, the Central Committee will convene a Congress of the Communist League in a suitable place just as soon as circumstances allow. Prussian Rhineland and Westphalia recently received a visit from

14. The Workers Brotherhood was founded by the Communist League member Stephan Born in Berlin in September 1848. It was composed primarily of handicraft workers and tended to follow an economist line rather than the revolutionary line of Marx and the *Neue Rheinische Zeitung* (see Introduction, p. 40). It survived the defeat of the revolution, and maintained a semiclandestine organization for some years after its banning in 1851.

an emissary of the Cologne central district. The report on the result of this trip has not yet reached Cologne. We request all central districts to send similar emissaries round their regions and to report on their success as soon as possible. Finally we should like to report that in Schleswig-Holstein contacts have been established with the army: we are still awaiting the more detailed report on the influence which the League can hope to gain here.

iii. Switzerland

The report of the emissary is still being awaited. It will therefore not be possible to provide more exact information until the next circular.

iv. France

Contacts with the German workers in Besançon and other places in the Jura will be re-established from Switzerland. In Paris Ewerbeck,[15] the League member who has been up till now at the head of the commune there, has announced his resignation from the League, as he considers his literary activities to be more important. Contact has therefore been interrupted for the present and must be resumed with particular caution, as the Parisians have enlisted a large number of people who are absolutely un-fitted for the League and who were formerly even directly opposed to it.

v. England

The London district is the strongest in the whole League. It has earned particular credit by covering single-handedly the League's expenses for several years – in particular those for the journeys of the League's emissaries. It has been strengthened recently by the recruitment of new elements and it continues to lead the German Workers Educational Association[16] here, as well as the more resolute section of the German refugees in England.

15. August Ewerbeck was a doctor of medicine, and a leading member of the League of the Just in Paris before its transformation into the Communist League.
16. See p. 26, n. 35.

The Central Committee is in touch with the decisively revolutionary parties of the French, English and Hungarians by way of members delegated for this purpose.

Of all the parties involved in the French revolution it is in particular the genuine proletarian party headed by Blanqui which has joined us. The delegates of the Blanquist secret society are in regular and official contact with the delegates of the League, to whom they have entrusted important preparatory work for the next French revolution.[17]

The leaders of the revolutionary wing of the Chartists are also in regular and close contact with the delegates of the Central Committee. Their journals are being made available to us.[18] The break between this revolutionary, independent workers' party and the faction headed by O'Connor,[19] which tends more towards a policy of reconciliation, has been considerably accelerated by the delegates of the League.

The Central Committee is similarly in contact with the most progressive section of the Hungarian refugees. This party is important because it includes many excellent military experts, who would be at the League's disposal in the event of revolution.

The Central Committee requests the central districts to distribute this letter among their members as soon as possible and to submit their own reports soon. It urges all League members to the most intense activity, especially now that the situation has become so critical that it cannot be long before another revolution breaks out.

17. See p. 57.

18. ibid. This refers in particular to Harney's *Red Republican*, in which the first English translation of the Communist Manifesto was published in November 1850.

19. Feargus O'Connor was the founder and editor of the *Northern Star*, the most influential Chartist newspaper, to which Engels had contributed before 1848. Marx and Engels discussed the different Chartist tendencies in their Review of May–October 1850, above, pp. 308–10.

Minutes of the Central Committee Meeting of 15 September 1850[1]

Meeting of the Central Committee held on 15 September 1850
Present: Marx, Engels, Schramm, Pfänder, Bauer, Eccarius, Schapper, Willich, Lehmann
Apologies from Fränkel.[2]

The minutes of the previous meeting were not at hand, because this was an extraordinary meeting. They were therefore not read out.

MARX: It was not possible to hold the Friday meeting because of a clash with the meeting of the Association's committee.[3] The meeting has to take place today because Willich called a district assembly, the legality of which I won't go into here. I want to present the following motion, which divides into three articles:

1. As soon as this meeting is concluded, the seat of the Central Committee shall be transferred from London to Cologne and its powers handed over to the district committee there. This decision

1. This document was first published in the *International Review of Social History*, vol. I, part 2. Amsterdam, 1956, and is translated here from the text of that journal.
2. Konrad Schramm was a journalist and the publisher of the *Neue Rheinische Zeitung Revue*; Karl Pfänder was a miniature painter, a member of the old League of the Just and later a member of the General Council of the First International; Johann Georg Eccarius was a tailor, also a member of the old League and a future member of the General Council of the International; Albert Lehmann was a worker, formerly a leading member of the League of the Just, and Fränkel was also a worker. When the Communist League split, Schramm, Pfänder and Eccarius took the side of Marx and Engels, Lehmann, Fränkel and Willich that of Schapper; Bauer joined neither side, and emigrated to Australia soon after. Though a majority in the Central Committee, Marx's group were a minority in the London district of the League, also in the German Workers Educational Association and the Social-Democratic Refugee Committee, both of which they left consequent on the split.
3. i.e. the committee of the German Workers Educational Association.

shall be transmitted to members of the League in Paris, Belgium and Switzerland. The new Central Committee shall itself be responsible for transmitting the decision within Germany.

Reason: I was opposed to Schapper's proposal for an all-German district committee in Cologne, because it would destroy the unity of the central authority. Our motion makes this unnecessary. There are a number of further reasons. The minority of the Central Committee is in open rebellion against the majority. This was manifested both in the vote of censure at the last meeting and in the general assembly now called by the district, as well as in the Association and among the refugees.[4] It is therefore impossible to keep the Central Committee here. The unity of the Central Committee can no longer be preserved: it would have to split and two leagues would be set up. Since the interest of the party[5] must take precedence, however, I suggest this as a way out.

2. The existing statutes of the League shall be repealed. The new Central Committee shall be assigned the task of drawing up new statutes.

Reason: The statutes adopted at the 1847 Congress were altered by the London Central Committee. The political situation has now changed once more. The last London statutes watered down the articles which dealt with matters of principle. Both sets of statutes are in use in one place or another; in some places neither is used, or people have taken it upon themselves to produce their own, i.e., there is total anarchy in the League. Furthermore, the more recent statutes have been made public and are thus of no further use. The essence of my motion is therefore that genuine statutes should replace this situation in which there are really none.[6]

3. In London, two districts shall be set up, which are to have absolutely no relations with one another. The only link between them shall be that they both belong to the League and correspond with the same Central Committee.

4. Presumably a reference to the Social-Democratic Refugee Committee.
5. i.e. the workers movement, see p. 28 n. 40.
6. The original statutes of the Communist League are those printed in *MEW* 4, pp. 596–601. The statement of principles contained in the first paragraph is quoted in the Introduction to this volume, above, p. 28. The 'watering down' was done by the new London Central Committee formed in autumn 1848, after Marx had dissolved the Cologne Central Committee in May. These new statutes were published consequent on their seizure by the Prussian police in March 1849.

Reason: It is precisely for the unity of the League that two districts must be set up here. Besides personal antagonisms, differences of principle have come to light, even within the Association. During our last debate in particular,[7] on the question of 'The position of the German proletariat in the next revolution', views were expressed by members of the minority of the Central Committee which directly contradict our second-to-last circular[8] and even the Manifesto. A national German approach has replaced the universal conception of the Manifesto, flattering the national sentiments of German artisans. The *will*, rather than the actual conditions, was stressed as the chief factor in the revolution. We tell the workers: If you want to change conditions and make yourselves capable of government, you will have to undergo fifteen, twenty or fifty years of civil war. Now they are told: We must come to power immediately or we might as well go to sleep. The word 'proletariat' has been reduced to a mere phrase, like the word 'people' was by the democrats. To make this phrase a reality one would have to declare the entire petty bourgeoisie to be proletarians, i.e. *de facto* represent the petty bourgeoisie and not the proletariat. In place of actual revolutionary development one would have to adopt the revolutionary phrase. This debate has finally exposed the differences of principle which underlie the personal animosities, and the time has come for intervention. It is these very differences which the two groups have taken as their slogans, and various League members have described the defenders of the Manifesto as reactionaries. An attempt has been made to make them unpopular through this, but this doesn't bother them at all, since they are not after popularity. In this situation the majority would have the right to dissolve the London district and expel the members of the minority for contradicting the principles of the League. I do not propose this course, because it would lead to fruitless quarrelling and because by conviction these people are communists, even though the views they have expressed are anti-communist and could at most be called social-democratic. It will be seen, however, that to stay together would be a pure waste of time. Schapper has often spoken of separation, well, I am taking separation seriously. I believe I have found a way for us to separate without destroying the party.

I want to state that, as far as I am concerned, I have no wish for

7. There seems to be no record of this debate.
8. The March Address.

more than a dozen people to be in our district, as few as possible, and I gladly leave the whole troop to the minority. If you accept this suggestion, we shall clearly be unable to remain in the same Association: I and the majority will resign from the Great Windmill Street Association. Finally, it is not a question of hostile relations between the two groups; on the contrary, we want to abolish the tension by abolishing all relations whatsoever. We shall still be together in the League and in the party, but we shall not maintain relations which can only be injurious.

SCHAPPER: Just as the proletariat cut itself off from the Montagne and the press in France, so here the people who speak for the party on matters of principle are cutting themselves off from those who organize within the proletariat. I am in favour of moving the Central Committee, and also of altering the statutes. I also believe that the new revolution will bring forth people who themselves will lead it, and do so better than all the people who had a name in 1848. As far as splits on questions of principle are concerned, it was Eccarius who proposed the question which provoked this debate. I expressed the view which is being challenged here because I have always had strong feelings on the matter. It boils down to whether we do the beheading at the outset or whether we are ourselves beheaded. The workers will have their turn in France, and thereby *we* will in Germany. If that was not the case I would certainly give the whole thing up and then I could have a different material position. If our turn comes, we can take the measures necessary to secure the power of the proletariat. I am a fanatical supporter of this view. No doubt I shall be sent to the guillotine in the next revolution but I shall return to Germany. If you want to set up two districts, well and good. The League will cease to exist and then we shall meet again in Germany and perhaps be able to come together again there. Marx is a personal friend of mine, but if you want separation, well and good. We'll go alone and you'll go alone. But then two leagues ought to be set up – one for those whose influence derives from their pens and the other for those who work in other ways. I don't hold with the view that the bourgeoisie will come to power in Germany, and I am a fanatical enthusiast in this respect. If I wasn't, I wouldn't give an iota for the whole business. But if we have two districts here in London, two associations, two refugee committees, then we might as well have two leagues and complete separation.

MARX: Schapper has misunderstood my motion. As soon as the motion is accepted we will separate, the two districts will separate, and the people involved will have no further connection with each other. They will be in the same League, however, and under the same Central Committee. You will even retain the great mass of the League membership. As far as personal sacrifices are concerned, I have made as many as anyone else, but they have been for the class and not for individual people. As for enthusiasm, there is not much enthusiasm involved in belonging to a party which you believe will become the government. I have always resisted the momentary opinion of the proletariat. We are devoted to a party which would do best not to assume power just now. The proletariat, if it should come to power, would not be able to implement proletarian measures immediately, but would have to introduce petty-bourgeois ones. Our party can only become the government when conditions allow *its* views to be put into practice. Louis Blanc provides the best example of what happens when power is assumed prematurely.[9] Moreover, in France the proletarians will not come to power alone, but with the peasants and the petty bourgeoisie, and it is the latter's measures that they will have to implement, not their own. The Paris Commune[10] is proof that it is not necessary to be part of the government in order to get something done. Anyway, why don't some of the other members of the minority say what they think, especially Citizen Willich, since at the time they all unanimously approved the circular. We *cannot* and do not want to split the League; we merely want to divide the London district into two separate districts.

ECCARIUS: I proposed the question, and intended to bring the matter up for discussion anyway. As far as Schapper's view is concerned, I have elaborated in the Association why I regard it as illusory and why I do not believe that our party will come to power immediately in the next revolution. Our party will be more important in the clubs than in the government.

9. Marx is referring to Blanc's membership of the Provisional Government set up in France after the February revolution, and the false position Blanc put himself in as a representative of the Paris working class in a bourgeois government; see 'The Class Struggles in France', in *Surveys from Exile*, pp. 44, 53–4.

10. Not, of course, the Commune of 1871, but the Commune (i.e. municipal council) of Paris which played a major role during the first French revolution.

Citizen Lehmann left without a word, as did Citizen Willich.

Article 1 accepted by all. Schapper abstained.
Article 2 accepted by all. Schapper the same.
Article 3 similarly accepted. Schapper the same.

SCHAPPER [*expressing his protest against us all*]: We are now completely separated. I have my acquaintances and friends in Cologne, who will follow me rather than you.

MARX: We have concluded the matter in accordance with the statutes, and the decisions of the Central Committee are valid.

After the minutes had been read Marx and Schapper stated that neither had written to Cologne on the subject.

Schapper was asked if he had any objections to the minutes. He said he had none, since he regarded all objections as superfluous.

Eccarius proposed that the minutes be signed by everyone. Schapper said he would not sign.

These proceedings took place in London, 15 September 1850. Read out, approved and signed.

K. MARX, *Chairman of the Central Committee*
F. ENGELS, *Secretary*
HENRY BAUER
C. SCHRAMM
J. G. ECCARIUS
C. PFÄNDER

Note on Previous Editions of the Works of Marx and Engels

Until recently there existed no complete edition of the works of Marx and Engels in any language. The Marx-Engels Institute, under its director D. Riazanov, began to produce such an edition in the late 1920s; the collapse of the project in 1935 was no doubt connected with Riazanov's dismissal and subsequent disappearance. However, eleven indispensable volumes did emerge between 1927 and 1935, under the title *Karl Marx – Friedrich Engels: Historisch-Kritische Gesamtausgabe*, commonly referred to as the *MEGA* edition. The *MEGA* contains works of both men down to 1848, and their correspondence, but nothing more. For the next thirty years, the field was held by the almost inaccessible Russian edition, the Marx-Engels *Sochineniya* (twenty-nine volumes, 1928–46).

Only in 1968 did the East Germans complete the first German definitive edition, the forty-one volume *Marx-Engels Werke* (*MEW*). Until then, the works of Marx and Engels existed only in separate editions and smaller collections on specific themes. For this reason, the translations into English have followed the same pattern, the only general selection being the *Marx-Engels Selected Works* (*MESW*), now expanded to a three-volume edition. Recently, however, the major gaps in the English translations have begun to be filled up. Lawrence and Wishart have produced a complete translation of *Theories of Surplus Value*, as well as the first adequate translation of *A Contribution to the Critique of Political Economy* and Marx's book on *The Cologne Communist Trial*. They plan to issue a complete English-language edition of even greater scope than the *MEW*, though this will inevitably take many years to complete. The Pelican Marx Library occupies an intermediate position between the *MESW* and the complete edition. It brings together the most important of Marx's larger works, the three volumes of *Capital* and the *Grundrisse*, as well as three volumes of political writings and an *Early Writings* volume.

Chronology of Works by Marx and Engels

Date[1]	Author[2]	Title	English edition[3]
1843	M	*Critique of Hegel's Doctrine of the State*	P *EW*
1843	M	*On the Jewish Question*	P *EW*
1843–4	M	*A Contribution to the Critique of Hegel's Philosophy of Right: Introduction*	P *EW*
1844	M	*Excerpts from James Mill's* Elements of Political Economy	P *EW*
1844	E	*Outlines of a Critique of Political Economy*	*EPM* App.
1844	M	*Economic and Philosophical Manuscripts*	P *EW*
1844	M	*Critical Notes on the Article 'The King of Prussia and Social Reform. By a Prussian'*	P *EW*
1844	M & E	*The Holy Family, or a Critique of Critical Critique*	LW 1957

1. Date of composition, except for *Capital*, where the date of first publication is given.

2. M = Marx, E = Engels.

3. The following abbreviations are used:

EPM App.: Appendix to Marx, *Economic and Philosophical Manuscripts of 1844*, Lawrence and Wishart, 1959.

LW: Lawrence and Wishart.

MESW: *Karl Marx and Frederick Engels, Selected Works in Three Volumes*, Progress Publishers, 1969.

P: Pelican Marx Library.

P *EW*: *Early Writings* (Pelican Marx Library).

P *FI*: *The First International and After* (Pelican Marx Library).

P *R1848*: *The Revolutions of 1848* (Pelican Marx Library).

P *SE*: *Surveys from Exile* (Pelican Marx Library).

Date	Author	Title	English edition
1844–5	E	*Condition of the Working Class in England*	Blackwell 1958
1845	M	*Theses on Feuerbach*	*MESW I*
1845–6	M & E	*The German Ideology*	LW 1964
1846–7	M	*The Poverty of Philosophy*	LW 1956
1847	M & E	*Speeches on Poland*	P *R1848*
1847	M	*Wage Labour and Capital*	*MESW I*
1847–8	M & E	*Manifesto of the Communist Party*	P *R1848*
1848	M & E	*Speeches on Poland*	P *R1848*
1848	M & E	*Demands of the Communist Party in Germany*	P *R1848*
1848–9	M & E	*Articles in the* Neue Rheinische Zeitung	P *R1848* (selection)
1850 (March)	M & E	*Address of the Central Committee to the Communist League*	P *R1848*
1850 (June)	M & E	*Address of the Central Committee to the Communist League*	P *R1848*
1850	M & E	*Reviews from the* Neue Rheinische Zeitung Revue	P *R1848*
1850	M	*The Class Struggles in France: 1848 to 1850*	P *SE*
1850	E	*The Peasant War in Germany*	LW 1956
1851–2	E	*Revolution and Counter-Revolution in Germany*	*MESW I*
1852	M	*The Eighteenth Brumaire of Louis Bonaparte*	P *SE*
1852	M	*Revelations on the Cologne Communist Trial*	LW 1970
1856	M	*Speech at the Anniversary of the* People's Paper	P *SE*
1857–8	M	*Grundrisse*	P
1859	M	*A Contribution to the Critique of Political Economy*	LW 1971
1852–61	M & E	*Articles in the* New York Daily Tribune	P *SE* (selections)
1861	M	*Articles in* Die Presse *on the Civil War in the United States*	P *SE* (selections)
1861–3	M	*Theories of Surplus Value*, Vol. 1 Vol. 2 Vol. 3	LW 1967 LW 1970 LW 1972
1863	M	*Proclamation on Poland*	P *SE*

Date	Author	Title	English edition
1864	M	*Inaugural Address of the International Working Men's Association*	P *FI*
1864	M	*Provisional Rules of the International Working Men's Association*	P *FI*
1865	E	*The Prussian Military Question and the German Workers' Party*	P *FI* (extract)
1865	M	*Wages, Prices, and Profit*	*MESW II*
1866	E	*What Have the Working Classes to Do with Poland?*	P *FI*
1867	M	*Capital*, Vol. 1	P
1867	M	*Instructions for Delegates to the Geneva Congress*	P *FI*
1868	M	*Report to the Brussels Congress*	P *FI*
1869	M	*Report to the Basel Congress*	P *FI*
1870	M	*The General Council to the Federal Council of French Switzerland* (a circular letter)	P *FI*
1870	M	*First Address of the General Council on Franco-Prussian War*	P *FI*
1870	M	*Second Address of the General Council on the Franco-Prussian War*	P *FI*
1871	M	First draft of *The Civil War in France*	P *FI*
1871	M & E	*On the Paris Commune*	LW 1971
1871	M	*The Civil War in France*	P *FI*
1871	M & E	*Resolution of the London Conference on Working-Class Political Action*	P *FI*
1872	M & E	*The Alleged Splits in the International*	P *FI*
1872	M	*Report to the Hague Congress*	P *FI*
1872–3	E	*The Housing Question*	*MESW II*
1874	M	*Political Indifferentism*	P *FI*
1874	E	*On Authority*	*MESW II*
1874–5	M	*Conspectus of Bakunin's Book* Statism and Anarchy	P *FI* (extract)
1875	M & E	*For Poland*	P *FI*
1875	M	*Critique of the Gotha Programme*	P *FI*
1876–8	E	*Anti-Dühring*	LW 1955
1879	M & E	*Circular Letter to Bebel, Liebknecht, Bracke, et al.*	P *FI*
1879–80	M	*Marginal Notes on Adolph Wagner's* Lehrbuch der politischen Ökonomie	P *Capital*
1880	E	*Socialism: Utopian and Scientific*	*MESW III*

Date	Author	Title	English edition
1880	M	*Introduction to the Programme of the French Workers' Party*	P *FI*
1873–83	E	*Dialectics of Nature*	LW 1954
1884	E	*The Origin of the Family, Private Property, and the State*	*MESW III*
1885	M	*Capital*, Vol. 2	P
1886	E	*Ludwig Feuerbach and the End of Classical German Philosophy*	*MESW III*
1894	M	*Capital*, Vol. 3	P

Index

absolutism, *see* Monarchy, absolute
Academic Legion, 174, 181
Adam (Blanquist), 57
agrarian reform/revolution, 97, 104, 107, 153
Alexander I [of Russia] (1777–1825), 106n, 144n, 269n
Algeria, 225, 271
Aliens Bill, 304
Alsace-Lorraine, 118, 242
Amsterdam, 286, 291, 318
Anekdota, 12
aristocratic critique of bourgeois society, 87–9
Arndt, Ernst Moritz (1769–1860), 267
artisans:
  proletarianization, 30, 77, 80
  political position, 9, 24, 26, 40, 341
Auersperg, Karl, Graf von (1783–1859), 172–3
Auerswald, Rudolf von (1795–1866), 160, 200, 204, 205n; *see also* Hansemann ministry
Augsburger Allgemeine Zeitung, 168
Australia, 274, 296–7, 300–302, 339n
Austria:
  and March revolutions, 38, 41;
  and German unification, 47–9, 51, 108, 175–6;
  and Hungarian revolution, 45, 47, 164n, 213, 223–6, 304n;
  and pan-Slavism, 234, 236, 244, 268;
  and partition of Poland, 49, 100n, 215;
  camarilla, 170, 175, 178, 223;
  early history, 214–19 *passim*;
  reliance on Slavs, 52, 125n, 172–81 *passim*, 185, 213, 216–17, 223, 230, 239, 241;
  rivalry with Prussia, 267, 295, 302, 310–13;

rule in Italy, 41, 126n, 127, 238–40, 308;
  suppresses Polish uprisings, 102, 102n, 147, 216–17, 240;
  Vienna Reichstag, 165n, 174, 178;
  see also Holy Alliance
Austro-Slavism, 125n, 220n; *see also* pan-Slavism

Babeuf, François-Noël (Gracchus) (1760–97), 23–4, 94
Baden, 48, 53, 311, 332, 333n, 335
Bakunin, Mikhail Alexandrovich (1814–76), 51–2, 64n, 227–45 *passim*
Bank of England, 197, 287–91
Barrot, Odilon (1791–1873), 130n
Bassermann, Friedrich Daniel (1811–55), 168, 180, 187, 310n, 311
Bauer, Bruno (1809–82), 11–19 *passim*
Bauer, Edgar (1820–86), 13, 17, 19
Bauer, Heinrich, 38, 111, 331n, 339, 344
Baumstark, Eduard (1807–89), 134
Bavaria, 279, 295n, 322, 335
Becker, Hermann Heinrich (1820–85), 167
Beckerath, Hermann von (1801–70), 157, 160
Belgium:
  and pan-Germanism, 242
  Communist activity in, 37, 99n, 102n, 334–5, 340
  constitutionalism in, 104, 206
  workers' movement in, 41, 63, 101
Berlin:
  counter-revolution in, 45, 177–8, 181–5, 226, 246
  March days in, 38, 159, 180, 190, 193, 310
  Marx and Engels in, 10, 17

MORE ABOUT PENGUINS
AND PELICANS

Penguinews, which appears every month, contains details of all the new books issued by Penguins as they are published. From time to time it is supplemented by *Penguins in Print*, which is a complete list of all available books published by Penguins. (There are well over four thousand of these.)

A specimen copy of *Penguinews* will be sent to you free on request. For a year's issues (including the complete lists) please send 30p if you live in the United Kingdom, or 60p if you live elsewhere. Just write to Dept EP, Penguin Books Ltd, Harmondsworth, Middlesex, enclosing a cheque or postal order, and your name will be added to the mailing list.

Note: *Penguinews* and *Penguins in Print* are not available in the U.S.A. or Canada

THE PELICAN MARX LIBRARY

(Published in association with *New Left Review*)

GRUNDRISSE

Foundations of the Critique of Political Economy

First complete English translation by Martin Nicolaus

For years Karl Marx had planned to continue the work begun in
Das Kapital with further books, in which he proposed to take up and
expand many of the ideas and questions he had already raised.
The *Grundrisse* – which was the outline of this massive plan –
was left by him, at his death, in the form of notes and partly
completed sections. Though long available in the Moscow archives,
it was not published in German until 1939 and this is its first
appearance in English.

The *Grundrisse* throws light on many obscure corners of Marx's
thought and, in this light, the English reader can now assess how far
his economic and philosophic outlook changed and how far it
has simply been misinterpreted. For here is a major part of
Marx's work which was unknown even to Lenin.

SURVEYS FROM EXILE

Edited by David Fernbach

During the 1850s, after Marx had found asylum in England, he was
more completely isolated than at any other time. To this period
belong *The Class Struggles in France*, in which he brilliantly
analyses the French political and social groupings after 1848, and
The Eighteenth Brumaire of Louis Napoleon, a similar study of the
coup d'état of 1851. Both are printed in this volume.

After perfecting his English, Marx began to interpret, in a series
of articles for the American (and German) press, the English
political scene and British rule in India, and, on the outbreak of the
American Civil War, he wrote at length on that conflict for a liberal
paper in Vienna. Samples of these extensive writings, by
which Marx earned a scanty living, appear in this volume, along
with other reviews, speeches and political statements.

Not for sale in the U.S.A. or Canada